A Sociological Tapestry
Classical and Contemporary Readings in Sociology

Edited by

Teri A. Milner
Irene Fiala

Edinboro University

KENDALL/HUNT PUBLISHING COMPANY
4050 Westmark Drive   Dubuque, Iowa 52002

Copyright © 2003 by Kendall/Hunt Publishing Company

ISBN 0-7575-0188-5

Kendall/Hunt Publishing Company has the exclusive rights to reproduce this work, to prepare derivative works from this work, to publicly distribute this work, to publicly perform this work and to publicly display this work.

All rights reserved. No part of this publication may be reproduced, stored in a retrieval system, or transmitted, in any form or by any means, electronic, mechanical, photocopying, recording, or otherwise, without the prior written permission of Kendall/Hunt Publishing Company.

Printed in the United States of America
10 9 8 7 6 5 4 3 2 1

Contents

Preface   vii

PART I   **Impact of Society on the Individual**   1
(Introduction to Part I by the editors)

Chapter 1   **The Sociological Perspective**   5
The Promise   7
C. Wright Mills
Reading Comprehension Activity Sheet   13

Chapter 2   **Theory and Research**   15
Some Conditions of Obedience and Disobedience to Authority   17
Stanley Milgram
Reading Comprehension Activity Sheet   29
Racism and Research: The Case of the Tuskegee Syphilis Study   31
Allan M. Brandt
Reading Comprehension Activity Sheet   43

Chapter 3   **Culture**   45
Body Ritual among the Nacirema   47
Horace Miner
Reading Comprehension Activity Sheet   53
The Narcirema and the Tsiruot   55
Joel Savishinsky
Reading Comprehension Activity Sheet   61
The Prevalence of Female Circumcision in Two Nigerian Communities   63
Ehigie Ebomoyi
Reading Comprehension Activity Sheet   75

Chapter 4   Socialization   77

Final Note on a Case of Extreme Isolation   79
Kingsley Davis
Reading Comprehension Activity Sheet   87

The Miseducation of Boys: Changing the Script   89
Myra Sadker and David Sadker
Reading Comprehension Activity Sheet   95

Chapter 5   Deviance, Crime, and Social Control   97

Becoming a Marihuana User   99
Howard S. Becker
Reading Comprehension Activity Sheet   111

Fraternities and Rape on Campus   113
Patricia Yancey Martin and Robert A. Hummer
Reading Comprehension Activity Sheet   129

Chapter 6   Social Groups and Formal Organizations   131

The Effects of Group Pressure on the Modification and Distortion of Judgments   133
Solomon E. Asch
Reading Comprehension Activity Sheet   145

Women of the Klan   147
Kathleen M. Blee
Reading Comprehension Activity Sheet   159

PART II   Stratification and Issues of Inequality   161
(Introduction to Part II by the editors)

Chapter 7   Social Class   165

Class, Status, Party   167
Max Weber
Reading Comprehension Activity Sheet   175

The Uses of Poverty: The Poor Pay All   177
Herbert J. Gans
Reading Comprehension Activity Sheet   183

Chapter 8   Gender   185

Sex and Temperament in Three Primitive Societies: The Malleability of Gender Roles   187
Margaret Mead
Reading Comprehension Activity Sheet   193

Sexual Terrorism 195
Carole J. Sheffield
Reading Comprehension Activity Sheet 215

Chapter 9 Race and Ethnicity 217

The Problem of the Twentieth Century Is the Problem of the Color Line 219
W.E.B. Du Bois
Reading Comprehension Activity Sheet 227

Angry Women are Building: Issues and Struggles Facing American Indian Women Today 229
Paula Gunn Allen
Reading Comprehension Activity Sheet 233

Chapter 10 Sexual Orientation 235

He Defies You Still: The Memoirs of a Sissy 237
Tommi Avicolli
Reading Comprehension Activity Sheet 243

The New Gay Struggle 245
Richard Lacayo
Reading Comprehension Activity Sheet 251

PART III Social Institutions 253
(Introduction to Part III by the editors)

Chapter 11 Marriages and Families 257

The Way We Really Are 259
Stephanie Coontz
Reading Comprehension Activity Sheet 269

The Two Marriages 271
Jessie Bernard
Reading Comprehension Activity Sheet 281

Ten Myths That Perpetuate Corporal Punishment 283
Murray A. Straus
Reading Comprehension Activity Sheet 295

Chapter 12 Education 297

Learning the Student Role: Kindergarten as Academic Boot Camp 299
Harry L. Gracey
Reading Comprehension Activity Sheet 307

Civilize Them with a Stick 309
Mary Crow Dog and Richard Erdoes
Reading Comprehension Activity Sheet 317

Chapter 13 Religion 319

The Elementary Forms of the Religious Life 321
Emile Durkheim
Reading Comprehension Activity Sheet 327

Miami's Little Havana: Yard Shrines, Cult Religion, and Landscape 329
James R. Curtis
Reading Comprehension Activity Sheet 339

Chapter 14 Politics and the Government 341

The Power Elite 343
C. Wright Mills
Reading Comprehension Activity Sheet 351

The My Lai Massacre: A Military Crime of Obedience 353
Herbert Kelman and V. Lee Hamilton
Reading Comprehension Activity Sheet 369

Chapter 15 Social Change and Social Movements 371

The McDonaldization of Society 373
George Ritzer
Reading Comprehension Activity Sheet 381

Appendix

Student Information Sheet 383
Course Assessment Sheet 385

Preface

The "sociological imagination" (coined by C. Wright Mills in 1959) is a quality of m̶ will help you see what is going on in the world, in your community, and in your da̶. The power of the sociological perspective lies not just in changing individual lives, ̶ transforming society. The more we learn how "the system" operates, the more we may wa̶ to change it in some way. People are "social beings," so it makes sense to explore and analyze the personal troubles in our lives in a historical and structural context, so that we understand those troubles as being interwoven in a broader set of public issues.

This reader, *A Sociological Tapestry*, suggests in its title the "interwoven" nature of the discipline. We have selected readings from classical authors and contemporary authors to enhance your sociological imagination. It is our aim for you to find excitement and engagement in these readings. Interestingly, once you begin to read you may notice that the classical readings were, for the most part, written by men who use "man" and male pronouns to apply to all people. These classical authors reflected the conventional and academic writing practices of their time. If they had the chance to revise their essays today their writing style would reflect the human experience in a more inclusive manner.

It is important to remember that society shapes individuals' lives and, of equal importance, that individuals also shape society. We increasingly are living in an interconnected world, so it is essential that we evaluate every aspect of social life to become better informed and active participants in that world.

Teri A. Milner, Ph.D.
Irene Fiala, Ph.D.
Department of Sociology
Edinboro University of Pennsylvania

PART I
Impact of Society on the Individual

In this first section, the articles are selected to coincide with most "Introduction to Sociology" textbooks: the sociological perspective, the sociological investigation (theory and research), the components of culture, and the socialization process. The selected readings are intended to stimulate discussion in the classroom setting, and to encourage continued discussion outside of the classroom. These discussions should not be limited only to the research presented here, but rather should be a starting point in the evaluation of social interaction, social structure, and social inequalities.

In the first article, C. Wright Mills explains the need for a "sociological imagination" in transforming personal troubles into public issues. By examining the historical, structural, and cultural contexts of social phenomena, we can better understand our lives and the world around us. Being unemployed, being divorced, and even perhaps being a victim of a crime are deeply personal and troubling experiences. However, by closely examining the structural aspects of society, we can begin to see that shifts in the economy, changes in the perception of divorce and in divorce laws, and even cultural forces (for example, the culture of violence which exists in our society) make life more difficult for everyone. You may already have a "sociological imagination" and not even realize it. You may also start to use that perspective more and more as you become more critical in analyzing your surroundings.

The second article illustrates why the emergence of ethical concerns are so important when conducting research. In a now famous study, Stanley Milgram devised an experiment in which study participants administered electric shocks to another person when ordered to do so. While the results of Milgram's study carried weight, meaning, and purpose, the results also sparked controversy and protest. The Tuskegee Study, also demonstrates why ethical rules should and

d. There is no clear consensus on a complete set of ethical guidelines [for] conducting research involving human subjects; however, it is professionally agreed that subjects should be fully aware of their role in the study, much like the practice of informed consent. In addition, subjects should not be [subjected] to unnecessary stress, manipulation, or personal risk. In the past, sociologists (and social scientists generally) often displayed arrogance in their treatment of research subjects. Let's hope lessons have been learned from past mistakes.

The next set of readings focuses on the issues of culture and cultural relativity. In sociology, the term "culture" refers to all the elements of human society that are socially, rather than biologically, transmitted. Taking a closer look at one's own culture can provide ways of explaining and understanding human behavior, belief systems, values, and ideologies. If we were then to take a close look at another culture, would it look the same? Cultural relativists assert that concepts are socially constructed, and that they vary cross-culturally (and over time). Thus, a particular culture is relative only to that particular society. The mannerisms, dress, language, rituals, norms of behavior, and system of beliefs are all relative to that particular culture, and at that particular time in history. How would that culture look to an "outsider"? How would our own culture look to an outsider?

Social control mechanisms are developed by social groups of all kinds, to enforce or encourage conformity, and to deal with behavior that violates accepted norms. Sociologists usually distinguish between two basic processes of social control. First, the process of socialization, the internalization of norms and values, is used as a social control mechanism. This process is generally so powerful that individuals conform, not out of fear of punishment, but because they want to. Second, sanctions with regard to rule-breakers and non-conformists usually exist in any given society. Sanctions may be positive (rewarding conforming conduct) or may be negative (punishing non-conforming conduct). What happens, however, when non-conforming behavior (for example, smoking marijuana) becomes a rewarding in its own right (especially when punishment seems like a remote possibility)? As a result, the deviant identity becomes internalized into a positive and often salient identity.

The last set of articles focuses on our group associations, and the impact they have on our lives. Interacting within groups is a very dynamic process. One such process, the tendency of group members to conform their opinions and judgments to those of the group, is known as "groupthink." If everyone in your group were telling you that one line was longer than the other (when in reality both lines are equal in length), would you disagree with the group and state that they are of equal length, or would you go along with the overall consensus of the group? Our group associations usually fall into two categories: primary and secondary group associations. According to Charles Horton Cooley, primary group associations are characterized as small, intimate groups in which members are engaged in fact-to-face, emotion-based interactions that are stable and long-lasting. On the other hand, secondary group associations are characterized as large, impersonal groups in which members are engaged in goal-oriented relationships for a limited amount of time. What is interesting, however, it that sometimes meaning and agency can stem from these secondary group associations.

chapter 1

The Sociological Perspective

The Promise
C. Wright Mills

The Promise

C. Wright Mills

Nowadays men often feel that their private lives are a series of traps. They sense that within their everyday worlds, they cannot overcome their troubles, and in this feeling, they are often quite correct. What ordinary men are directly aware of and what they try to do are bounded by the private orbits in which they live; their visions and their powers are limited to the close-up scenes of job, family, neighborhood; in other miliux[1], they move vicariously and remain spectators. And the more aware they become, however vaguely, of ambitions and of threats which transcend their immediate locales, the more trapped they seem to feel.

Underlying this sense of being trapped are seemingly impersonal changes in the very structure of continent-wide societies. The facts of contemporary history are also facts about the success and the failure of individual men and women. When a society is industrialized, a peasant becomes a worker; a feudal lord is liquidated or becomes a businessman. When classes rise or fall, a person is employed or unemployed; when the rate of investment goes up or down, a person takes new heart or goes broke. When wars happen, an insurance salesperson becomes a rocket launcher; a store clerk, a radar operator; a wife or husband lives alone; a child grows up without a parent. Neither the life of an individual nor the history of a society can be understood without understanding both.

Yet men do not usually define the troubles they endure in terms of historical change and institutional contradiction. The well-being they enjoy, they do not usually impute to the big ups and downs of the societies in which they live. Seldom aware of the intricate connection between the patterns of their own lives and the course of world history, ordinary men do not usually know what this connection means for the kinds of men they are becoming and for the kinds of history-making in which they might take part. They do not posses the quality of mind essential to grasp the interplay of man and society, of biography and history, of self and world. They cannot cope with their personal troubles in such ways as to control the structural transformations that usually lie behind them.

From *The Sociological Imagination* by C. Wright Mills, copyright © 2000 by Oxford University Press, Inc. Used by permission of Oxford University Press, Inc.

Surely it is no wonder. In what period have so many men been so totally exposed at so fast a pace to such earthquakes of change? That Americans have not known such catastrophic changes as have the men and women of other societies is due to historical facts that are now quickly becoming "merely history." The history that now affects every man is world history. Within this scene and this period, in the course of a single generation, one sixth of mankind is transformed from all that is feudal and backward into all that is modern, advanced, and fearful. Political colonies are freed; new and less visible forms of imperialism installed. Revolutions occur; men feel the intimate grip of new kinds of authority. Totalitarian societies rise, and are smashed to bits—or succeed fabulously. After two centuries of ascendancy, capitalism is shown up as only one way to make society into an industrial apparatus. After two centuries of hope, even formal democracy is restricted to a quite small portion of mankind. Everywhere in the underdeveloped world, ancient ways of life are broken up and vague expectations become urgent demands. Everywhere in the overdeveloped world, the means of authority and of violence become total in scope and bureaucratic in form. Humanity itself now lies before us, the super-nation at either pole concentrating its most coordinated and massive efforts upon the preparation of World War Three.

The very shaping of history now outpaces the ability of men to orient themselves in accordance with cherished values. And which values? Even when they do not panic, men often sense that older ways of feeling and thinking have collapsed and that newer beginnings are ambiguous to the point of moral stasis. Is it any wonder that ordinary men feel they cannot cope with the larger worlds with which they are so suddenly confronted? That they cannot understand the meaning of their epoch for their own lives? That—in defense of selfhood—they become morally insensible, trying to remain altogether private men? Is it any wonder that they come to be possessed by a sense of the trap?

It is not only information that they need—in this Age of Fact, information often dominates their attention and overwhelms their capacities to assimilate it. It is not only the skills of reason that they need—although their struggles to acquire these often exhaust their limited moral energy.

What they need, and what they feel they need, is a quality of mind that will help them to use information and to develop reason in order to achieve lucid summations of what is going on in the world and of what may be happening within themselves. It is this quality, I am going to contend, that journalists and scholars, artists and publics, scientists and editors are coming to expect of what may be called the *sociological imagination*.

1

The sociological imagination enables its possessor to understand the larger historical scene in terms of its meaning for the inner life and the external career of a variety of individuals. It enables him to take into account how individuals, in the welter of their daily experience, often become falsely conscious of their social positions. Within that welter, the framework of modern society is sought, and within that framework the psychologies of a variety of men and women are formulated. By such means the personal uneasiness of individuals is focused upon explicit troubles and the indifference of publics is transformed into involvement with public issues.

The first fruit of this imagination—and the first lesson of the social science that embodies it—is the idea that the individual can understand his own experience and gauge his own fate only by locating himself within his period, that he can know her own chances in life only by becoming aware of those of all individuals in his circumstances. In many ways it is a terrible lesson; in many ways a magnificent one. We do not know the limits of man's capacities for supreme effort or willing degradation, for agony or glee, for pleasurable brutality or the sweetness of reason. Buy in our time we have come to know that the limits of "human nature" are frighteningly broad. We have come to know that every individual lives, from one generation to the next, in some society; that he lives out a biography, and lives it out within some historical sequence. By the fact of this living, he contributes, however minutely, to the shaping of this society and to the course of its history, even as he is made by society and by its historical push and shove.

The sociological imagination enables us to grasp history and biography and the relations between the two within society. That is its task and its promise. To recognize this task and this promise is the mark of the classic social analyst. It is characteristic of Herbert Spencer—turgid, polysyllabic, comprehensive; of E. A. Ross—graceful, muckraking, upright; of Auguste Comte and Emile Durkheim; of the intricate and subtle Karl Mannheim. It is the quality of all that is intellectually excellent in Karl Marx; it is the clue to Thorstein Veblen's brilliant and ironic insight, to Joseph Schumpeter's many-sided constructions of reality; it is the basis of the psychological sweep of W. E. H. Lecky no less than of the profundity and clarity of Max Weber. And it is the signal of what is best in contemporary studies of man and society.

No social study that does not come back to the problems of biography, of history and of their intersections within a society has completed its intellectual journey. Whatever the specific problems of the classic social analysts, however limited or however broad the features of social reality they have examined, those who have been imaginatively aware of the promise of their work have consistently asked three sorts of questions:

1. What is the structure of this particular society as a whole? What are its essential components, and how are they related to one another? How does it differ from other varieties of social order? Within it, what is the meaning of any particular feature for its continuance and for its change?
2. Where does this society stand in human history? What are the mechanics by which it is changing? What is its place within and its meaning for the development of humanity as a whole? How does any particular feature we are examining affect, and how is it

affected by, the historical period in which it moves? And this period—what are its essential features? How does it differ from other periods? What are its characteristic ways of history-making?
3. What varieties of men and women now prevail in this society and in this period? And what varieties are coming to prevail? In what ways are they selected and formed, liberated and repressed, made sensitive and blunted? What kinds of "human nature" are revealed in the conduct and character we observe in this society in this period? And what is the meaning for "human nature" of each and every feature of the society we are examining?

Whether the point of interest is a great power state or a minor literary mood, a family, a prison, a creed—these are the kinds of questions the best social analysts have asked. They are the intellectual pivots of classic studies of individuals in society—and they are the questions inevitably raised by any mind possessing the sociological imagination. For that imagination is the capacity to shift from one perspective to another—from the political to the psychological; from examination of a single family to comparative assessment of the national budgets of the world; from the theological school to the military establishment; from considerations of an oil industry to studies of contemporary poetry. It is the capacity to range from the most impersonal and remote transformations to the most intimate features of the human self—and to see the relations between the two. Back of its use there is always the urge to know the social and historical meaning of the individual in the society and in the period in which he has his quality and his being.

That, in brief, is why it is by means of the sociological imagination that men now hope to grasp what is going on in the world, and to understand what is happening in themselves as minute points of the intersections of biography and history within society. In large part, contemporary man's self-conscious view of himself as at least an outsider, if not a permanent stranger, rests upon an absorbed realization of social relativity and of the transformative power of history. The sociological imagination is the most fruitful form of this self-consciousness. By its use men whose mentalities have swept only a series of limited orbits often come to feel as if suddenly awakened in a house with which they had only supposed themselves to be familiar. Correctly or incorrectly, they often come to feel that they can now provide themselves with adequate summations, cohesive assessments, comprehensive orientations. Older decisions that once appeared sound now seem to them products of a mind unaccountably dens. Their capacity for astonishment is made lively again. They acquire a new way of thinking, they experience a transvaluation of values: in a word, by their reflection and by their sensibility, they realize the cultural meaning of the social sciences.

2

Perhaps the most fruitful distinction with which the sociological imagination works is between "the personal troubles of milieu" and "the public issues of social structure." This distinction is an essential tool of the sociological imagination and a feature of all classic work in social science.

Troubles occur within the character of the individual and within the range of his immediate relations with others; they have to do with his self and with those limited areas of social life of which he is directly and personally aware. Accordingly, the statement and the resolution of troubles properly lie within the individual as a biographical entity and within the scope of his immediate milieu—the social setting that is directly open to his personal experience and to some extent his willful activity. A trouble is a private matter: values cherished by an individual are felt by him to be threatened.

Issues have to do with matters that transcend these local environments of the individual and the range of her inner life. They have to do with the organization of many such milieux into the institutions of an historical society as a whole, with the ways in which various milieux overlap and interpenetrate to form the larger structure of social and historical life. An issue is a public matter: some value cherished by publics is felt to be threatened. Often there is a debate about what that value really is and about what it is that really threatens it. This debate is often without focus if only because it is the very nature of an issue, unlike even widespread trouble, that it cannot very well be defined in terms of the immediate and everyday environments of ordinary people. An issue, in fact, often involves a crisis in institutional arrangements, and often too it involves what Marxists call "contradictions" or "antagonisms."

In these terms, consider unemployment. When, in a city of 100,000, only one is unemployed, that is his personal trouble, and for its relief we properly look to the character of the individual, his skills and his immediate opportunities. But when in a nation of 50 million employees, 15 million people are unemployed, that is an issue, and we may not hope to find its solution within the range of opportunities open to any one individual. The very structure of opportunities has collapsed. Both the correct statement of the problem and the range of possible solutions require us to consider the economic and political institutions of the society, and not merely the personal situations and character of a scatter of individuals.

Consider war. The personal problem of war, when it occurs, may be how to survive it or how to die in it with honor; how to make money out of it; how to climb into the higher safety of the military apparatus; or how to contribute to the war's termination. In short, according to one's values, to find a set of milieux and within it to survive the war or make one's death in it meaningful. But the structural issues of war have to do with its causes; with what types of men it throws up into command; with its effects upon economic and political, family and religious institutions, with the unorganized irresponsibility of a world of nation-states.

Consider marriage. Inside a marriage a man and a woman may experience personal troubles, but when the divorce rate during the first four years of marriage is 250 out of every 1,000 attempts, this is an indication of a structural issue having to do with the institutions of marriage and the family and other institutions that bear upon them.

Or consider the metropolis—the horrible, beautiful, ugly, magnificent sprawl of the great city. For many upper-class people the personal solution to "the problem of the city" is to have an apartment with private garage under it in the heart of the city and forty miles out, a house by Henry Hill, garden by Garrett Eckbo, on a hundred acres of private land. In these two controlled environments—with a small staff at each end and a private helicopter connection—most people could solve many of the problems of personal milieux caused by the facts of the city. But all this, however splendid, does not solve the public issues that the structural fact of the city poses. What should be done with this wonderful monstrosity? Break it all up into scattered units, combining residence and work? Refurbish it as it stands? Or, after evacuation, dynamite it and build new cities according to new plans in new places? What should those plans be? And who is to decide and to accomplish whatever choice is made? These are structural issues; to confront them and to solve them requires us to consider political and economic issues that affect innumerable milieux.

In so far as an economy is so arranged that slumps occur, the problem of unemployment becomes incapable of personal solution. In so far as war is inherent in the nation-state system and in the uneven industrialization of the world, the ordinary individual in his restricted milieu will be powerless—with or without psychiatric aid—to solve the troubles this system or lack of system imposes upon him. In so far as the family as an institution turns women into darling little slaves and men into their chief providers and unweaned dependents, the problem of a satisfactory marriage remains incapable of purely private solution. In so far as the overdeveloped megalopolis and the overdeveloped automobile are built-in features of the overdeveloped society, the issues of urban living will not be solved by personal ingenuity and private wealth.

What we experience in various and specific milieux, I have noted, is often caused by structural changes. Accordingly, to understand the changes of many personal milieux we are required to look beyond them. And the number and variety of such structural changes increase as the institutions within which we live become more embracing and more intricately connected with one another. To be aware of the idea of social structure and to use it with sensibility is to be capable of tracing such linkages among a great variety of milieux. To be able to do that is to possess the sociological imagination.

Notes

1. *milieux*—derived from the French. Translates as "social environments."

Name: _____   Class: _____

Date: _____   Section: _____

Reading Comprehension Activity Sheet

The Promise, C. Wright Mills

1. According to C. Wright Mills, what exactly is a "sociological imagination"? _____

_____
_____
_____
_____
_____
_____
_____
_____
_____
_____
_____

2. How would developing and utilizing your "sociological imagination" be beneficial to you? ____

_____
_____
_____
_____
_____
_____
_____
_____
_____
_____
_____
_____
_____
_____

chapter 2

Theory and Research

Some conditions of Obedience and Disobedience to Authority
Stanley Milgram

Research and Racism: The Case of the Tuskegee Syphilis Study
Allan M. Brandt

Some Conditions of Obedience and Disobedience to Authority

Stanley Milgram

The situation in which one agent commands another to hurt a third turns up time and again as a significant theme in human relations. . . . We describe an experimental program, recently concluded at Yale University, in which a particular expression of this conflict is studied by experimental means.

In its most general form the problem may be defined thus: if X tells Y to hurt Z, under what conditions will Y carry out the command of X and under what conditions will he refuse. In the more limited form possible in laboratory research, the question becomes: if an experimenter tells a subject to hurt another person, under what conditions will the subject go along with this instruction, and under what conditions will he refuse to obey. The laboratory problem is not so much a dilution of the general statement as one concrete expression of the many particular forms this question may assume.

One aim of the research was to study behavior in a strong situation of deep consequence to the participants, for the psychological forces operative in powerful and lifelike forms of the conflict may not be brought into play under diluted conditions. . . .

Terminology

If Y follows the command of X we shall say that he has obeyed X; if he fails to carry out the command of X, we shall say that he has disobeyed X. The terms to *obey* and to *disobey*, as used here, refer to the subject's overt action only, and carry no implication for the motive or experiential states accompanying the action. . . .

From *Human Relations* by Stanley Milgram. Copyright © 1965 by Stanley Milgram. Reprinted by permission of the Estate.

A subject who complies with the entire series of experimental commands will be termed an *obedient* subject; one who at any point in the command series defies the experimenter will be called a *disobedient* or *defiant* subject. As used in this report, the terms refer only to the subject's performance in the experiment, and do not necessarily imply a general personality disposition to submit to or reject authority.

Subject Population

The subjects used in all experimental conditions were male adults, residing in the greater New Haven and Bridgeport [Connecticut] areas, aged 20 to 50 years, and engaged in a wide variety of occupations. Each experimental condition described in this report employed 40 fresh subjects and was carefully balanced for age and occupational types. The occupational composition for each experiment was: workers, skilled and unskilled: 40 per cent; white collar, sales, business: 40 per cent; professionals: 20 per cent. The occupations were intersected with three age categories (subjects in 20s, 30s, and 40s, assigned to each condition in the proportions of 20, 40, and 40 per cent respectively).

The General Laboratory Procedure

The focus of the study concerns the amount of electric shock a subject is willing to administer to another person when ordered by an experimenter to give the 'victim' increasingly more severe punishment. The act of administering shock is set in the context of a learning experiment, ostensibly designed to study the effect of punishment on memory. Aside from the experimenter, one naïve subject and one accomplice perform in each session. On arrival each subject is paid $4.50. After a general talk by the experimenter, telling how little scientists know about the effect of punishment on memory, subjects are informed that one member of the pair will serve as teacher and one as learner. A rigged drawing is held so that the naïve subject is always the teacher, and the accomplice becomes the learner. The learner is taken to an adjacent room and strapped into an 'electric chair'.

The naïve subject is told that it is his task to teach the learner a list of paired associates, to test him on the list, and to administer punishment whenever the learner errs in the test. Punishment takes the form of electric shock, delivered to the learner by means of a shock generator controlled by the naïve subject. The teacher is instructed to increase the intensity of electric shock one step on the generator on each error. The learner, according to plan, provides many wrong answers, so that before long the naïve subject must give him the strongest shock on the generator. Increases in shock level are met by increasingly insistent demands from the learner that the experiment be stopped because of the growing discomfort to him. However, in clear terms the experimenter orders the teacher to continue with the procedure in disregard of the learner's protests. *Thus, the naïve subject must resolve a conflict between two mutually incompatible demands from the social field. He may continue to follow the orders of the experimenter and shock the learner with increasing severity, or he may refuse to follow the orders of the experimenter and heed the learner's pleas. The experimenter's authority operates not in a free field, but against ever-mounting countervailing pressures from the person being punished.*

A few technical points need to be considered before the findings of the study are described. For the purpose of delivering shock, a simulated shock generator is used, with 30 clearly marked voltage levels that range from 15 to 450 volts (and each activated by one of 30 individual lever switches set in a horizontal line). The naïve subject is given a sample shock of 45 volts to convince him of the authenticity of the instrument. The generator bears verbal designations that range from 'Slight Shock' to 'Danger: Severe Shock'.

The responses of the victim are standardized on tape, and each protest is coordinated to a particular voltage level on the shock generator. Starting with 75 volts the learner begins to grunt and moan. At 150 volts he demands to be let out of the experiment. At 180 volts he cries out that he can not longer stand the pain. At 300 volts he refused to provide any more answers to the memory test, insisting that he is no longer a participant in the experiment and must be freed. In response to this last tactic, the experimenter instructs the naïve subject to treat the absence of an answer as equivalent to a wrong answer, and to follow the usual shock procedure. The experimenter reinforces his demand with the statement: 'You have no other choice, you must go on!' (This imperative is used whenever the naïve subject tries to break off the experiment.) If the subject refuses to give the next higher level of shock, the experiment is considered at an end. A quantitative value is assigned to the subject's performance based on the maximum intensity shock he administered before breaking off. Thus any subject's score may range from zero (for a subject unwilling to administer the first shock level) to 30 (for a subject who proceeds to the highest voltage level on the board). For any particular subject and for any particular experimental condition the degree to which participants have followed the experimenter's orders may be specified with a numerical value, corresponding to the metric on the shock generator. . . .

Immediacy of the Victim

This series consisted of four experimental conditions. In each condition the victim was brought 'psychologically' closer to the subject giving him shocks.

In the first condition (Remote Feedback) the victim was placed in another room and could not be heard or seen by the subject, except that, at 300 volts, he pounded on the wall in protest. After 315 volts he no longer answered or was heard from.

The second condition (Voice Feedback) was identical to the first except that voice protests were introduced. As in the first condition the victim was placed in an adjacent room, but his complaints could be heard clearly through a door left slightly ajar, and through the walls of the laboratory.

The third experimental condition (Proximity) was similar to the second, except that the victim was now placed in the same room as the subject, and 1½ feet from him. Thus he was visible as well as audible, and voice cues were provided.

The fourth, and final, condition of this series (Touch-Proximity) was identical to the third, with this exception: the victim received a shock only when his hand rested on a shockplate. At the 150-vold level the victim again demanded to be let free and, in this condition, refused to place his hand on the shockplate. The experimenter ordered the naïve subject to force the victim's hand onto the plate. Thus obedience in this condition required that the subject have physical contact with the victim in order to give him punishment beyond the 150-volt level.

Forty adult subjects were studied in each condition. The data revealed that obedience was significantly reduced as the victim was rendered more immediate to the subject. The mean maximum shock for the conditions is shown in *Figure 1*.

Expressed in terms of the proportion of obedient of defiant subjects, the findings are that 34 per cent of the subjects defied the experimenter in the Remote condition, 37.5 per cent in Voice Feedback, 60 per cent in Proximity, and 70 per cent in Touch-Proximity.

How are we to account for this effect? A first conjecture might be that as the victim was brought closer the subject became more aware of the intensity of his suffering and regulated his behavior accordingly. This makes sense, but our evidence does not support the interpre-

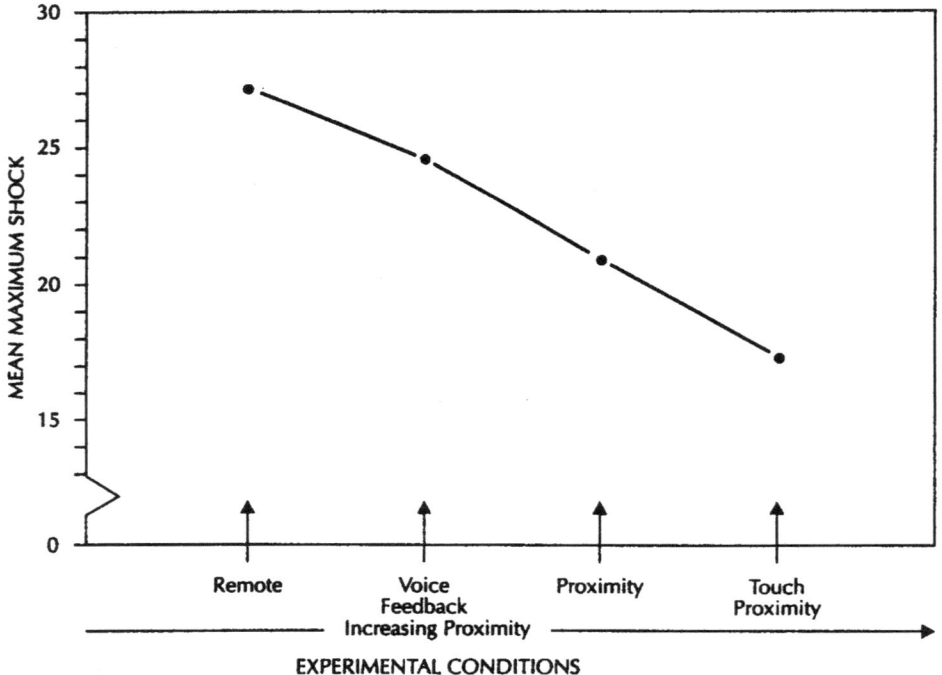

FIGURE 1
Mean Maxima in Proximity Series

tation. There are no consistent differences in the attributed level of pain across the four conditions (i.e. the amount of pain experienced by the victim as estimated by the subject and expressed on a 14-point scale). But it is easy to speculate about alternative mechanisms:

Empathic cues. In the Remote and to a lesser extent the Voice Feedback condition, the victim's suffering possesses an abstract, remote quality for the subject. He is aware, but only in a conceptual sense, that his actions cause pain to another person; the fact is apprehended, but not felt. The phenomenon is common enough. The bombardier can reasonably suppose that his weapons will inflict suffering and death, yet this knowledge is divested of affect, and does not move him to a felt, emotional response to the suffering resulting from his actions. . . .

Denial and narrowing of the cognitive field. The Remote condition allows a narrowing of the cognitive field so that the victim is put out of mind. The subject no longer considers the act of depressing a lever relevant to moral judgement, for it is no longer associated with the victim's suffering. When the victim is close it is more difficult to exclude him phenomenologically. . . . The mechanism of denial can no longer be brought into play. One subject in the Remote condition said: 'It's funny how you really begin to forget that there's a guy out there, even though you can hear him. For a long time I just concentrated on pressing the switches and reading the words.'

Reciprocal fields. If in the Proximity condition the subject is in an improved position to observe the victim, the reverse is also true. The actions of the subject now come under proximal scrutiny by the victim. Possibly, it is easier to harm a person when he is unable to observe our actions than when he can see what we are doing. His surveillance of the action directed against him may give rise to shame, or guilt, which may then serve to curtail the action. . . .

Phenomenal unity of act. In the Remote conditions it is more difficult for the subject to gain a sense of *relatedness* between his own actions and the consequences of these actions for the victim. There is a physical and spatial separation of the act and its consequences. The subject depresses a lever in one room, and protests and cries are heard from another. The two events are in correlation, yet they lack a compelling phenomenological unity. . . .

Incipient group formation. Placing the victim in another room not only takes him further from the subject, but the subject and the experimenter are drawn relatively closer. There is incipient group formation between the experimenter and the subject, from which the victim is excluded. The wall between the victim and the others deprives him of an intimacy which the experimenter and subject feel. In the Remote condition, the victim is truly an outsider, who stands alone, physically and psychologically.

When the victim is placed close to the subject, it becomes easier to form an alliance with him against the experimenter. Subjects no longer have to face the experimenter alone. They have an ally who is close at hand and eager to collaborate in a revolt against the experiment. Thus, the changing set of spatial relations leads to a potentially shifting set of alliances over the several experimental conditions.

Acquired behavior dispositions. It is commonly observed that laboratory mice will rarely fight with their litter mates. . . . [T]he organism learns that it is safer to be aggressive toward others at a distance, and precarious to be so when the parties are within arm's reach. Through a pattern of rewards and punishments, he acquires a disposition to avoid aggression at close quarters, a disposition which does not extend to harming others at a distance. And this may account for experimental findings in the remote and proximal experiments. . . .

Closeness of Authority

If the spatial relationship of the subject and victim is relevant to the degree of obedience, would not the relationship of subject to experimenter also play a part?

There are reasons to feel that, on arrival, the subject is oriented primarily to the experimenter rather than to the victim. He has come to the laboratory to fit into the structure that the experimenter—not the victim—would provide. He has come less to understand his behavior than to *reveal* that behavior to a competent scientist, and he is willing to display himself as the scientist's purposes require. Most subjects seem quite concerned about the appearance they are making before the experimenter, and one could argue that this preoccupation in a relatively new and strange setting makes the subject somewhat insensitive to the triadic nature of the social situation. . . .

In a series of experiments we varied the physical closeness and degree of surveillance of the experimenter. In one condition the experimenter sat just a few feet away from the subject. In a second condition, after giving initial instructions the experimenter left the laboratory and gave his orders by telephone; in still a third condition the experimenter was never seen, providing instructions by means of a tape recording activated when the subjects entered the laboratory.

Obedience dropped sharply as the experimenter was physically removed from the laboratory. The number of obedient subjects in the first condition (Experimenter Present) was almost three times as great as in the second, where the experimenter gave his orders by telephone. Twenty-six subjects were fully obedient in the first condition, and only 9 in the second. . . . Subjects seemed able to take a far stronger stand against the experimenter when they did not have to encounter him face to face, and the experimenter's power over the subject was severely curtailed.

Moreover, when the experimenter was absent, subjects displayed an interesting form of behavior that had not occurred under his surveillance. Though continuing with the experiment, several subjects administered lower shocks than were required and never informed the experimenter of their deviation from the correct procedure. . . . Indeed, in telephone conversations some subjects specifically assured the experimenter that they were raising the shock level according to instruction, whereas in fact they were repeatedly using the lowest shock on the board. This form of behavior is particularly interesting: although these subjects acted in a way that clearly undermined the avowed purposes of the experiment, they found it easier to handle the conflict in this manner than to precipitate an open break with authority. . . .

Experiments in this series show that the physical *presence* of an authority is an important force contributing to the subject's obedience or defiance. Taken together with the first experimental series on the proximity of the victim, it would appear that something akin to fields of force, diminishing in effectiveness with increasing psychological distance from their source, have a controlling effect on the subject's performance. As the victim is brought closer, the subject finds it harder to administer shocks to him. When the victim's position is held constant relative to the subject, and the authority is made more remote, the subject finds it easier to break off the experiment. This effect is substantial in both cases, but manipulation of the experimenter's position yielded the more powerful results. Obedience to destructive commands is highly dependent on the proximal relations between authority and subject.

Tensions

The description of final scores does not fully convey the character of the subjects' performance, and it would be useful to interrupt our reporting of quantitative relationships to remark on the subjects' general reaction to the situation.

One might suppose that a subject would simply break off or continue as his conscience and temperament dictated. Yet this is very far from what happened. There were powerful reactions of tension and emotional strain in a substantial proportion of the participants. Persons were observed to sweat, tremble, stutter, bite their lips, and groan as they found themselves increasingly implicated in the experimental conflict. Some sense of the subjects' mood can be gotten from a transcript of their remarks at break-off point. Here are the remarks of two defiant subjects:

> Is he banging? . . . Is he hurt out there? Well, I don't want to be responsible for anything that happens to him. No, I can't go on with it. I don't know whether he's all right or not. I mean he may have a heart condition or something; I wouldn't feel right doing it. He's banging for help. He's evidently in trouble or he wouldn't bang . . . I don't see any sense to this—to knocking him out or something. I just can't see it.
> (*Subject refuses to administer shocks*) [*Subject 0108*]
>
> The man is banging. He wants to get out . . . I'm sorry. If the man wants to get out I'd just as soon stop . . . I don't want to administer any more [extremely excited] . . . I will gladly refund the check, but I will not harm this man . . . I'm sorry, I will not give him any more if he obviously wants to get out. There is no money in the world that will make me hurt another individual. [*Subject 010X*]

And here is a transcript from an obedient subject. He began the experiment calmly, but became increasingly tense as the experiment proceeded. After administering the 150-volt shock, he began to address the experimenter in agitated tones:

> *150 volts delivered.* You want me to keep going?
> *165 volts delivered.* That guy is hollering in there. There's a lot of them here. He's liable to have heart condition. You want me to go?
> *180 volts delivered.* He can't stand it! I'm not going to kill that man in there! You hear him hollering? He's hollering. He can't stand it. What if something happens to him? . . . I'm not

going to get that man sick in there. He's hollering in there. You know what I mean? I mean I refuse to take responsibility. He's getting hurt in there. He's in there hollering. Too many left here. Geez, if he gets them wrong. There's too many of them left. I mean who is going to take responsibility if anything happens to that gentleman?
[*The experimenter accepts responsibility.*] All right.
195 volts delivered. You see he's hollering. Hear that. Gee, I don't know. [*The experimenter says: 'the experiment requires that you go on.'*]—I know it does sir, but I mean—hugh—he don't know what he's in for. He's up to 195 volts.
210 volts delivered
225 volts delivered
240 volts delivered. Aw, no. You mean I've got to keep going up with the scale? No sir. I'm not going to kill that man! I'm not going to give him 450 volts! [*The experimenter says: 'The experiment requires that you go on.'*]—I know it does, but that man is hollering in there, sir. . . .

Despite his numerous, agitated objections, which were constant accompaniments to his actions, the subject unfailingly obeyed the experimenter, proceeding to the highest shock level on the generator. He displayed a curious dissociation between word and action. Although at the verbal level he had resolved not to go on, his actions were fully in accord with the experimenter's commands. This subject did not want to shock the victim, and he found it an extremely disagreeable task, but he was unable to invent a response that would free him from *E*'s authority. Many subjects cannot find the specific verbal formula that would enable them to reject the role assigned to them by the experimenter. Perhaps our culture does not provide adequate models for disobedience. . . .

Background Authority

In psychophysics, animal learning, and other branches of psychology, the fact that measures are obtained at one institution rather than another is irrelevant to the interpretation of the findings, so long as the technical facilities for measurement are adequate and the operations are carried out with competence.

But it cannot be assumed that this holds true for the present study. The effectiveness of the experimenter's commands may depend in an important way on the larger institutional context in which they are issued. The experiments described thus far were conducted at Yale University, an organization which most subjects regarded with respect and sometimes awe. In post-experimental interviews several participants remarked that the locale and sponsorship of the study gave them confidence in the integrity, competence, and benign purposes of the personnel; many indicated that they would not have shocked the learner if the experiments had been done elsewhere.

This issue of background authority seemed to us important for an interpretation of the results that had been obtained thus far; moreover it is highly relevant to any comprehensive theory of human obedience. Consider, for example, how closely our compliance with the imperatives of others is tied to particular institutions and locales in our day-to-day activities.

On request, we expose our throats to a man with a razor blade in the barber shop, but would not do so in a shoe store; in the latter setting we willingly follow the clerk's request to stand in our stockinged feet, but resist the command in a bank. In the laboratory of a great university, subjects may comply with a set of commands that would be resisted if given elsewhere. *One must always question the relationship of obedience to a person's sense of the context in which he is operating.*

To explore the problem we moved our apparatus to an office building in industrial Bridgeport and replicated experimental conditions, without any visible tie to the university.

Bridgeport subjects were invited to the experiment through a mail circular similar to the one used in the Yale study, with appropriate changes in letterhead, etc. As in the earlier study, subjects were paid $4.50 for coming to the laboratory. The same age and occupational distributions used at Yale, and the identical personnel, were employed.

The purpose in relocating in Bridgeport was to assure a complete dissociation from Yale, and in this regard we were fully successful. On the surface, the study appeared to be conducted by RESEARCH ASSOCIATES OF BRIDGEPORT, an organization of unknown character (the title had been concocted exclusively for use in this study).

The experiments were conducted in a three-room office suite in a somewhat run-down commercial building located in the downtown shopping area. The laboratory was sparsely furnished, though clean, and marginally respectable in appearance. When subjects inquired about professional affiliations, they were informed only that we were a private firm conducting research for industry. . . .

There was no noticeable reduction in tension for the Bridgeport subjects. And the subjects' estimation of the amount of pain felt by the victim was slightly, though not significantly, higher than in the Yale study.

A failure to obtain complete obedience in Bridgeport would indicate that the extreme compliance found in New Haven subjects was tied closely to the background authority of Yale University; if a large proportion of the subjects remained fully obedient, very different conclusions would be called for.

As it turned out, the level of obedience in Bridgeport, although somewhat reduced, was not significantly lower than that obtained at Yale. A large proportion of the Bridgeport subjects were fully obedient to the experimenter's commands (48 per cent of the Bridgeport subjects delivered the maximum shock *vs.* 65 per cent in the corresponding condition at Yale). . . .

Levels of Obedience and Defiance

One general finding that merits attention is the high level of obedience manifested in the experimental situation. Subjects often expressed deep disapproval of shocking a man in the face of his objections, and others denounced it as senseless and stupid. Yet many subjects complied even while they protested. The proportion of obedient subjects greatly exceeded the expectations of the experimenter and his colleagues. At the outset, we had conjectured that subjects would not, in general, go above the level of 'Strong Shock'. In practice, many subjects were willing to administer the most extreme shocks available when commanded by the experimenter. For some subjects the experiment provides an occasion for aggressive release. And for others it demonstrates the extent to which obedient dispositions are deeply ingrained, and are engaged irrespective of their consequences for others. Yet this is not the whole story. Somehow, the subject becomes implicated in a situation from which he cannot disengage himself. . . .

Many people, not knowing much about the experiment, claim that subjects who go to the end of the board are sadistic. Nothing could be more foolish as an overall characterization of these persons. It is like saying that a person thrown into a swift-flowing stream is necessarily a fast swimmer, or that he has great stamina because he moves so rapidly relative to the bank. The context of action must always be considered. The individual, upon entering the laboratory, becomes integrated into a situation that carries its own momentum. The subject's problem then is how to become disengaged from a situation which is moving in an altogether ugly direction.

The fact that disengagement is so difficult testifies to the potency of the forces that keep the subject at the control board. Are these forces to be conceptualized as individual motives and expressed in the language of personality dynamics, or are they to be seen as the effects of social structure and pressures arising from the situational field?

A full understanding of the subject's action will, I feel, require that both perspectives be adopted. The person brings to the laboratory enduring dispositions toward authority and aggression, and at the same time he becomes enmeshed in a social structure that is no less an objective fact of the case. . . .

Postscript

Almost a thousand adults were individually studied in the obedience research, and there were many specific conclusions regarding the variables that control obedience and disobedience to authority. Some of these have been discussed briefly in the preceding sections, and more detailed reports will be released subsequently.

There are now some other generalizations I should like to make, which do not derive in any strictly logical fashion from the experiments as carried out, but which, I feel, ought to be made. They are formulations of an intuitive sort that have been forced on me by observation of many subjects responding to the pressures of authority. The assertions represent a painful alteration in my own thinking; and since they were acquired only under the repeated impact of direct observation, I have no illusion that they will be generally accepted by persons who have not had the same experience.

With numbing regularity good people were seen to knuckle under the demands of authority and perform actions that were callous and severe. Men who are in everyday life responsible and decent were seduced by the trappings of authority, by the control of their perceptions, and by the uncritical acceptance of the experimenter's definition of the situation, into performing harsh acts.

What is the limit of such obedience? At many points we attempted to establish a boundary. Cries from the victim were inserted; not good enough. The victim claimed heart trouble; subjects still shocked him on command. The victim pleaded that he be let free, and his answers no longer registered on the signal box; subjects continued to shock him. At the outset we had not conceived that such drastic procedures would be needed to generate disobedience, and each step was added only as the ineffectiveness of the earlier techniques became clear. The final effort to establish a limit was the Touch-Proximity condition. But the very first subject in this condition subdued the victim on command, and proceeded to the highest shock level. A quarter of the subjects in this condition performed similarly.

The results, as seen and felt in the laboratory, are to this author disturbing. They raise the possibility that human nature, or—more specifically—the kind of character produced in American democratic society, cannot be counted on to insulate its citizens from brutality and inhumane treatment at the direction of malevolent authority. A substantial proportion of people do what they are told to do, irrespective of the content of the act and without limitations of conscience, so long as they perceive that the command comes from a legitimate authority. If in this study an anonymous experimenter could successfully command adults to subdue a fifty-year-old man, and force on him painful electric shocks against his protests, one can only wonder what government, with its vastly greater authority and prestige, can command of its subjects. There is, of course, the extremely important question of whether malevolent political institutions could or would arise in American society. The present research contributes nothing to this issue.

Name: _____   Class: _____

Date: _____   Section: _____

Reading Comprehension Activity Sheet

Some Conditions of Obedience and Disobedience to Authority, Stanley Milgram

1. Briefly describe Milgram's experiment. _____

_____

_____

_____

_____

_____

_____

_____

_____

_____

_____

_____

_____

2. How did the four experimental conditions impact the outcome of the study? What additional conditions produced differing results? _____

_____

_____

_____

_____

_____

_____

_____

_____

_____

_____

_____

_____

3. Milgram states that the results of his study are disturbing. Why? _____

Racism and Research
The Case of the Tuskegee Syphilis Study

Allan M. Brandt

In 1932 the U.S. Public Health Service (USPHS) initiated an experiment in Macon County, Alabama, to determine the natural course of untreated, latent syphilis in black males. The test comprised 400 syphilitic men, as well as 200 uninfected men who served as controls. The first published report of the study appeared in 1936 with subsequent papers issued every four to six years, through the 1960s. When penicillin became widely available by the early 1950s as the preferred treatment for syphilis, the men did not receive therapy. In fact on several occasions, the USPHS actually sought to prevent treatment. Moreover, a committee at the federally operated Center for Disease Control decided in 1969 that the study should be continued. Only in 1972, when accounts of the study first appeared in the national press, did the Department of Health, Education, and Welfare halt the experiment. At that time seventy-four of the test subjects were still alive; at least twenty-eight, but perhaps more than 100 had died directly from advanced syphilitic lesions. In August 1972, HEW appointed an investigatory panel which issued a report the following year. The panel found the study to have been "ethically unjustified," and argues that penicillin should have been provided to the men.

This article attempts to place the Tuskegee Study in a historical context and to assess its ethical implications. Despite the media attention which the study received, the HEW *Final Report,* and the criticism expressed by several professional organizations, the experiment has been largely misunderstood. The most basic questions of *how* the study was undertaken in the first place and *why* it continued for forty years were never addressed by the HEW investigation. Moreover, the panel misconstrued the nature of the experiment, failing to consult

From *Hastings Center Report* by Allan M. Brandt. Copyright © The Hastings Center. Reprinted by permission.

important documents available at the National Archives which bear significantly on its ethical assessment. Only by examining the specific ways in which values are engaged in scientific research can the study be understood.

Racism and Medical Opinion

A brief review of the prevailing scientific thought regarding race and heredity in the early twentieth century is fundamental for an understanding of the Tuskegee Study. By the turn of the century, Darwinism had provided a new rationale for American racism. Essentially primitive peoples, it was argued, could not be assimilated into a complex, white civilization. Scientists speculated that in the struggle for survival the Negro in America was doomed. Particularly prone to disease, vice, and crime, black Americans could not be helped by education of philanthropy. Social Darwinists analyzed census data to predict the virtual extinction of the Negro in the Twentieth century, for they believed the Negro race in America was in the throes of a degenerative evolutionary process.

The medical profession supported these findings of late nineteenth- and early twentieth-century anthropologists, ethnologists, and biologists. Physicians studying the effects of emancipation on health concluded almost universally that freedom had caused the mental, moral, and physical deterioration of the black population. They substantiated this argument by citing examples in the comparative anatomy of the black and white races. As Dr. W. T. English wrote: "A careful inspection reveals the body of the negro a mass of minor defects and imperfections from the crown of the head to the soles of the feet. . . ." Cranial structures, wide nasal apertures, receding chins, projecting jaws, all typed the Negro as the lowest species in the Darwinian hierarchy.

Interest in racial differences centered on the sexual nature of blacks. The Negro, doctors explained, possessed an excessive sexual desire, which threatened the very foundations of white society. As one physician noted in the *Journal of the American Medical Association,* "The negro springs from a southern race, and as such his sexual appetite is strong; all of this environments stimulate this appetite, and as a general rule his emotional type of religion certainly does not decrease it." Doctors reported a complete lack of morality on the part of blacks:

> Virtue in the negro race is like angels' visits—few and far between. In a practice of sixteen years I have never examined a virgin negro over fourteen years of age.

A particularly ominous feature of this overzealous sexuality, doctors argued, was the black males' desire for white women. "A perversion from which most races are exempt," wrote Dr. English, "prompts the negro's inclination towards white women, whereas other races incline towards females of their own." Though English estimated the "gray matter of the negro brain" to be at least a thousand years behind that of the white races, his genital organs were overdeveloped. As Dr. William Lee Howard noted:

> The attacks on defenseless white women are evidences of racial instincts that are about as amenable to ethical culture as is the inherent odor of the race.... When education will reduce the size of the negro's penis as well as bring about the sensitiveness of the terminal fibers which exist in the Caucasian, then will it also be able to prevent the African's birthright to sexual madness and excess.

One southern medical journal proposed "Castration Instead of Lynching," as retribution for black sexual crimes. "An impressive trial by a ghost-like kuklux klan [sic] and a 'ghost' physician or surgeon to perform the operation would make it an event the 'patient' would never forget," noted the editorial.

According to these physicians, lust and immorality, unstable families, and reversion to barbaric tendencies made blacks especially prone to venereal diseases. One doctor estimated that over 50 percent of all Negroes over the age of twenty-five were syphilitic. Virtually free of disease as slaves, they were now overwhelmed by it, according to informed medical opinion. Moreover, doctors believed that treatment for venereal disease among blacks was impossible, particularly because in its latent stage the symptoms of syphilis become quiescent. As Dr. Thomas W. Murrell wrote:

> They come for treatment at the beginning and at the end. When there are visible manifestations or when harried by pain, they readily come, for as a race they are not averse to physic; but tell them not, though they look well and feel well, that they are still diseased. Here ignorance rates science a fool. . . .

Even the best educated black, according to Murrell, could not be convinced to seek treatment for syphilis. Venereal disease, according to some doctors, threatened the future of the race. The medical profession attributed the low birth rate among blacks to the high prevalence of venereal disease which caused stillbirths and miscarriages. Moreover, the high rates of syphilis were thought to lead to increased insanity and crime. One doctor writing at the turn of the century estimated that the number of insane Negroes had increased thirteen-fold since the end of the Civil War. Dr. Murrell's conclusion echoed the most informed anthropological and ethnological data:

> So the scourge sweeps among them. Those that are treated are only half cured, and the effort to assimilate a complex civilization driving their diseases minds until the results are criminal records. Perhaps here, in conjunction with tuberculosis, will be the end of the negro problem. Disease will accomplish what man cannot do.

This particular configuration of ideas formed the core of medical opinion concerning blacks, sex, and disease in the early twentieth century. Doctors generally discounted socioeconomic explanations of the state of black health, arguing that better medical care could not alter the evolutionary scheme. These assumptions provide the backdrop for examining the Tuskegee Syphilis Study.

The Origins of the Experiment

In 1929, under a grant from the Julius Rosenwald Fund, the USPHS conducted studies in the rural South to determine the prevalence of syphilis among blacks and explore possibilities for mass treatment. The USPHS found Macon County, Alabama, in which the town of Tuskegee is located to have the highest syphilis rate of the six counties surveyed. The Rosenwald Study concluded that mass treatment could be successfully implemented among rural blacks. Although it is doubtful that the necessary funds would have been allocated even in the best economic conditions, after the economy collapsed in 1929, the findings were ignored. It is, however, ironic that the Tuskegee Study came to be based on findings of the Rosenwald Study that demonstrated the possibilities of mass treatment.

Three years later, in 1932, Dr. Taliaferro Clark, Chief of the USPHS Venereal Disease Division and author of the Rosenwald Study report, decided that conditions in Macon County merited renewed attention. Clark believed the high prevalence of syphilis offered an "unusual opportunity" for observation. From its inception, the USPHS regarded the Tuskegee Study as a classic "study in nature," rather than an experiment. As long as syphilis was so prevalent in Macon and most of the blacks went untreated throughout life, it seemed only natural to Clark that it would be valuable to observe the consequences. He described it as a "ready-made situation." Surgeon General H. S. Cumming wrote to R. R. Moton, Director of the Tuskegee Institute:

> The recent syphilis control demonstration carried out in Macon County, with the financial assistance of the Julius Rosenwald Fund, revealed the presence of an unusually high rate in this county and, what is more remarkable, the fact that 99 per cent of this group was entirely without previous treatment. This combination, together with the expected cooperation of your hospital, offers an unparalleled opportunity for carrying on this piece of scientific research which probably cannot be duplicated anywhere else in the world.

Although no formal protocol appears to have been written, several letters of Clark and Cumming suggest what the USPHS hoped to find. Clark indicated that it would be important to see how disease affected the daily lives of the men:

> 1. In 1865, Claude Bernard, the famous French physiologist, outlined the distinction between a "study in nature" and experimentation. A study in nature required simple observation, an essentially passive act, while experimentation demanded intervention which altered the original condition. The Tuskegee Study was thus clearly not a study in nature. The very act of diagnosis altered the original conditions. "It is on this very possibility of acting or not acting on a body," wrote Bernard, "that the distinction will exclusively rest between sciences called sciences of observation and sciences called experimental."
>
>   The results of these studies of case records suggest the desirability of making a further study of the effect of untreated syphilis on the human economy among people now living and engaged in their daily pursuits.

It also seems that the USPHS believed the experiment might demonstrate that antisyphilitic treatment was unnecessary. As Cumming noted: "It is expected the results of this study may have a marked bearing on the treatment, or conversely the non-necessity of treatment, of cases of latent syphilis." . . .

Selecting the Subjects

Clark sent Dr. Raymond Vonderlehr to Tuskegee in September 1932 to assemble a sample of men with latent syphilis for the experiment. The basic design of the study called for the selection of syphilitic black males between the ages of twenty-five and sixty, a thorough physical examination including x-rays, and finally, a spinal tap to determine the incidence of neuro-syphilis. They had no intention of providing any treatment for the infected men. The USPHS originally scheduled the whole experiment to last six months; it seemed to be both a simple and inexpensive project.

The task of collecting the sample, however, proved to be more difficult than the USPHS had supposed. Vonderlehr canvassed the largely illiterate, poverty-stricken population of sharecroppers and tenant farmers in search of test subjects. If his circulars requested only men over twenty-five to attend his clinics, none would appear, suspecting he was conducting draft physicals. Therefore, he was forced to test large numbers of women and men who did not fit the experiments' specifications. This involved considerable expense since the USPHS had promised the Macon County Board of Health that it would treat those who were infected, but not included in the study. Clark wrote to Vonderlehr about the situation: "It never once occurred to me that we would be called upon to treat a large part of the county as return for the privilege of making this study. . . . I am anxious to keep the expenditures for treatment down to the lowest possible point because it is the one item of expenditure in connection with the study most difficult to defend despite our knowledge of the need therefor." Vonderlehr responded: "If we could find from 100 to 200 cases . . . we would not have to do another Wassermann on useless individuals. . . ."

Significantly, the attempt to develop the sample contradicted the prediction the USPHS had made initially regarding the prevalence of the disease in Macon County. Overall rates of syphilis fell well below expectations; as opposed to the USPHS projection of 35 percent, 20 percent of those tested were actually disease. Moreover, those who had sought and received previous treatment far exceeded the expectations of the USPHS. Clark noted in a letter to Vonderlehr:

> I find your report of March 6th quite interesting but regret the necessity for Wassermanning [sic] . . . such a large number of individuals in order to uncover this relatively limited number of untreated cases.

Further difficulties arose in enlisting the subjects to participate in the experiment, to be "Wassermanned," and to return for a subsequent series of examinations. Vonderlehr found that only the offer of treatment elicited the cooperation of the men. They were told they were ill and were promised free care. Offered therapy, they became willing subjects. The USPHS did not tell the men that they were participants in an experiment; on the contrary, the subjects believed they were being treated for "bad blood"—the rural South's colloquialism for syphilis. They thought they were participating in a public health demonstration similar to the one that had been conducted by the Julius Rosenwald Fund in Tuskegee several years earlier. In the end, the men were so eager for medical care that the number of defaulters in the experiment proved to be insignificant.

To preserve the subjects' interest, Vonderlehr gave most of the men mercurial ointment, a noneffective drug, while some of the younger men apparently received inadequate dosages of neoarsphenamine. This required Vonderlehr to write frequently to Clark requesting supplies. He feared the experiment would fail if the men were not offered treatment. . . .

The readiness of the test subjects to participate of course contradicted the notion that blacks would not seek or continue therapy.

The final procedure of the experiment was to be a spinal tap to test for evidence of neuro-syphilis. The USPHS presented this purely diagnostic exam, which often entails considerable pain and complications, to the men as a "special treatment." Clark explained to Moore:

> We have not yet commenced the spinal punctures. This operation will be deferred to the last in order not to unduly disturb our field work by any adverse reports by the patients subjected to spinal puncture because of some disagreeable sensations following this procedure. These negroes are very ignorant and easily influenced by things that would be of minor significance in a more intelligent group.

The letter to the subjects announcing the spinal tap read:

> Some time ago you were given a thorough examination and since that time we hope you have gotten a great deal of treatment for bad blood. You will now be given your last chance to get a second examination. This examination is a very special one and after it is finished you will be given a special treatment if it is believed you are in a condition to stand it. . . .
> REMEMBER THIS IS YOUR LAST CHANCE FOR SPECIAL FREE TREATMENT. BE SURE TO MEET THE NURSE.

The HEW investigation did not uncover this crucial fact: the men participated in the study under the guise of treatment.

Despite the fact that their assumption regarding prevalence and black attitudes toward treatment had proved wrong, the USPHS decided in the summer of 1933 to continue the study. Once again, it seemed only "natural" to pursue the research since the sample already existed, and with depressed economy, the cost of treatment appeared prohibitive—although there is no indication it was ever considered. Vonderlehr first suggested extending the study in letters to Clark and Wenger:

> At the end of this project we shall have a considerable number of cases presenting various complications of syphilis, who have received only mercury and may still be considered

untreated in the modern sense of therapy. Should these cases be followed over a period of from five to ten years many interesting facts could be learned regarding the course and complications of untreated syphilis.

"As I see it," responded Wenger, "we have no further interest in these patients *until they die.*" Apparently, the physicians engaged in the experiment believed that only autopsies could scientifically confirm the findings of the study.

Bringing the men to autopsy required the USPHS to devise a further series of deceptions and inducements. Wenger warned Vonderlehr that the men must not realize that they would be autopsied:

> There is one danger in the latter plan and that is if the colored population become aware that accepting free hospital care means a post-mortem, every darkey will leave Macon County and it will hurt [Dr. Eugene] Dibble's hospital.

The USPHS offered several inducements to maintain contact and to procure the continued cooperation of the men. Eunice Rivers, a black nurse, was hired to follow their health and to secure approval for autopsies. She gave the men non-effective medicines—"spring tonic" and aspirin—as well as transportation and hot meals on the days of their examinations. More important, Nurse Rivers provided continuity to the project over the entire forty-year period. By supplying "medicinals," the USPHS was able to continue to deceive the participants, who believed that they were receiving therapy from the government doctors Deceit was integral to the study. When the test subjects complained about spinal taps one doctor wrote:

> They simply do not like spinal punctures. A few of those who were tapped are enthusiastic over the results but to most, the suggestion causes violent shaking of the head; others claim they were robbed of their procreative powers (regardless of the fact that I claim it stimulates them).

Letters to the subjects announcing an impending USPHS visit to Tuskegee explained: "[The doctor] wants to make a special examination to find out how you have been feeling and whether the treatment has improved your health." In fact, after the first six months of the study, the USPHS had furnished no treatment whatsoever.

Finally, because it proved difficult to persuade the men to come to the hospital when they became severely ill, the USPHS promised to cover their burial expenses. The Milbank Memorial Fund provided approximately $50 per man for this purpose beginning in 1935. This was a particularly strong inducement as funeral rites constituted an important component of the cultural life of rural blacks. One report of the study concluded, "Without this suasion it would, we believe, have been impossible to secure the cooperation of the group and their families."

Reports of the study's findings, which appeared regularly in the medical press beginning in 1936, consistently cited the ravages of untreated syphilis. The first paper, read at the 1936 American Medical Association annual meeting, found "that syphilis in this period [latency] tends to greatly increase the frequency of manifestations of cardiovascular disease." Only 16 percent of the subjects gave no sign of morbidity as opposed to 61 percent of the controls. Ten years later, a report noted coldly, "The fact that nearly twice as large a proportion of the syphilitic individuals as of the control group has died is a very striking one." Life expectancy, concluded the doctors, is reduced by about 20 percent.

A 1955 article found that slightly more than 30 percent of the test group autopsied had died *directly* from advanced syphilitic lesions of either the cardiovascular or the central nervous system. Another published account stated, "Review of those still living reveals that an appreciable number have late complications of syphilis which probably will result, for some at least, in contributing materially to the ultimate cause of death." In 1950, Dr. Wenger had concluded, "We now know, where we could only surmise before, that we have contributed to their ailments and shortened their lives." As black physician Vernal Cave, a member of the HEW panel, later wrote, "They proved a point, then proved a point, then proved a point."

During the forty years of the experiment the USPHS had sought on several occasions to ensure that the subjects did not receive treatment from other sources. To this end, Vonderlehr met with groups of local black doctors in 1934, to ask their cooperation in not treating the men. Lists of subjects were distributed to Macon County physicians along with letters requesting them to refer these men back to the USPHS if they sought care. The USPHS warned the Alabama Health Department not to treat the test subjects when they took a mobile VD unit into Tuskegee in the early 1940s. In 1941, the Army drafted several subjects and told them to begin antisyphilitic treatment immediately. The USPHS supplied the draft board with a list of 256 names they desired to have excluded from treatment, and the board complied.

In spite of these efforts, by the early 1950s many of the men had secured some treatment on their own. By 1952, almost 30 percent of the test subjects had received some penicillin, although only 7.5 percent had received what could be considered adequate doses. Vonderlehr wrote to one of the participating physicians, "I hope that the availability of antibiotics has not interfered too much with this project." A report published in 1955 considered whether the treatment that some of the men had obtained had "defeated" the study. The article attempted to explain the relatively low exposure to penicillin in an age of antibiotics, suggesting as a reason: "the stoicism of these men as a group; they still regard hospitals and medicines with suspicion and prefer an occasional dose of time-honored herbs or tonics to modern drugs." The authors failed to note that the men believed they already were under the care of the government doctors and thus saw no need to seek treatment elsewhere. Any treatment which the men might have received, concluded the report, had been insufficient to compromise the experiment.

When the USPHS evaluated the status of the study in the 1960s they continued to rationalize the racial aspects of the experiment. For example, the minutes of a 1965 meeting at the Center for Disease Control recorded:

Racial issue was mentioned briefly. Will not affect the study. Any questions can be handled by saying these people were at the point that therapy would no longer help them. They are getting better medical care than they would under any other circumstances.

A group of physicians met again at the CDC in 1969 to decide whether or not to terminate the study. Although one doctor argued that the study should be stopped and the men treated, the consensus was to continue. Dr. J. Lawton Smith remarked, "You will never have another study like this; take advantage of it." A memo prepared by Dr. James B. Lucas, Assistant Chief of the Venereal Disease Branch, state: "Nothing learned will prevent, find, or cure a single case of infectious syphilis or bring us closer to our basic mission of controlling venereal disease in the United States." He concluded, however, that the study should be continued "along its present lines." When the first accounts of the experiment appeared in the national press in July 1972, data were still being collected and autopsies performed.

The HEW Final Report

Hew finally formed the Tuskegee Syphilis Study Ad Hoc Advisory Panel on August 28, 1972, in response to criticism that the press descriptions of the experiment had triggered. The panel, composed of nine members, five of them black, concentrated on two issues. First, was the study justified in 1932 and had the men given their informed consent? Second, should penicillin have been provided when it became available in the early 1950s? The panel was also charged with determining if the study should be terminated and assessing current policies regarding experimentation with human subjects. The group issued their report in June 1973.

By focusing on the issues of penicillin therapy and informed consent, the *Final Report* and the investigation betrayed a basic misunderstanding of the experiment's purposes and design. The HEW report implied that the failure to provide penicillin constituted the study's major ethical misjudgment; implicit was the assumption that no adequate therapy existed prior to penicillin. Nonetheless medical authorities firmly believed in the efficacy of arsenotherapy for treating syphilis at the time of the experiment's inception in 1932. The panel further failed to recognize that the entire study had been predicated on nontreatment. Provision of effective medication would have violated the rational of the experiment—to study the natural course of the disease until death. On several occasions, in fact, the USPHS had prevented the men from receiving proper treatment. Indeed, there is no evidence that the USPHS ever considered providing penicillin.

The other focus of the *Final Report*—informed consent—also served to obscure the historical facts of the experiment. In light of the deceptions and exploitations which the experiment perpetrated, it is an understatement to declare, as the *Report* did, that the experiment was "ethically unjustified," because it failed to obtain informed consent from the subjects. The *Final Report's* statement, "Submitting voluntarily is not informed consent," indicated that the panel believed that the men had volunteered *for the experiment*. The records in the National Archives make clear that the men did not submit voluntarily to an experiment; they were told and they believed that they were getting free treatment from expert government doctors for a serious disease. The failure of the HEW *Final Report* to expose this critical fact—that the USPHS lied to the subjects—calls into question the thoroughness and credibility of their investigation.

Failure to place the study in a historical context also made it impossible for the investigation to deal with the essentially racist nature of the experiment. The panel treated the study as an aberration, well-intentioned but misguided. Moreover, concern that the *Final Report* might be viewed as a critique of human experimentation in general seems to have severely limited the scope of the inquiry. The *Final Report* is quick to remind the reader on two occasions: "The position of the Panel must not be construed to be a general repudiation of scientific research with human subjects." The *Report* assures as that a better designed experiment could have been justified:

> It is possible that a scientific study in 1932 of untreated syphilis, properly conceived with a clear protocol and conducted with suitable subjects who fully understood the implications of their involvement, might have been justified in the pre-penicillin era. This is especially true when one considers the uncertain nature of the results of treatment of late latent syphilis and the highly toxic nature of therapeutic agents then available.

This statement is questionable in view of the proven dangers of untreated syphilis known in 1932.

Since the publication of the HEW *Final Report,* a defense of the Tuskegee Study has emerged. These arguments, most clearly articulated by Dr. R. H. Kampmeier in the *Southern Medical Journal,* center on the limited knowledge of effective therapy for latent syphilis when the experiment began. Kampmeier argues that by 1950, penicillin would have been of no value for these men. Others have suggested that the men were fortunate to have been spared the highly toxic treatments of the earlier period. Moreover, even these contemporary defenses assume that the men never would have been treated anyway. As Dr. Charles Barnett of Stanford University wrote in 1974, "The lack of treatment was not contrived by the USPHS but was an established fact of which they proposed to take advantage." Several doctors who participated in the study continued to justify the experiment. Dr. J. R. Heller, who on one occasion had referred to the test subjects as the "Ethiopian population," told reporters in 1972:

> I don't see why they should be shocked or horrified. There was no racial side to this. It just happened to be in a black community. I feel this was a perfectly straightforward study, perfectly ethical, with controls. Part of our mission as physicians is to find out what happens to individuals with disease and without disease.

These apologies, as well as the HEW *Final Report,* ignore many of the essential ethical issues which they study poses, The Tuskegee Study reveals the persistence of beliefs within the medical profession about the nature of blacks, sex, and disease—beliefs that had tragic repercussions long after their alleged "scientific" bases were known to be incorrect. Most strikingly, the entire health of a community was jeopardized by leaving a communicable disease untreated. There can be little doubt that the Tuskegee researchers regarded their subjects as less than human. As a result, the ethical canons of experimenting on human subjects were completely disregarded.

The study also raises significant questions about professional self-regulation and scientific bureaucracy. Once the USPHS decided to extend the experiment in the summer of 1933, it was unlikely that the test would be halted short of the men's deaths. The experiment was widely reported for forty years without evoking any significant protest within the medical community. Nor did any bureaucratic mechanism exist within the government for the periodic reassessment of the Tuskegee experiment's ethics and scientific value. The USPHS sent physicians to Tuskegee every several years to check on the study's progress, but never subjected the morality or usefulness of the experiment to serious scrutiny. Only the press accounts of 1972 finally punctured the continued rationalizations of the USPHS and brought the study to an end. Even the HEW investigation was compromised by fear that it would be considered a threat to future human experimentation.

In retrospect the Tuskegee Study revealed more about the pathology of racism than it did about the pathology of syphilis; more about the nature of scientific inquiry than the nature of the disease process. The injustice committed by the experiment went well beyond the facts outlined in the press and the HEW *Final Report*. The degree of deception and damages have been seriously underestimated. As this history of the study suggests, the notion that science is a value-free discipline must be rejected. The need for greater vigilance in assessing the specific ways in which social values and attitudes affect professional behavior is clearly indicated.

Name: _____ Class: _____

Date: _____ Section: _____

Reading Comprehension Activity Sheet

Racism and Research: The Case of the Tuskegee Syphilis Study, Allan M. Brandt

1. Briefly describe the Tuskegee Syphilis Study. _____

   _____

   _____

   _____

   _____

   _____

   _____

   _____

   _____

   _____

   _____

   _____

   _____

2. How did the race of the study participants impact the rationale for developing and continuing such a study? _____

   _____

   _____

   _____

   _____

   _____

   _____

   _____

   _____

   _____

   _____

   _____

3. Brandt states that the Tuskegee Study was unethical for many reasons. Briefly discuss the ethical issues that the study poses. _____

chapter 3

Culture

Body Ritual among the Nacirema
Horace Miner

The Nacirema and the Tsiruot
Joel Savishinsky

The Prevalence of Female Circumcision in Two Nigerian Communities
Ehigie Ebomoyi

Body Ritual among the Nacirema

Horace Miner

The anthropologist has become so familiar with the diversity of ways in which different people behave in similar situations that he is not apt to be surprised by even the most exotic customs. In fact, if all of the logically possible combinations of behavior have not been found somewhere in the world, he is apt to suspect that they must be present in some yet undescribed tribe. The point has, in fact, been expressed with respect to clan organization by Murdock (1949, 71). In this light, the magical beliefs and practices of the Nacirema present such unusual aspects that it seems desirable to describe them as an example of the extremes to which human behavior can go.

Professor Linton first brought the ritual of the Nacirema to the attention of anthropologists twenty years ago (1936, 326), but the culture of this people is still very poorly understood. They are a North American group living in the territory between the Canadian Cree, the Yaqui and Tarahumare of Mexico, and the Carib and Arawak of the Antilles. Little is known of their origin, although tradition states that they came from the east. . . .

Nacirema culture is characterized by a highly developed market economy which has evolved in a rich natural habitat. While much of the people's time is devoted to economic pursuits, a large part of the fruits of these labors and a considerable portion of the day are spent in ritual activity. The focus of this activity is the human body, the appearance and health of which loom as a dominant concern in the ethos of the people. While such a concern is certainly not unusual, its ceremonial aspects and associated philosophy are unique.

The fundamental belief underlying the whole system appears to be that the human body is ugly and that its natural tendency is to debility and disease. Incarcerated in such a body, man's only hope is to avert these characteristics through the use of ritual and ceremony. Every household has one or more shrines devoted to this purpose. The more powerful individuals in the society have several shrines in their houses and, in fact, the opulence of a

From *American Anthropologist,* June 1956, 58:3 by Horace Miner. Copyright © 1956 by American Anthropological Association.

house is often referred to in terms of the number of such ritual centers it possesses. Most houses are of wattle and daub construction, but the shrine rooms of the more wealthy are walled with stone. Poorer families imitate the rich by applying pottery plaques to their shrine walls.

While each family has at least one such shrine, the rituals associated with it are not family ceremonies but are private and secret. The rites are normally only discussed with children, and then only during the period when they are being initiated into these mysteries. I was able, however, to establish sufficient rapport with the natives to examine these shrines and to have the rituals described to me.

The focal point of the shrine is a box or chest which is built into the wall. In this chest are kept the many charms and magical potions without which no native believes he could live. These preparations are secured from a variety of specialized practitioners. The most powerful of these are the medicine men, whose assistance must be rewarded with substantial gifts. However, the medicine men do not provide the curative potions for their clients, but decide what the ingredients should be and then write them down in an ancient and secret language. This writing is understood only by the medicine men and by the herbalists who, for another gift, provide the required charm.

The charm is not disposed of after it has served its purpose, but is placed in the charm-box of the household shrine. As these magical materials are specific for certain ills, and the real or imagined maladies of the people are many, the charm-box is usually full to overflowing. The magical packets are so numerous that people forget what their purposes were and fear to use them again. While the natives are very vague on this point, we can only assume that the idea in retaining all the old magical materials is that their presence in the charm-box, before which the body rituals are conducted, will in some way protect the worshipper.

Beneath the charm-box is a small font. Each day every member of the family, in succession, enters the shrine room, bows his head before the charm-box, mingles different sorts of holy water in the font, and proceeds with a brief rite of ablution. The holy waters are secured from the Water Temple of the community, where the priests conduct elaborate ceremonies to make the liquid ritually pure.

In the hierarchy of magical practitioners, and below the medicine men in prestige, are specialists whose designation is best translated as "holy-mouth-men." The Nacirema have an almost pathological horror of and fascination with the mouth, the condition of which is believed to have a supernatural influence on all social relationships. Were it not for the rituals of the mouth, they believe that their teeth would fall out, their gums bleed, their jaws shrink, their friends desert them, and their lovers reject them. They also believe that a strong relationship exists between oral and moral characteristics. For example, there is a ritual ablution of the mouth for children which is supposed to improve their moral fiber.

The daily body ritual performed by everyone includes a mouth-rite. Despite the fact that these people are so punctilious about care of the mouth, this rite involves a practice which strikes the uninitiated stranger as revolting. It was reported to me that the ritual consists of inserting a small bundle of hog hairs into the mouth, along with certain magical powders, and then moving the bundle in a highly formalized series of gestures.

In addition to the private mouth-rite, the people seek out a holy-mouth-man once or twice a year. These practitioners have an impressive set of paraphernalia, consisting of a variety of augers, awls, probes, and prods. The use of these items in the exorcism of the evils of the mouth involves almost unbelievable ritual torture of the client. The holy-mouth-man opens the client's mouth and, using the above mentioned tools, enlarges any holes which decay may have created in the teeth. Magical materials are put into these holes. If there are not naturally occurring holes in the teeth, large sections of one or more teeth are gouged out so that the supernatural substance can be applied. In the client's view, the purpose of these ministrations is to arrest decay and to draw friends. The extremely sacred and traditional character of the rite is evident in the fact that the natives return to the holy-mouth-men year after year, despite the fact that their teeth continue to decay.

It is to be hoped that, when a thorough study of the Nacirema is made, there will be careful inquiry into the personality structure of these people. One has but to watch the gleam in the eye of a holy-mouth-man, as he jabs an awl into an exposed nerve, to suspect that a certain amount of sadism is involved. If this can be established, a very interesting pattern emerges, for most of the population shows definite masochistic tendencies. It was to these that Professor Linton referred in discussing a distinctive part of the daily body ritual which is performed only by men. This part of the rite includes scraping and lacerating the surface of the face with a sharp instrument. Special women's rites are performed only four times during each lunar month, but what they lack in frequency is made up in barbarity. As part of this ceremony, women bake their heads in small ovens for about an hour. The theoretically interesting point is that what seems to be a preponderantly masochistic people have developed sadistic specialists.

The medicine men have an imposing temple, or *latipso,* in every community of any size. The more elaborate ceremonies required to treat very sick patients can only be performed at this temple. These ceremonies involve not only the thaumaturge but a permanent group of vestal maidens who move sedately about the temple chambers in distinctive costume and headdress.

The *latipso* ceremonies are so harsh that it is phenomenal that a fair proportion of the really sick natives who enter the temple ever recover. Small children whose indoctrination is still incomplete have been known to resist attempts to take them to the temple because "that is where you go to die." Despite this fact, sick adults are not only willing but eager to undergo the protracted ritual purification, if they can afford to do so. No matter how ill the supplicant or how grave the emergency, the guardians of many temples will not admit a client if he cannot give a rich gift to the custodian. Even after one has gained and survived the ceremonies, the guardians will not permit the neophyte to leave until he makes still another gift.

The supplicant entering the temple is first stripped of all his or her clothes. In everyday life the Nacirema avoids exposure of his body and its natural functions. Bathing and excretory acts are performed only in the secrecy of the household shrine, where they are ritualized as part of the body-rites. Psychological shock results from the fact that body secrecy is suddenly lost upon entry into the *latipso*. A man, whose own wife has never seen him in an excretory act, suddenly finds himself naked and assisted by a vestal maiden while he performs his natural functions into a sacred vessel. This sort of ceremonial treatment is necessitated by the fact that the excreta are used by a diviner to ascertain the course and nature of the client's sickness. Female clients, on the other hand, find their naked bodies are subjected to the scrutiny, manipulation and prodding of the medicine men.

Few supplicants in the temple are well enough to do anything but lie on their hard beds. The daily ceremonies, like the rites of the holy-mouth-men, involve discomfort and torture. With ritual precision, the vestals awaken their miserable charges each dawn and roll them about on their beds of pain while performing ablutions, in the formal movements of which the maidens are highly trained. At other times they insert magic wands in the supplicant's mouth or force him to eat substances which are supposed to be healing. From time to time the medicine men come to their clients and jab magically treated needles into their flesh. The fact that these temple ceremonies may not cure, and may even kill the neophyte, in no way decreases the people's faith in the medicine men.

There remains one other kind of practitioner, known as a "listener." This witchdoctor has the power to exorcise the devils that lodge in the heads of people who have been bewitched. The Nacirema believe that parents bewitch their own children. Mothers are particularly suspected of putting a curse on children while teaching them the secret body rituals. The counter-magic of the witchdoctor is unusual in its lack of ritual. The patient simply tells the "listener" all his troubles and fears, beginning with the earliest difficulties he can remember. The memory displayed by the Nacirema in these exorcism sessions is truly remarkable. It is not uncommon for the patient to bemoan the rejection he felt upon being weaned as a babe, and a few individuals even see their troubles going back to the traumatic effects of their own birth.

In conclusion, mention must be made of certain practices which have their base in native esthetics but which depend upon the pervasive aversion to the natural body and its functions. There are ritual fasts to make fat people think and ceremonial feasts to make thin people fat. Still other rites are used to make women's breasts larger if they are small, and smaller if they are large. General dissatisfaction with breast shape is symbolized in the fact that the ideal form is virtually outside the range of human variation. A few women afflicted with almost inhuman hyper-mammary development are so idolized that they make a handsome living by simply going from village to village and permitting the natives to stare at them for a fee.

Reference has already been made to the fact that excretory functions are ritualized, routinized, and relegated to secrecy. Natural reproductive functions are similarly distorted. Intercourse is taboo as a topic and scheduled as an act. Efforts are made to avoid pregnancy by the use of magical materials or by limiting intercourse to certain phases of the moon. Conception is actually very infrequent. When pregnant, women dress so as to hide their condition. Parturition takes place in secret, without friends or relatives to assist, and the majority of women do not nurse their infants.

Our review of the ritual life of the Nacirema has certainly shown them to be a magic-ridden people. It is hard to understand how they have managed to exist so long under the burdens which they have imposed upon themselves. But even such exotic customs as these take on real meaning when they are viewed with the insight provided by Malinowski when he wrote (1948, 70):

> Looking from far and above, from our high places of safety in the developed civilization, it is easy to see all the crudity and irrelevance of magic. But without its power and guidance early man could not have mastered his practical difficulties as he has done, nor could man have advanced to the higher stages of civilization.

References

Anton, Ralph. 1936. *The Study of Man.* New York: Appleton-Century.
Malinowski, Bronislaw. 1948. *Magic, Science, and Religion.* Glencoe, IL: Free Press.
Murdock, George P. 1949. *Social Structure.* New York: Macmillan.

The Nacirema and the Tsiruot

Joel Savishinsky

Shortly after the mid-point of the 20th century, anthropological attention shifted to a newly discovered North American people called the Nacirema.[1] These people were emphatic in their feeling that they were blessed. Their land was prosperous, and many of their leaders enlightened. When acknowledging their good fortune, or asking for victory in their wars, the Nacirema prayed to their totem animal, the eagle, or thanked the spirits of their founding male ancestors. They did this by singing sacred songs in unison before they engaged in ritual combats called *strops,* or by reciting a special prayer before their ritual banner as it hung from the top of a smooth totem pole. The Nacirema often decorated their homes and sacred buildings with painted or carved images of the tribe's patriarchs, who were usually shown wearing powdered mats of fiber on their heads, and holding the feathers of birds in their hands, which they used to scratch mystical symbols onto the surface of large flat leaves.

In their daily lives the Nacirema worked hard, but they also believed in magic. To earn their livelihood, many of them spent long hours inside a large box. They sat behind long pieces of wood on which there were piles of bleached leaves covered with small symbols, and by the end of the day the Nacirema had to move these leaves from one side of the wooden surface to the other, making sure that all the symbols were in their proper, sacred order. The Nacirema who did this well were then allowed to go to places called *serots*, where they found food that was already cleaned, and cooked, and wrapped up for them. Very few Nacirema knew where the food came from, or how it got there, and most didn't even bother to think much about this. The food was just there. It always seemed to be there, and so the Nacirema knew that their leaders and gods indeed had powerful magic. Among the more religious Nacirema, before a meal was eaten, a prayer would be said to thank their chief spirit for magically giving them so much sustenance.

Reprinted from *International Journal of Intercultural Relations,* Joel Shavishinsky, Copyright © with permission from Elsevier, UK.

The Nacirema were so busy so much of the time, working in their boxes with the symbol-covered leaves, that they usually sent their children and their elders away to places called *slooks* and *gnisrun* homes. There they were cared for by strangers so that the adult Nacirema could work enough to pay their leaders a kind of tribute called *sex-at*. All Nacirema leaders took as much *sex-at* as they could get from the people, and the people generally went along with this because they felt that having to give out *sex-at* was as natural and inevitable and unavoidable as dying. Actually, the Nacirema did not *like sex-at,* or being mortal, or the fact that they had to give even more *sex-at* when, at last, they did die. But their usual reaction, as one of their popular storytellers once said, was just to shrug, apply their favorite pain-killing device, the *noisivelet,* and mutter: "so it goes."

The Nacirema at least took comfort in the fact that their leaders used their *sex-at* to build the *slooks* and *gnisrun* homes that the young and the old were always sent to. Indeed, though the Nacirema often missed their children and their elderly parents, they commonly moved to live in villages far away from these kin. When they did this, the Nacirema would send messages back to their distant relatives, folding these up inside thin leaves on the outside of which they put small pictures of revered, mythic figures, such as their great spirit, *Sivle*. As is true of important deities in other world religions, the figure of *Sivle* took many forms, and the Nacirema variously worshipped him in either his young or his mature incarnation. Each year, in fact, many Nacirema claimed to see apparitions of *Sivle*, and millions made an annual pilgrimage to his home, *Dnal-ecarg*. They also sang a popular song about going to this sacred site, similarly entitled *Dnal-ecarg,* which had been composed by one of their great poets, *Luap No-mis*.

While the Nacirema generally took great pride in their culture, they were also uneasy and restless about it, and unsure whether people in other tribes might be enjoying some things that they didn't even know about. This insecurity led to a great paradox in the Nacirema way of life. The paradox was that the Nacirema liked to leave the homeland they loved so much in order to search for clues to a better life. They did this by travelling among strangers who ate unusual foods, and followed exotic customs, and who spoke languages that few Nacirema could even name. These travels were called sruot, and a Nacirema who left his or her homeland to undertake such a quest for the pursuit of happiness and the meaning of life was called a *tsiruot*.

When *tsiruots* set out on a journey, they usually travelled in groups because, as much as they wanted to leave their compatriots behind, they were also afraid to be parted from them. Even those Nacirema who travelled alone always carried mementos of their clan with them. The most common of these amulets were small green leaves with pictures of their dead patriarchs. So much did the Nacirema *tsiruots* value these soft fetishes that they assumed that any foreigner whom they met would gladly give them whatever they wanted in exchange for some leaves. The Nacirema were always fascinated to discover that people from other places also had leaves, but *tsiruots* were frequently puzzled and confused by the strange pictures, colors and symbols that these other people painted on them. In their own villages, it was only Nacirema children who used brightly colored leaves, and even then the leaves were just part of a divination game the children played with dotted cubes of ivory, called *ecid,* which they threw on the ground. The children would scream and cheer at the pattern of dots, and then trade special leaves—with names like *Klaw-draob* and *Krap-ecalp.* Later in life, when Nacirema grew up to be *tsiruots,* they often forgot who and where they were, and used other people's colored leaves as if they were still playing this childhood game of *Yloponom.*

When the Nacirema became *tsiruots,* they were sometimes delighted, and other times disappointed, with what they found. In some of the lands the Nacirema went to, they found dark-skinned people living in the forests and deserts in the way that their own great-great-ancestors had, i.e., by hunting animals, gathering plants, or growing small gardens. The Nacirema thought this was wonderful; many a *tsiruot* even thought it was quaint. They praised and revered the foreign people who reminded them of their ancestors, and who knew where their food came from, and who lived in this old way. The Nacirema called them by the honorific name *El-bon segavas.* The only time a Nacirema *tsiruot* got upset with the *segavas* was when they saw them cutting down the forests to make pastures to feed their herds of *Elttac.* Later, back home in their own land, many Nacirema would sit together over their favorite meal of *reg-rub-mah,* and shake their heads over what the *segavas* were doing to the world.

People from Nacirema villages have now been travelling for so many years that some of their ideas about being a *tsiruot* have changed during this time. Years ago, when the Nacirema first began to go on *sruot,* they were shocked when they encountered people who behaved differently from them. Often it was a matter of size or number, such as foreigners who grew large lips, or who took six wives, or who downsized their enemies' heads. But more recently, the Nacirema have tended to be offended and upset when the foreigners they meet act, instead, just like the Nacirema do, such as by constructing tall ugly boxes, or cutting down trees, or throwing garbage in their rivers, or even eating traditional Nacirema foods, such as *Scam-gib.* When the Nacirema see themselves imitated now, they are annoyed rather than flattered. Apparently, suggested one of their pundits, the Nacirema want the world to envy but not copy them.

Though the Nacirema sometimes criticize the foreigners they meet when they are on *sruot,* in their heart of hearts, they truly think of themselves as helpful and understanding people. They like to send foreigners gifts containing lots of their green leaves with the patriarchal pictures, as well as examples of such national treasures as their *cisum,* and their *smlif,* and their *skoob.* In that spirit of helpfulness, a Nacirema once made up a list of suggestions for how foreigners should act when they meet a Nacirema *tsiruot:*

(1) Try to speak to the Nacirema in their own language, and not yours. The Nacirema get very upset—some have apparently gone into shock—when they discover that other people do not understand their language.

Some Basic Nacirema Vocabulary
(in order of appearance)

Nacirema:	a member of a semi-nomadic, industrial culture, comprised largely of the children of immigrants and the descendants of slaves
Tsiruot:	a Nacirema who travels in a quest for pleasure and enlightenment, usually in two weeks stretches
Strops:	the Nacirema's most popular form of ritual combat
Serots:	non-denominational places for Nacirema worship, where people acquire merit and credit
Slooks:	places of confinement that all young Nacirema are sent to in order to be cured of idealism and curiosity
Gnisrun homes:	sterile environments for playing the game *og-nib*
Sex-at:	financial tribute paid by the Nacirema to their leaders
Noisi-velet:	A Nacirema tool for performing non-surgical lobotomies
Sivle:	a great Nacirema god, variously worshipped in his youthful and mature incarnations
Dnal-ecarg:	the last home of the god *Sivle*, now used as a shrine and pilgrimage site
Laup No-mis:	a revered poet and composer who brings back creative foreign ideas when he himself goes on *sruot*
Sruot:	the main form of pilgrimage found in Nacirema culture
Ecid:	spotted ivory cubes believed to hold the secrets to fate and good fortune
Klaw-draob and Krap-ecalp:	mythic places that Nacirema children are taught they can live in some day if they work hard, and have talent and ambition; skill with *ecid* also helps in getting there
El-bon segavas:	the people whom the Nacirema would be if they could be someone else, so long as they could still have running water
El-uac:	animals once held sacred by the Nacirema, but now blamed for destroying forests
Reg-rub-mah:	a favorite Nacirema dish, traditionally prepared outdoors, and cooked by men using modern versions of old hunting weapons
Scam-Gib:	The Nacirema national food
Cisum:	what Nacirema listen and dance to before kissing
smlif:	collective visions, acquired by Nacirema in dark rooms, and achieved without the use of drugs
Skoob:	what Nacirema take to bed when they can't find a partner
Sarepo paos:	a form of daily penance imposed on female Nacirema hermits who have chosen a life of vicarious lust
Sar-emac:	Nacirema devices for helping people remember places they were at but never really saw

(2) If you don't understand them, pretend that you do. The Nacirema love to be understood almost as much as they love to be loved.

(3) When your people put on a show for the Nacirema, let them think it is for real. Though they try hard, the Nacirema have a lot of difficulty distinguishing between theatre and ritual. They tend to assume that anything that is staged is authentic. Most, in fact, would be appalled and surprised by the notion of "stages authenticity"[2]. This may be because they are exposed to a lot of damaging rays called *sarepo paos* when they use the painkiller *noisivelet*.

(4) Finally, remember that each Nacirema *tsiruot* is on a quest for happiness and enlightenment, and that they have given away a lot of patriarchal green leaves to achieve these things and visit you. Be as gracious as you can be and remember that, however bad it gets, the Nacirema won't stay for long. Eventually, they go home, where they will force their friends to look at the images of you they have made with their *saremac*. It is these friends who will suffer even more than you, and it is they who truly deserve your compassion.

References

MacCannell, D. (1976). *The Tourist. A New Theory of The Leisure Class.* New York: Schocken Books.

Miner, H. (1956). Body ritual among the Nacirema. *American Anthropologist,* 58, 504–505.

Notes

1. Credit is due to the anthropologist Horace Miner, who first discovered the Nacirema and wrote about their bizarre yet strangely familiar culture (Miner, 1956).
2. The concept of "stages authenticity" is taken from MacCannell (1976).

Name: _____ Class: _____

Date: _____ Section: _____

Reading Comprehension Activity Sheet

The Narcirema and the Tsiruot, Joel Savishinsky

1. What are some cultural characteristics of the Narcirema and the Tsiruot in Savishinsky's article?

   _____
   _____
   _____
   _____
   _____
   _____
   _____
   _____
   _____
   _____

2. Who are the Tsiruot? Tsiruot were travellers who traveled in groups on a quest for the pursuit of happiness & the meaning of life.

3. How does reading Miner's and Savishinsky's articles help you to expand your "sociological imagination"?

The Prevalence of Female Circumcision in Two Nigerian Communities

Ehigie Ebomoyi

The practice of female circumcision is widespread not only in Africa but also in other continents of the world (Hathout, 1968). Its origin dates well back into history and could have originated as an initiation ceremony of young girls into womanhood (Bella, 1980). A Greek papyrus dated 163 B.C. made specific reference to female circumcision. Although female circumcision was said to be prevalent in all continents of the world, the practice was more common among the Phoenicians, Hittites, Ethiopians, Arabians, Syrians, Malaysians, Indonesians, and Africans (Baasher, 1977). Researchers have contended that no single continent was exempt from this custom of female mutilation. Currently, this practice has long been extirpated in many continents except in some of the African Countries (Assaad, 1982). Sanderson 1981) gives a conservative estimate of 70 million women in Africa who are affected.

Types of Female Circumcision

Female circumcision is the excision of the little hood that covers the clitoris, but the term is also used to include the partial or complete surgical removal of all or part of the female genitalia (Onadeko & Adekunle, 1982). Infibulation refers to the removal of the hood, the entire clitoris, the labial minora, and the adjacent medial part of the labial majors. Additionally, the two sides of the vulva are sewn together by catgut sutures, making allowance for a small opening for urine and menstrual flow (Anonymous, 1981; . . .). There are four major types of female circumcision practiced. Circumcision proper is recognized as type 1. This is the circumferential excision of the hood of the clitoris. This surgical technique is sometimes

From *Sex Roles* by Ehigie Ebomoyi. Reprinted by permission of the Kluwer Academic Publishers.

performed in the United States to redress the failure to attain orgasm by women experiencing frigidity or phimosis of the female prepuce (Rathmann, 1959).

The second type involves the excision of the hood of the clitoris and the glans clitoridis, or the clitoris completely. The third type is referred to as infibulation or Pharaonic circumcision. As previously described, the entire clitoris, including the whole of the labial minora, and at least the anterior two thirds and often the whole of the medial part of the labial majora, are excised. The two sides of the vulva are then stitched together either with a silk or catgut sutures (in the Sudan), or by thorns in Somalia. This procedure obliterates the vaginal introitus except for a small orifice made posteriorly to allow for the passage of urine and menstrual blood (Cook, 1976). The fourth type, which was practiced by the Pitta-Patta ethnic group of the Australian aborigines, necessitates the enlargement of the vagina orifice at puberty by surgically tearing it downwards or splitting the perineum with a locally fashioned stone knife (Cook, 1976; Melly, 1935).

In Nigeria, the practice of female circumcision varies among different ethnic groups and the type of operation depends on the religious and traditional beliefs of the people. In southern Nigeria, where Christianity and Animism are the predominant faiths, the procedure commonly employed among the Ibos is the surgical removal of the clitoris with or without the labia minora (Agugua & Egwuatu, 1982). Among the Edo and Yoruba ethnic groups of southern Nigeria, clitoridectomy is the type widely practiced. Among the former ethnic group, the traditional healer is labeled as a quack if he or she tampers with either the labia minora or the labia majors. In northern Nigeria, only the partial excision of the clitoris is employed and the same procedure is adopted in the north of Ghana (Ebomoyi, 1985).

Several medical complications are regularly experienced with infibulation and the fourth type that necessitates the splitting of the perineum with a stone knife. The adverse consequences include septicaemia, partial labial fusion, implantation dermoid, introital stenosis, urinary tract infection, and hemorrhage (Agugua & Egwuatu, 1982; Asuen, 1977; Dareer, 1983; Ebomoyi, 1985).

This study was conducted in the northwestern area of Nigeria where the majority of female children are circumcised in early infancy. However, the age and period at which female circumcision is performed varied according to the ethnic group. The Yorubas in Oyo State, Urhobo, and the Edo ethnic groups of Bendel State in southern Nigeria, perform this practice in infancy and early childhood. The Isoko ethnic group of Bendel State and the Hausas in the northern states circumcise their females just before marriage. The Igbos in Abakaliki celebrate this ritual at puberty, and the Ogbaru ethnic group in Anambra State and the Igbomina-Ekiti ethnic group in Kwara State circumcise their females at the third trimester of first pregnancy (Adetoro & Ebomoyi, 1986; Iregbulem, 1980; Mustapha, 1966).

The present study was designed to assess the prevalence of female circumcision in two communities in Kwara State, Nigeria. Also assessed were the factors underlying the practice of female circumcision, the willingness of respondents to circumcise their daughters, and the effective approach to eliminate this harmful practice.

Methods

Questionnaire interviews were conducted at two communities in the outskirts of Ilorin, the capital of Kwara State, Nigeria, which has a population of about 400,000 (Watts, 1984). The two study sties were Shao and Okelele. Using the "dejure" technique, the population census conducted in Shao by the writer revealed that there were 434 houses with 3,756 females and 3,510 males. The village contained two primary health care (PHC) centers and three outpatient medicine stores. The census of Okelele reported by Watts (1984) revealed that there were 328 houses at Okelele inhabited by 1,733 females and 1,808 males. The community contains a PHC center and over five patient medicine stores. In each of the two communities, males and females of childbearing age made up over 58% of the total population. Since each of the two communities was relatively small, every house was visited and a stratified random sampling technique was used to select an equal number of male and female respondents. A total of 2,300 respondents were interviewed in the two communities. Every house was visited, 575 men and the same number of women of reproductive age were interviewed, and information on age, sex, marital status, religion, ethnic group, occupation, and state of origin was noted. The respondents were asked to explain their knowledge of and attitudes toward female circumcision. Inquiry was also made into the sociocultural rationales underlying the practice of female circumcision and the suitable strategy to eliminate this practice.

Findings

A total of 1,150 men and 1,150 women were interviewed at the two communities on the outskirts of Ilorin. Over 90% of the female respondents were themselves circumcised in their childhood. In the two communities, females were generally circumcised in their infancy when they were 7–10 days old. However, the circumcision of a sickly child is postponed to a much later period, but it must be performed before she attains puberty.

Summarized in Table 3.1 are the stated rationales underlying the practice of female circumcision in the two communities. The main justification for female circumcision given by over 58% of the respondents from each community was that the practice constituted part of their cultural heritage. From [the tables presented in this chapter] it can be observed that [the majority] of the persons interviewed agreed that they will circumcise any daughter born to them. As shown in Table 3.2, the significant others whose views were highly respected in the practice of female circumcision included grandfathers, fathers, grandmothers, and mothers. In Nigeria, grandparents are the custodians of culture and morality. Among the various age cohorts, respondents willing to circumcise any daughter born to them were over 50% (Table 3.3). Presented in Table 3.4 is the educational status of respondents by their willingness to circumcise a daughter. Again, respondents willing to circumcise a daughter at each educational level was over 50%.

TABLE 3.1
Rationales Underlying the Practice of Female Circumcision at Shao and Okelele, Kwara State, Nigeria

Rationales	Okelele (N = 1,150)	Shao (N = 1,150)
Traditional and cultural heritage	58.6	69.3
Circumcision can prevent female promiscuity.	13.3	8.4
Circumcision can prevent clitoral growth.	10.5	7.6
Circumcision enhances female fertility.	3.5	6.0
Circumcision enhances the cleaniness of the vagina.	3.5	0.3
Circumcision prevents the clitoris from infection.	0.8	0.8

TABLE 3.2
Significant Others Who Care More for Female Circumcision in the Family

Significant Others	Okelele		Shao	
	N	%	N	%
Grandfathers	690	60.0	609	53.0
Fathers	420	36.5	466	40.5
Mothers	29	2.5	35	3.0
Grandmothers	11	1.0	29	2.5
Brothers	—	—	11	1.0
Sisters	—	—	—	—
Total	1,150	100.0	1,150	100.0

In both communities well over 50% of the persons interviewed did not feel female circumcision should be discouraged on any of the following grounds: pain, severe bleeding, interference with orgasm, permanent emotional trauma, tetanus infection, and complication of childbirth (Table 3.5).

On the suggested strategies to eliminate female circumcision (Table 3.6), over 46% of the persons interviewed did not feel eradication of the practice is necessary. However, over 36% of the respondents in each community suggested health education, and over 9% recommended government legislation against female circumcision.

TABLE 3.3
Attitude of Respondents toward the Circumcision of a Daughter by Age

	Okelele								Shao						
	Agree		Disagree		Neutral		Total		Agree		Disagree		Neutral		Total	
Age	N	%	N	%	N	%	N	%	N	%	N	%	N	%	N	%
15–19	66	5.7	18	1.5	2	0.2	86	7.5	68	5.9	9	0.8	—	—	77	6.7
20–29	59	5.2	20	1.7	1	0.1	80	6.9	60	5.2	24	2.0	—	—	84	7.3
30–39	150	13.0	46	4.0	4	0.4	200	17.5	170	14.8	39	3.4	2	0.2	211	18.3
40–49	190	16.5	60	5.2	—	—	150	13.0	206	17.9	59	5.1	1	0.1	266	23.1
50–59	220	19.1	40	3.5	—	—	260	22.6	230	20.0	64	5.6	5	0.4	299	26.0
60+	354	30.8	20	1.7	—	—	374	32.5	213	18.5	—	—	—	—	213	18.6
Total	1,039	90.2	204	17.7	7	0.7	1,150	100.0	947	82.3	195	16.9	8	0.7	1,150	100.0

TABLE 3.4
Education Status of Respondents by Their Willingness to Circumcise a Daughter

	Okelele ($N = 1,150$)								Shao ($N = 1,150$)							
	Agree		Disagree		Neutral		Total		Agree		Disagree		Neutral		Total	
	N	%	N	%	N	%	N	%	N	%	N	%	N	%	N	%
Illiterates	642	55.8	23	2.0	23	2.0	688	59.8	691	60.1	24	2.1	—	—	715	62.2
Primary (1–6 years of schooling)	231	20.1	28	2.4	25	2.2	284	24.7	181	15.8	25	2.2	46	4	253	22.0
Vocational/secondary (7–12 years of schooling)	116	10.1	16	1.4	46	4.0	178	15.5	102	8.9	46	4.0	33	2.9	182	15.8
Total	989	86.0	67	5.8	94	8.2	1,150	100.0	974	84.8	95	8.3	79	6.9	1,150	100.0

TABLE 3.5
Comparison of Respondents' Opinion of Female Circumcision

Variables of Female Circumcision	Okelele ($N = 1,150$)								Shao ($N = 1,150$)							
	Agree		Disagree		Neutral		Total		Agree		Disagree		Neutral		Total	
	N	%	N	%	N	%	N	%	N	%	N	%	N	%	N	%
Female circumcision should be discouraged because it is very painful.	109	9.5	983	85.5	58	5.0	1,150	100	144	12.5	1,006	87.5	—	—	1,150	100
Female circumcision can be the cause of excessive bleeding.	277	19.7	865	75.3	58	5.0	1,150	100	130	11.3	1,009	87.7	11	1	1,150	100
Female circumcision can be the vehicle for tetanus infection.	290	25.2	802	69.8	58	5.0	1,150	100	139	12.1	1,101	87.9	—	—	1,150	100

Variables of Female Circumcision	Okelele (N = 1,150)								Shao (N = 1,150)							
	Agree		Disagree		Neutral		Total		Agree		Disagree		Neutral		Total	
	N	%	N	%	N	%	N	%	N	%	N	%	N	%	N	%
Female circumcision can facilitate complication in childbirth.	320	27.8	765	66.5	65	5.7	1,150	100	137	11.9	1,002	87.1	11	1	1,150	100
Female circumcision may hinder orgasm.	132	11.5	931	81.0	87	7.5	1,150	100	173	15.1	974	84.7	3	0.3	1,150	100
Female circumcision may lead to permanent emotional scars from the initial pains.	100	8.8	97	84.8	75	6.5	1,150	100	172	15.0	977	84.9	1	0.1	1,150	100

TABLE 3.6
Percentage Distribution of Suggested Strategies to Eradicate Female Circumcision by Sex

Suggested Strategies	Okelele (N = 1,150)			Shao (N = 1,150)		
	Male (%)	Female (%)	Total (%)	Male (%)	Female (%)	Total (%)
Health education	36.5	48.0	42.25	38.1	51.0	44.5
Government legislation	13.5	1.5	7.50	9.5	2.5	6.0
Eradication of the practice is unnecessary.	50.0	40.5	50.25	52.4	46.5	49.5

Discussion

The findings from this study revealed that the majority of the female respondents in the two communities surveyed were not only circumcised but supported the practice of female circumcision. Although over 58.0% of the respondents agreed that female circumcision is part of the traditional and cultural heritage in the two communities surveyed, the view that female circumcision can prevent female promiscuity ranks second of all the reasons advanced for their desire to continue the practice. That female circumcision can prevent clitoral growth and that it will enhance childbirth were ranked as third and fourth salient rationales (Table 3.1). As elicited from the study sample, the circumcision of female children in the two communities is performed about seven days after delivery of the infant. For the sickly female infant, circumcision can be postponed but must be performed before she attains puberty. For this category of female children, they can be exposed to both physical and psychological trauma. In situations where female circumcision is performed by the unskilled traditional healer, who works under septic conditions and without prior hematological problem-related consideration, several complications can ensue. These include genital sepsis, septicaemia, partial labia fusion, hemorrhage, implantation dermoid, deep scarred tissues, apareurda dyspareunia, and tetanus (Adetoro & Ebomoyi, 1986; Taba, 1980).

The two uniovular twins, who are the traditional healers performing circumcision in the study area, opined that the complications associated with female circumcision occur when done by unskilled traditional healers. Their contention was that this practice cannot be wiped out in their lifetime because of the traditional essence of the practice.

The practice of female circumcision is ethnically linked in Nigerian communities. There are quite a few ethnic groups where the practice is not acceptable to the general public. These include the Egbas and Ijebus of Ogun State, the Itshekiris of Bendel State, and some calabarians of the Cross River State of Nigeria. Earlier researchers in Senegal have observed similar ethnic differences where the Fula and Toucoulese women circumcise their daughters, and the Wolofs refrain from circumcision (Onadeko & Adekunle, 1985).

[In this study, it was] . . . observed that the majority of the respondents . . . were willing to circumcise any daughter born to them. However, . . . males in the two communities were [more] willing [than females] to have any of their daughters circumcised. As presented in Table 3.2 the majority of the significant others who cared more for female circumcision were grandfathers and fathers in the two communities. This observation was confirmed by Dareer (1983) who maintained that fathers generally play a passive role that really amounts to indirect approval and that "they do in the fact participate in the subjection of their daughters and sisters to the ordeal." (p. 143).

Control of Women's Illicit Sexuality and Reproduction

Shao and Okelele have a family system in which a female can have only one husband while the male is free to be polygamous. As a result, there is a strong need in this male-dominated society to restrict women's sexuality. Viewed from the materialistic perspective, because marriage is an event that both fathers and daughters look forward to, efforts are made by fathers to protect their daughter's virginity and their reputation for virginity until marriage. In communities such as Okelele and Shao, where both polygamy and the extended family system are in evidence, it is little wonder that the fraternal interest group is strong and there is overwhelming support for the fathers' motives. In these Yoruba communities, circumcision is also adopted as a form of contraceptive for the potential mother. Because it is widely believed sperm can easily contaminate a nursing mother's milk and thereby harm the baby (Oni, 1986), during the nursing period, the mother has to abstain from sexual intercourse for the 18 months that she needs to breast-feed her baby. It is locally believed that, because she was circumcised it is easier for her to endure a sexless life for the period she nurses her baby (Anonymous, 1981).

In many African societies where marriage and childbearing are essential for women, those who are uncircumcised are stigmatized as uncouth and may not be able to attract a husband. So excision is performed to attenuate sexual desire and make women less vulnerable to illicit sexual behavior before or after marriage (Epelboin & Epelboin, 1979).

In the two communities studied, respondents who were generally willing to circumcise any daughter born to them were the older and less literate persons. As can be observed from Table 3.4 over 55% of the respondents who supported the circumcision of their daughter were illiterate. Those of them with primary education who supported female circumcision were less than 21%. The preponderance of activists who oppose female circumcision are educated women and concerned learned males (Onadeko & Adekunle, 1985; *Women in Nigeria,* 1977).

The main justification for female circumcision given by 58.6% and 69.3% of those interviewed at Okelele and Shao, respectively, was that the practice was part of their cultural heritage. In both communities, well over 66% of the persons interviewed did not feel female circumcision should be discouraged on any on the following grounds: pain, severe bleeding, interference with orgasm, tetanus infection, and complication of childbirth.

The contention by a prominent African leader (Kenyata, 1959) has been that, by eradicating female circumcision, a fundamental African tradition will be destroyed or extirpated. The practice is harmful, and just as facial marks and scarifications have been allowed to disappear, female circumcision should be abolished.

Home visitors and PHC workers should assist women to identify and solve their most important problems. The issue of female circumcision can be effectively tackled by multidisciplinary teams in which women are motivated to be leaders. The rights of women are not only a question of justice but also of social progress. Collaboration with enlightened African women organizations such as the Association of African Women for Research and Development can invest efforts in launching and supporting programs aimed at reducing or eliminating the excessive control that African men currently exert over their women counterparts. Additionally, nongovernmental organizations such as the World Health Organization, UNICEF and other international organizations in Europe and America, have prominent roles to play in enhancing the status of women in most African societies.

In traditional and homogenous cultural settings such as Okelele and Shao, the ability to bear children is highly revered. Quite often housewives engage in intrafamilial competition in terms of the number and sex of children they are able to bear. Generally males are preferred, owing to property rights and the perpetuation of family names. So it is a fulfillment of the women's life to have children—without children she is nothing at all (Alausa, Ebomoyi, Parakoyi, Omonisi, & Alade, 1985; Hosken, 1976).

The respondents in this study were of the opinion that the practice of female circumcision was aimed at promoting sexual morality among women and enhancing safe delivery among women. Additionally, the practice was said to ensure infantile survival. Public health efforts directed at discouraging the practice of female circumcision must provide precise information capable of invalidating the erroneous views currently upheld about the essence of female circumcision, not only in Nigeria but also in most developing African societies. The various dangers associated with the practice must be made known. Sex education of women can assist in reducing the unwanted physical, psychological, and social torture inflicted upon women as a result of this practice.

Legislation can also be adopted if people are sufficiently made aware of the dangers associated with female circumcision. Legislation should be the last resort, but the education of men, women, and traditional healers should create an awareness that would enable people to give up the practice of female circumcision in order to enhance the general health status not only of women but also of the community at large.

References

Adetoro, O., & Ebomoyi, E. Health implications of traditional female circumcision in pregnancy. *Asia-Oceania Journal of Obstetrics and Gynaecology,* 1986, 12(4), 489–492.

Agugua, N., & Egwuatu, V. Female circumcision management of urinary complication. *Journal of Tropical Pediatrics,* October 1982, 28, 248–252.

Alausa, O. K., Ebomoyi, E., Parakoyi, B. D., Omonisi, K., & Alade, I. The health needs of people. *An International Journal of Health Development World Health Forum,* 1985, 6(4), 348–349.

Anonymous. The battle against female circumcision. *New African,* 1981, 168, 42.

Assaad, F. The sexual mutilation of women. *An International Journal of Health Development World Health Forum,* 1982, 3(4) 391–394.

Asuen, M. Maternal septicaemia and death after circumcision. *Tropical Doctor,* October 1977, 7, 177–178.

Baasher, T. *Psychological aspects of female circumcision.* WHO Eastern Mediterranean Region, 1977.

Bella, H. Female circumcision. *African Health,* 1980, 2, 31–32.

Cook, R. *Damage to physical health from pharaonic circumcision (infibulation) of females: A review of medical literature.* WHO/EMRO Tech. Publ. Vol. 2, 1976, 138–144.

Dareer, A. Attitudes of Sudanese people to the practice of female circumcision. *International Journal of Epidemiology,* 1983, 12, 138–144.

Ebomoyi, E. Female circumcision: An inhuman practice. *An International Journal of Health Development World Health Forum,* 1985 6(3), 236–237.

Epelboin, S., & Epelboin, A. Female circumcision. *People,* 1979, 24–29.

Hathout, H. M. Some aspects of female circumcision. *Journal of Obstetrics Gynaecology,* 1968, 79, 505–507.

Hosken, F. P. Female circumcision and fertility in Africa. *Women and Health,* 1976, 1(6) 3–11.

Iregbulem, L. M. Post circumcision vulval adhesions in Nigeria. *British Journal Plastic Surgery,* 1990, 33, 83–86.

Kenyata, J. *Facing Mount Kenya.* London: Secker and Warburg, 1959.

Melly, J. M. Infibulation. *Lancet,* 1935, 2, 1272.

Mustapha, A. Z. Female circumcision and infibulation in the Sudan. *Journal of Obstetrics and Gynaecology,* 1966, 73, 302–306.

Onadeko, M. O., & Adekunle, V. L. Female circumcision in Nigeria: A fact or farce? *Journal of Tropical Pediatrics,* 1985, 31, 180–194.

Oni, G. A. Contraceptive use and breast feeding: Their inverse relationship and policy concern. *East African Medical Journal,* 1986, 63(8), 522–529.

Rathmann, W. G. Female circumcision: Indications and new techniques. *General Practitioners,* 1959, 20, 115–120.

Sanderson, L. P. *Against the mutilation of women: The struggle against unnecessary suffering.* London: Ithala Press, 1981.

Taba, H. A. Female circumcision. *Tropical Doctor,* 1980, 10, 21–23.

Watts, S. J. Marriage migration: A neglected form of long-term mobility. A case study from Ilorin, Nigeria. *International Migration Review,* 1984, 17, 682–698.

Women in Nigeria: New Female Circumcision. Lexington, MA: (n.p.), 1977.

Name: _____ Class: _____

Date: _____ Section: _____

Reading Comprehension Activity Sheet

The Prevalence of Female Circumcision in Two Nigerian Communities, Ehigie Ebomoyi

1. What are the four major types of female circumcision practiced? _____

_____

_____

_____

_____

_____

_____

_____

_____

_____

2. What cultural factors were given to support the continuation of female circumcision?

_____

_____

_____

_____

_____

_____

_____

_____

_____

_____

3. Is it "ethnocentric" to support the eradication of the practice? _____

chapter 4

Socialization

Final Note on a Case of Extreme Isolation
Kingsley Davis

The Miseducation of Boys: Changing the Script
Myra Sadker and David Sadker

Final Note on a Case of Extreme Isolation

Kingsley Davis

Early in 1940 there appeared ... an account of a girl called Anna.[1] She had been deprived of normal contact and had received a minimum of human care for almost the whole of her first six years of life. At this time observations were not complete and the report had a tentative character. Now, however, the girl is dead, and with more information available,[2] it is possible to give a fuller and more definitive description of the case from a sociological point of view.

Anna's death, caused by hemorrhagic jaundice, occurred on August 6, 1942. Having been born on March 1 or 6,[3] 1932, she was approximately ten and a half years of age when she died. The previous report covered her development up to the age of almost eight years; the present one recapitulates the earlier period on the basis of new evidence and then covers the last two and half years of her life.

Early History

The first few days and weeks of Anna's life were complicated by frequent changes of domicile. It will be recalled that she was an illegitimate child, the second such child born to her mother, and that her grandfather, a widowed farmer in whose house the mother lived, strongly disapproved of this new evidence of the mother's indiscretion. This fact led to the baby's being shifted about.

Two weeks after being born in a nurse's private home, Anna was brought to the family farm, but the grandfather's antagonism was so great that she was shortly taken to the house of one of her mother's friends. At this time a local minister became interested in her and took her to his house with an idea of possible adoption. He decided against adoption, however, when he discovered that she had vaginitis. The infant was then taken to a children's home in

From *American Journal of Sociology* by Kingsley Davis. Reprinted by permission of Marta Seoane, widow of Kingsley Davis.

the nearest large city. This agency found that at the age of only three weeks she was already in a miserable condition, being "terribly galled and otherwise in very bad shape." It did not regard her as a likely subject for adoption but took her in for a while anyway, hoping to benefit her. After Anna had spent nearly eight weeks in this place, the agency notified her mother to come to get her. The mother responded by sending a man and his wife to the children's home with a view to their adopting Anna, but they made such a poor impression on the agency that permission was refused. Later the mother came herself and took the child out of the home and then gave her to this couple. It was in the home of this pair that a social worker found the girl a short time thereafter. The social worker went to the mother's home and pleaded with Anna's grandfather to allow the mother to bring the child home. In spite of threats, he refused. The child, by then more than four months old, was next taken to another children's home in a nearby town. A medical examination at this time revealed that she had impetigo, vaginitis, umbilical hernia, and a skin rash.

Anna remained in this second children's home for nearly three weeks, at the end of which time she was transferred to a private foster-home. Since, however, the grandfather would not, and the mother could not, pay for the child's care, she was finally taken back as a last resort to the grandfather's house (at the age of five and half months). There she remained, kept on the second floor in an attic-like room because her mother hesitated to incur the grandfather's wrath by bringing her downstairs.

The mother, a sturdy woman weighing about 180 pounds, did a man's work on the farm. She engaged in heavy work such as milking cows and tending hogs and had little time for her children. Sometimes she went out at night, in which case Anna was left entirely without attention. Ordinarily, it seems, Anna received only enough care to keep her barely alive. She appears to have been seldom moved from one position to another. Her clothing and bedding were filthy. She apparently had no instruction, no friendly attention.

It is little wonder that, when finally found and removed from the room in the grandfather's house at the age of nearly six years, the child could not talk, walk, or do anything that showed intelligence. She was in an extremely emaciated and undernourished condition, with skeletonlike legs and a bloated abdomen. She had been fed on virtually nothing except cow's milk during the years under her mother's care.

Anna's condition when found, and her subsequent improvement, have been described in the previous report. It now remains to say what happened to her after that.

Later History

In 1939, nearly two years after being discovered, Anna had progressed, as previously reported, to the point where she could walk, understand simple commands, feed herself, achieve some neatness, remember people, etc. But she still did not speak, and, though she was much more like a normal infant of something over one year of age in mentality, she was far from normal for her age.

On August 30, 1939, she was taken to a private home for retarded children, leaving the county home where she had been for more than a year and a half. In her new setting she made some further progress, but not a great deal. In a report of an examination made November 6 of the same year, the head of the institution pictured the child as follows:

> Anna walks about aimlessly, makes periodic rhythmic motions of her hands, and, at intervals, makes guttural and sucking noises. She regards her hands as if she had seen them for the first time. It was impossible to hold her attention for more than a few seconds at a time—not because of distraction due to external stimuli but because of her inability to concentrate. She ignored the task in hand to gaze vacantly about the room. Speech is entirely lacking. Numerous unsuccessful attempts have been made with her in the hope of developing initial sounds. I do not believe that this failure is due to negativism or deafness but that she is not sufficiently developed to accept speech at this time. . . . The prognosis is not favorable. . . .

More than five months later, on April 25, 1940, a clinical psychologist, the late Professor Francis N. Maxfield, examined Anna and reported the following: large for her age; hearing "entirely normal"; vision apparently normal; able to climb stairs; speech in the "babbling stage" and "promise for developing intelligible speech later seems to be good." He said further that "on the Merrill-Palmer scale she made a mental score of 19 months. On the Vineland social maturity scale she made a score of 23 months."[4]

Professor Maxfield very sensibly pointed out that prognosis is difficult in such cases of isolation. "It is very difficult to take scores on tests standardized under average conditions of environment and experience," he wrote, "and interpret them in a case where environment and experience have been so unusual." With this warning he gave it as his opinion at that time that Anna would eventually "attain an adult mental level of six or seven years."[5]

The school for retarded children, on July 1, 1941, reported that Anna had reached 46 inches in height and weighed 60 pounds. She could bounce and catch a ball and was said to conform to group socialization, though as a follower rather than a leader. Toilet habits were firmly established. Food habits were normal, except that she still used a spoon as her sole implement. She could dress herself except for fastening her clothes. Most remarkable of all, she had finally begun to develop speech. She was characterized as being at about the two-year level in this regard. She could call attendants by name and bring in one when she was asked to. She had a few complete sentences to express her wants. The report concluded that there was nothing peculiar about her, except that she was feeble-minded—"probably congenital in type."[6]

A final report from the school made on June 22, 1942, and evidently the last report before the girl's death, pictured only a slight advance over that given above. It said that Anna could follow directions, string beads, identify a few colors, build with blocks, and differentiate between attractive and unattractive pictures. She had a good sense of rhythm and loved a doll. She talked mainly in phrases but would repeat words and try to carry on a conversation. She was clean about clothing. She habitually washed her hands and brushed her teeth.

She would try to help other children. She walked well and could run fairly well, though clumsily. Although easily excited, she had a pleasant disposition.

Interpretation

Such was Anna's condition just before her death. It may seem as if she had not made much progress, but one must remember the condition in which she had been found. One must recall that she had no glimmering of speech, absolutely no ability to talk, no sense of gesture, not the least capacity to feed herself even when the food was put in front of her, and no comprehension of cleanliness. She was so apathetic that it was hard to tell whether or not she could hear. And all this at the age of nearly six years. Compared with this condition, her capacities at the time of her death seem striking indeed, though they do not amount to much more than a two-and-a-half-year mental level. One conclusion therefore seems safe, namely, that her isolation prevented a considerable amount of mental development that was undoubtedly part of her capacity. Just what her original capacity was, of course, is hard to say; but her development after her period of confinement (including the ability to walk and run, to play, to dress, fit into a social situation, and, above all, to speak) shows that she had at least this capacity—capacity that never could have been realized in her original condition of isolation.

A further question is this: What would she have been like if she had received a normal upbringing from the moment of birth? A definitive answer would have been impossible in any case, but even an approximate answer is made difficult by her dearly death. If one assumes, as was tentatively surmised in the previous report, that it is "almost impossible for any child to learn to speak, think, and act like a normal person after a long period of early isolation," it seems likely that Anna might have had a normal or near-normal capacity, genetically speaking. On the other hand, it was pointed out that Anna represented "a marginal case, [because] she was discovered before she had reached six years of age," an age "young enough to allow for some plasticity."[7] while admitting, then, that Anna's isolation *may* have been the major cause (and was certainly a minor cause) of her lack of rapid mental progress during the four and a half years following her rescue from neglect, it is necessary to entertain the hypothesis that she was congenitally deficient.

In connection with this hypothesis, one suggestive though by no means conclusive circumstance needs consideration, namely, the mentality of Anna's forebears. Information on this subject is easier to obtain, as one might guess, on the mother's than on the father's side. Anna's maternal grandmother, for example, is said to have been college educated and wished to have her children receive a good education, but her husband, Anna's stern grandfather, apparently a shrewd, hard-driving, calculating farmowner, was so penurious that her ambitions in this direction were thwarted. Under the circumstances her daughter (Anna's mother) managed, despite having to do hard work on the farm, to complete the eighth grade in a country school. Even so, however, the daughter was evidently not very smart. "A schoolmate of [Anna's mother] stated that she was retarded in schoolwork; was very gullible at this age; and that her morals even at this time were discussed by other students." Two tests administered to her on March 4, 1938, when she was thirty-two years of age, showed that she was mentally deficient. On the Stanford Revision of the Binet-Simon Scale her performance was equivalent to that of a child of eight years, giving her an I.Q. of 50 and indicating mental deficiency of "middle-grade moron type."[8]

As to the identity of Anna's father, the most persistent theory holds that he was an old man about seventy-four years of age at the time of the girl's birth. If he was the one, there is no indication of mental or other biological deficiency, whatever one may think of his morals. However, someone else may actually have been the father.

To sum up: Anna's heredity is the kind that *might* have given rise to innate mental deficiency, though not necessarily.

Comparison with Another Case

Perhaps more to the point than speculation about Anna's ancestry would be a case for comparison. If a child could be discovered who had been isolated about the same length of time as Anna but had achieved a much quicker recovery and a greater mental development, it would be a stronger indication that Anna was deficient to start with.

Such a case does exist. It is the case of a girl found at about the same time as Anna and under strikingly similar circumstances. A full description of the details of this case has not been published, but in addition to newspaper reports, an excellent preliminary account by a speech specialist, Dr. Marie K. Mason, who played an important role in the handling of the child, has appeared.[9] Also the late Dr. Francis N. Maxfield, clinical psychologist at Ohio State University, as was Dr. Mason, has written an as yet unpublished but penetrating analysis of the case.[10] Some of his observations have been included in Professor Zingg's book on feral man.[11] The following discussion is drawn mainly from these enlightening materials. The writer, through the kindness of Professors Mason and Maxfield, did have a chance to observe the girl in April, 1940, and to discuss the features of her case with them.

Born apparently one month later than Anna, the girl in question, who has been given the pseudonym Isabelle, was discovered in November, 1938, nine months after the discovery of Anna. At the time she was found she was approximately six and a half years of age. Like Anna, she was an illegitimate child and had been kept in seclusion for that reason. Her mother was a deaf-mute, having become so at the age of two, and it appears that she and Isabelle had spent most of their time together in a dark room shut off from the rest of the mother's family. As a result Isabelle had no chance to develop speech; when she communicated with her mother, it was by means of gestures. Lack of sunshine and inadequacy of diet had caused Isabelle to become rachitic. Her legs in particular were affected; they "were so bowed that as she stood erect the soles of her shoes came nearly flat together, and she got about with a skittering gait."[12] Her behavior toward strangers, especially men, was almost that of a wild animal, manifesting much fear and hostility. In lieu of speech she made only a strange croaking sound. In many ways she acted like an infant. "She was apparently utterly unaware of relationships of any kind. When presented with a ball for the first time, she held it in the palm of her hand, then reached out and stroked my face with it. Such behavior is comparable to that of a child of six months."[13] At first it was even hard to tell whether or not she could hear, so unused were her senses. Many of her actions resembled those of deaf children.

It is small wonder that, once it was established that she could hear, specialists working with her believed her to be feeble-minded. Even on nonverbal tests her performance was so low as to promise little for the future. Her first score on the Stanford-Binet was 19 months, practically at the zero point of the scale. On the Vineland social maturity scale her first score was 39, representing an age level of two and a half years.[14] "The general impression was that she was wholly uneducable and that any attempt to teach her to speak, after so long a period of silence, would meet with failure."[15]

In spite of this interpretation, the individuals in charge of Isabelle launched a systematic and skillful program of training. It seemed hopeless at first. The approach had to be through pantomime and dramatization, suitable to an infant. It required one week of intensive effort before she even made her first attempt at vocalization. Gradually she began to respond, however, and, after the first hurdles had at least been overcome, a curious thing happened. She went through the usual stages of learning characteristic of the years from one to six not only in proper succession but far more rapidly than normal. In a little over two months after her first vocalization she was putting sentences together. Nine months after that she could identify words and sentences on the printed page, could write well, could add to ten, and could retell a story after hearing it. Seven months beyond this point she had a vocabulary of 1,500–2,000 words and was asking complicated questions. Starting from an educational level of between one and three years (depending on what aspect one considers), she had reached a normal level by the time she was eight and a half years old. In short, she covered in two years the stages of learning that ordinarily require six.[16] Or, to put it another way, her I.Q. trebled in a year and a half.[17] The speed with which she reached the normal level of mental development seems analogous to the recovery of body weight in a growing child after an illness, the recovery being achieved by an extra fast rate of growth for a period after the illness until normal weight for the given age is again attained.

When the writer saw Isabelle a year and a half after her discovery, she gave him the impression of being a very bright, cheerful, energetic little girl. She spoke well, walked and ran without trouble, and sang with gusto and accuracy. Today she is over fourteen years old and has passed the sixth grade in a public school. Her teachers say that she participates in all school activities as normally as other children. Though older than her classmates, she has fortunately not physically matured too far beyond their level.[18]

Clearly the history of Isabelle's development is different from that of Anna's. In both cases there was an exceedingly low, or rather blank, intellectual level to begin with. In both cases it seemed that the girl might be congenitally feeble-minded. In both a considerably higher level was reached later on. But the Ohio girl achieved a normal mentality within two years, whereas Anna was still marked inadequate at the end of four and a half years. This difference in achievement may suggest that Anna had less initial capacity. But an alternative hypothesis is possible.

One should remember that Anna never received the prolonged and expert attention that Isabelle received. The result of such attention, in the case of the Ohio girl, was to give her speech at an early stage, and her subsequent rapid development seems to have been a consequence of that. "Until Isabelle's speech and language development, she had all the characteristics of a feeble-minded child." Had Anna, who, from the standpoint of psychometric tests and early history, closely resembled this girl at the start, been given a mastery of speech at an earlier point by intensive training, her subsequent development might have been much more rapid.[19]

The hypothesis that Anna began with a sharply inferior mental capacity is therefore not established. Even if she were deficient to start with, we have no way of knowing how much so. Under ordinary conditions she might have been a dull normal or, like her mother, a moron. Even after the blight of her isolation, if she had lived to maturity, she might have finally reached virtually the full level of her capacity, whatever it may have been. That her isolation did have a profound effect upon her mentality, there can be no doubt. This is proved by the substantial degree of change during the four and a half years following her rescue.

Consideration of Isabelle's case serves to show, as Anna's case does not clearly show, that isolation up to the age of six, with failure to acquire any form of speech and hence failure to grasp nearly the whole world of cultural meaning, does not preclude the subsequent acquisition of these. Indeed, there seems to be a process of accelerated recovery in which the child goes through the mental stages at a more rapid rate than would be the case in normal development. Just what would be the maximum age at which a person could remain isolated and still retain the capacity for full cultural acquisition is hard to say. Almost certainly it would not be as high as age fifteen; it might possibly be as low as age ten. Undoubtedly various individuals would differ considerably as to the exact age.

Anna's is not an ideal case for showing the effects of extreme isolation, partly because she was possibly deficient to begin with, partly because she did not receive the best training available, and partly because she did not live long enough. Nevertheless, her case is instructive when placed in the record with numerous other cases of extreme isolation. This and the previous article about her are meant to place her in the record. It is to be hoped that other cases will be described in the scientific literature as they are discovered (as unfortunately they will be), for only in these rare cases of extreme isolation is it possible "to observe *concretely separated* two factors in the development of human personality which are always otherwise only analytically separated, the biogenic and the sociogenic factors."[20]

Notes

[1] Kingsley Davis, "Extreme Social Isolation of a Child," *American Journal of Sociology,* XLV (January, 1940), 554–65.

[2] Sincere appreciation is due to the officials in the Department of Welfare, Commonwealth of Pennsylvania, for their kind cooperation in making available the records concerning Anna and discussing the case frankly with the writer. Helen C. Hubbell, Florentine Hackbusch, and Eleanor Meckelnburg were particularly helpful, as was Fanny L. Matchette. Without their aid neither of the reports on Anna could have been written.

[3] The records are not clear as to which day.

[4] Letter to one of the state officials in charge of the case.

[5] *Ibid.*

[6] Progress report of the school.

[7] Davis, *op. cit.,* p. 564.

[8] The facts set forth here as to Anna's ancestry are taken chiefly from a report of mental tests administered to Anna's mother by psychologists at a state hospital where she was taken for this purpose after the discovery of Anna's seclusion. This excellent report was not available to the writer when the previous paper on Anna was published.

[9] Marier K. Mason, "Learning to Speak after Six and One-Half Years of Silence," *Journal of Speech Disorders,* VII (1942), 295–304.

[10] Francis N. Maxfield, "What Happens When the Social Environment of a Child Approaches Zero." The writer is greatly indebted to Mrs. Maxfield and to Professor Horace B. English, a colleague of Professor Maxfield, for the privilege of seeing this manuscript and other materials collected on isolated and feral individuals.

[11] J. A. L. Singh and Robert M. Zingg, *Wolf-Children and Feral Man* (New York: Harper & Bros., 1941), pp. 248–51.

[12] Maxfield, unpublished manuscript cited above.

[13] Mason, *op. cit.,* p. 299.

[14] Maxfield, unpublished manuscript.

[15] Mason, *op. cit.,* p. 299.

[16] *Ibid.,* pp. 300–304.

[17] Maxfield, unpublished manuscript.

[18] Based on a personal letter from Dr. Mason to the writer, May 13, 1946.

[19] This point is suggested in a personal letter from Dr. Mason to the writer, October 22, 1946.

[20] Singh and Zingg, *op. cit.,* pp. xxi–xxii, in a foreword by the writer.

Glossary

Socialization: The process of learning cooperative group living.

Learning state: The knowledge and ability individuals are expected to have attained a particular age.

Name: _____ Class: _____

Date: _____ Section: _____

Reading Comprehension Activity Sheet

Final Note on a Case of Extreme Isolation, Kingsley Davis

1. Discuss Anna's early life and the condition she was in when found at the age of six.

   _____
   _____
   _____
   _____
   _____
   _____
   _____
   _____
   _____
   _____
   _____

2. According to Davis, was Anna's lack of normal development due to her heredity or her upbringing? _____

   _____
   _____
   _____
   _____
   _____
   _____
   _____
   _____
   _____
   _____

3. Most sociologists concur that children are not born with instincts or the innate drives that will make them human, and that humanness is acquired through human interaction and socialization. Would you agree or disagree with this statement? (Use information from the Davis article to support your answer.)

The Miseducation of Boys
Changing the Script

Myra Sadker and David Sadker

Boys confront frozen boundaries of the male role at every turn of school life. They grow up learning lines and practicing moves from a timeworn script: Be cool, don't show emotion, repress feelings, be aggressive, compete and win. As the script is internalized, boys learn to look down on girls and to distance themselves from any activity considered feminine. Dutifully they follow the lines of the script, but now changes are being made in the plot. Today's schoolboys are learning lines for a play that is closing. Consider these statistics:

- From elementary school through high school, boys received lower report card grades. By middle school they are far more likely to be grade repeaters and dropouts.[1]
- Boys experience more difficulty adjusting to school. They are nine times more likely to suffer form hyperactivity and higher levels of academic stress.[2]
- The majority of students identified for special education programs are boys. They represent 58 percent of those in classes for the mentally retarded, 71 percent of the learning disabled, and 80 percent of those in programs for the emotionally disturbed.[3]
- In school, boys' misbehavior results in more frequent penalties, including corporal punishment. Boys comprise 71 percent of all school suspensions.[4]

Beyond academic problems, conforming to a stereotypic role takes a psychological toll:

- Boys are three times more likely to become alcohol dependent and 50 percent more likely to use illicit drugs. Men account for more than 90 percent of alcohol- and drug-related arrests.[5]

Reprinted with the permission of Scribner, an imprint of Simon & Schuster Adult Publishing Group, from *Failing at Fairness* by Myra M. Sadker and David Sadker. Copyright © 1994 by Myra M. Sadker and David Sadker.

- Risk-taking behavior goes beyond drug and alcohol abuse. The leading cause of death among fifteen- to twenty-four-year-old white males is accidents. Teenage boys are more likely to die from gunshot wounds than from all natural causes combined.[6]
- Many boys are encouraged to pursue unrealistically high career goals. When these are not attained, males often feel like failures, and a lifelong sense of frustration may follow.[7]
- Males commit suicide two to three times more frequently than females.[8]

The problems for minority males are more devastation:

- Approximately one in every three black male teenagers is unemployed, and those who are working take home paychecks with 30 percent less salary than white workers.[9] It is estimated that 25 percent of black youths' income results directly from crime and that one in every six African-American males is arrested by age nineteen.[10]
- The odds of a young white woman being a murder victim are one in 369; for a young white man, one in 131; for an African-American woman, one in 104; and for an African-American man, a shocking one in 21. Homicide is the leading cause of death for young black men.[11]

City by city, the statistics are even more alarming. In New York City, about three out of four black males never make it to graduation, and in Milwaukee, 94 percent of all expelled students are African-American boys.[12] Milwaukee, Detroit, and Chicago consider black males an "endangered academic species" and have resorted to some radical solutions.

Milwaukee was one of the first cities to create black male academies, public schools that serve only African-American boys. The idea spread to other metropolitan areas, along with the notion that the best teachers for black boys are black men. At Matthew Henson Elementary School in a poor, drug-infested section of Baltimore, Richard Boynton teaches a class of young black students. Most of them grew up without fathers, so Boynton's responsibilities go beyond the classroom. "There are three things I enforce," he said, "three things I want them to know in that room: responsibility, respect, and self-control. I feel that these three things will not only carry you through school, they'll carry you through life."[13] So Boynton checks to make sure that all the boys have library cards. On weekends he takes them to the Smithsonian or to play ball in the park. "It's almost as if I have twenty-seven sons," he said. Boynton tries to create a school that will turn each of his "sons" on to education. But not everyone is convinced that teaching black males separately is the best approach.

"I read these things, and I can't believe that we're actually regressing like this," said African-American psychologist Kenneth Clark. "Why are we talking about segregating and stigmatizing black males?"[14] Clark's stinging observations are particularly potent since his research paved the way for the 1954 *Brown* decision that desegregated America's schools. Other critics charge that black male academies are little more than a return to the cries of "woman peril," scapegoating female teachers, criticizing black mothers, and ignoring the needs of African-American girls. NOW, the ACLU, and several courts have found separate black male education to be an example of sex discrimination and a violation of the law.

Morningside Elementary School in Prince Georges County, Maryland, is not a black male academy, but its students take special pride in their school team, the Master Knights. Tuesdays and Thursdays are team days, and the members, wearing blue pants and white shirts, devote recess and afternoons to practice. But the Knights, the majority of whom are young black boys, differ from other school teams. Their practices take place in the school library, and the arena in which they compete is chess.

The idea for the team originated in the office of Beulah McManus, the guidance counselor. When children, most often African-American boys, were referred to her as behavior problems, she pulled out a worn chess set. Somehow the game got boys talking, and eventually they found out they enjoyed chess, with its emphasis on tactics and skill, and the chance to complete on a field where size and strength mattered less than brains. As Gregory Bridges, the twelve-year-old president of the Master Knights, said, "When you see someone who is big and bad on the streets, you hardly see anyone who plays chess. . . . You have to have patience and a cool head, and that patience carries outside the chess club."[15] While Morningside emphasizes the importance of getting African-American boys excited about education, girls are not excluded, says principal Elsie Neely. In fact, the school is trying to recruit more female players for next year.

While Morningside stresses extracurricular activities in order to involve boys, some teachers are bringing lessons that challenge the male sex role stereotype directly into the classroom. Often they use the growing number of children's books that show boys expanding their roles. In a fourth-grade class we watched a teacher encouraging boys to push the borders of the male stereotype. As we observed her lesson, we were struck by how much effort it took to stretch outmoded attitudes. She began by writing a letter on the board.

Dear Adviser:
   My seven-year-old son wants me to buy him a doll. I don't know what to do. Should I go ahead and get it for him? Is this normal, or is my son sick? Please help!
                   Waiting for your answer,
                   Concerned

"Suppose you were an advice columnist, like Ann Landers," the teachers said to the class, "and you received a letter like this. What would you tell this parent? Write a letter answering 'Concerned,' and then we'll talk about your recommendations."

For the next twenty minutes she walked around the room and gave suggestions about format and spelling. When she invited the students to read their letters, Andy volunteered.

Dear Concerned:
   You are in big trouble. Your son in sick, sick, sick! Get him to a psychiatrist fast. And if he keeps asking for a doll, get him bats and balls and guns and other toys boys should play with.
                   Hope this helps,
                   Andy

Several other students also read their letters, and most, like Andy, recommended that the son be denied a doll. Then the teacher read Charlotte Zolotow's *William's Doll,* the story of a boy who is ridiculed by other children when he says he wants a doll. Not until his grandmother visits does he get his wish so that, as the wise woman says, he can learn to be a father one day.

As the teacher was reading, several students began to fidget, laugh, and whisper to one another. When she asked the fourth graders how they liked the book, one group of boys, the most popular clique in the class, acted as if the story was a personal insult. Their reaction was so hostile, the teacher had trouble keeping order. We heard their comments:

"He's a fag."

"He'd better learn how boys are supposed to behave, or he'll never get to be a man."

"Dolls are dumb. It's a girly thing to do."

"If you saw him playing with that baby doll, I'd take it away. Maybe a good kick in the pants would teach him."

Next the teacher played the song "William Wants a Doll" from the *Free to Be You and Me* album. Several boys began to sing along in a mocking tone, dragging out the word *doll* until it became two syllables: "William wants a do-oll, William wants a do-oll." As they chanted, they pointed to Bill, the star athlete of the class. Both boys and girls whispered and laughed as Bill, slumped in his chair, looked ready to explode.

Belatedly the teacher realized the problem of the name coincidence; she assured the class that there was nothing wrong with playing with dolls, that it teaches both girls and boys how to become parents when they grow up. When the students began to settle down, she gave them her next instructions: "I'd like you to reread your letters and make any last-minute corrections. If you want to change your advice, you may, but you don't have to."

Later we read the students' letters. Most of them said a seven-year-old boy should not get a doll. But after listening to William's story, six modified their advice, having reached a similar conclusion: "Oh, all right. Give him a doll if you have to. But no baby dolls or girl dolls. Make sure it's a Turtle or a G.I. Joe."

For some nontraditional programs, reading *William's Doll* is just a first step. At Germantown Friends School in Philadelphia, parenting classes begin in elementary school where children learn to observe, study, and interact with infants. By the sixth grade both boys and girls are in charge of caring for babies at school. Programs that make child-rearing a central and required part of school life find that boys become more nurturant and caring in their relationships with others.

Schools in New York City and other communities are downplaying aggression and encouraging cooperation through programs in conflict resolution. In these courses students learn how to negotiate and compromise while they avoid attitudes and actions that lead to violence. Students learn techniques in how to control anger, to listen carefully to others, and to seek common ground.

These innovative courses are rare. Most schools are locked in a more traditional model, one that promotes competition over cooperation, aggression over nurturing, and sports victories rather than athletic participation. Some boys thrive on this traditional male menu, and most students derive some benefit. But the school program is far from balanced, and the education served to boys is not always healthy despite the extra portions they receive.

From their earliest days at school, boys learn a destructive form of division—how to separate themselves from girls. Once the school world is divided, boys can strive to climb to the top of the male domain, thinking that even if they fall short, they still are ahead of the game because they are not girls. Boys learn in the classroom that they can demean girls at will. Schools that do not permit racist, ethnic, or religious slights still tolerate sexism as a harmless bigotry.

In *American Manhood,* Anthony Rotundo writes that men need to regain "access to stigmatized parts of themselves—tenderness, nurturance, the desire for connection, the skills of cooperation—that are helpful in personal situations and needed for the social good."[16] Studies support Rotundo's contention: Males who can call on a range of qualities, tenderness as well as toughness, are viewed by others as more intelligent, likable, and mentally healthy than rigidly stereotyped men.[17] But boys cannot develop these repressed parts of themselves without abandoning attitudes that degrade girls. Until gender equity becomes a value promoted in every aspect of school, boys, as victims of their own miseducation, will grow up to be troubled men; they will be saddened by unmet expectations, unable to communicate with women as equals, and unprepared for modern life.

Notes

1. Brophy, Jere, and Thomas Good. "Feminization of American Elementary Schools," *Phi Delta Kappan* 54 (1973), pp. 564–66.
    Sadker, Myra, and David Sadker. *Sex Equity Handbook for Schools.* New York: Longman, 1982.
2. Kessler, R., and J. McRae. "Trends in the Relationship Between Sex and Psychological Distress, 1957–76," *American Sociological Review* 46 (1981).
    McLanahan, S. S., and J. L. Glass. "A Note on the Trend in Sex Differences in Psychological Distress," *Journal of Health and Human Stress* 2 (1976).
3. Sadker, David, and Myra Sadker, updated by Mary Jo Strauss. "The Report Card #1: The cost of Sex Bias in Schools and Society." Distributed by the Mid-Atlantic Equity Center, Washington, D.C., and the New England Center for Equity Assistance, Andover, Massachusetts, 1989.
4. Duke, D. L. "Who Misbehaves? A High School Studies Its Discipline Problems," *Educational Administration Quarterly* 12 (1976), pp. 65–85.
    Office for Civil Rights. *1986 Elementary and Secondary Civil Rights Survey, State and National Summary of Projected Data.* Washington, DC: U.S. Department of Education, 1988.

5. Kimbrell, Andrew. "A Time for Men to Pull Together," *Utne Reader* (May–June 1991), pp. 66–75.
    Watts, W. David, and Loyd S. Wright. "The Relationship of Alcohol, Tobacco, Marijuana, and Other Illegal Drug Use to Delinquency Among Mexican-American, Black, and White Adolescent Males," *Adolescence* 25:97 (Spring 1990), pp. 171–81.
6. Unpublished data of the National Center for Health Statistics, Public Health Service, U.S. Department of Health and Human Services, 1986.
    "Death Rates from Accidents and Violence: 1970 to 1985," *Statistical Abstract of the United States,* 1988. Washington, DC: Bureau of the Census, U.S. Department of Commerce, 1988.
    Poinsett, Alvin. "Why Our children Are Killing One Another," *Ebony* 43 (December 1987).
    Children's Defense Fund. *The State of America's Children: 1992.* Washington, DC: Children's Defense Fund, 1992.
7. Pleck, Joseph, and Robert Brannon (eds.). "Male Roles and the Male Experience," *Journal of Social Issues* 34 (1978), pp. 1–4.
    Komarovsky, M. *Dilemmas of Masculinity: A Study of College Youth.* New York: Norton, 1976.
    Sadker and Sadker, *Sex Equity Handbook for Schools.*
8. Lester, David. *Why People Kill Themselves: A 1990s Summary of Research Findings on Suicide Behavior,* third edition. Springfield, IL: Charles C. Thomas, 1992.
    Maris R. W. *Pathways to Suicide: A Survey of Self-Destructive Behaviors.* Baltimore, MD: Johns Hopkins Press, 1981.
9. Dewart, J. (ed.) *The State of Black America, 1989.* Washington, DC: National Urban League, 1989.
    Garibaldi, Antoine M. *Educating Black Male Youth: A Moral and Civic Imperative.* New Orleans: Orleans Parish School Board, 1988.
    Collison, Michelle N.-K. "More Young Black Men Choosing Not to Go to College," *Chronicle of Higher Education* 34:15 (December 9, 1987), pp. A1, 26–27.
    Gibbs, Jewelle Taylor (ed.). *Young, Black, and Male in America: An Endangered Species.* Dover, MA: Auburn House, 1988.
10. Whitaker, Charles. "Do Black Males Need Special Schools?" *Ebony* (March 1991), pp. 17–18, 20.
11. Simons, Janet M., Belva Finlay, and Alice Yang. *The Adolescent Young Adult Fact Book.* Washington, DC: Children's Defense Fund, 1991.
    Children's Defense Fund. *The State of America's Children: 1992,* p. 52.
12. Lawton, Millicent. "Two Schools Aimed for Black Males Set in Milwaukee," *Education Week* X:6 (October 10, 1990), pp. 1, 8.
13. Dunkel, Tom. "Self-Segregated Schools Seek to Build Self-Esteem," *The Washington Times* (March 11, 1991), pp. E1–2.
14. Clark quoted in Whitaker, "Do Black Males Need Special Schools?" p. 18.
15. Leff, Lisa. "Maneuvering to Win Young Minds, P. G. School Chess Club Teaches Boys Self-Discipline, Self-Esteem," *The Washington Post* (May 17, 1993), pp. A1, A3.
16. Rotundo, E. Anthony. *American Manhood.* New York: Basic Books, 1993, p. 291.
17. Cramer, Robert Ervin, et al. "Motivating and Reinforcing Functions of the Male Sex Role: Social Analogues of Partial Reinforcement, Delay of Reinforcement, and Intermittent Shock," *Sex Roles* 20:9–10 (1989), pp. 551–73.

Name: _____ Class: _____

Date: _____ Section: _____

Reading Comprehension Activity Sheet

The Miseducation of Boys: Changing the Script, Myra Sadker and David Sadker

1. How are boys being "miseducated," and what are the consequences of this miseducation?

   _____
   _____
   _____
   _____
   _____
   _____
   _____
   _____
   _____
   _____
   _____

2. This article illustrates the concept of "gender polarization" (the fact that women and men are cast as opposites and placed into two mutually exclusive categories). What are some benefits of being educated (socialized) to have a wide range of both feminine and masculine qualities?

   _____
   _____
   _____
   _____
   _____
   _____
   _____
   _____
   _____
   _____

3. Do you think it is more acceptable for boys to have feminine qualities or for girls to have masculine qualities?

chapter 5

Deviance, Crime, and Social Control

Becoming a Marihuana User
Howard S. Becker

Fraternities and Rape on Campus
Patricia Yancey Martin
Robert A. Hummer

Becoming a Marihuana User

Howard S. Becker

An unknown, but probably quite large, number of people in the United States use marihuana. They do this in spite of the fact that it is both illegal and disapproved.

The phenomenon of marihuana use has received much attention, particularly from psychiatrists and law enforcement officials. The research that has been done, as is often the case with research on behavior that is viewed as deviant, is mainly concerned with the question: why do they do it? Attempts to account for the use of marihuana lean heavily on the premise that the presence of any particular kind of behavior in an individual can best be explained as the result of some trait which predisposes or motivates him to engage in that behavior. In the case of marihuana use, this trait is usually identified as psychological, as a need for fantasy and escape from psychological problems the individual cannot face.[1]

I do not think such theories can adequately account for marihuana use. In fact, marihuana use is an interesting case for theories of deviance, because it illustrates the way deviant motives actually develop in the course of experience with the deviant activity. To put a complex argument in a few words: Instead of the deviant motives leading to the deviant behavior, it is the other way around; the deviant behavior in time produces the deviant motivation. Vague impulses and desires—in this case, probably most frequently a curiosity about the kind of experience the drug will produce—are transformed into definite patterns of action through the social interpretation of a physical experience which is in itself ambiguous. Marihuana use is a function of the individual's conception of marihuana and of the uses to which it can be put, and this conception develops as the individual's experience with the drug increases.[2]

The research reported [here] deals with the career of the marihuana user, [specifically, with] the development of the individual's immediate physical experience with marihuana . . .

From *American Journal of Sociology,* 59, 1953, 235–242. Reprinted by permission of The University of Chicago Press.

What we are trying to understand here is the sequence of changes in attitude and experience which lead to the use of marihuana for pleasure. This way of phrasing the problem requires a little explanation. Marihuana does not produce addiction, at least in the sense that alcohol and the opiate drugs do. The user experiences no withdrawal sickness and exhibits no ineradicable craving for the drug.[3] The most frequent pattern of use might be termed "recreational." The drug is used occasionally for the pleasure the user finds in it, a relatively casual kind of behavior in comparison with that connected with the use of addicting drugs. The report of the New York City Mayor's Committee on Marihuana emphasizes this point:

> A person may be a confirmed smoker for a prolonged period, and give up the drug voluntarily without experiencing any craving for it or exhibiting withdrawal symptoms. He may, at some time later on, go back to its use. Others may remain infrequent users of the cigarette, taking one or two a week, or only when the "social setting" calls for participation. From time to time we had one of our investigators associate with a marihuana user. The investigator would bring up the subject of smoking. This would invariably lead to the suggestion that they obtain some marihuana cigarettes. They would seek a "tea-pad," and if it was closed the smoker and our investigator would calmly resume their previous activity, such as the discussion of life in general or the playing of pool. There were apparently no signs indicative of frustration in the smoker at not being able to gratify the desire for the drug. We consider this point highly significant since it is so contrary to the experience of users of other narcotics. A similar situation occurring in one addicted to the use of morphine, cocaine or heroin would result in a compulsive attitude on the part of the addict to obtain the drug. If unable to secure it, there would be obvious physical and mental manifestations of frustration. This may be considered presumptive evidence that there is no true addiction in the medical sense associated with the use of marihuana.[4]

In using the phrase "use for pleasure," I mean to emphasize the noncompulsive and casual character of the behavior. (I also mean to eliminate from consideration here those few cases in which marihuana is used for its prestige value only, as a symbol that one is a certain kind of person, with no pleasure at all being derived from its use.)

The research I am about to report was not so designed that it could constitute a crucial test of the theories that relate marihuana use to some psychological trait of the user. However, it does show that psychological explanations are not in themselves sufficient to account for marihuana use and that they are, perhaps, not even necessary. Researchers attempting to prove such psychological theories have run into two great difficulties, never satisfactorily resolved, which the theory presented here avoids. In the first place, theories based on the existence of some predisposing psychological trait have difficulty in accounting for that group of users, who turn up in sizable numbers in every study,[5] who do not exhibit the trait or traits which are considered to cause the behavior. Second, psychological theories have difficulty in accounting for the great variability over time of a given individual's behavior with reference to the drug. The same person will at one time be unable to use the drug for pleasure, at a later stage be able and willing to do so, and still later again be unable to use it in this way. These changes, difficult to explain from a theory based on the user's needs for "escape" are readily understandable as consequences of changes in his conception of the drug. Similarly, if we think of the marihuana user as someone who has learned to view marihuana as something that can give him pleasure, we have no difficulty in understanding the existence of psychologically "normal" users.

In doing the study, I used the method of analytic induction. I tried to arrive at a general statement of the sequence of changes in individual attitude and experience which always occurred when the individual became willing and able to use marihuana for pleasure, and never occurred or had not been permanently maintained when the person was unwilling to use marihuana for pleasure. The method requires that *every* case collected in the research substantiate the hypothesis. If one case is encountered which does not substantiate it, the researcher is required to change the hypothesis to fit the case which has proven his original idea wrong.[6]

To develop and test my hypothesis about the genesis of marihuana use for pleasure, I conducted fifty interviews with marihuana users. I had been a professional dance musician for some years when I conducted this study and my first interviews were with people I had met in the music business. I asked them to put me in contact with other users who would be willing to discuss their experiences with me. Colleagues working on a study of users of opiate drugs made a few interviews available to me which contained, in addition to material on opiate drugs, sufficient material on the use of marihuana to furnish a test of my hypothesis.[7] Although in the end half of the fifty interviews were conducted with musicians, the other half covered a wide range of people, including laborers, machinists, and people in the professions. The sample is, of course, in no sense "random": it would not be possible to draw a random sample, since no one knows the nature of the universe from which it would have to be drawn.

In interviewing users, I focused on the history of the person's experience with marihuana, seeking major changes in his attitude toward it and in his actual use of it, and the reasons for these changes. Where it was possible and appropriate, I used the jargon of the user himself.

The theory starts with the person who has arrived at the point of willingness to try marihuana. . . . He knows others use marihuana to "get high," but he does not know what this means in any concrete way. He is curious about the experience, ignorant of what it may turn out to be, and afraid it may be more than he has bargained for. The steps outlined below, if he undergoes them all and maintains the attitudes developed in them, leave him willing and able to use the drug for pleasure when the opportunity presents itself.

Learning the Technique

The novice does not ordinarily get high the first time he smokes marihuana, and several attempts are usually necessary to induce this state. One explanation of this may be that the drug is not smoked "properly," that is, in a way that insures sufficient dosage to produce real symptoms of intoxication. Most users agree that it cannot be smoked like tobacco if one is to get high:

> Take in a lot of air, you know, and . . . I don't know how to describe it, you don't smoke it like a cigarette, you draw in a lot of air and get it deep down in your system and then keep it there. Keep it there as long as you can.

Without the use of some such technique[8] the drug will produce no effects, and the user will be unable to get high:

> The trouble with people like that [who are not able to get high] is that they're just not smoking it right, that's all there is to it. Either they're not holding it down long enough, or they're getting too much air and not enough smoke, or the other way around or something like that. A lot of people just don't smoke it right, so naturally nothing's gonna happen.

If nothing happens, it is manifestly impossible for the user to develop a conception of the drug as an object which can be used for pleasure, and use will therefore not continue. The first step in the sequence of events that must occur if the person is to become a user is that he must learn to use the proper smoking technique so that his use of the drug will produce effects in terms of which his conception of it can change.

Such a change is, as might be expected, a result of the individual's participation in groups in which marihuana is used. In them the individual learns the proper way to smoke the drug. This may occur through direct teaching:

> I was smoking like I did an ordinary cigarette. He said, "No, don't do it like that." He said, "Suck it, you know, draw in and hold it in your lungs till you . . . for a period of time."
> I said, "Is there any limit of time to hold it?"
> He said, "No, just till you feel that you want to let it out, let it out." So I did that three or four times.

Many new users are ashamed to admit ignorance and, pretending to know already, must learn through the more indirect means of observation and imitation:

> I came on like I had turned on many times before, you know. I didn't want to seem like a punk to this cat. See, like I didn't know the first thing about it—how to smoke it, or what was going to happen, or what. I just watched him like a hawk—I didn't take my eyes off him for a second, because I wanted to do everything just as he did it. I watched how he held it, how he smoked it, and everything. Then when he gave it to me I just came on cool, as though I knew exactly what the score was. I held it like he did and took a poke just the way he did.

No one I interviewed continued marihuana use for pleasure without learning a technique that supplied sufficient dosage for the effects of the drug to appear. Only when this was learned was it possible for a conception of the drug as an object which could be used for pleasure to emerge. Without such a conception marihuana use was considered meaningless and did not continue.

Learning to Perceive the Effects

Even after he learns the proper smoking technique, the new user may not get high and thus not form a conception of the drug as something which can be used for pleasure. A remark made by a user suggested the reason for this difficulty in getting high and pointed to the next necessary step on the road to being a user:

> As a matter of fact, I've seen a guy who was high out of his mind and didn't know it.
> [How can that be, man?]
> Well, it's pretty strange, I'll grant you that, but I've see it. This guy got on with me, claiming that he'd never got high, one of those guys, and he got completely stoned. And he kept insisting that he wasn't high. So I had to prove to him that he was.

What does this mean? It suggests that being high consists of two elements: the presence of symptoms caused by marihuana use and the recognition of these symptoms and their connection by the user with his use of the drug. It is not enough, that is, that the effects be present; alone, they do not automatically provide the experience of being high. The user must be able to point them out to himself and consciously connect them with having smoked marihuana before he can have this experience. Otherwise, no matter what actual effects are produced, he considers that the drug has had no effect on him: "I figured it either had no effect on me or other people were exaggerating its effect on them, you know. I thought it was probably psychological, see." Such persons believe the whole thing is an illusion and that the wish to be high leads the user to deceive himself into believing that something is happening when, in fact, nothing is. They do not continue marihuana use, feeling that "it does nothing" for them.

Typically, however, the novice has faith (developed from his observation of users who do get high) that the drug actually will produce some new experience and continues to experiment with it until it does. His failure to get high worries him, and he is likely to ask more experienced users or provoke comments from them about it. In such conversations he is made aware of specific details of his experience which he may not have noticed or may have noticed but failed to identify as symptoms of being high:

> I didn't get high the first time. . . . I don't think I held it in long enough. I probably let it out, you know, you're a little afraid. The second time I wasn't sure, and he [smoking companion] told me, like I asked him for some of the symptoms or something, how would I know, you know. . . . So he told me to sit on a stool. I sat on—I think I sat on a bar stool—and he said, "Let your feet hang," and then when I got down my feet were real cold, you know.
> And I started feeling it, you know. That was the first time. And then about a week after that, sometime pretty close to it, I really got on. That was the first time I got on a big laughing kick, you know. Then I really knew I was on.

One symptom of being high is an intense hunger. In the next case the novice becomes aware of this and gets high for the first time:

> They were just laughing the hell out of me because like I was eating so much. I just scoffed [ate] so much food, and they were just laughing at me, you know. Sometimes I'd be looking at them, you know, wondering why they're laughing, you know, not knowing what I was doing. [Well, did they tell you why they were laughing eventually?] Yeah, yeah, I come back, "Hey, man, what's happening?" Like, you know, like I'd ask, "What's happening?" and all of

a sudden I feel weird, you know. "Man, you're on, you know. You're on pot [high on marihuana]." I said, "No, am I?" Like I don't know what's happening.

The learning may occur in more indirect ways:

> I heard little remarks that were made by other people. Somebody said, "My legs are rubbery," and I can't remember all the remarks that were made because I was very attentively listening for all these cues for what I was supposed to feel like.

The novice, then, eager to have this feeling, picks up from other users some concrete referents of the term "high" and applies these notions to his own experience. The new concepts make it possible for him to locate these symptoms among his own sensations and to point out to himself a "something different" in his experience that he connects with drug use. It is only when he can do this that he is high. In the next case, the contrast between two successive experiences of a user makes clear the crucial importance of the awareness of the symptoms in being high and re-emphasizes the important role of interaction with other users in acquiring the concepts that make this awareness possible:

> [Did you get high the first time you turned on?] Yeah, sure. Although, come to think of it, I guess I really didn't. I mean, like that first time it was more or less of a mild drunk. I was happy, I guess, you know what I mean. But I didn't really know I was high, you know what I mean. It was only after the second time I got high that I realized I was high the first time. Then I knew that something different was happening.
>
> [How did you know that?] How did I know? If what happened to me that night would of happened to you, you would've known, believe me. We played the first tune for almost two hours—one tune! Imagine, man! We got on the stand and played this one tune, we started at nine o'clock. When we got finished I looked at my watch, it's a quarter to eleven. Almost two hours on one tune. And it didn't seem like anything.
>
> I mean, you know, it does that to you. It's like you have much more time or something. Anyway, when I saw that, man, it was too much. I knew I must really be high or something if anything like that could happen. See, and then they explained to me that's what it did to you, you had a different sense of time and everything. So I realized that's what it was. I knew then. Like the first time, I probably felt that way, you know, but I didn't know what's happening.

It is only when the novice becomes able to get high in this sense that he will continue to use marihuana for pleasure. In every case in which use continued, the user had acquired the necessary concepts with which to express to himself the fact that he was experiencing new sensations caused by the drug. That is, for use to continue, it is necessary not only to use the drug so as to produce effects but also to learn to perceive these effects when they occur. In this way marihuana acquires meaning for the user as an object which can be sued for pleasure.

With increasing experience the user develops a greater appreciation of the drug's effects; he continues to learn to get high. He examines succeeding experiences closely, looking for new effects, making sure the old ones are still there. Out of this there grows a stable set of categories for experiencing the drug's effects whose presence enables the user to get high with ease.

Users, as they acquire this set of categories, become connoisseurs. Like experts in fine wines, they can specify where a particular plant was grown and what time of year it was harvested. Although it is usually not possible to know whether these attributions are correct, it is true that they distinguish between batches of marihuana, not only according to strength, but also with respect to the different kinds of symptoms produced.

The ability to perceive the drug's effects must be maintained if use is to continue; if it is lost, marihuana use ceases. Two kinds of evidence support this statement. First, people who become heavy users of alcohol, barbiturates, or opiates do not continue to smoke marihuana, largely because they lose the ability to distinguish between its effects and those of the other drugs.[9] They no longer know whether the marihuana gets them high. Second, in those few cases in which an individual uses marihuana in such quantities that he is always high, he is apt to feel the drug has not effect on him, since the essential element of a noticeable difference between feeling high and feeling normal is missing. In such a situation, use is likely to be given up completely, but temporarily, in order that the user may once again be able to perceive the difference.

Learning to Enjoy the Effects

One more step is necessary if the user who has now learned to get high is to continue use. He must learn to enjoy the effects he has just learned to experience. Marihuana-produced sensations are not automatically or necessarily pleasurable. The taste for such experience is a socially acquired one, not different in kind from acquired tastes for oysters or dry martinis. The user feels dizzy, thirsty; his scalp tingles; he misjudges time and distances. Are these things pleasurable? He isn't sure. If he is to continue marihuana use, he must decide that they are. Otherwise, getting high, while a real enough experience, will be an unpleasant one he would rather avoid.

The effects of the drug, when first perceived, may be physically unpleasant or at least ambiguous:

> It started taking effect, and I didn't know what was happening, you know, what it was, and I was very sick. I walked around the room, walking around the room trying to get off, you know; it just scared me at first, you know. I wasn't used to that kind of feeling.

In addition, the novice's naïve interpretation of what is happening to him may further confuse and frighten him, particularly if he decides, as many do, that he is going insane:

> I felt I was insane, you know. Everything people done to me just wigged me. I couldn't hold a conversation, and my mind would be wandering, and I was always thinking, oh, I don't know, weird things, like hearing music different. . . . I get the feeling that I can't talk to anyone. I'll goof completely.

Given these typically frightening and unpleasant first experiences, the beginner will not continue use unless he learns to redefine the sensations as pleasurable:

> It was offered to me, and I tried it. I'll tell you one thing. I never did enjoy it at all. I mean it was just nothing that I could enjoy. [Well, did you get high when you turned on?] Oh, yeah, I got definite feelings from it. But I didn't enjoy them. I mean I got plenty of reactions, but they were mostly reactions of fear. [You were frightened?] Yes. I didn't enjoy it. I couldn't seem to relax with it, you know. If you can't relax with a thing, you can't enjoy it, I don't think.

In other cases the first experiences were also definitely unpleasant, but the person did become a marihuana user. This occurred, however, only after a later experience enabled him to redefine the sensations as pleasurable:

> [This man's first experience was extremely unpleasant, involving distortion of spatial relationships and sounds, violent thirst, and panic produced by these symptoms.] After the first time I didn't turn on for about, I'd say, ten months to a year. . . . It wasn't a moral thing; it was because I'd gotten so frightened, bein' so high. An' I didn't want to go through that again, I mean, my reaction was, "Well, if this is what they call bein' high, I don't dig [like] it." . . . So I didn't turn on for a year almost, accounta that. . . .
>
> Well, my friends started, an' consequently I started again. But I didn't have any more, I didn't have that same initial reaction, after I started turning on again.
>
> [In interaction with his friends he became able to find pleasure in the effects of the drug and eventually became a regular user.]

In no case will use continue without a redefinition of the effects as enjoyable.

This redefinition occurs, typically, in interaction with more experienced users who, in a number of ways, teach the novice to find pleasure in this experience which is at first so frightening.[10] They may reassure him as to the temporary character of the unpleasant sensations and minimize their seriousness, at the same time calling attention to the more enjoyable aspects. An experienced user describes how he handles newcomers to marihuana use:

> Well, they get pretty high sometimes. The average person isn't ready for that, and it is a little frightening to them sometimes. I mean, they've been high on lush [alcohol], and they get higher that way than they've ever been before, and they don't know what's happening to them. Because they think they're going to keep going up, up, up till they lose their minds or begin doing weird things or something. You have to like reassure them, explain to them that they're not really flipping or anything, that they're gonna be all right. You have to just talk them out of being afraid. Keep talking to them, reassuring, telling them it's all right. And come on with your own story, you know: "The same thing happened to me. You'll get to like that after awhile." Keep coming on like that; pretty soon you talk them out of being scared. And besides they see you doing it and nothing horrible is happening to you, so that gives them more confidence.

The more experienced user may also teach the novice to regulate the amount he smokes more carefully, so as to avoid any severely uncomfortable symptoms while retaining the pleasant ones. Finally, he teaches the new user that he can "get to like it after awhile." He teaches him to regard those ambiguous experiences formerly defined as unpleasant as enjoyable. The older user in the following incident is a person whose tastes have shifted in this way, and his remarks have the effect of helping others to make a similar redefinition:

> A new user had her first experience of the effects of marihuana and became frightened and hysterical. She "felt like she was half in and half out of the room" and experienced a number of alarming physical symptoms. One of the more experienced users present said, "She's dragged because she's high like that. I'd give anything to get that high myself. I haven't been that high in years."

In short, what was once frightening and distasteful becomes, after a taste for it is built up, pleasant, desired, and sought after. Enjoyment is introduced by the favorable definition of the experience that one acquires from others. Without this, use will not continue, for marihuana will not be for the user an object he can use for pleasure.

In addition to being a necessary step in becoming a user, this represents an important condition for continued use. It is quite common for experienced users suddenly to have an unpleasant or frightening experience, which they cannot define as pleasurable, either because they have used a larger amount of marihuana than usual or because the marihuana they have used turns out to be of a higher quality than they expected. The user has sensations which go beyond any conception he has of what being high is and is in much the same situation as the novice, uncomfortable and frightened. He may blame it on an overdose and simply be more careful in the future. But he may make this the occasion for a rethinking of his attitude toward the drug and decide that it no longer can give him pleasure. When this occurs and is not followed by a redefinition of the drug as capable of producing pleasure, use will cease.

The likelihood of such a redefinition occurring depends on the degree of the individual's participation with other users. Where this participation is intensive, the individual is quickly talked out of his feeling against marihuana use. In the next case, on the other hand, the experience was very disturbing, and the aftermath of the incident cut the person's participation with other users to almost zero. Use stopped for three years and began again only when a combination of circumstances, important among which was a resumption of ties with users, made possible a redefinition of the nature of the drug:

> It was too much, like I only made about four pokes, and I couldn't even get it out of my mouth, I was so high, and I got real flipped. In the basement, you know, I just couldn't stay in there anymore. My heart was pounding real hard, you know, and I was going out of my mind; I thought I was losing my mind completely. So I cut out of this basement, and this other guy, he's out of his mind, told me, "Don't, don't leave me, man. Stay here." And I couldn't.
>
> I walked outside, and it was five below zero, and I thought I was dying, and I had my coat open; I was sweating, I was perspiring. My whole insides were all . . . , and I walked about two blocks away, and I fainted behind a bush. I don't know how long I laid there. I

woke up, and I was feeling the worst, I can't describe it at all, so I made it to a bowling alley, man, and I was trying to act normal, I was trying to shoot pool, you know, trying to act real normal, and I couldn't lay and I couldn't stand up and I couldn't sit down, and I went up and laid down where some guys that spot pins lay down, and that didn't help me, and I went down to a doctor's office. I was going to go in there and tell the doctor to put me out of my misery . . . because my heart was pounding so hard, you know. . . . So then all weekend I started flipping, seeing things there and going through hell, you know, all kinds of abnormal things. . . . I just quit for a long time then.

[He went to a doctor who defined the symptoms for him as those of a nervous breakdown caused by "nerves" and "worries." Although he was no longer using marihuana, he had some recurrences of the symptoms which led him to suspect that "it was all his nerves."] So I just stopped worrying, you know; so it was about thirty-six months later I started making it again. I'd just take a few pokes, you know. [He first resumed use in the company of the same user-friend with whom he had been involved in the original incident.]

A person, then, cannot begin to use marihuana for pleasure, or continue its sue for pleasure, unless he learns to define its effects as enjoyable, unless it becomes and remains an object he conceives of as capable of producing pleasure.

In summary, an individual will be able to use marihuana for pleasure only when he goes through a process of learning to conceive of it as an object which can be used in this way. No one becomes a user without (1) learning to smoke the drug in a way which will produce real effects; (2) learning to recognize the effects and connect them with drug use (learning, in other words, to get high); and (3) learning to enjoy the sensations he perceives. In the course of this process he develops a disposition or motivation to use marihuana which was not and could not have been present when he began use, for it involves and depends on conceptions of the drug which could only grow out of the kind of actual experience detailed above. On completion of this process he is willing and able to use marihuana for pleasure.

He had learned, in short, to answer "Yes" to the question: "Is it fun?" The direction his further use of the drug takes depends on his being able to continue to answer "Yes" to this question and, in addition, on his being able to answer "Yes" to other questions which arise as he becomes aware of the implications of the fact that society disapproves of the practice: "Is it expedient?" Is it moral?" Once he has acquired the ability to get enjoyment by using the drug, use will continue to be possible for him. Considerations of morality and expediency, occasioned by the reactions of society, may interfere and inhibit use, but use continues to be a possibility in terms of his conception of the drug. The act becomes impossible only when the ability to enjoy the experience of being high is lost, through a change in the user's conception of the drug occasioned by certain kinds of experience with it.

Notes

1. See, as examples of this approach, the following: Eli Marcovitz and Henry J. Meyers, "The Marihuana Addict in the Army," *War Medicine,* VI (December, 1944), 382–391; Herbert S. Gaskill, "Marihuana, an Intoxicant," *American Journal of Psychiatry,* CII (September, 1945),

202–204; Sol Charen and Luis Perelman, "Personality Studies of Marihuana Addicts," *American Journal of Psychiatry,* CII (March, 1946), 674–682.
2. This theoretical point of view stems from George Herbert Mead's discussion of objects in *Mind, Self, and Society* (Chicago: University of Chicago Press, 1934), pp. 277–280.
3. Cf. Rogers Adams, "Marihuana," *Bulletin of the New York Academy of Medicine,* XVIII (November, 1942), 705–730.
4. The New York City Mayor's Committee on Marihuana, *The Marihuana Problem in the City of New York* (Lancaster, Pennsylvania: Jacques Cattell Press, 1944), pp. 12–13.
5. Cf. Lawrence Kolb, "Marihuana," *Federal Probation,* II (July, 1938), 22–25; and Walter Bromberg, "Marihuana: A Psychiatric Study," *Journal of the American Medical Association,* CXIII (July 1, 1939), 11.
6. The method is described in Alfred R. Lindesmith, *Opiate Addiction* (Bloomington, Indiana: Principia Press, 1947), chap. 1. There has been considerable discussion of this method in the literature. See, particularly, Ralph H. Turner, "The quest for Universals in Sociological Research," *American Sociological Review,* 18 (December, 1953), 604–611, and the literature cited there.
7. I wish to thank Solomon Kobrin and Harold Finestone for making these interviews available to me.
8. A pharmacologist notes that this ritual is in fact an extremely efficient way of getting the drug into the blood stream. See R. P. Walton, *Marihuana: America's New Drug Problem* (Philadelphia: J. B. Lippincott, 1938), p. 48.
9. "Smokers have repeatedly stated that the consumption of whiskey while smoking negates the potency of the drug. They find it very difficult to get 'high' while drinking whiskey and because of that smokers will not drink while using the 'weed.'" (New York City Mayor's Committee on Marihuana, *The Marihuana Problem in the City of New York, op. cit.,* p. 13.)
10. Charen and Perelman, *op. cit.,* p. 679.

Fraternities and Rape on Campus

Patricia Yancey Martin
Robert A. Hummer

Rapes are perpetrated on dates, at parties, in chance encounters, and in specially planned circumstances. That group structure and processes, rather than individual values or characteristics, are the impetus for many rape episodes was documented by Blanchard (1959) 30 years ago (also see Geis 1971), yet sociologists have failed to pursue this theme (for an exception, see Chancer 1987). A recent review of research (Muehlenhard and Linton 1987) on sexual violence, or rape, devotes only a few pages to the situational context of rape events, and these are conceptualized as potential risk factors for individuals rather than qualities of rape-prone social contexts.

Many rapes, far more than come to the public's attention, occur in fraternity houses on college and university campuses, yet little research has analyzed fraternities at American colleges and universities as rape-prone contexts (cf. Ehrhart and Sandler 1985). Most of the research on fraternities reports on samples of individual fraternity men. One group of studies compares the values, attitudes, perceptions, family socioeconomic status, psychological traits (aggressiveness, dependence), and so on, of fraternity and nonfraternity men (Bohrnstedt 1969; Fox, Hodge, and Ward 1987; Kanin 1967; Lemire 1979; Miller 1973). A second group attempts to identify the effects of fraternity membership over time on the values, attitudes, beliefs, or moral precepts of members (Hughes and Winston 1987; Marlowe and Auvenshine 1982; Miller 1973; Wilder, Hoyt, Doren, Hauck, and Zettle 1978; Wilder, Hoyt, Surbeck, Wilder, and Carney 1986). With minor exceptions, little research addresses the group and organizational context of fraternities or the social construction of fraternity life (for exceptions, see Letchworth 1969; Longino and Kart 1973; Smith 1964).

Gary Tash, writing as an alumnus and trial attorney in his fraternity's magazine, claims that over 90 percent of all gang rapes on college campuses involve fraternity men (1988, p. 2). Tash provides no evidence to substantiate this claim, but students of violence against

From *Gender and Society,* 3 December 1989, pp. 213–224. Reprinted by permission of Sage Publications, Inc.

women have been concerned with fraternity men's frequently reported involvement in rape episodes (Adams and Abarbanel 1988). Ehrhart and Sandler (1985) identify over 50 cases of gang rapes on campus perpetrated by fraternity men, and their analysis points to many of the conditions that we discuss here. Their analysis is unique in focusing on conditions in fraternities that make gang rapes of women by fraternity men both feasible and probable. They identify excessive alcohol use, isolation from external monitoring, treatment of women as prey, use of pornography, approval of violence, and excessive concern with competition as precipitating conditions to gang rape (also see Merton 1985; Roark 1987).

The study reported here confirmed and complemented these findings by focusing on both conditions and processes. We examined dynamics associated with the social construction of fraternity life, with a focus on processes that foster the use of coercion, including rape, in fraternity men's relations with women. Our examination of men's social fraternities on college and university campuses as groups and organizations led us to conclude that fraternities are a physical and sociocultural context that encourages the sexual coercion of women. We make no claims that all fraternities are "bad" or that all fraternity men are rapists. Our observations indicated, however, that rape is especially probable in fraternities because of the kinds of organizations they are, the kinds of members they have, the practices their members engage in, and a virtual absence of university or community oversight. Analyses that lay blame for rapes by fraternity men on "peer pressure" are, we feel, overly simplistic (cf. Burkhart 1989; Walsh 1989). We suggest, rather, that fraternities create a sociocultural context in which the use of coercion in sexual relations with women is normative and in which the mechanisms to keep this pattern of behavior in check are minimal at best and absent at worst. We conclude that unless fraternities change in fundamental ways, little improvement can be expected.

Methodology

Our goal was to analyze the group and organizational practices and conditions that create in fraternities an abusive social context for women. We developed a conceptual framework from an initial case study of an alleged gang rape at Florida State University that involved four fraternity men and an 18-year-old coed. The group rape took place on the third floor of a fraternity house and ended with the "dumping" of the woman in the hallway of a neighboring fraternity house. According to newspaper accounts, the victim's blood-alcohol concentration, when she was discovered, was .349 percent, more than three times the legal limit for automobile driving and an almost lethal amount. One law enforcement officer reported that sexual intercourse occurred during the time the victim was unconscious: "She was in a life-threatening situation" (*Tallahassee Democrat,* 1988b). When the victim was found, she was comatose and had suffered multiple scratches and abrasions. Crude words and a fraternity symbol had been written on her thighs (*Tampa Tribune,* 1988). When law enforcement officials tried to investigate the case, fraternity members refused to cooperate. This led, eventually, to a five-year ban of the fraternity from campus by the university and by the fraternity's national organization.

In trying to understand how such an event could have occurred, and how a group of over 150 members (exact figures are unknown because the fraternity refused to provide a membership roster) could hold rank, deny knowledge of the event, and allegedly lie to a grand jury, we analyzed newspaper articles about the case and conducted open-ended interviews with a variety of respondents about the case and about fraternities, rapes, alcohol use, gender relations, and sexual activities on campus. Our data included over 100 newspaper articles on the initial gang rape case; open-ended interviews with Greek (social fraternity and sorority) and non-Greek (independent) students ($N = 20$); university administrators ($N = 8$, five men, three women); and alumni advisers to Greek organizations ($N = 6$). Open-ended interviews were held also with judges, public and private defense attorneys, victim advocates, and state prosecutors regarding the processing of sexual assault cases. Data were analyzed using the grounded theory method[1] (Glaser 1978; Martin and Turner 1986). In the following analysis, concepts generated from the data analysis are integrated with the literature on men's social fraternities, sexual coercion, and related issues.

Fraternities and the Social Construction of Men and Masculinity

Our research indicated that fraternities are vitally concerned—more than with anything else—with masculinity (cf. Kanin 1967). They work hard to create a macho image and context and try to avoid any suggestion of "wimpishness," effeminacy, and homosexuality. Valued members display, or are willing to go along with, a narrow conception of masculinity that stresses competition, athleticism, dominance, winning, conflict, wealth, material possessions, willingness to drink alcohol, and sexual prowess vis-à-vis women.

Valued Qualities of Members

When fraternity members talked about the kind of pledges they prefer, a litany of stereotypical and narrowly masculine attributes and behaviors was recited and feminine or woman-associated qualities and behaviors were expressly denounced (cf. Merton 1985). Fraternities seek men who are "athletic," "big guys," good in intramural competition, "who can talk college sports." Males "who are willing to drink alcohol," "who drink socially," or "who can hold their liquor" are sought. Alcohol and activities associated with the recreational use of alcohol are cornerstones of fraternity social life. Nondrinkers are viewed with skepticism and rarely selected for membership.[2]

Fraternities try to avoid "geeks," nerds, and men said to give the fraternity a "wimpy" or "gay" reputation. Art, music, and humanities majors, majors in traditional women's fields (nursing, home economics, social work, education), men with long hair, and those whose appearance or dress violate current norms are rejected. Clean-cut, handsome men who dress well (are clean, neat, conforming, fashionable) are preferred. One sorority woman commented that "the top ranking fraternities have the best looking guys."

One fraternity man, a senior, said his fraternity recruited "some big guys, very athletic" over a two-year period to help overcome its image of wimpiness. His fraternity had won the interfraternity competition for highest grade point-average several years running but was looked down on as "wimpy, dancy, even gay." With their bigger, more athletic recruits, "our reputation improved; we're a much more recognized fraternity now." Thus a fraternity's reputation and status depends on members' possession of stereotypically masculine qualities. Good grades, campus leadership, and community service are "nice" but masculinity dominance—for example, in athletic events, physical size of members, athleticism of members—counts most.

Certain social skills are valued. Men are sought who "have good personalities," are friendly, and "have the ability to relate to girls" (cf. Longino and Kart 1973). One fraternity man, a junior, said: "We watch a guy [a potential pledge] talk to women . . . we want guys who can relate to girls." Assessing a pledge's ability to talk to women is, in part, a preoccupation with homosexuality and a conscious avoidance of men who seem to have effeminate manners or qualities. If a member is suspected of being gay, he is ostracized and informally drummed out of the fraternity. A fraternity with a reputation as wimpy or tolerant of gays is ridiculed and shunned by other fraternities. Militant heterosexuality is frequently used by men as a strategy to keep each other in line (Kimmel 1987).

Financial affluence or wealth, a male-associated value in American culture, is highly valued by fraternities. In accounting for why the fraternity involved in the gang rape that precipitated our research project had been recognized recently as "the best fraternity chapter in the United States," a university official said: "They were good-looking, a big fraternity, had lots of BMWs [expensive, German-made automobiles]." After the rape, newspaper stories described the fraternity members' affluence, noting the high number of members who owned expensive cars (*St. Petersburg Times,* 1988).

THE STATUS AND NORMS OF PLEDGESHIP

A pledge (sometimes called an associate member) is a new recruit who occupies a trial membership status for a specific period of time. The pledge period (typically ranging from 10 to 15 weeks) gives fraternity brothers an opportunity to assess and socialize new recruits. Pledges evaluate the fraternity also and decide if they want to become brothers. The socialization experience is structured partly through assignment of a Big Brother to each pledge. Big Brothers are expected to teach pledges how to become a brother and to support them as they progress through the trial membership period. Some pledges are repelled by the pledging experience, which can entail physical abuse; harsh discipline; and demands to be subordinate, follow orders, and engage in demeaning routines and activities, similar to those used by the military to "make men out of boys" during boot camp.

Characteristics of the pledge experience are rationalized by fraternity members as necessary to help pledges unite into a group, rely on each other, and join together against outsiders. The process is highly masculinist in execution as well as conception. A willingness to submit to authority, follow orders, and do as one is told is viewed as a sign of loyalty, togetherness and unity. Fraternity pledges who find the pledge process offensive often drop out. Some do this by openly quitting, which can subject them to ridicule by brothers and other pledges, or they may deliberately fail to make the grades necessary for initiation or transfer schools and decline to reaffiliate with the fraternity on the new campus. One fraternity pledge who quit the fraternity he had pledged described an experience during pledgeship as follows:

> This one guy was always picking on me. No matter what I did, I was wrong. One night after dinner, he and two other guys called me and two other pledges into the chapter room. He said, "Hers, X, hold this 25 pound bag of ice at arms' length 'til I tell you to stop." I did it even though my arms and hands were killing me. When I asked if I could stop, he grabbed me around the throat and lifted me off the floor. I thought he would choke me to death. He cussed me and called me all kinds of names. He took one of my fingers and twisted it until it nearly broke.... I stayed in the fraternity for a few more days, but then I decided to quite. I hated it. Those guys are sick. They like seeing you suffer.

Fraternities' emphasis on toughness, withstanding pain and humiliation, obedience to superiors, and using physical force to obtain compliance contributes to an interpersonal style that de-emphasizes caring and sensitivity but fosters intragroup trust and loyalty. If the least macho or most critical pledges drop out, those who remain may be more receptive to, and influenced by, masculinist values and practices that encourage the use of force in sexual relations with women and the covering up of such behavior (cf. Kanin 1967).

NORMS AND DYNAMICS OF BROTHERHOOD

Brother is the status occupied by fraternity men to indicate their relations to each other and their membership in a particular fraternity organization or group. Brother is a male-specific status; only males can become brothers, although women can become "Little Sisters," a form of pseudomembership. "Becoming a brother" is a rite of passage that follows the consistent and often lengthy display by pledges of appropriately masculine qualities and behaviors. Brothers have a quasi-familial relationship with each other, are normatively said to share bonds of closeness and support, and are sharply set off from nonmembers. Brotherhood is a loosely defined term used to represent the bonds that develop among fraternity members and the obligations and expectations incumbent upon them (cf. Marlowe and Auvenshine [1982] on fraternities' failure to encourage "moral development" in freshman pledges).

Some of our respondents talked about brotherhood in almost reverential terms, viewing it as the most valuable benefit of fraternity membership. One senior, a business-school major who had been affiliated with a fairly high-status fraternity throughout four years on campus, said:

> Brotherhood spurs friendship for life, which I consider its best aspect, although I didn't see it that way when I joined. Brotherhood bonds and unites. It instills values of caring about one another, caring about community, caring about ourselves. The values and bonds [of brotherhood] continually develop over the four years [in college] while normal friendships come and go.

Despite this idealization, most aspects of fraternity practice and conception are more mundane. Brotherhood often plays itself out as an overriding concern with masculinity and, by extension, femininity. As a consequence, fraternities comprise collectivities of highly masculinized men with attitudinal qualities and behavioral norms that predispose them to sexual coercion of women (cf. Kanin 1967; Merton 1985; Rapaport and Burkhart 1984). The norms of masculinity are complemented by conceptions of women and femininity that are equally distorted and stereotyped and that may enhance the probability of women's exploitation (cf. Ehrhart and Sandler 1985; Sanday 1981, 1986).

PRACTICES OF BROTHERHOOD

Practices associated with fraternity brotherhood that contribute to the sexual coercion of women include a preoccupation with loyalty, group protection and secrecy, use of alcohol as a weapon, involvement in violence and physical force, and an emphasis on competition and superiority.

Loyalty, Group Protection, and Secrecy Loyalty is a fraternity preoccupation. Members are reminded constantly to be loyal to the fraternity and to their brother. Among other ways, loyalty is played out in the practices of group protection and secrecy. The fraternity must be shielded from criticism. Members are admonished to avoid getting the fraternity in trouble and to bring all problems "to the chapter" (local branch of a national social fraternity) rather than to outsiders. Fraternities try to protect themselves from close scrutiny and criticism by the Interfraternity Council (a quasi-governing body composed of representatives from all social fraternities on campus), their fraternity's national office, university officials, law enforcement, the media, and the public. Protection of the fraternity often takes precedence over what is procedurally, ethically, or legally correct. Numerous examples were related to us of fraternity brothers' lying to outsiders to "protect the fraternity."

Group protection was observed in the alleged gang rape case with which we began our study. Except for one brother, a rapist who turned state's evidence, the entire remaining fraternity membership was accused by university and criminal justice officials of lying to protect the fraternity. Members consistently failed to cooperate even though the alleged crimes were felonies, involved only four men (two of whom were not even members of the local chapter), and the victim of the crime nearly died. According to a grand jury's findings, fraternity officers repeatedly broke appointments with law enforcement officials, refused to provide police with a list of members, and refused to cooperate with police and prosecutors investigating the case (*Florida Flambeau,* 1988).

Secrecy is a priority value and practice in fraternities, partly because full-fledged membership is premised on it (for confirmation, see Ehrhart and Sandler 1985; Longino and Kart 1973; Roark 1987). Secrecy is also a boundary-maintaining mechanism, demarcating ingroup from out-group, us from them. Secret rituals, handshakes, and mottoes are revealed to pledge brothers as they are initiated into full brotherhood. Since only brothers are supposed to know a fraternity's secrets, such knowledge affirms membership in the fraternity and separates a brother from others. Extending secrecy tactics from protection of private knowledge to protection of the fraternity from criticism is a predictable development. Our interviews indicated that individual members knew the difference between right and wrong, but fraternity norms that emphasize loyalty, group protection, and secrecy often overrode standards of ethical correctness.

Alcohol as Weapon Alcohol use by fraternity men is normative. They use it on weekdays to relax after class and on weekends to "get drunk," "get crazy," and "get laid." The use of alcohol to obtain sex from women is pervasive—in other words, it is used as a weapon against sexual reluctance. According to several fraternity men whom we interviewed, alcohol is the major tool used to gain sexual mastery over women (cf. Adams and Abarbanel 1988; Ehrhart and Sandler 1985). One fraternity man, a 21-year-old senior, described alcohol use to gain sex as follows: "There are girls that you know will fuck, then some you have to put some effort into it. . . . You have to buy them drinks or find out if she's drunk enough. . . ."

A similar strategy is used collectively. A fraternity man said that at parties with Little Sisters: "We provide them with 'hunch punch' and things get wild. We get them drunk and most of the guys end up with one." " 'Hunch punch,'" he said, "is a girls' drink made up of overproof alcohol and powdered Kool-Aid, no water or anything, just ice. It's very strong. Two cups will do a number on a female." He had plans in the next academic term to surreptitiously give hunch punch to women in a "prim and proper" sorority because "having sex with prim and proper sorority girls is definitely a goal." These women are a challenge because they "won't openly consume alcohol and won't get openly drunk as hell." Their sororities have "standards committees" that forbid heavy drinking and easy sex.

In the gang rape case, our sources said that many fraternity men on campus believed the victim had a drinking problem and was thus an "easy make." According to newspaper accounts, she had been drinking alcohol on the evening she was raped; the lead assailant is alleged to have given her a bottle of wine after she arrived at his fraternity house. Portions of the rape occurred in a shower, and the victim was reportedly so drunk that her assailants had difficulty holding her in a standing position (*Tallahassee Democrat,* 1988a). While raping her, her assailants repeatedly told her they were members of another fraternity under the apparent belief that she was too drunk to know the difference. Of course, if she was too drunk to know who they were, she was too drunk to consent to sex (cf. Allgeier 1986; Tash 1988).

One respondent told us that gang rapes are wrong and can get one expelled, but he seemed to see nothing wrong in sexual coercion one-on-one. He seemed unaware that the use of alcohol to obtain sex from a woman is grounds for a claim that rape occurred (cf. Tash 1988). Few women on campus (who also may not know these grounds) report date rapes, however; so the odds of detection and punishment are slim for fraternity men who use alcohol for "seduction" purposes (cf. Byington and Keeter 1988; Merton 1985).

Violence and Physical Force Fraternity men have a history of violence (Ehrhart and Sandler 1985; Roark 1987). Their record of hazing, fighting, property destruction, and rape has caused them problems with insurance companies (Bradford 1986; Pressley 1987). Two university officials told us that fraternities "are the third riskiest property to insure behind toxic waste dumps and amusement parks." Fraternities are increasingly defendants in legal actions brought by pledges subjected to hazing (Meyer 1986; Pressley 1987) and by women who were raped by one or more members. In a recent alleged gang rape incident at another Florida university, prosecutors failed to file charges but the victim filed a civil suit against the fraternity nevertheless (*Tallahassee Democrat,* 1989).

Competition and Superiority Interfraternity rivalry fosters in-group identification and out-group hostility. Fraternities stress pride of membership and superiority over other fraternities as major goals. Interfraternity rivalries take many forms, including competition for desirable pledges, size of pledge class, size of membership, size and appearance of fraternity house, superiority in intramural sports, highest grade-point averages, giving the best parties, gaining the best or most campus leadership roles, and, of great importance, attracting and displaying "good looking women." Rivalry is particularly intense over members, intramural sports, and women (cf. Messner 1989).

Fraternities' Commodification of Women

In claiming that women are treated by fraternities as commodities, we mean that fraternities knowingly, and intentionally, *use* women for their benefit. Fraternities use women as bait for new members, as servers of brother's needs, and as sexual prey.

WOMEN AS BAIT

Fashionably attractive women help a fraternity attract new members. As one fraternity man, a junior, said, "They are good bait." Beautiful, social women are believed to impress the right kind of pledges and give the impression that the fraternity can deliver this type of woman to its members. Photographs of shapely, attractive coeds are printed in fraternity brochures and videotapes that are distributed and shown to potential pledges. The women pictured are often dressed in bikinis, at the beach, and are pictured hugging the brothers of the fraternity. One university official says such recruitment materials give the message: "Hey, they're here for you, you can have whatever you want," and "we have the best looking women. Join us and you can have them too." Another commented: "Something's wrong when males join an all-male organization as the best place to meet women. It's so illogical."

Fraternities compete in promising access to beautiful women. One fraternity man, a senior, commented that "the attraction of girls [i.e., a fraternity's success in attracting women] is a big status symbol for fraternities." One university official commented that the use of women as a recruiting tool is so well entrenched that fraternities that might be willing to forgo it say they cannot afford to unless other fraternities do so as well. One fraternity man said, "Look, if we don't have Little Sisters, the fraternities that do will get all the good pledges." Another said, "We won't have as good a rush [the period during which new members are assessed and selected] if we don't have these women around."

In displaying good-looking, attractive, skimpily dressed, nubile women to potential members, fraternities implicitly, and sometimes explicitly promise sexual access to women. One fraternity man commented that "part of what being in a fraternity is all about is the sex" and explained how his fraternity uses Little Sisters to recruit new members:

> We'll tell the sweetheart [the fraternity's term for Little Sister], "You're gorgeous; you can get him." We'll tell her to fake a scam and she'll go hang all over him during a rush party, kiss him, and he thinks he's done wonderful and wants to join. The girls think it's great too. It's flattering for them.

WOMEN AS SERVERS

The use of women as servers is exemplified in the Little Sister program. Little Sisters are undergraduate women who are rushed and selected in a manner parallel to the recruitment of fraternity men. They are affiliated with the fraternity in a formal but unofficial way and are able, indeed required, to wear the fraternity's Greek letters. Little Sisters are not full-fledged fraternity members, however; and fraternity national offices and most universities do not register or regulate them. Each fraternity has an officer called Little Sister Chairman who oversees their organization and activities. The Little Sisters elect officers among themselves, pay monthly dues to the fraternity, and have well-defined roles. Their dues are used to pay for the fraternity's social events, and Little Sisters are expected to attend and hostess fraternity parties and hang around the house to make it a "nice place to be." One fraternity man, a senior, described Little Sisters this way: "They are very social girls, willing to join in, be affiliated with the group, devoted to the fraternity." Another member, a sophomore, said: "Their sole purpose is social—attend parties, attract new members, and 'take care' of the guys."

Our observations and interviews suggested that women selected by fraternities as Little Sisters are physically attractive, possess good social skills, and are willing to devote time and energy to the fraternity and its members. One undergraduate woman gave the following job description for Little Sisters to a campus newspaper:

> It's not just making appearances at all the parties but entails many more responsibilities. You're

going to be expected to go to all the intramural games to cheer the brothers on, support and encourage the pledges, and just be around to bring some extra life to the house. [As a Little Sister] you have to agree to take on a new responsibility other than studying to maintain your grades and managing to keep your checkbook from bouncing. You have to make time to be a part of the fraternity and support the brothers in all they do. (*The Tomahawk,* 1988)

The title of Little Sister reflects women's subordinate status; fraternity men in a parallel role are called Big Brothers. Big Brothers assist a sorority primarily with the physical work of sorority rushes, which, compared to fraternity rushes, are more formal, structured, and intensive. Sorority rushes take place in the daytime and fraternity rushes at night so fraternity men are free to help. According to one fraternity member, Little Sister status is a benefit to women because it gives them a social outlet and "the protection of the brothers." The gender-stereotypic conceptions and obligations of these Little Sister and Big Brother statuses indicate that fraternities and sororities promote a gender hierarchy on campus that fosters subordination and dependence in women, thus encouraging sexual exploitation and the belief that it is acceptable.

WOMEN AS SEXUAL PREY

Little Sisters are a sexual utility. Many Little Sisters do not belong to sororities and lack peer support for refraining from unwanted sexual relations. One fraternity man (whose fraternity has 65 members and 85 Little Sisters) told us they had recruited "wholesale" in the prior year to "get lots of new women." The structural access to women that the Little Sister program provides and the absence of normative supports for refusing fraternity members' sexual advances may make women in this program particularly susceptible to coerced sexual encounters with fraternity men.

Access to women for sexual gratification is a presumed benefit of fraternity membership, promised in recruitment materials and strategies and through brothers' conversations with new recruits. One fraternity man said: "We always tell the guys that you get sex all the time, there's always new girls. . . . After I became a Greek, I found out I could be with females at will." A university official told us that, based on his observations, "no one [i.e., fraternity men] on this campus wants to have 'relationships.' They just want to have fun [i.e., sex]." Fraternity men plan and execute strategies aimed at obtaining sexual gratification, and this occurs at both individual and collective levels.

Individual strategies include getting a woman drunk and spending a great deal of money on her. As for collective strategies, most of our undergraduate interviewees agreed that fraternity parties often culminate in sex and that this outcome is planned. One fraternity man said fraternity parties often involve sex and nudity and can "turn into orgies." Orgies may be planned in advance, such as the Bowery Ball party held by one fraternity. A former fraternity member said of this party:

> The entire idea behind this is sex. Both men and women come to the party wearing little or nothing. There are pornographic pinups on the walls and usually porno movies playing on

the TV. The music carries sexual overtones.... They just get schnockered [drunk] and, in most cases, they also get laid.

When asked about the women who come to such a party, he said: "Some Little Sisters just won't go.... The girls who do are looking for a good time, girls who don't know what it is, things like that."

Other respondents denied that fraternity parties are orgies but said that sex is always talked about among the brothers and they all know "who each other is doing it with." One member said that most of the time, guys have sex with their girlfriends "but with socials, girlfriends aren't allowed to come and it's their [members'] big chance [to have sex with other women]." The use of alcohol to help them get women into bed is a routine strategy at fraternity parties.

Conclusions

In general, our research indicated that the organization and membership of fraternities contribute heavily to coercive and often violent sex. Fraternity houses are occupied by same-sex (all men) and same-age (late teens, early twenties) peers whose maturity and judgment is often less than ideal. Yet fraternity houses are private dwellings that are mostly off-limits to, and away from scrutiny of, university and community representatives, with the result that fraternity house events seldom come to the attention of outsiders. Practices associated with the social construction of fraternity brotherhood emphasize a macho conception of men and masculinity, a narrow, stereotyped conception of women and femininity, and the treatment of women as commodities. Other practices contributing to coercive sexual relations and the cover-up of rapes include excessive alcohol use, competitiveness, and normative support for deviance and secrecy (cf. Bogal-Allbritten and Allbritten 1985; Kanin 1967). Some Fraternity practices exacerbate others. Brotherhood norms require "sticking together" regardless of right or wrong, thus rape episodes are unlikely to be stopped or reported to outsiders, even when witnesses disapprove. The ability to use alcohol without scrutiny by authorities and alcohol's frequent association with violence, including sexual coercion, facilitates rape in fraternity houses. Fraternity norms that emphasize the value of maleness and masculinity over femaleness and femininity and that elevate the status of men and lower the status of women in members' eyes undermine perceptions and treatment of women as persons who deserve consideration and care (cf. Ehrhart and Sandler 1985; Merton 1985).

Androgynous men and men with a broad range of interests and attributes are lost to fraternities through their recruitment practices. Masculinity of a narrow and stereotypical type helps create attitudes, norms, and practices that predispose fraternity men to coerce women sexually, both individually and collectively (Allgeier 1986; Hood 1989; Sanday 1981, 1986). Male athletes on campus may be similarly disposed for the same reasons (Kirshenbaum 1989; Telander and Sullivan 1989).

Research into the social contexts in which rape crimes occur and the social constructions associated with these contexts illuminate rape dynamics on campus. Blanchard (1959) found that group rapes almost always have a leader who pushes others into the crime. He also found that the leader's latent homosexuality, desire to show off to his peers, or fear of failing to prove himself a man are frequently an impetus. Fraternity norms and practices contribute to the approval and use of sexual coercion as an accepted tactic in relations with women. Alcohol-induced compliance is normative, whereas, presumably, use of a knife, gun, or threat of bodily harm would not be because the woman who "drinks too much" is viewed as "causing her own rape" (cf. Ehrhart and Sandler 1985).

Our research led us to conclude that fraternity norms and practices influence members to view the sexual coercion of women, which is a felony crime, as sport, a contest, or a game (cf. Sato 1988). This sport is played not between men and women but between men and men. Women are the pawns or prey in the interfraternity rivalry game; they prove that a fraternity is successful or prestigious. The use of women in this way encourages fraternity men to see women as objects and sexual coercion as sport. Today's societal norms support young women's right to engage in sex at their discretion and coercion is unnecessary in a mutually desired encounter. However, nubile young women say they prefer to be "in a relationship" to have sex, while young men say they prefer to "get laid" without a commitment (Muehlenhard and Linton 1987). These differences may reflect, in part, American puritanism and men's fears of sexual intimacy or perhaps intimacy of any kind. In a fraternity context, getting sex without giving emotionally demonstrates "cool" masculinity. More important, it poses no threat to the bonding and loyalty, the fraternity brotherhood (cf. Farr 1988). Drinking large quantities of alcohol before having sex suggests that "scoring" rather than intrinsic sexual pleasure is a primary concern of fraternity men.

Unless fraternities' composition, goals, structures, and practices change in fundamental ways, women on campus will continue to be sexual prey for fraternity men. As all-male enclaves dedicated to opposing faculty and administration and to cementing in-group ties, fraternity members eschew any hint of homosexuality. Their version of masculinity transforms women, and men with womanly characteristics, into the out-group. "Womanly men" are ostracized; feminine women are used to demonstrate members' masculinity. Encouraging renewed emphasis on their founding values (Longino and Kart 1973), service orientation and activities (Lemire 1979), or members' moral development (Marlowe and Auvenshine 1982) will have little effect on fraternities' treatment of women. A case for or against fraternities cannot be made by studying individual members. The fraternity qua group and organization is at issue. Located on campus along with many vulnerable women, embedded in a sexist society, and caught up in masculinist goals, practices, and values, fraternities' violation of women—including forcible rape—should come as no surprise.

Notes

1. "Grounded theory method" means that the researcher's ideas about the data are developed as an ongoing process while he or she is in the field—that is, while gathering the data; the method relies heavily on common sense and speculation. This method is in contrast to the classical sci-

entific method in which the researcher begins with a hypothesis and then gathers data to test it.—Ed.
2. Recent bans by some universities on open-keg parties at fraternity houses have resulted in heavy drinking before coming to a party and an increase in drunkenness among those who attend. This may aggravate, rather than improve, the treatment of women by fraternity men at parties.

References

Adams, Aileen and Gail Abarbanel. 1988. *Sexual Assault on Campus: What Colleges Can Do.* Santa Monica, CA: Rape Treatment Center.

Allgeier, Elizabeth. 1986. "Coercive Versus Consensual Sexual Interactions." G. Stanley Hall Lecture to American Psychological Association Annual Meeting, Washington, DC, August.

Blanchard, W. H. 1959. "The Group Process in Gang Rape." *Journal of Social Psychology* 49:259–66.

Bogal-Allbritten, Rosemarie B. and William L. Allbritten. 1985. "The Hidden Victims: Courtship Violence Among College Students." *Journal of College Student Personnel* 43:201–4.

Bohrnstedt, George W. 1969. "Conservatism, Authoritarianism and Religiosity of Fraternity Pledges." *Journal of College Student Personnel* 27:36–43.

Bradford, Michael. 1986. "Tight Market Dries Up Nightlife at University." *Business Insurance* (March 2): 2, 6.

Burkhart, Barry. 1989. Comments in Seminar on Acquaintance/Date Rape Prevention: A National Video Teleconference, February 2.

Byington, Diane B. and Karen W. Keeter. 1988. "Assessing Needs of Sexual Assault Victims on a University Campus." Pp. 23–31 in *Student Services: Responding to Issues and Challenges.* Chapel Hill: University of North Carolina Press.

Chancer, Lynn S. 1987. "New Bedford, Massachusetts, March 6, 1983–March 22, 1984: The 'Before and After' of a Group Rape." *Gender & Society* 1:239–60.

Ehrhart, Julie K. and Bernice R. Sandler. 1985. *Campus Gang Rape: Party Game?* Washington, DC: Association of American Colleges.

Farr, K. A. 1988. "Dominance Bonding through the Good Old Boys Sociability Network." *Sex Roles* 18:259–77.

Florida Flambeau. 1988. "Pike Members Indicted in Rape." (May 19): 1, 5.

Fox, Elaine, Charles Hodge, and Walter Ward. 1987. "A Comparison of Attitudes Held by Black and White Fraternity Members." *Journal of Negro Education* 56:521–34.

Geis, Gilbert. 1971. "Group Sexual Assaults." *Medical Aspects of Human Sexuality* 5:101–13.

Glaser, Barney G. 1978. *Theoretical Sensitivity: Advances in the Methodology of Grounded Theory.* Mill Valley, CA: Sociology Press.

Hood, Jane. 1989. "Why Our Society Is Rape-Prone." *New York Times,* May 16.

Hughes, Michael J. and Roger B. Winston, Jr. 1987. "Effects of Fraternity Membership on Interpersonal Values." *Journal of College Student Personnel* 45:405–11.

Kanin, Eugene J. 1967. "Reference Groups and Sex Conduct Norm Violations." *The Sociological Quarterly* 8:495–504.

Kimmel, Michael, ed. 1987. *Changing Men: New Directions in Research on Men and Masculinity.* Newbury Park, CA: Sage.

Kirshenbaum, Jerry. 1989. "Special Report, An American Disgrace: A Violent and Unprecedented

Lawlessness Has Arisen Among College Athletes in All Parts of the Country." *Sports Illustrated* (February 27): 16–19.
Lemire, David. 1979. "One Investigation of the Stereotypes Associated with Fraternities and Sororities." *Journal of College Student Personnel* 37:54–57.
Letchworth, G. E. 1969. "Fraternities Now and in the Future." *Journal of College Student Personnel* 10:118–22.
Longino, Charles F., Jr., and Cary S. Kart. 1973. "The College Fraternity: An Assessment of Theory and Research." *Journal of College Student Personnel* 31:118–25.
Marlowe, Anne F. and Dwight C. Auvenshine. 1982. "Greek Membership: Its Impact on the Moral Development of College Freshmen." *Journal of College Student Personnel* 40:53–57.
Martin, Patricia Yancey and Barry A. Turner. 1986. "Grounded Theory and Organizational Research." *Journal of Applied Behavioral Science* 22:141–57.
Merton, Andrew. 1985. "On Competition and Class: Return to Brotherhood." *Ms.* (September):60–65, 121–22.
Messner, Michael. 1989. "Masculinities and Athletic Careers." *Gender & Society* 3:71–88.
Meyer, T. J. 1986. "Fight Against Hazing Rituals Rages on Campuses." *Chronicle of Higher Education* (March 12):34–36.
Miller, Leonard D. 1973. "Distinctive Characteristics of Fraternity Members." *Journal of college Student Personnel* 31:126–28.
Muehlenhard, Charlene L. and Melaney A. Linton. 1987. "Date Rape and Sexual Aggression in Dating Situations: Incidence and Risk Factors." *Journal of Counseling Psychology* 34:186–96.
Pressley, Sue Anne. 1987. "Fraternity Hell Night Still Endures." *Washington Post* (August 11):B1.
Rapaport, Karen and Barry R. Burkhart. 1984. "Personality and Attitudinal Characteristics of Sexually Coercive College Males." *Journal of Abnormal Psychology* 93:216–21.
Roark, Mary L. 1987. "Preventing Violence on College Campuses." *Journal of Counseling and Development* 65:367–70.
St. Petersburg Times. 1988. "A Greek Tragedy." (May 29):1F, 6F.
Sanday, Peggy Reeves. 1981. "The Socio-Cultural Context of Rape: A Cross-Cultural Study." *Journal of Social Issues* 37:5–27.
———. 1986. "Rape and the Silencing of the Feminine." Pp. 84–101 in *Rape,* edited by S. Tomaselli and R. Porter. Oxford: Basil Blackwell.
Sato, Ikuya. 1988. "Play Theory of Delinquency: Toward a General Theory of 'Action.' " *Symbolic Interaction* 11:191–212.
Smith, T. 1964. "Emergence and Maintenance of Fraternal Solidarity." *Pacific Sociological Review* 7:29–37.
Tallahassee Democrat. 1988a. "FSU Fraternity Brothers Charged" (April 27):1A, 12A.
———. 1988b. "FSU Interviewing Students About Alleged Rape" (April 24):1D.
———. 1989. "Woman Sues Stetson in Alleged Rape" (March 19):3B.
Tampa Tribune. 1988. "Fraternity Brothers Charged in Sexual Assault of FSU Coed" (April 27):6B.
Tash, Gary B. 1988. "Date Rape." *The Emerald of Sigma Pi Fraternity* 75(4):1–2.
Telander, Rich and Robert Sullivan. 1989. "Special Report, You Reap What You Sow." *Sports Illustrated* (February 27):20–34.

The Tomahawk. 1988. "A Look Back at Rush, A Mixture of Hard Work and Fun." (April/May):3D.

Walsh, Claire. 1989. Comments in Seminar on Acquaintance/Date Rape Prevention: A National Video Teleconference, February 2.

Wilder, David H., Arlyne E. Hoyt, Dennis M. Doren, William E. Hauck, and Robert D. Zettle. 1978. "The Impact of Fraternity and Sorority Membership on Values and Attitudes." *Journal of College Student Personnel* 36:445–49.

Wilder, David H., Arlyne E. Hoyt, Beth Shuster Surbeck, Janet C. Wilder, and Patricia Imperatrice Carney. 1986. "Greek Affiliation and Attitude Change in College Students." *Journal of College Student Personnel* 44:510–19.

Name: _____ Class: _____

Date: _____ Section: _____

Reading Comprehension Activity Sheet

Fraternities and Rape on Campus, Patricia Yancey Martin and Robert A. Hummer

1. It is through the socialization process that individuals internalize the norms, morals, and values of the society. Why does the prevalence of rape on college campuses continue despite its being defined as immoral and illegal? (Use specific information from the article to support your answer.) _____

_____

_____

_____

_____

_____

_____

_____

_____

_____

_____

2. What are some fraternity sociocultural characteristics that encourage the sexual coercion of women? _____

_____

_____

_____

_____

_____

_____

_____

_____

_____

_____

3. Describe the "commodification of women" that often takes place in fraternities. _____

chapter 6

Social Groups and Formal Organizations

The Effects of Group Pressure on the Modification and
Distortion of Judgments
Solomon E. Asch

Women of the Klan
Kathleen M. Blee

The Effects of Group Pressure on the Modification and Distortion of Judgments

Solomon E. Asch

We shall here describe in summary form the conception and first findings of a program of investigation into the conditions of independence and submission to group pressure. This program is based on a series of earlier studies conducted by the writer while a Fellow of the John Simon Guggenheim Memorial Foundation. . . . Our immediate object was to study the social and personal conditions that induce individuals to resist or to yield to group pressures when the latter are perceived to be *contrary to fact*. The issues which this problem raises are of obvious consequence for society; it can be of decisive importance whether or not a group will, under certain conditions, submit to existing pressures. Equally direct are the consequences for individuals and our understanding of them, since it is a decisive fact about a person whether he possesses the freedom to act independently, or whether he characteristically submits to group pressures.

The problem under investigation requires the direct observation of certain basic processes in the interaction between individuals, and between individuals and groups. To clarify these seems necessary if we are to make fundamental advances in the understanding of the formation and reorganization of attitudes, of the functioning of public opinion, and of the operation of propaganda. Today we do not possess an adequate theory of these central psycho-social processes. Empirical investigation has been predominantly controlled by general propositions concerning group influence which have as a rule been assumed but not

Reprinted with the permission of Scribner, a Division of Simon & Schuster Adult Publishing Group, from *Groups, Leadership, and Men: Research in Human Relations* edited by Harold Guetzkow. Copyright © 1951 and copyright renewed 1979 by Harold Guetzkow.

tested. With few exceptions investigation has relied upon descriptive formulations concerning the operation of suggestion and prestige, the inadequacy of which is becoming increasingly obvious, and upon schematic applications of stimulus-response theory.

The [References list] articles representative of the current theoretical empirical situation. Basic to the current approach has been the axiom that group pressures characteristically induce psychological changes *arbitrarily,* in far-reaching disregard of the material properties of the given conditions. This mode of thinking has almost exclusively stressed the slavish submission of individuals to group forces, has neglected to inquire into their possibilities for independence and for productive relations with the human environment, and has virtually denied the capacity of men under certain conditions to rise above group passion and prejudice. It was our aim to contribute to a clarification of these questions, important both for the theory and for their human implications, by means of direct observation of the effects of groups upon the decisions and evaluations of individuals.

The Experiment and First Results

To this end we developed an experimental technique which has served as the basis for the present series of studies. We employed the procedure of placing an individual in a relation of radical conflict with all the other members of a group, of measuring its effect upon him in quantitative terms, and of describing its psychological consequences. A group of eight individuals was instructed to judge a series of simple, clearly structured perceptual relations—to match the length of a given line with one of three unequal lines. Each member of the group announced his judgments publicly. In the midst of this monotonous "test" one individual found himself suddenly contradicted by the entire group, and this contradiction was repeated again and again in the course of the experiment. The group in question had, with the exception of one member, previously met with the experimenter and received instructions to respond at certain points with wrong—and unanimous—judgments. The errors of the majority were large (ranging between 1/2″ and 1 3/4″) and of an order not encountered under control conditions. The outstanding person—the critical subject—(whom we had placed in the position of *a minority of one* in the midst of a *unanimous majority*), was the object of investigation. He faced, possibly for the first time in his life, a situation in which a group unanimously contradicted the evidence of his senses.

This procedure was the starting point of the investigation and the point of departure for the study of further problems. Its main features were the following: (1) The critical subject was submitted to two contradictory and irreconcilable forces—the evidence of his own experience of an utterly clear perceptual fact and the unanimous evidence of a group of equals. (2) Both forces were part of the immediate situation; the majority was concretely present, surrounding the subject physically. (3) The critical subject, who was requested together with all others to state his judgments publicly, was obliged to declare himself and to take a definite stand vis-à-vis the group. (4) The situation possessed a self-contained character. The critical subject could not avoid or evade the dilemma by reference to conditions external to the experimental situation. (It may be mentioned at this point that the forces generated by the given conditions acted so quickly upon the critical subjects that instances of suspicion were rare.)

The technique employed permitted a simple quantitative measure of the "majority effect" in terms of the frequency of errors in the direction of the distorted estimates of the majority. At the same time we were concerned from the start to obtain evidence of the ways in which the subjects perceived the group, to establish whether they became doubtful, whether they were tempted to join the majority. Most important, it was our object to establish the grounds of the subject's independence or yielding—whether, for example, the yielding subject was aware of the effect of the majority upon him, whether he abandoned his judgment deliberately or compulsively. To this end we constructed a comprehensive set of questions which served as the basis of an individual interview immediately following the experimental period. Toward the conclusion of the interview each subject was informed fully of the purpose of the experiment, of his role and of that of the majority. The reactions to the disclosure of the purpose of the experiment became in fact an integral part of the procedure. We may state here that the information derived from the interview became an indispensable source of evidence and insight into the psychological structure of the experimental situation, and in particular, of the nature of the individual differences. Also, it is not justified or advisable to allow the subject to leave without giving him a full explanation of the experimental conditions. The experimenter has a responsibility to the subject to clarify his doubts and to state the reasons for placing him in the experimental situation. When this is done most subjects react with interest and many express gratification at having lived through a striking situation which has some bearing on wider human issues.

Both the members of the majority and the critical subjects were male college students. We shall report the results for a total of fifty critical subjects in this experiment. In Table 6.1 we summarize the successive comparison trials and the majority estimates.

The quantitative results are clear and unambiguous:

1. There was a marked movement toward the majority. One-third of all the estimates in the critical group were errors identical with or in the direction of the distorted estimates of the majority. The significance of this finding becomes clear in the light of the virtual absence of errors in control groups, the members of which recorded their estimates in writing. The relevant data of the critical and control groups are summarized in Table 6.2.
2. At the same time the effect of the majority was far from complete. The preponderance of estimates in the critical group (68 percent) was correct despite the pressure of the majority.
3. We found evidence of extreme individual differences. There were in the critical group subjects who remained independent without exception, and there were those who went nearly all the time with the majority. (The maximum possible number of errors was 12, while the actual range of errors was 0–11). One-fourth of the critical subjects was completely independent; at the other extreme, one-third of the group displaced the estimates toward the majority in one-half or more of the trials.

TABLE 6.1
Lengths of Standard and Comparison Lines

Trials	Length of Standard Line (in inches)	Comparison Lines (in inches)			Correct Response	Group Response	Majority Error (in inches)
		1	2	3			
1	10	8.75	10	8	2	2	—
2	2	2	1	1.50	1	1	—
3	3	3.75	4.25	3	3	1*	+0.75
4	5	5	4	6.50	1	2*	−1.00
5	4	3	5	4	3	3	—
6	3	3.75	4.25	3	3	2*	+1.25
7	8	6.25	8	6.75	2	3*	−1.25
8	5	5	4	6.50	1	3*	+1.50
9	8	6.25	8	6.75	2	1*	−1.75
10	10	8.75	10	8	2	2	—
11	2	2	1	1.50	1	1	—
12	3	3.75	4.25	3	3	1*	+0.75
13	5	5	4	6.50	1	2*	−1.00
14	4	3	5	4	3	3	—
15	3	3.75	4.25	3	3	2*	+1.25
16	8	6.25	8	6.75	2	3*	−1.25
17	5	5	4	6.50	1	3*	+1.50
18	8	6.25	8	6.75	2	1*	−1.75

*Starred figures designate the erroneous estimates by the majority.

TABLE 6.2
Distribution of Errors in Experimental and Control Groups

Number of Critical Errors	Critical Group* Frequency (No. of Trials = 50)	Control Group Frequency (No. of Trials = 37)
0	13	35
1	4	1
2	5	1
3	6	
4	3	
5	4	
6	1	
7	2	
8	5	
9	3	
10	3	
11	1	
12	0	
Total	50	37
Mean	3.84	0.08

*All errors in the critical group were in the direction of the majority estimates.

The differences between the critical subjects in their reactions to the given conditions were equally striking. There were subjects who remained completely confident throughout. At the other extreme were those who became disoriented, doubt-ridden, and experienced a powerful impulse not to appear different from the majority.

For purposes of illustration we include a brief description of one independent and one yielding subject.

INDEPENDENT

After a few trials he appeared puzzled, hesitant. He announced all disagreeing answers in the form of "Three, sir; two, sir"; not so with the unanimous answers. At trial 4 he answered immediately after the first member of the group, shook his head, blinked, and whispered to his neighbor: "Can't help it, that's one." His later answers came in a whispered voice, accompanied by a deprecating smile. At one point he grinned embarrassedly, and whispered explosively to his neighbor: "I always disagree—darn it!" During the questioning, this subject's constant refrain was: "I called them as I saw them, sir." He insisted that his estimates were right without, however, committing himself as to whether the others were wrong, remarking that "that's the way I see them and that's the way they see them." If he had to make a practical decision under similar circumstances, he declared, "I would follow my own view, though part of my reason would tell me that I might be wrong." Immediately following the experiment the majority engaged this subject in a brief discussion. When they pressed him to say whether the entire group was wrong and he alone right, he turned upon them defiantly, exclaiming: "You're *probably* right, but you may be wrong!" To the disclosure of the experiment this subject reacted with the statement that he felt "exultant and relieved," adding, "I do not deny that at times I had the feeling: 'to heck with it, I'll go along with the rest.'"

YIELDING

This subject went with the majority in 11 out of 12 trials. He appeared nervous and somewhat confused, but he did not attempt to evade discussion; on the contrary, he was helpful and tried to answer to the best of his ability. He opened the discussion with the statement: "If I'd been the first I probably would have responded differently"; this was his way of stating that he had adopted the majority estimates. The primary factor in his case was loss of confidence. He perceived the majority as a decided group, acting without hesitation: "If they had been doubtful I probably would have changed, but they answered with such confidence." Certain of his errors, he explained, were due to the doubtful nature of the comparisons; in such instances he went with the majority. When the object of the experiment was explained, the subject volunteered: "I suspected about the middle—but tried to push it out of my mind." It is of interest that his suspicion was not able to restore his confidence and diminish the power of the majority. Equally striking is his report that he assumed the experiment to involve an "illusion" to which the others, but not he, were subject. This assumption too did not help to free him; on the contrary, he acted as if his divergence from the majority was a sign of defect. The principal impression this subject produced was of one so caught up by immediate difficulties that he lost clear reasons for his actions, and could make no reasonable decisions.

A First Analysis of Individual Differences

On the basis of the interview data described earlier, we undertook to differentiate and describe the major forms of reaction to the experimental situation, which we shall now briefly summarize.

Among the *independent* subjects we distinguished the following main categories:

1. Independence based on *confidence* in one's perception and experience. The most striking characteristic of these subjects is the vigor with which they withstand the group opposition. Though they are sensitive to the group, and experience the conflict, they show a resilience in coping with it, which is expressed in their continuing reassurance on their perception and the effectiveness with which they shake off the oppressive group opposition.

2. Quite different are those subjects who are independent and *withdrawn*. These do not react in a spontaneously emotional way, but rather on the basis of explicit principles concerning the necessity of being an individual.
3. A third group of independent subjects manifest considerable tension and *doubt,* but adhere to their judgments on the basis of a felt necessity to deal adequately with the task.

The following were the main categories of reaction among the *yielding* subjects, or those who went with the majority during one-half or more of the trials.

1. *Distortion of perception* under the stress of group pressure. In this category belong a very few subjects who yield completely, but are not aware that their estimates have been displaced or distorted by the majority. These subjects report that they came to perceive the majority estimates as correct.
2. *Distortion of judgment.* Most submitting subjects belong to this category. The factor of greatest importance in this group is a decision the subjects reach that their perceptions are inaccurate, and that those of the majority are correct. These subjects suffer from primary doubt and lack of confidence; on this basis they feel a strong tendency to join the majority.
3. *Distortion of action.* The subjects in this group do not suffer a modification of perception nor do they conclude that they are wrong. They yield because of an overmastering need not to appear different from or inferior to others, because of an inability to tolerate the appearance of defectiveness in the eyes of the group. These subjects suppress their observations and voice the majority position with awareness of what they are doing.

The results are sufficient to establish that independence and yielding are not psychologically homogeneous, that submission to group pressure (and freedom from pressure) can be the result of different psychological conditions. It should also be noted that the categories described [previously], being based exclusively on the subjects' reactions to the experimental conditions, are descriptive, not presuming to explain why a given individual responded in one way rather than another. The further exploration of the basis for the individual differences is a separate task upon which we are now at work.

Experimental Variations

The results described are clearly a joint function of two broadly different sets of conditions. They are determined first by the specific external conditions, by the particular character of the relation between social evidence and one's own experience. Second, the presence of pronounced individual differences points to the important role of personal factors, of factors connected with the individual's character structure. We reasoned that there are group conditions which would produce independence in all subjects, and that there probably are group conditions which would induce intensified yielding in many, though not in all. Accordingly we followed the procedure of *experimental variation,* systematically altering the quality of social evidence by means of systematic variation of group conditions. Secondly, we deemed it reasonable to assume that behavior under the experimental social pressure is significantly related to certain basic, relatively permanent characteristics of the individual. The investigation has moved in both of these directions. Because the study of the character-qualities which may be functionally connected with independence and yielding is still in progress, we shall limit the present account to a sketch of the representative experimental variations.

The Effect of Non-Unanimous Majorities

Evidence obtained from the basic experiment suggested that the condition of being exposed *alone* to the opposition of a "compact majority" may have played a decisive role in determining the course and strength of the effects observed. Accordingly we undertook to investigate in a series of successive variations the effects of *non-unanimous* majorities. The technical problem of altering the uniformity of a majority is, in terms of our procedure, relatively simple. In most instances we merely directed one or more members of the instructed group to deviate from the majority in prescribed ways. It is obvious that we cannot hope to compare the performance of the same individual in two situations on the assumption that they remain independent of one another. At best we can investigate the effect of an earlier upon a later experimental condition. The comparison of different experimental situations therefore requires the use of different but comparable groups of critical subjects. This is the procedure we have followed. In the variations to be described we have maintained the conditions of the basic experiment (e.g., the sex of the subjects, the size of the majority, the content of the task, and so on) save for the specific factor that was varied. The following were some of the variations we studied:

1. *The presence of a "true partner."* (a) In the midst of the majority were two naive, critical subjects. The subjects were separated spatially, being seated in the fourth and eighth positions, respectively. Each therefore heard his judgment confirmed by one other person (provided the other person remained independent), one prior to, the other subsequently to announcing his own judgment. In addition, each experienced a break in the unanimity of the majority. There were six pairs of critical subjects. (b) In a further variation the "partner" to the critical subject was a member of the group who had been instructed to respond correctly throughout. This procedure permits the exact control of the partner's responses. The partner was always seated in the fourth position; he therefore announced his estimates in each case before the critical subject.

The results clearly demonstrate that a disturbance of the unanimity of the majority markedly increased the independence of the critical subjects. The frequency of pro-majority errors dropped to 10.4 percent of the total number of estimates in variation (a), and to 5.5 percent in variation (b). These results are to be compared with the frequency of yielding to the unanimous majorities in the basic experiment, which was 32 percent of the total number of estimates. It is clear that the presence in the field of *one other* individual who responded correctly was sufficient to deplete the power of the majority, and in some cases to destroy it. This finding is all the more striking in the light of other variations which demonstrate the effect of even small minorities provided they are unanimous. Indeed, we have been able to show that a unanimous majority of three is, under the given conditions, far more effective than a majority of eight containing one dissenter. That critical subjects will under these conditions free themselves of a majority of seven and join forces with one other person in the minority is, we believe, a result significant for theory. It points to a fundamental psychological difference between the condition of being alone and having a minimum of human support. It further demonstrates that the effects obtained are not the result of a summation of influences proceeding from each member of the group; it is necessary to conceive the results as being relationally determined.

2. *Withdrawal of a "true partner."* What will be the effect of providing the critical subject with a partner who responds correctly and then withdrawing him? The critical subject started with a partner who responded correctly. The partner was a member of the majority who had been instructed to respond correctly and to "desert" to the majority in the middle of the experiment. This procedure permits the observation of the same subject in the course of transition from one condition to another. The withdrawal of the partner produced a powerful and unexpected result. We had assumed that the critical subject, having gone through the experience of opposing the majority with a minimum of support, would maintain his independence when alone. Contrary to this expectation, we found that the experience of having had and then lost a partner restored the majority effect to its full force, the proportion of errors rising to 28.5 percent of all judgments, in contrast to the preceding level of 5.5 percent. Further experimentation is needed to establish whether the critical subjects were responding to the sheer fact of being alone, or to the fact that the partner abandoned them.

3. *Late arrival of a "true partner."* The critical subject started as a minority of one in the midst of a unanimous majority. Toward the conclusion of the experiment one member of the majority "broke" away and began announcing correct estimates. This procedure, which reverses the order of conditions of the preceding experiment, permits the observation of the transition from being alone to being a member of a pair against a majority. It is obvious that those critical subjects who were independent when alone would continue to be so when joined by another partner. The variation is therefore of significance primarily for those subjects who yielded during the first phase of the experiment. The appearance of the late partner exerts a freeing effect, reducing the level to 8.7 percent. Those who had previously yielded also became markedly more independent but not completely so, continuing to yield more than previously independent subjects. The reports of the subjects do not cast much light on the factors responsible for the result. It is our impression that having once committed himself to yielding, the individual finds it difficult and painful to change his direction. To do so is tantamount to a public admission that he has not acted rightly. He therefore follows the precarious course he has already chosen in order to maintain an outward semblance of consistency and conviction.

4. *The presence of a "compromise partner."* The majority was consistently extremist, always matching the standard with the most unequal line. One instructed subject (who, as in the other variations, preceded the critical subject) also responded incorrectly, but his estimates were always intermediate between the truth and the majority position. The critical subject therefore faced an extremist majority whose unanimity was broken by one more moderately erring person. Under these conditions the frequency of errors was reduced but not significantly. However, the lack of unanimity determined in a strikingly consistent way the *direction* of the errors. The preponderance of the errors, 75.7 percent of the total, was moderate, whereas in a parallel experiment in which the majority was unanimously extremist (i.e., with the "compromise" partner excluded), the incidence of moderate errors was reduced to 42 percent of the total. As might be expected, in a unanimously moderate majority, the errors of the critical subjects were without exception moderate.

The Role of Majority Size

To gain further understanding of the majority effect, we varied the size of the majority in several different variations. The majorities, which were in each case unanimous, consisted of sixteen, eight, four, three, and two persons, respectively. In addition, we studied the limiting case in which the critical subject was opposed by one instructed subject. Table 6.3 contains the means and the range of errors under each condition.

With the opposition reduced to one, the majority effect all but disappeared. When the opposition proceeded from a group of two, it produced a measurable though small distortion, the errors being 12.8 percent of the total number of estimates. The effect appeared in full force with a majority of three. Larger majorities of four, eight, and sixteen did not produce effects greater than a majority of three.

The effect of a majority is often silent, revealing little of its operation to the subject, and often hiding it from the experimenter. To examine the range of effects it is capable of inducing, decisive variations of conditions are necessary. An indication of one effect is furnished by the following variation in which the conditions of the basic experiment were simply reversed. Here the majority, consisting of a group of sixteen, was naive; in the midst of it we

TABLE 6.3
Errors of Critical Subjects with Unanimous Majorities of Different Size

	Control	Size of Majority					
		1	2	3	4	8	16
Number of trials	37	10	15	10	10	50	12
Mean number of errors	0.08	0.33	1.53	4.0	4.2	3.84	3.75
Range of errors	0–2	0–1	0–5	1–12	0–11	0–11	0–10

placed a single individual who responded wrongly according to instructions. Under these conditions the members of the naive majority reacted to the lone dissenter with amusement and disdain. Contagious laughter spread through the group at the droll minority of one. Of significance is the fact that the members lack awareness that they draw their strength from the majority, and that their reactions would change radically if they faced the dissenter individually. In fact, the attitude of derision in the majority turns to seriousness and increased respect as soon as the minority is increased to three. These observations demonstrate the role of social support as a source of power and stability, in contrast to the preceding investigations which stressed the effects of withdrawal of social support, or to be more exact, the effects of social opposition. Both aspects must be explicitly considered in a unified formulation of the effects of group conditions on the formation and change of judgments. . . .

Summary

We have investigated the effects upon individuals of majority opinions when the latter were seen to be in a direction contrary to fact. By means of a simple technique we produced radical divergence between a majority and a minority, and observed the ways in which individuals coped with the resulting difficulty. Despite the stress of the given conditions, a substantial proportion of individuals retained their independence throughout. At the same time a substantial minority yielded, modifying their judgments in accordance with the majority. Independence and yielding are a joint function of the following major factors:

1. *The character of the stimulus situation:* Variations in structural clarity have a decisive effect: with diminishing clarity of the stimulus-conditions the majority effect increases.
2. *The character of the group forces.* Individuals are highly sensitive to the structural qualities of group opposition. In particular, we demonstrated the great importance of the factor of unanimity. Also, the majority effect is a function of the size of group opposition.
3. *The character of the individual.* There were wide, and indeed, striking differences among individuals within the same experimental situation. The hypothesis was proposed that these are functionally dependent on relatively enduring character differences, in particular those pertaining to the person's social relations.

References

Asch, S. E. Studies in the principles of judgments and attitudes: II. Determination of judgments by group and by ego-standards. *Journal of Social Psychology,* 1940, 12, 433–465.

Asch, S. E. The doctrine of suggestion, prestige and imitation in social psychology. *Psychological Review,* 1948, 55, 250–276.

Asch, S. E., Block, H., and Hertzman, M. Studies in the principles of judgments and attitudes. I. Two basic principles of judgment. *Journal of Psychology,* 1938, 5, 219–251.

Coffin, E. E. Some conditions of suggestion and suggestibility: A study of certain attitudinal and situational factors influencing the process of suggestion. *Psychological Monographs,* 1941, 53, No. 4.

Lewis, H. B. Studies in the principles of judgments and attitudes: IV. The operation of prestige suggestion. *Journal of Social Psychology,* 1941, 14, 229–256.

Lorge, I. Prestige, suggestion, and attitudes. *Journal of Social Psychology,* 1936, 7, 386–402.

Miller, N. E. and Dollard, J. *Social Learning and Imitation.* New Haven: Yale University Press, 1941.

Moore, H. T. The comparative influence of majority and expert opinion. *American Journal of Psychology,* 1921, 32, 16–20.

Sherif, M. A study of some social factors in perception. *Archives of Psychology, N.Y.,* 1935, No. 187.

Thorndike, E. L. *The Psychology of Wants, Interests, and Attitudes.* New York: D. Appleton-Century Company, Inc., 1935.

Name: _____   Class: _____

Date: _____   Section: _____

Reading Comprehension Activity Sheet

The Effects of Group Pressure on the Modification of Judgments, Solomon E. Asch

1. What are the main objectives of Asch's study? Briefly describe the experiment. _____
   _____
   _____
   _____
   _____
   _____
   _____
   _____
   _____
   _____
   _____

2. What factors contributed to a substantial minority of study participants' modifying their judgments? _____
   _____
   _____
   _____
   _____
   _____
   _____
   _____
   _____
   _____
   _____
   _____
   _____
   _____

Women of the Klan

Kathleen M. Blee

Judge R. M. Mann of the second division circuit court in Little Rock, Arkansas, officially chartered the Women of the Ku Klux Klan on June 10, 1923. Its national headquarters were set up in a three-room office in the Ancient Order of United Workmen hall in Little Rock, Arkansas, at some distance from the male Klan's Atlanta headquarters to symbolize the purported independence of the new women's order form its male counterpart.[1]

Membership in the WKKK was open to white Gentile female native-born citizens over 18 years of age who owed no allegiance to any foreign government or sect, that is, who were not Catholic, Socialist, Communist, or so forth. Applicants were required to have been resident in a Klan jurisdiction for at least six months and to be endorsed by at least two Klanswomen or a WKKK kleagle or Imperial Commander. Klanswomen swore to investigate "carefully and personally" the qualifications and background of every candidate they proposed for office. Dues of $10 included one robe and helmet but did not apply to wives of men who were members of the original Klan or a similar organization during Reconstruction. The national offices of the WKKK were supported (in lavish style) by a portion of all dues; an Imperial Tax (a per capita assessment); profits from the sale of regalia, uniforms, stationery, jewelry, and costumes; and by interest and profits from investments.[2]

... The WKKK declared itself an organization "by women, for women, and of women [that] no man is exploiting for his individual gain." The structure of the new women's Klan, worked out in a meeting of WKKK leaders in Asheville, North Carolina, would focus on specific functions and each would have a corresponding task department. The major areas of work for the WKKK's initial efforts were Americanism, education, public amusements, legislation, child welfare and delinquency, citizenship, civics, law enforcement, disarmament, peace, and politics.[3]

...

The charter membership of the new WKKK numbered 125,000 women. Most lived in the Midwest, Northwest, and Ozarks region, strongholds of the KKK. Not satisfied with a

From *Women of the Klan: Racism and Gender in the 1920's,* copyright © 1991 by the Regents of the University of California. Reprinted by permission.

membership drawn from among the wives, sisters, sweethearts, and mothers of Klansmen, [WKKK leaders] immediately embarked on a recruiting trip throughout the West and Northwest, increasing the WKKK's overall membership and giving the new organization visibility in other regions. [Leaders] also hired female field agents and kleagles who worked with KKK kleagles to bring the message of the women's Klan to all areas of the country. WKKK kleagles, initially often the wives and sisters of KKK officers, worked on a commission basis, retaining a percentage of the initiation dues collected from each new Klanswoman. Organizers used techniques proven effective in the men's Klan: they recruited through personal, family, and work contacts and held highly publicized open meetings to reach politically inactive women and women not from Klan families. In addition, WKKK kleagles worked to recruit women through existing organizations. Female nativist and patriotic societies, in particular, were courted by WKKK organizers who sought to persuade them to merge into the new national women's Klan organizaiton.[4]

Organizers for the women's Klan were effective. Within four months, the WKKK claimed that its membership had doubled to 250,000. By November 1923, 36 states had chapters of the Women of the Ku Klux Klan. Throughout 1924 the WKKK continued to grow, accepting girls over 16 years old and chartering 50 locals a week in 1924. The following year an influential anti-Klan commentator declared that at least three million women had been initiated into the women's Klan. His estimate was no doubt inflated, perhaps by projecting from the recruitment successes of the strong Ohio and Indiana WKKK realms; indeed, modern scholars judge the entire 1920s Klan to have enrolled no more than three to five million members. It is clear, however, that the WKKK attracted a great many women within a short time.[5]

It is impossible to determine the exact number or location of WKKK chapters across the country in the absence of organizational records, but we can estimate the expansion of the women's Klan by examining the pages of Klan periodicals. During the mid-1920s the *Fellowship Forum* published news about WKKK chapters, women's rights organizations, and women's clubs—mingled with recipes and fashion tips. The September 1925 issue carried news from local WKKK chapters in 11 states: New York, Connecticut, Pennsylvania, Michigan, Ohio, Virginia, West Virginia, Kansas, Oklahoma, Texas, and Colorado. Most chapters were located in small towns; the exceptions were those of Oklahoma City and Norfolk. The Following September, in 1926, the *Fellowship Forum* included news from WKKK chapters in 16 states: New York, Pennsylvania, Maryland, Virginia, Georgia, Florida, Illinois, Indiana, Ohio, Iowa, Minnesota, Wisconsin, Michigan, Nebraska, California, Washington, and in the District of Columbia as well. Again, most chapters were located outside major metropolitan areas although most members of the WKKK, as of the male Ku Klux Klan, probably resided in large or middle-sized cities. Other issues of the *Fellowship Forum* show a similar geographical dispersion of the women's Klan. Many chapters clustered in Pennsylvania, Ohio, Indiana, Michigan, and New York—states where the KKK was also strong—but chapters existed in the West, on the Atlantic Coast, and along the North-South border.[6]

In chartering its new women's organization, the Klan emphasized the role of women as helpmates to Klansmen. Women's cooperation and assistance were needed, Klansmen insisted, to ensure that the political agenda of the men's Klan could be implemented. The KKK press talked often of the WKKK as its "women's auxiliary" and argued that the men's Klan had created the WKKK with the same ideals and principles as its father organization.[7]

Klansmen were unsure, however, about what Klan membership would mean for women. Women might be convenient symbols for mobilizing men into the Klan, but women's actual political participation was another matter. An early advertisement written by the KKK to solicit members for an organization of Klanswomen illustrates the men's ambivalence. Although it was a recruitment pitch for the WKKK, the advertisement also pointed to a fearful potential in political involvement to masculinize women. Many worry, the ad suggested, that "giving [women] the ballot would foster masculine boldness and restless independence, which might detract from the modesty and virtue of womanhood." To this dilemma, the KKK posed as a solution the creation of a separate organization for Klanswomen. The WKKK would allow women to be politically active without "sacrifice of that womanly dignity and modesty we all admire." The key to the delicate balancing act between a "masculine" and a "feminine" political involvement, according to the KKK, was acquiescence of Klanswomen in the political agenda of Klansmen. By adopting as a whole the Klan's agenda of support for white Protestantism, the English language, public schools, the Bible, and immigration restrictions, women could exercise their newly granted enfranchisement without relying on "masculine" traits of political judgment and strategizing.[8]

A related tactic of recruitment for the women's organization stressed women's political *potential*. Although ostensibly supporting women's involvement in politics, this approach emphasized women's ignorance and limited abilities in the political arena. Excluded from the world of political debate, white Protestant women had developed only a "moral influence" in politics. Their special roles in the family and home gave women good political instincts, the Klan argued, but not mature political judgment. Women now needed to be taught (by men) those principles and attitudes that the world of politics required: clear thinking, intelligence, and collective and individual responsibility for maintaining the principles of Anglo-Saxon Protestantism. Women might have gained the ballot by law, but the ability to use it intelligently required further education—an education the Klan was prepared to provide through its women's organization.

. . .

The WKKK advertised its ability to champion the goals of white womanhood as a standard recruiting tool for new members. Its Washington chapter, for example, argued that white Protestant native-born women had common political interests and would be more effective in pursuing those interests if they were politically organized. Their recruitment advertisement posed a number of questions for women to consider:

- *Are you interested in the welfare of our nation?*
- *As an enfranchised woman are you interested in better government?*

- *Do you not wish for the protection of pure womanhood?*
- *Shall we uphold the sanctity of the American home?*
- *Should we not interest ourselves in better education for our children?*
- *Do we not want American teachers in our American schools?*

"Patriotic women," those who answered these questions in the affirmative, were needed in the women's Klan. Protestant white women, the WKKK insisted, shared a concern for their children's education and the welfare of the country. It is the "duty of the American Mother" to stamp out vice and immorality in the nation. Joining the Klan was an effective avenue for the political work that white Protestant women needed to do.[9]

The Women's Klan

To understand the nature of the new women's Klan, we need to examine the beliefs, organizations, rituals, and activities of the WKKK in comparison with those of the men's order. But we must use caution in our comparison. When Klanswomen swore to uphold the "sanctity of the home and chastity of womanhood" they echoed the words, but not necessarily the sentiments, of their male Klan counterparts. Although a simple listing of WKKK and KKK principles and rituals would suggest that there was little difference between the two organizations, we must understand how these were interpreted and justified by each organization.

Beliefs

On one level, many principles of the new women's Klan appear identical to the racist and xenophobic politics of the first and second men's Klans. The WKKK supported militant patriotism, national quotas for immigration, racial segregation, and antimiscegenation laws. Klanswomen cited the need to safeguard the "eternal supremacy" of the white race against a "rising tide of color" and decried Catholic and Jewish influence in politics, the schools, the media, and the business world. [Lulu] Markwell [of Arkansas, the first Imperial Commander of the WKKK,] . . . saw the mission of the women's Klan as "fighting for the same principles as the Knights of the Ku Klux Klan," although she reserved for the WKKK a special interest in "work peculiar to women's organization, such as social welfare work [and] the prevention of juvenile delinquency."[10]

Like the men's Klan, the WKKK often used politically palatable symbols to present its agenda of nativism and racial hatred to the public. It called for separation of church from state when crusading against Roman Catholic political influence, for free public schools when seeking to destroy parochial schools, and for the purity of race when seeking racial segregation and restricted immigration. In private, the racial bigotry of the WKKK was fully as vicious as that of the KKK, as in Klanswomen's condemnation of "mulatto leaders forced to remain members of the negro group [who] aspire to white association because of their white blood [thus] boldly preaching racial equality."[11]

But if many of the WKKK's basic principles followed existing doctrines of the men's Klan, women and men did not always have a common perception of the problems that required Klan action. Klansmen of the 1920s denounced interracial marriage for its destructive genetic outcomes; their Klan forefathers fought interracial sexuality to maintain white men's sexual access to white and black women. Klanswomen, however, saw a different danger in miscegenation: the destruction of white marriages by untrustworthy white men who "betray their own kind."

In many cases, women and men in the Klan took different messages from common symbols. Klansmen praised womanhood to underscore the correctness of male supremacy; Klanswomen used the symbol to point out the inequities that women faced in society and politics. Klansmen sought political inspiration in the "great achievements" of white American Protestantism, but Klanswomen read history differently. Rather than mimicking the men's empty gestures of praise for "true American women" in the past, the WKKK complained that women had been excluded from public politics throughout most of this glorious history, even though "our mothers have ever been Klanswomen at heart, sharing with our fathers the progress and development of our country." Klanswomen embraced the KKK's racist, anti-Catholic, and anti-Semitic agenda and symbols of American womanhood but they used these to argue as well for equality for white Protestant women.[12]

Organization

For the most part the WKKK adopted the militaristic hierarchical style of the KKK. An Excellent Commander served as president, with a four-year term of office and responsibility for issuing, suspending, and revoking the charters of locals and realms (state organizations). Next in the chain of command was the klaliff (vice-president), who acted as presiding officer of the Imperial Klonvokation; the klokard (lecturer), responsible for disseminating Klankraft; and the kludd (chaplain), who presided over Klan ritual. Other major officers included the kligrapp (secretary), bonded for $25,000 to handle minor Klan funds; the Klabee (treasurer), bonded for $50,000 to handle major Klan funds; and the officers of Klan ritual and ceremony, including the kladd (conductor), klagoro (inner guard), klexter (outer guard), night hawk (in charge of candidates), klokan (investigator and auditor), and kourier (messenger).

Each realm or group of realms of the WKKK was organized by a Major Kleagle with subjurisdictions organized by minor kleagles and supervised by a series of Realm Commanders and Imperial Commanders. Upon retirement from office, Excellent Commanders became Klan Regents, Realm Commander became Grand Regents, and Imperial Commanders became Imperial Regents. In keeping with the military arrangement of the WKKK, nearly all offices were subdivided into further levels of authority. The rank of kourier, for example, was subdivided into that of kourier private, corporal, sergeant, lieutenant, captain, major, and colonel. Ranks carried more than symbolic authority, as failure to obey the command of an officer was defined as insubordination and could bring harsh punishment.[13]

The similarity between the organization of the male and female Klans is significant. Consistently, WKKK denied that it was like the auxiliary of a fraternal association, "merely a social order for social purposed." Instead, Klanswomen embraced the mixture of individualism and deference to authority that characterized the male Klan. Like Klansmen, Klanswomen had at least ostensible opportunities to rise within the organization through individual effort and talent; both organizations used a strict command hierarchy. In this, the WKKK claimed to stand apart from the outside world that discouraged women from individual efforts and achievements. By valuing both obedience and individual effort, the WKKK would "inculcate patriotism, upbuild character, and develop true clannishness among women."[14]

Other features of the WKKK show the contrasting aspects of obedience and commonality that characterized the KKK. Like their male counterparts, Klanswomen typically wore white robes with masks and helmets, although some chapters used red robes. Masks were clearly intended to disguise the identity of Klanswomen in public, but the WKKK insisted that masks had only a symbolic purpose. Through masking Klanswomen hid their individuality as well as identity, exemplifying the Klan motto "not for self, but for others." Similar claims were made about Klan robes. Although in fact officers' robes had more colors and accoutrements, Klanswomen asserted that their robes symbolized the equality of all women within Klankraft. Robes set Klanswomen apart from the invidious world of social class distinctions in fashion, leveling the divisions of wealth so pervasive in alien society." As we look upon a body of women robed in white we realize that we are on a common level of sisterhood and fraternal union."[15]

The detailed laws and regulations of the WKKK ensured obedience to authority. Women, no less than men, were expected to conduct themselves according to klannish principles. The WKKK treated as major offenses those of treason to the Klan, violating the oath of allegiance, disrespect of virtuous womanhood, violation of the U.S. Constitution, the "pollution" of Caucasian blood through miscegenation, and other acts unworthy of a Klanswoman. Minor offenses included profane language or vulgarity during a klonklave, acts against the best interest of the Klan or a Klanswoman, and refusal or failure to obey the Excellent Commander. The Excellent Commander assessed penalties for minor offenses; a tribunal handled major offenses. Violators faced reprimand, suspension, banishment forever, or complete ostracism.

Ritual

At least as central as laws and hierarchy to both women's and men's Klans was an elaborate and intricate web of ceremonials, rites, and protocols designed to increase members' commitment to the order and to sharpen the distinctions between insiders and outsiders ("aliens"). Like the men's Klan, the WKKK used threatening, frightening, and challenging rituals to ensure loyalty and instill fear in its members. Both the WKKK and the KKK referred to themselves as "invisible empires," conveying the Klan's aspirations to universal jurisdiction. Secret klannish words gave members an immediate way to recognize sister and brother Klan members. In Klan ceremonies, days of the week were not Sunday, Monday, and so forth as in the alien world but were desperate, dreadful, desolate, doleful, dismal, deadly, and dark. Weeks of the month became weird, wonderful, wailing, weeping, and woeful. January through December were labeled appalling, frightful, sorrowful, mournful, horrible, terrible, alarming, furious, fearful, hideous, gloomy, and bloody.

The Klan changed historical time as well, setting it to the ascendancy of white Gentile Americans. The reign of Incarnation included all time up to the American Revolution. A first reign of Reincarnation lasted from the beginning of the revolutionary war until the organization of the first Ku Klux Klan in 1866. A second reign of Reincarnation extended from 1866 to 1872, the collapse of the first KKK. The third reign of Reincarnation began in 1915, the reorganization of the KKK, and extended from the present into the future.[16]

The naturalization klonklave was typical of women's Klan rituals. An altar was placed in the center of a room or in an open-air gathering place surrounded by stations with water, a Bible, a flag, and a sword. WKKK officers entered the klonklave, kissed the flag, proceeded to the altar, and saluted the Excellent Commander or other presiding officer, raising their masks to reveal their identities to this official. When all officers were assembled, the kladd certified that everyone present was a valid member of the WKKK. The entrance to the building or park was secured by the klexter and klagoro and then all masks were removed.

Once assembled, officers were questioned about the seven sacred symbols of Klankraft in a ritualized catechism oddly patterned after the catechism ritual of the Roman Catholic church. Each officer repeated a litany of symbols: the Bible (God), fiery cross (sacrifice and service), flag (U.S. Constitution), sword (law enforcement and national defense), water (purity of life and unity of purpose), mask (secrecy, unselfishness, and banishment of individuality), and robe (purity and equality). Between each restatement of Klan doctrine, the audience and officers sang a Christian hymn.

During the naturalization ceremony, a klokard led the class of candidates through the oath of admission. Candidates swore that they were serious, qualified for admission, believers in klannishness, and willing to practice klannishness toward other Klanswomen and work for the eternal maintenance of white supremacy. Candidates then were greeted by officers and members and congratulated for their "womanly decision to forsake the world of selfishness and fraternal alienation and emigrate to the delectable bounds of the Invisible Empire and become its loyal citizens." At this point, the Excellent Commander conferred the obligation and oath of admission on the assembled candidates and baptized the new members by pouring water and saying:

> With this transparent, life-giving, powerful God-given fluid, more precious and far more significant than all the sacred oils of the ancients, I set you apart from the women of your daily

association to the great and honorable task you have voluntarily allotted yourselves as citizens of the Invisible Empire, Women of the Ku Klux Klan. As Klanswomen, may your character be as transparent, your life purpose as powerful, your motive in all things as magnanimous and as pure, and your Klannishness as real and as faithful as the manifold drops herein.

As a quartet of Klanswomen sang and the assembly prayed, the klannish initiates responded with their own ritual. They dipped fingers in water and touched their shoulders, saying "In body," and their foreheads, saying "In mind," then waved their hands in the air, saying "In spirit," and made a circle above their heads saying "In life." The klokard then imparted the secret signs and words of the Klan. The ceremony closed with an opportunity to raise issues from the floor (probably an infrequent occurrence), followed by a restatement of the need for secrecy in the presence of aliens. The night hawk extinguished the fiery cross, the kludd performed a benediction, and the klonklave was declared closed.[17]

Ceremonies for higher levels in the WKKK followed a similar pattern, although more was required of the candidates. Acceptance into the second-degree obligation, the highest rank below officer level, required candidates to make pledges against slandering other Klanswomen or Klansmen, against materialism, and against selfishness and similar temptations. Candidates for advanced degrees also made greater pledges of duty, swearing that "when pleasure interferes with my duty as Klanswoman . . . I will set aside pleasure"; they affirmed their loyalty, vowing not to recommend "faithless, contemptuous, careless, or indifferent" women for advancement in the order.[18]

Activities

It is difficult to compare the political practices of the women's and men's Klans, as both varied considerably across the nation and over time but the national agendas of each organization give some indication of the differences. The political agenda of the men's Klan ranged from infiltration into legislative and judicial politics on the state, municipal, and county level to acts of violence and terroristic intimidation against Jews, Catholics, and blacks. Many Klansmen, though, used the KKK as primarily a male fraternity, a social club of like-minded white Protestants.[19]

The women's Klan similarly showed a range of activities and purposes. On a national level, the women's Klan worked to legitimate the violence and terrorism of the men's order. It published and distributed a detailed guide to the proper display of the American flag and a pocket-sized version of the U.S. Constitution and circulated a card reminding Protestants to attend church faithfully; each item prominently displayed the WKKK logo. The WKKK involved itself in national legislative politics, although without much success. It actively supported the creation of a federal Department of Education to bolster public schools and undermine parochial education and opposed U.S. membership in the World court. Although it claimed to be interested in safeguarding white Protestant children and the home, the WKKK opposed a 1924 bill outlawing child labor on the grounds that it was "a

Communistic, Bolshevistic scheme." That same year Klanswomen were active in blocking an attempt by anti-Klan forces to introduce a plank in the national Democratic party platform condemning the Ku Klux Klan.[20]

At times the women's Klan sought to portray itself as an organization of social work and social welfare. One national WKKK speaker announced that she left social work for the "broader field of Klankraft" because of the Klan's effectiveness in promoting morality and public welfare. Many chapters claimed to collect food and money for the needy, although these donations typically went to Klan families, often to families of Klan members arrested for rioting and vigilante activities. A powerful Florida WKKK chapter operated a free day nursery, charging that Catholic teachers had ruined the local public schools.[21]

Some WKKK chapters ran homes for wayward girls. These homes served two purposes: to protect the virtue of Protestant women who were tempted by a life of vice and to underscore the danger faced by delinquent girls placed in Catholic-controlled reform schools. The Shreveport, Louisiana, WKKK chapter, for example, based its fund-raising for a Protestant girls' home on the story of a woman whose unhappy fate it was to be sent to a Catholic reform home after being convicted of selling whiskey and prostituting her teenaged daughters.[22]

Another activity of many WKKK locals was the crusade against liquor and vice. WKKK chapters worked to "clean up" a motion picture industry in which they claimed Jewish owners spewed a steady diet of immoral sex onto the screen. Other chapters fought against liquor, as evidenced by the case of Myrtle Cook, a Klanswoman and president of the Vinton, Iowa, WCTU, who was assassinated for documenting the names of suspected bootleggers. In death, Cook was eulogized by Klanswomen and WCTU members alike; all business in Vinton was suspended for the two hours of the funeral.[23]

WKKK chapters in many states were active also in campaigns to prohibit prenuptial religious agreements about future children, bar interracial marriage, outlaw the Knights of Columbus (a Catholic fraternal society), remove Catholic encyclopedias from public schools, bar the use of Catholic contractors by public agencies, and exclude urban (i.e., Jewish and Catholic) vacationers in majority-Protestant suburban resorts.[24]

Some WKKK locals, though, functioned largely for the personal and financial success of their members. F. C. Dunn of Lansing, Michigan, made a fortune after introducing her invention, a new antiseptic powder, at a local WKKK meeting.[25]

Klanswomen tended not to be involved in physical violence and rioting, but there were exceptions. In the aftermath of a 1924 Klan riot in Wilkinsburg, Pennsylvania, Mamie H. Bittner, a 39-year-old mother of three children and member of the Homestead, Pennsylvania, WKKK testified that she, along with thousands of other Klanswomen paraded through town, carrying heavy maple riot clubs. Moreover, Bittner claimed that the WKKK was teaching its members to murder and kill in the interest of the Klan.[26]

The activities of the women's Klan were shaped largely by the existing political agenda of the men's Klan. It is not accurate, however, to portray the WKKK as a dependent auxiliary of the men's order. Klanswomen created a distinctive ideology and political agenda that infused the Klan's racist and nativist goals with ideas of equality between white Protestant women and men. The ideology and politics of Klanswomen and Klansmen were not identical, though at many points they were compatible. But women and men of the Klan movement sometimes found themselves in contention as women changed from symbols to actors in the Klan.

The difference between the women's and men's Klan grew from an underlying message in the symbol of white womanhood. By using gender and female sexual virtue as prime political symbols, the Klan shaped its identity through intensely masculinist themes, as an organization of real men. Clearly, this was an effective recruitment strategy for the first Klan. But in the 1920s, as both financial and political expediency and significant changes in women's political roles prompted the Klan to accept female members, an identity based on symbols of masculine exclusivity and supremacy became problematic. In addition, if Klansmen understood that defending white womanhood meant safeguarding white Protestant supremacy and male supremacy, many women heard the message differently. The WKKK embraced ideas of racial and religious privilege but rejected the messages of white female vulnerability. In its place Klanswomen substituted support for women's rights and a challenge to white men's political and economic domination.

Notes

1. *Arkansas Gazette,* June 10, 1923, 1.
2. WKKK, *Constitution and Laws* (WKKK, 1927).
3. *Fellowship Forum,* Feb. 23, 1924, p. 6; Nov. 17, 1923, p. 6; *Imperial Night-Hawk,* Oct. 31, 1923, p. 1; Aug. 1, 1923, p. 8.
4. *The Truth;* also, *Fiery Cross,* July 13, 1923, p. 1; Sue Wilson Abbey ("The Ku Klux Klan in Arizona, 1921–25," *Journal of Arizona History* 14 [Spring 1973]: 10–30) discusses how Tom Akers was sent to organize the Phoenix, Arizona, chapter of the WKKK in 1923; Loucks, *The Ku Klux Klan in Pennsylvania,* pp. 150–56; *Arkansas Gazette,* June 10, 1925, p. 1.
5. *Arkansas Gazette,* Oct. 7, 1923, p. 12; see also *Imperial Night-Hawk,* Oct. 31, 1923, p. 1; *New York Times,* Nov. 7, 1923, p. 15; Kenneth Jackson, *The Ku Klux Klan;* William M. Likins, *The Ku Klux Klan, Its Rise and Fall; Patriotism Capitalized or Religion Turned into Gold* (privately published, 1925).
6. See Kenneth Jackson, *The Ku Klux Klan; Fellowship Forum,* 1924–1928.
7. *Imperial Night-Hawk,* June 13, 1923, p. 5; Aug. 8, 1923, p. 6.
8. *Fiery Cross,* Mar. 2, 1923, p. 4; *Fellowship Forum,* June 2, 1923, p. 8.
9. *Watcher on the Tower,* Sept. 15, 1923, p. 12.
10. *Imperial Night-Hawk,* June 20, 1923, p. 8.
11. WKKK, *Ideals of the Women of the Ku Klux Klan* (WKKK, 1923), pp. 2–3, 4–5; WKKK, *Women of America!,* pp. 6–7, 9–10, 13–14 (WKKK, ca. 1923); WKKK, *Kreed* (WKKK, ca. 1924).
12. WKKK, *Women of America!;* WKKK, *Constitution and Laws,* pp. 6–7; WKKK, *Kreed;* WKKK, *Ideals,* pp. 2–3, 4–5; *Imperial Night-Hawk,* June 20, 1923, p. 8; May 14, 1924, p. 7; advertisement in *Dawn,* Aug. 11, 1923, p. 2.

13. WKKK, *Constitution and Laws*. From statement by Victoria Rogers, Major Kleagle for the Realm of Illinois, in *Dawn,* Feb. 2, 1924, p. 12.
14. WKKK, *Women of America!*
15. WKKK, *Catalogue of Official Robes and Banners* (WKKK, ca. 1923); WKKK, *Kloran or Ritual of the WKKK* (WKKK, 1923).
16. WKKK, *Constitution and Laws.*
17. WKKK, *Kloran or Ritual of the WKKK*. The *New York Times* (Aug. 19, 1923, p. 2) has detailed coverage of a naturalization ceremony involving 700 members of the women's Klan in Allenwood, New Jersey.
18. WKKK, *Second Degree Obligation of the Women of the Ku Klux Klan* (WKKK, n.d.); see also WKKK, *Installation Ceremonies of the Women of the Ku Klux Klan* (WKKK, n.d.).
19. Hiram Evans, *The Menace* and *The Attitude of the Knights of the Ku Klux Klan toward the Roman Catholic Hierarchy* (KKK, ca. 1923).
20. WKKK, *Flag Book* (WKKK, 1923); Ku Klux Klan record collection (hereafter cited as KKK), Indiana State Library; WKKK, *U.S. Constitution* (WKKK, n.d.); *Fiery Cross,* Oct. 10, 1924, p. 5; *Fellowship Forum,* July 5, 1924, pp. 6–7.
21. *Fellowship Forum,* Sept. 19, 1925, p. 6; July 5, 1924; Mar. 3, 1926, p. 6. The anonymous speaker is identified only as a "Klan female speaker." January 1925 issues of the *Fellowship Forum* have other examples of such self-promotion, as does that of May 1, 1926, p. 7; see also Chalmers, *Hooded Americanism.*
22. *Imperial Night-Hawk,* May 9, 1923, p. 2; see also *New York Times,* July 11, 1926, p. 7.
23. *Arkansas Gazette,* Sept. 8, 1925, p. 1; *Fiery Cross,* Mar. 30, 1923, p. 5; *Fellowship Forum,* Jan. 24, 1925, p. 6; *New York Times,* Sept. 9, 1925, p. 1; Sept. 19, 1925, p. 20; Sept. 11, 1925, p. 5.
24. *New York Times,* June 3, 1923, sect. 1, pt. 2, p. 8; *Fellowship Forum,* Jan. 24, 1925, p. 6; *New York Times,* Mar. 21, 1922, p. 6; Dec. 8, 1922, p. 9; *Imperial Night-Hawk,* May 9, 1923, p. 3; *Fiery Cross,* Oct. 10, 1924, p. 5; *Fellowship Forum,* Jan. 17, 1925, p. 6; July 5, 1924, p. 6. For a detailed analysis of the conflict over the Klan during the 1924 election, especially during the Democratic party convention, see Lee Allen, "The McAdoo Campaign for the Presidential Nomination of 1924," *Journal of Southern History* 29 (1963): 211–18; "The Klan and the Democrats," *Literary Digest,* June 14, 1924, pp. 12–13; Rice, *Ku Klux Klan;* Chalmers, *Hooded Americanism,* pp. 282–90.
25. *Fiery Cross,* July 18, 1924, p. 6. In an odd twist—"because of their affiliation with the KKK"—two women were excluded from the will of a third woman with whom they had lived for 16 years (will of Alice Reid, filed in surrogate's court in Brooklyn in 1928 and reported in the *New York Times,* Oct. 10, 1928, p. 16).
26. Testimony of Mamie H. Bittner in U.S. District Court for the Western District of Pennsylvania, *Knights of the Ku Klux Klan, Plaintiff, v. Rev. John F. Strayer et al., Defendants,* 1928 (Equity 1897 in National Archives–Philadelphia Branch; William M. Likins, *The Trial of the Serpent* (n.p., 1928), pp. 64–67.

Name: _____   Class: _____

Date: _____   Section: _____

Reading Comprehension Activity Sheet

Women of the Klan, Kathleen M. Blee

1. Why was the WKKK implemented? _____

_____
_____
_____
_____
_____
_____
_____
_____
_____
_____
_____

2. Compare and contrast the characteristics of the WKKK with the KKK. _____

_____
_____
_____
_____
_____
_____
_____
_____
_____
_____
_____

3. Through a secondary group association, how did women of the Klan find meaning and agency in their arena?

PART II
Stratification and Issues of Inequality

In American culture, the principle of individual effort leading to social rewards has been institutionalized in all of the dominant social settings. We teach our children the idea that "individual hard work and effort will be rewarded" and (implicitly) that failure is the result of not working hard enough. We socialize our children by reaffirming these values through such statements as "Keep your nose to the grindstone," "Pull yourself up by your own bootstrap," and "Quitters never win."

Not generally recognized is the impact that an ascribed status (that is, sex, race/ethnicity, and age) has on either an individual's life chances or the statuses that we are able to achieve. Other statuses, such as those involving sexual orientation and even marital status, influence how others see us in society and how they in turn treat us. We fail to see that, although we espouse the virtue of individuality, the fact is that our position relative to others will determine the kind of access we have to social rewards. It is almost "un-American" to suggest that people in the United States, the "land of opportunity," are denied opportunities (or perhaps bestowed with particular advantages) because of their race, sex, or even age.

"Social stratification" refers to the differential division of people (and categories of people) into layers according to their relative power, prestige, and privilege. In addition, society ranks these categories of people in a hierarchy. Thus, some categories are seen as superior, others inferior; as valued, others devalued. People occupying similar positions share similar life chances, enjoy similar social rewards, and encounter similar difficulties. The idea of social strata is one in which entire categories of people have differential access to social resources and social opportunities.

The first set of readings will examine social class. Most Americans believe that they occupy a "middle-class" position, almost as if being something other than middle-class is also somehow "un-American." To talk about social class is to begin a discussion of inequality among groups of people. Our social class determines so much of our life chances, from the quality and quantity of education we receive, to the quality and quantity of our health care, to our likelihood of being a victim of crime. Social class influences where we live, what types of illnesses and injuries we incur, and even how and when we die. Even the kinds of jobs available to us, the hobbies we enjoy, and the activities we engage in are functions of social class. Our social class also influences the stability of our marriage(s) and type of family structure, the place in which we worship, and even the make and model of the car we drive. There is virtually no life circumstance that is not influenced by social class. Social class is something that is often hard to define, and yet something of which most Americans has an almost intuitive understanding of. Social class is more than being about individual effort, since entire groups of people have similar social experiences, opportunities presented, or opportunities denied, based upon their income, their accumulated wealth, and their social power.

The second set of readings deals with the issue of gender. As a social construct, the idea will be presented that gender represents socially prescribed attitudes and behaviors based upon biological sex. Notions such as "Boys will be boys" and "Pink is for girls" will be demonstrated to represent social ideas placed within a particular historical context, representing cultural values, and perpetuated through social institutions. Just as importantly as recognizing that gender reflects a social construct is the fact that gender is also used to stratify men and women. Men and women, in the United States as well as abroad, have differential access to social rewards. Women are denied opportunities that are made available to men, and even today in the 21st century, women encounter discrimination in hiring and promotion practice in employment, admittance to academic programs, and inclusion in various social activities. Moreover, women are also substantially more likely than men to experience violence in their homes and sexual harassment in the workplace. Whether in corporate boardrooms, in the classrooms, or in the locker rooms, women and men experience different access to social rewards. One result of gender stratification is the inequality that women experience relative to the paycheck, as evidenced by the fact that women earn approximately 74 cents for every dollar that a man earns.

The third set of readings represents the social constructs of race and ethnicity. Again, we see that social rewards are differentially distributed because of a person's perceived race or ethnicity. Entire categories of people are presented with social advantage or denied opportunities, due to their membership in a particular group. Although racial discrimination was outlawed through such legislation as the Civil Rights Act, Title VII, discrimination institutionalized through normative practices continues to exist. Perhaps more unsettling is that with recent terrorist acts, legislation such as the Patriot Act has passed through Congress. Under the guise of patriotism, this legislation has the potential effect of fostering prejudicial attitudes and legitimating discriminatory behavior that acts such as Title VII tried to reduce or eliminate.

The final set of readings addresses a person's sexual orientation. Heterosexuals are typically unaware of the prejudice and discrimination, both individual and institutionalized, that homosexuals encounter. Homosexuals continue to be denied equal access to the institution of marriage and the benefits that are accorded in marriage, such as tax breaks; insurance policies such as medical, dental, vision, and life; and adoption of children. Certain sexual acts between consenting same-sex adult individuals (acts that are not necessarily illegal for opposite-sex couples) continue to be illegal in many states. Furthermore, violence against homosexuals, in the form of "gay-bashing" like that perpetrated against Matthew Sheppard, continues.

chapter 7

Social Class

Class, Status, Party
Max Weber

The Uses of Poverty: The Poor Pay All
Herbert J. Gans

Class, Status, Party

Max Weber

Economically Determined Power and the Social Order

Law exists when there is a probability that an order will be upheld by a specific staff of men who will use physical or psychical compulsion with the intention of obtaining conformity with the order, or of inflicting sanctions for infringement of it.[1] The structure of every legal order directly influences the distribution of power, economic or otherwise, within its respective community. This is true of all legal orders and not only that of the state. In general, we understand by "power" the chance of a man or of a number of men to realize their own will in a communal action even against the resistance of others who are participating in the action.

"Economically conditioned" power is not, of course, identical with "power" as such. On the contrary, the emergence of economic power may be the consequence of power existing on other grounds. Man does not strive for power only in order to enrich himself economically. Power, including economic power, may be valued "for its own sake." Very frequently the striving for power is also conditioned by the social "honor" it entails. Not all power, however, entails social honor: The typical American Boss, as well as the typical big speculator, deliberately relinquishes social honor. Quite generally, "mere economic" power, and especially "naked" money power, is by no means a recognized basis of social honor. Nor is power the only basis of social honor. Indeed, social honor, or prestige, may even be the basis of political or economic power, and very frequently has been. Power, as well as honor, may be guaranteed by the legal order, but, at least normally, it is not their primary source. The legal order is rather an additional factor that enhances the chance to hold power or honor; but it cannot always secure them.

The way in which social honor is distributed in a community between typical groups participating in this distribution we may call the "social order." The social order and the

From *Economy and Society,* Volume II by Max Weber, copyright © 1978 by The Regents of the University of California. Reprinted by permission.

economic order are, of course, similarly related to the "legal order." However, the social and the economic order are not identical. The economic order is for us merely the way in which economic goods and services are distributed and used. The social order is of course conditioned by the economic order to a high degree, and in its turn reacts upon it.

Now: "classes," "status groups," and "parties" are phenomena of the distribution of power within a community.

Determination of Class-Situation by Market-Situation

In our terminology, "classes" are not communities; they merely represent possible, and frequent, bases for communal action. We may speak of a "class" when (1) a number of people have in common a specific causal component of their life chances, insofar as (2) this component is represented exclusively by economic interests in the possession of goods and opportunities for income, and (3) is represented under the conditions of the commodity or labor markets [These points refer to "class situation," which we may express more briefly as the typical chance for a supply of goods, external living conditions, and personal life experiences, insofar as this chance is determined by the amount and kind of power, or lack of such, to dispose of goods or skills for the sake of income in a given economic order. The term "class" refers to any group of people that is found in the same class situation.]

It is the most elemental economic fact that the way in which the disposition over material property is distributed among a plurality of people, meeting competitively in the market for the purpose of exchange, in itself creates specific life chances. According to the law of marginal utility this mode of distribution excludes the non-owners from competing for highly valued goods; it favors the owners and, in fact, gives them a monopoly to acquire such goods. Other things being equal, this mode of distribution monopolizes the opportunities for profitable deals for all those who, provided with goods, do not necessarily have to exchange them. It increases, at least generally, their power in price wars with those who, being propertyless, have nothing to offer but their services in native form or goods in a form constituted through their own labor, and who above all are compelled to get rid of these products in order barely to subsist. This mode of distribution gives to the propertied a monopoly on the possibility of transferring property from the sphere of use as a "fortune," to the sphere of "capital goods"; that is, it gives them the entrepreneurial function and all chances to share directly or indirectly in returns on capital. All this holds true within the area in which pure market conditions prevail. "Property" and "lack of property" are, therefore, the basic categories of all class situations. It does not matter whether these two categories become effective in price wars or in competitive struggles.

Within these categories, however, class situations are further differentiated: on the one hand, according to the kind of property that is usable for returns; and, on the other hand, according to the kind of services that can be offered in the market. Ownership of domestic buildings; productive establishments; warehouses; stores, agriculturally usable land, large and small holdings—quantitative differences with possibly qualitative consequences; ownership of mines; cattle; men (slaves); disposition over mobile instruments of production, or capital goods of all sorts, especially money or objects that can be exchanged for money easily and at any time; disposition over products of one's own labor or of others' labor differing according to their various distances from consumability; disposition over transferable monopolies of any kind—all these distinctions differentiate the class situations of the propertied just as does the "meaning" which they can and do give to the utilization of property, especially to property which has money equivalence. Accordingly, the propertied, for instance, may belong to the class of rentiers or to the class of entrepreneurs.

Those who have no property but who offer services are differentiated just as much according to their kinds of services as according to the way in which they make use of these services, in a continuous or discontinuous relation to a recipient. But always this is the generic connotation of the concept of class: that the kind of chances in the *market* is the decisive moment which presents a common condition for the individual's fate. "Class situation" is in this sense, ultimately "market situation." The effect of naked possession *per se,* which among cattle breeders gives the nonowning slave or serf into the power of the cattle owner, is, only a forerunner of real "class" formation. However, in the cattle loan and in the naked severity of the law of debts in such communities, for the first time mere "possession" as such emerges as decisive for the fate of the individual. This is very much in contrast to the agricultural communities based on labor. The creditor-debtor relation becomes the basis of "class situations" only in those cities where a "credit market," however primitive, with rates of interest increasing according to the extent of dearth and a factual monopolization of credits, is developed by a plutocracy. Therewith "class struggles" begin.

Those men whose fate is not determined by the chance of using goods or services for themselves on the market, e.g., slaves, are not, however, a "class" in the technical sense of the term. They are, rather, a "status group."

Communal Action Flowing from Class Interest

According to our terminology, the factor that creates "class" is unambiguously economic interest, and indeed, only those interests involved in the existence of the "market." Nevertheless, the concept of "class-interest" is an ambiguous one: Even as an empirical concept it is ambiguous as soon as one understands by it something other than the factual direction of interests following with a certain probability from the class situation for a certain "average" of those people subjected to the class situation. The class situation and other circumstances remaining the same, the direction in which the individual worker, for instance, is likely to pursue his interests may vary widely, according to whether he is constitutionally qualified for the task at hand to a high, to an average, or to a low degree. In the same way, the direction of interests may vary according to whether or not a *communal* action of a larger or smaller portion of those commonly affected by the "class situation," or even an association among them, e.g., a "trade union," has grown out of the class situation from which the individual may or may not expect promising results. [Communal action refers to that action which is oriented to the feeling of the actors that they belong together. Societal action, on the other hand, is oriented to a rationally motivated adjustment of interests.] The rise of societal or even of communal action from a common class situation is by no means a universal phenomenon.

The class situation may be restricted in its effects to the generation of essentially *similar* reactions, that is to say, within our terminology, of "mass actions." However, it may not have even this result. Furthermore, often merely an amorphous communal action emerges. For example, the "murmuring" of the workers known in ancient oriental ethics: the moral disapproval of the work-master's conduct, which in its practical significance was probably equivalent to an increasingly typical phenomenon of precisely the latest industrial development, namely, the "slowdown" (the deliberate limiting of work effort) of laborers by virtue of tacit agreement. The degree in which "communal action" and possibly "societal action," emerges from the "mass actions" of the members of a class is linked to general cultural conditions, especially to those of an intellectual sort. It is also linked to the extent of the contrasts that have already evolved, and is especially linked to the *transparency* of the connections between the causes and the consequences of the "class situation." For however different life chances may be, this fact in itself, according to all experience, by no means gives birth to "class action" (communal action by the members of a class). The fact of being conditioned and the results of the class situation must be distinctly recognizable. For only then the contrast of life chances can be felt not as an absolutely given fact to be accepted, but as a resultant from either (1) the given distribution of property, or (2) the structure of the concrete economic order. It is only then that people may react against the class structure not only through acts of an intermittent and irrational protest, but in the form of rational association. There have been "class situations" of the first category (1), of a specifically naked and transparent sort, in the urban centers of antiquity and during the Middle Ages: especially then, when great fortunes were accumulated by factually monopolized trading in industrial products of these locaities or in foodstuffs. Furthermore, under certain circumstances, in the rural economy of the most diverse periods, when agriculture was increasingly exploited in a profit-making manner. The most important historical example of the second category (2) is the class situation of the modern "proletariat."

Types of "Class Struggle"

Thus every class may be the carrier of any one of the possibly innumerable forms of "class action," but this is not necessarily so: In any case, a class does not in itself constitute a community. To treat "class" conceptually as having the same value as "community" leads to distortion. That men in the same class situation regularly react in mass actions to such tangible situations as economic ones in the direction of those interests that are most adequate to their average number is an important and after all simple fact for the understanding of historical events. Above all, this fact must not lead to that kind of pseudo-scientific operation with the concepts of "class" and "class interests" so frequently found these days, and which has found its most classic expression in the statement of a talented author, that the individual may be in error concerning his interests but that the "class" is "infallible" about its interests. Yet, if classes as such are not communities, nevertheless class situations emerge only on the basis of communalization. The communal action that brings forth class situations, however, is not basically action between members of the identical class; it is an action between members of different classes. Communal actions that directly determine the class situation of the worker and the entrepreneur are the labor market, the commodities market, and the capitalistic enterprise. But, in its turn, the existence of a capitalistic enterprise presupposes that a very specific communal action exists and that it is specifically structured to protect the possession of goods *per se,* and especially the power of individuals to dispose, in principal freely, over the means of production. The existence of a capitalistic enterprise is preconditioned by a specific kind of "legal order." Each kind of class situation, and above all when it rests upon the power of property *per se,* will become most clearly efficacious when all other determinants of reciprocal relations are, as far as possible, eliminated in their significance. It is in this way that the utilization of the power of property in the market obtains its most sovereign importance.

Now "status groups" hinder the strict carrying through of the sheer market principle. In the present context they are of interest to us only from this one point of view. Before we briefly consider them, note that not much of a general nature can be said about the more specific kinds of antagonism between "classes" (in our meaning of the term). The great shift, which has been going on continuously in the past, and up to our times, may be summarized, although at the cost of some precision: The struggle in which class situations are effective has progressively shifted from consumption credit toward, first, competitive struggles in the commodity market and, then, toward price wars on the labor market. The "class struggles" of antiquity—to the extent that they were genuine class struggles and not struggles between status groups—were initially carried on by indebted peasants, and perhaps also by artisans threatened by debt bondage and struggling against urban creditors. For debt bondage is the normal result of the differentiation of wealth in commercial cities, especially in seaport cities. A similar situation has existed among cattle breeders. Debt relationships as such produced class action up to the time of Cataline. Along with this, and with an increase in provision of grain for the city by transporting it from the outside, the struggle over the means of sustenance emerged. It centered in the first place around the provision of bread and the determination of the price of bread. It lasted throughout antiquity and the entire Middle Ages. The propertyless as such flocked together against those who actually and supposedly were interested in the dearth of bread. This fight spread until it involved all those commodities essential to the way of life and to handicraft production. There were only incipient discussions of wage disputes in antiquity and in the Middle Ages. But they have been slowly increasing up into modern times. In the earlier periods they were completely secondary to slave rebellions as well as to fights n the commodity market.

The propertyless of antiquity and of the Middle Ages protested against monopolies, pre-emption, forestalling, and the withholding of goods from the market in order to raise prices. Today the central issue is the determination of the price of labor.

This transition is represented by the fight for access to the market and for the determination of the price of products. Such fights went on between merchants and workers in the putting-out system of domestic handicraft during the transition to modern times. Since it is quite a general phenomenon we must mention here that the class antagonisms that are conditioned through the market situation are usually most bitter between those who actually and directly participate as opponents in price wars. It is not the rentier, the shareholder, and the banker who suffer the ill will of the worker, but almost exclusively the manufacturer and the business executives who are the direct opponents of workers in price wars. This is so in spite of the fact that it is precisely the cash boxes of the rentier, the share-holder, and the banker into which the more or less "unearned" gains flow, rather than into the pockets of the manufacturers or of the business executives. This simple state of affairs has very frequently been decisive for the role the class situation has played in the formation of political parties. For example, it has made possible the varieties of patriarchal socialism and the frequent attempts—formerly, at least—of threatened status groups to form alliances with the proletariat against the "bourgeoisie."

Status Honor

In contrast to classes, *status groups* are normally communities. They are, however, often of an amorphous kind. In contrast to the purely economically determined "class situation" we wish to designate as "status situation" every typical component of the life fate of men that is determined by a specific, positive or negative, social estimation of *honor.* This honor may be connected with any quality share by a plurality, and, of course, it can be knit to a class situation: Class distinctions are linked in the most varied ways with status distinctions. Property as such is not always recognized as a status qualification, but in the long run it is, and with extraordinary regularity. In the subsistence economy of the organized neighborhood, very often the richest man is simply the chieftain. However, this often means only an honorific preference. For example, in the so-called pure modern "democracy," that is, one devoid of any expressly ordered status privileges for individuals, it may be that only the families coming under approximately the same tax class dance with one another. This example is reported of certain smaller Swiss cities. But status honor need not necessarily be linked with a "class situation." On the contrary, it normally stands in sharp opposition to the pretensions of sheer property.

Both propertied and propertyless people can belong to the same status group, and frequently they do with very tangible consequences. This "equality" of social esteem may, however, in the long run become quite precarious. The "equality" of status among the American "gentlemen," for instance, is expressed by the fact that outside the subordination determined by the different functions of "business," it would be considered strictly repugnant—wherever the old tradition still prevails—if even the richest "chief," while playing billiards or cards in his club in the evening, would not treat his "clerk" as in every sense fully his equal in birthright. It would be repugnant if the American "chief" would bestow upon his "clerk" the condescending "benevolence" marking a distinction of "position," which the German chief can never dissever from his attitude. This is one of the most important reasons why in America the German "clubby-ness" has never been able to attain the attraction that the American clubs have.

Guarantees of Status Stratification

In content, status honor is normally expressed by the fact that above all else a specific *style of life* can be expected from all those who wish to belong to the circle. Linked with this expectation are restrictions on "social" intercourse (that is, intercourse which is not subservient to economic or any other of business's "functional" purposes). These restrictions may confine normal marriages to within the status circle and may lead to complete endogamous closure. As soon as there is not a mere individual and socially irrelevant imitation of another style of life, but an agreed-upon communal action of this closing character, the "status" development is under way.

In its characteristic form, stratification by "status groups" on the basis of conventional styles of life evolves at the present time in the United States out of the traditional democracy. For example, only the resident of a certain street ("the street") is considered as belonging to "society," is qualified for social intercourse, and is visited and invited. Above all, this differentiation evolves in such a way as to make for strict submission to the fashion that is dominant at a given time in society. This submission to fashion also exists among men in America to a degree unknown in Germany. Such submission is considered to be an indication of the fact that a given man *pretends* to qualify as a gentleman. This submission decides, at least *prima facie,* that he will be treated as such. And this recognition becomes just as important for his employment chances in "swank" establishments, and above all, for social intercourse and marriage with "esteemed" families, as the qualification for dueling among Germans in the Kaiser's day. As for the rest: certain families resident for a long time, and, of course, correspondingly wealthy, e.g., "F.F.V., i.e. First Families of Virginia," or the actual or alleged descendants of the "Indian Princes" Pocahontas, of the Pilgrim fathers, or of the Knickerbockers, the members of almost inaccessible sects and all sorts of circles setting themselves apart by means of any other characteristics and badges—all these elements usurp "status" honor. The development of status is essentially a question of stratification resting upon usurpation. Such usurpation is the normal origin of almost all status honor. But the road from this purely conventional situation to legal privilege, positive or negative, is easily traveled as soon as a certain stratification of the social order has in fact been "lived in" and has achieved stability by virtue of a stable distribution of economic power.

. . .
Status Privileges

For all practical purposes, stratification by status goes hand in hand with a monopolization of ideal and material goods or opportunities, in a manner we have come to know as typical. Besides the specific status honor, which always rests upon distance and exclusiveness, we find all sorts of material monopolies. Such honorific preferences may consist of the privilege of wearing special costumes, of eating special dishes taboo to others, of carrying arms—which is most obvious in its consequences—the right to pursue certain non-professional dilettante artistic practices, e.g., to play certain musical instruments. Of course, material monopolies provide the most effective motives for the exclusiveness of a status group; although, in themselves, they are rarely sufficient, almost always they come into play to some extent. Within a status circle there is the question of intermarriage: The interest of the families in the monopolization of potential bridegrooms is at least of equal importance and is parallel to the interest in the monopolization of daughters. The daughters of the circle must be provided for. With an increased inclosure of the status group, the conventional preferential opportunities for special employment grow into a legal monopoly of special offices for the members. Certain goods become objects for monopolization by status groups. In the typical fashion these include "entailed estates" and frequently also the possessions of serfs or bondsmen and, finally, special trades. This monopolization occurs positively when the status group is exclusively entitled to own and to manage them; and negatively when, in order to maintain its specific way of life, the status group must *not* own and manage them.

The decisive role of a "style of life" in status "honor" means that status groups are the specific bearers of all "conventions." In whatever way it may be manifest, all "stylization" of life either originates in status groups or is at least conserved by them. Even if the principles of status conventions differ greatly, they reveal certain typical traits, especially among those strata which are most privileged. Quite generally, among privileged status groups there is a status disqualification that operates against the performance of common physical labor. This disqualification is now "setting in" in America against the old tradition of esteem for labor. Very frequently every rational economic pursuit, and especially "entrepreneurial activity," is looked upon as a disqualification of status. Artistic and literary activity is also considered as degrading work as soon as it is exploited for income, or at least when it is connected with hard physical exertion. An example is the sculptor working like a mason in his dusty smock as over against the painter in his salon-like "studio" and those forms of musical practice that are acceptable to the status group.

Note

1. *Wirtschaft and Gesellschaft,* part III, chap. 4, pp. 631–40. The first sentence in paragraph one and the several definitions in this chapter which are in brackets do not appear in the original text. They have been taken from other contexts of *Wirtschaft und Gesellschaft.*

Name: _____ Class: _____

Date: _____ Section: _____

Reading Comprehension Activity Sheet

Class, Status, Party, Max Weber

1. Briefly describe the types of "class struggle" demonstrated by Weber. _____

_____
_____
_____
_____
_____
_____
_____
_____
_____
_____
_____

2. How does Weber distinguish "class" from "status"? _____

_____
_____
_____
_____
_____
_____
_____
_____
_____
_____
_____

3. How does "stratification by status" develop?

The Uses of Poverty: The Poor Pay All

Herbert J. Gans

Some twenty years ago Robert K. Merton applied the notion of functional analysis to explain the continuing though maligned existence of the urban political machine: if it continued to exist, perhaps it fulfilled latent—unintended or unrecognized—positive functions. Clearly it did. Merton pointed out how the political machine provided central authority to get things done when a decentralized local government could not act, humanized the services of the impersonal bureaucracy for fearful citizens, offered concrete help (rather than abstract law or justice) to the poor, and otherwise performed services needed or demanded by many people but considered unconventional or even illegal by formal public agencies.

Today, poverty is more maligned than the political machine ever was; yet it, too, is a persistent social phenomenon. Consequently, there may be some merit in applying functional analysis to poverty, in asking whether it also has positive functions that explain its persistence.

Merton defined functions as "those observed consequences [of a phenomenon] which make for the adaptation or adjustment of a given [social] system." I shall use a slightly different definition; instead of identifying functions for an entire social system, I shall identify them for the interest groups, socio-economic classes, and other population aggregates with shared values that "inhabit" a social system. I suspect that in a modern heterogeneous society, few phenomena are functional or dysfunctional for the society as a whole, and that most result in benefits to some groups and costs to others. Nor are any phenomena indispensable; in most instances, one can suggest what Merton calls "functional alternatives" or equivalents for them, i.e., other social patterns or policies that achieve the same positive functions but avoid the dysfunctions.

From *Social Policy*, by Herbert J. Gans. Copyright © 1971 by Social Policy Corporation. Reprinted by permission.

Associating poverty with positive functions seems at first glance to be unimaginable. Of course, the slumlord and the loan shark are commonly known to profit from the existence of poverty, but they are viewed as evil men, so their activities are classified among the dysfunctions of poverty. However, what is less often recognized, at least by the conventional wisdom, is that poverty also makes possible the existence or expansion of respectable professions and occupations, for example, penology, criminology, social work, and public health. More recently, the poor have provided jobs for professional and paraprofessional "poverty warriors," and for journalists and social scientists, this author included, who have supplied the information demanded by the revival of public interest in poverty.

Clearly, then, poverty and the poor may well satisfy a number of positive functions for many nonpoor groups in American society. I shall describe thirteen such functions—economic, social and political—that seem to me most significant.

The Functions of Poverty

First, the existence of poverty ensures that society's "dirty work" will be done. Every society has such work: physically dirty or dangerous, temporary, dead-end and underpaid, undignified and menial jobs. Society can fill these jobs by paying higher wages for "clean" work, or it can force people who have no other choice to do the dirty work—and at low wages. In America, poverty functions to provide a low-wage labor pool that is willing—or rather, unable to be *un*willing—to perform dirty work at low cost. Indeed, this function of the poor is so important that in some Southern states, welfare payments have been cut off during the summer months when the poor are needed to work in the fields. Moreover, much of the debate about the Negative Income Tax and the Family Assistance Plan [welfare programs] has concerned their impact on the work incentive, by which is actually meant the incentive of the poor to do the needed dirty work if the wages therefrom are no larger than the income grant. Many economic activities that involve dirty work depend on the poor for their existence: restaurants, hospitals, parts of the garment industry, and "truck farming," among others, could not persist in their present form without the poor.

Second, because the poor are required to work at low wages, they subsidize a variety of economic activities that benefit the affluent. For example, domestics subsidize the upper middle and upper classes, making life easier for their employers and freeing affluent women for a variety of professional, cultural, civic and partying activities. Similarly, because the poor pay a higher proportion of their income in property and sales taxes, among others, they subsidize many state and local governmental services that benefit more affluent groups. In addition, the poor support innovation in medical practice as patients in teaching and research hospitals and as guinea pigs in medical experiments.

Third, poverty creates jobs for a number of occupations and professions that serve or "service" the poor, or protect the rest of society from them. As already noted, penology would be minuscule without the poor, as would the police. Other activities and groups that flourish because of the existence of poverty are the numbers game, the sale of heroin and cheap wines and liquors, Pentecostal ministers, faith healers, prostitutes, pawn shops, and the peacetime army, which recruits its enlisted men mainly from among the poor.

Fourth, the poor buy goods others do not want and thus prolong the economic usefulness of such goods—day-old bread, fruit and vegetables that otherwise would have to be thrown out, secondhand clothes, and deteriorating automobiles and buildings. They also provide incomes for doctors, lawyers, teachers, and others who are too old, poorly trained or incompetent to attract more affluent clients.

In addition to economic functions, the poor perform a number of social functions:

Fifth, the poor can be identified and punished as alleged or real deviants in order to uphold the legitimacy of conventional norms. To justify the desirability of hard work, thrift, honesty, and monogamy, for example, the defenders of these norms must be able to find people who can be accused of being lazy, spendthrift, dishonest, and promiscuous. Although there is some evidence that the poor are about as moral and law-abiding as anyone else, they are more likely than middle-class transgressors to be caught and punished when they participate in deviant acts. Moreover, they lack the political and cultural power to correct the stereotypes that other people hold of them and thus continue to be thought of as lazy, spendthrift, etc., by those who need living proof that moral deviance does not pay.

Sixth, and conversely, the poor offer vicarious participation to the rest of the population in the uninhibited sexual, alcoholic, and narcotic behavior in which they are alleged to participate and which, being freed from the constraints of affluence, they are often thought to enjoy more than the middle classes. Thus many people, some social scientists included, believe that the poor not only are more given to uninhibited behavior (which may be true, although it is often motivated by despair more than by lack of inhibition) but derive more pleasure from it than affluent people (which research by Lee Rainwater, Walter Miller and others shows to be patently untrue). However, whether the poor actually have more sex and enjoy it more is irrelevant; so long as middle-class people believe this to be true, they can participate in it vicariously when instances are reported in a factual or fictional form.

Seventh, the poor also serve a direct cultural function when culture created by or for them is adopted by the more affluent. The rich often collect artifacts from extinct folk cultures of poor people; and almost all Americans listen to the blues, Negro spirituals, and country music, which originated among the Southern poor. Recently they have enjoyed the rock styles that were born, like the Beatles, in the slums, and in the last year, poetry written by ghetto children has become popular in literary circles. The poor also serve as culture heroes, particularly, of course, to the Left; but the hobo, the cowboy, the hipster, and the mythical prostitute with a heart of gold have performed this function for a variety of groups.

Eighth, poverty helps to guarantee the status of those who are not poor. In every hierarchical society, someone has to be at the bottom; but in American society, in which social mobility is an important goal for many and people need to know where they stand, the poor function as a reliable and relatively permanent measuring rod for status comparisons. This is particularly true for the working class, whose politics is influenced by the need to maintain status distinctions between themselves and the poor, much as the aristocracy must find ways of distinguishing itself from the *nouveaux riches.*

Ninth, the poor also aid the upward mobility of groups just above them in the class hierarchy. Thus a goodly number of Americans have entered the middle class through the profits earned from the provision of goods and services in the slums, including illegal or nonrespectable ones that upper-class and upper-middle-class businessmen shun because of their low prestige. As a result, members of almost every immigrant group have financed their upward mobility by providing slum housing, entertainment, gambling, narcotics, etc., to later arrivals—most recently to blacks and Puerto Ricans.

Tenth, the poor help to keep the aristocracy busy, thus justifying its continued existence. "Society" uses the poor as clients of settlement houses and beneficiaries of charity affairs; indeed, the aristocracy must have the poor to demonstrate its superiority over other elites who devote themselves to earning money.

Eleventh, the poor, being powerless, can be made to absorb the costs of change and growth in American society. During the nineteenth century, they did the backbreaking work that build the cities; today, they are pushed out of their neighborhoods to make room for "progress." Urban renewal projects to hold middle-class taxpayers in the city and expressways to enable suburbanites to commute downtown have typically been located in poor neighborhoods, since no other group will allow itself to be displaced. For the same reason, universities, hospitals, and civic centers also expand into land occupied by the poor. The major costs of the industrialization of agriculture have been borne by the poor, who are pushed off the land without recompense; and they have paid a large share of the human cost of the growth of American power overseas, for they have provided many of the foot soldiers for Vietnam and other wars.

Twelfth, the poor facilitate and stabilize the American political process. Because they vote and participate in politics less than other groups, the political system is often free to ignore them. Moreover, since they can rarely support Republicans, they often provide the Democrats with a captive constituency that has no other place to go. As a result, the Democrats can count on their votes, and be more responsive to voters—for example, the white working class—who might otherwise switch to the Republicans.

Thirteenth, the role of the poor in upholding conventional norms (see the *fifth* point, above) also has a significant political function. An economy based on the ideology of laissez faire requires a deprived populations that is allegedly unwilling to work or that can be considered inferior because it must accept charity or welfare in order to survive. Not only does the alleged moral deviancy of the poor reduce the moral pressure on the present political economy to eliminate poverty but socialist alternatives can be made to look quite unattractive if those who will benefit most from them can be descried as lazy, spendthrift, dishonest and promiscuous.

The Alternatives

I have described thirteen of the more important functions poverty and the poor satisfy in American society, enough to support the functionalist thesis that poverty, like any other social phenomenon, survives in part because it is useful to society or some of its parts. This analysis is not intended to suggest that because it is often functional, poverty *should* exist, or that it *must* exist. For one thing, poverty has many more dysfunctions that functions; for another, it is possible to suggest functional alternatives.

For example, society's dirty work could be done without poverty, either by automation or by paying "dirty workers" decent wages. Nor is it necessary for the poor to subsidize the many activities they support through their low-wage jobs. This would, however, drive up the costs of these activities, which would result in higher prices to their customers and clients. Similarly, many of the professionals who flourish because of the poor could be given other roles. Social workers could provide counseling to the affluent, as they prefer to do anyway; and the police could devote themselves to traffic and organized crime. Other roles would have to be found for badly trained or incompetent professionals now relegated to serving the poor, and someone else would have to pay their salaries. Fewer penologists would be employable, however. And Pentecostal religion probably could not survive without the poor—nor would parts of the second- and third-hand goods market. And in many cities, "used" housing that no one else wants would then have to be torn down at public expense.

Alternatives for the cultural functions of the poor could be found more easily and cheaply. Indeed, entertainers, hippies, and adolescents are already serving as the deviants needed to uphold traditional morality and as devotees of orgies to "staff" the fantasies of vicarious participation.

The status functions of the poor are another matter. In a hierarchical society, some people must be defined as inferior to everyone else with respect to a variety of attributes, but they need not be poor in the absolute sense. One could conceive of a society in which the "lower class," though last in the pecking order, received 75 percent of the median income, rather than 15–40 percent, as is now the case. Needless to say, this would require considerable income redistribution.

The contribution the poor make to the upward mobility of the groups that provide them with goods and services could also be maintained without the poor's having such low incomes. However, it is true that if the poor were more affluent, they would have access to enough capital to take over the provider role, thus competing with and perhaps rejecting the "outsiders." (Indeed, owing in part to antipoverty programs, this is already happening in a number of ghettos, where white storeowners are being replaced by blacks.) Similarly, if the poor were more affluent, they would make less willing clients for upper-class philanthropy, although some would still use settlement houses to achieve upward mobility, as they do now. Thus "Society" could continue to run its philanthropic activities.

The political functions of the poor would be more difficult to replace. With increased affluence the poor would probably obtain more political power and be more active politically. With higher incomes and more political power, the poor would be likely to resist paying the costs of growth and change. Of course, it is possible to imagine urban renewal and highway projects that properly reimburse the displaced people, but such projects would then become considerably more expensive, and many might never be built. This, in turn, would reduce the comfort and convenience of those who now benefit from urban renewal and expressways. Finally, hippies could serve also as more deviants to justify the existing political economy—as they already do. Presumably, however, if poverty were eliminated, there would be fewer attacks on that economy.

In sum, then, many of the functions served by the poor could be replaced if poverty were eliminated, but almost always at higher costs to others, particularly more affluent others. Consequently, a functional analysis must conclude that poverty persists not only because it fulfills a number of positive functions but also because many of the functional alternatives to poverty would be quite dysfunctional for the affluent members of society. A functional analysis thus ultimately arrives at much the same conclusion as radical sociology, except that radical thinkers treat as manifest what I describe as latent: that social phenomena that are functional for affluent or powerful groups and dysfunctional for poor or powerless ones persist; that when the elimination of such phenomena through functional alternatives would generate dysfunctions for the affluent or powerful, they will continue to persist; and that phenomena like poverty can be eliminated only when they become dysfunctional for the affluent or powerful, or when the powerless can obtain enough power to change society.

Postscript

Over the years, this article has been interpreted as either a direct attack on functionalism or a tongue-in-cheek satirical comment on it. Neither interpretation is true. I wrote the article for two reasons. First and foremost, I wanted to point out that there are, unfortunately, positive functions of poverty which have to be dealt with by antipoverty policy. Second, I was trying to show that functionalism is not the inherently conservative approach for which it has often been criticized, but that it can be employed in liberal and radical analyses.

Name: _____ Class: _____

Date: _____ Section: _____

Reading Comprehension Activity Sheet

The Uses of Poverty: The Poor Pay All, Herbert H. Gans

1. Gans states that poverty and the poor provide numerous functions or benefits for many non-poor groups in our society. Briefly describe the economic functions of poverty. _____

_____

_____

_____

_____

_____

_____

_____

_____

_____

_____

2. What are the social functions of poverty? _____

_____

_____

_____

_____

_____

_____

_____

_____

_____

_____

3. How could the functions of poverty be replaced if poverty were eliminated? _____

chapter 8

Gender

Sex and Temperament in Three Primitive Societies:
The Malleability of Gender Roles
Margaret Mead

Sexual Terrorism
Carole J. Sheffield

Sex and Temperament in Three Primitive Societies: The Malleability of Gender Roles

Margaret Mead

The Pacific Islands are an area where groups of men separated from each other by sea and mountain range, and lacking those political forms which bind men together into kingdoms, have developed strikingly different ways of life. . . .

The Mountain Arapesh

The mountain Arapesh are a mild, undernourished people who live in the steep, unproductive Torricelli Mountains of New Guinea, poor themselves, and always struggling to save enough to buy music and dance-steps and new fashions from the trading peoples of the seacoast, and to buy off the sorcerers among the fiercer people of the interior plains. Responsive and cooperative, they have developed a society in which, while there is never enough to eat, each man spends most of his time helping his neighbor, and committed to his neighbor's purposes. The greatest interest of both men and women is in growing things—children, pigs, coconut-trees—and their greatest fear that each generation will reach maturity shorter in stature than their forebears, until finally there will be no people under the palm-trees.

The Arapesh treat a baby as a soft, vulnerable, precious little object, to be protected, fed, cherished. Not only the mother, but the father also, must play this overall protective role. After birth the father abstains from work and sleeps beside the mother, and he must abstain from intercourse while the child is young, even with his other wife. . . .

From *Male and Female* by Margaret Mead. Copyright © 1949 by Margaret Mead. Reprinted by permission of HarperCollins Publishers, Inc. The excerpt combines text from *Male and Female* and *Sex and Temperament in Three Primitive Societies,* also by Margaret Mead.

The Arapesh system . . . [places] emphasis on the maternal, parental aspects of both men and women. Arapesh men and women are both snugly at home in their small mountain huts, caring together for their children. They have no use for a men's house except for ceremonials, and large houses are hard to build. Labour is always scarce and might better be put into feeding children. All the rites have been rephrased as protective, and the men keep the fierce impersonations of the supernatural guardian of the men's cult from showing his fierceness towards the women, and if possible, towards the initiates.

In such a society, small boys and girls grow up together, with parents of both sexes always before their eyes as models. Boys know that they are boys by their bodies, their names, and the skills they learn. Girls know they are girls by their bodies, their names, and the little carrying-bags that their mothers place on their heads. Both sexes sit happily around the fires on chill mornings and bubble their lips. Little girls see their mothers carry loads in net bags, and little boys see their fathers carry them on carrying-poles. . . . Both boys and girls have to guard their growth so that they will both be good parents. They will both be depleted by parenthood, a man no less than a woman. "You should have seen what a fine-looking man he was before he had all those children."

But what happens to the Arapesh male? What kind of preparation is it for living in the rough mountain country of New Guinea, surrounded by tribes who are fierce head-hunters and blackmailing sorcerers, to have learned that the major relationship to other people is either one of passive receptivity or one of provision of food and drink? He does not, within his own society, become a homosexual, although there is great ease and warmth and much giggling puppyishness among boys. But the reverse attitude—the desire to dominate, to intrude, which would provide a basis for active homosexuality—is too slightly cultivated, nor is there enough development of assertive resentment of passivity to fit into a type of homosexuality where active and passive roles are interchanged. The men in adulthood develop into heterosexual males. . . . They engage very little in warfare, they permit themselves to be blackmailed and bullied and intimidated and bribed by their more aggressive neighbors; they admire so deeply the artistic products of others that they have developed practically no art of their own. . . .

The Cannibal Mundugumor of the Yuat River

These robust, restive people live on the banks of a swiftly flowing river, but with no river lore. They trade with and prey upon the miserable, underfed bush-peoples who live on poorer land, devote their time to quarrelling and headhunting, and have developed a form of social organization in which every man's hand is against every other man. The women are as assertive and vigorous as the men; they detest bearing and rearing children, and provide most of the food, leaving the men free to plot and fight.

The Mundugumor women actively dislike child-bearing, and they dislike children. Children are carried in harsh opaque baskets that scratch their skins, later, high on their mother's shoulders, well away from the breast. Mothers nurse their children standing up, pushing them away as soon as they are the least bit satisfied. The occasional adopted newborn child is kept sharply hungry, so as to suck vigorously on a woman's breast until milk comes in. Here we find a character developing that stresses angry, eager avidity. In later life love-making is conducted like the first round of a prize-fight, and biting and scratching are important parts of foreplay. When the Mundugumor captured an enemy they ate him, and laughed as they told of it afterwards. When a Mundugumor became so angry that his anger turned even against himself, he got into a canoe and drifted down the river to be eaten by the next tribe. . . .

Boys and girls alike grow up in a world that is hostile and divided against itself. Boys are taught their place in society, their kinship terms, and elaborate sets of kinship prohibitions by their mothers, girls by their fathers. Both sexes are independent, hostile, vigorous, and both boys and girls come out with very similar personalities. There is no men's house in which all the men gather, for no two men sit down comfortably together. The unit of society is the compound, where a man's wives maintain an uneasy cooperation and his daughters a certain degree of solidarity, while each mother turns her son into an enemy both of his father and of his half-brothers. [The] initiation [rite into adulthood] is no longer a collective act in which males are welded together, but a display given by an important man, in which those who have not been initiated, whatever their age, can be cut and bullied by the already initiated. Girls are permitted to be initiated merely by observing taboos.

In such a society women are handicapped by their womanly qualities. Pregnancy and nursing are hated and avoided if possible, and men detest their wives for being pregnant. Men see women as a kind of human being over whom they will have to fight and through whom they can be injured. If one has no sister to give in exchange one will have to pay a valuable flute for a wife, and so we come to the curious position that flutes, those excessively male symbols of the male cult, which elsewhere can never be seen by women without endangering the entire male society, are equated with women, are nearly but not quite as valuable as women, and are something that women are permitted to see with less fuss than boys. The boys' whole concept of their identity is that of fighting males tied precariously through women to other fighting males. Women are masculinized to a point where every feminine feature is a drawback except their highly specific genital sexuality, men to a point where any aspect of their personalities that might hold an echo of the feminine or the maternal is a vulnerability and a liability.

The Lake-Dwelling Tchambuli

The Tchambuli people, who number only six hundred in all, have built their houses along the edge of one of the loveliest of New Guinea lakes, which gleams like polished ebony, with a backdrop of the distant hills behind which the Arapesh live. In the lake are purple lotus and great pink and white water lilies, white osprey and blue heron. Here the Tchambuli women, brisk, unadorned, managing and industrious, fish and go to market; the men, decorative and adorned, carve and paint and practice dance steps, their head-hunting tradition replaced by the simpler practice of buying victims to validate their manhood.

Adult males in Tchambuli are skittish, wary of each other, interested in art, in the theater, in a thousand petty bits of insult and gossip. Hurt feelings are rampant, not [a] violent angry response . . . but the pettishness of those who feel themselves weak and isolated. The men wear lovely ornaments, they do the shopping, they carve and paint and dance. Before the coming of British control head-hunting had been reduced to the ritual killing of bought captives, and they put up no effective resistance against the depreciations of the neighbouring Iatmuls, but fled inland instead, only to return when the Pax Britannica made it possible. Men whose hair was long enough wore curls, and the others made false curls out of rattan rings.

This is the only society in which I have worked where little girls of ten and eleven were more alertly intelligent and more enterprising than little boys. . . . in Tchambuli the minds of small males, teased, pampered, neglected, and isolated, had a fitful fleeting quality, and inability to come to grips with anything.

The Standardization of Sex-Temperament

We have now considered in detail the approved personalities of each sex among three primitive peoples. We found the Arapesh—both men and women—displaying a personality that, out of our historically limited preoccupations, we would call maternal in its parental aspects, and feminine in its sexual aspects. We found men, as well as women, trained to be cooperative, unaggressive, responsive to the needs and demands of others. We found no idea that sex was a powerful driving force either for men or for women. In marked contrast to these attitudes, we found among the Mundugumor that both men and women developed as ruthless, aggressive, positively sexed individuals, with the maternal cherishing aspects of personality at a minimum. Both men and women approximated to a personality type that we in our culture would find only in an undisciplined and very violent male. Neither the Arapesh nor the Mundugumor profit by a contrast between the sexes; the Arapesh ideal is the mild, responsive man married to the mild, responsive woman; the Mundugumor ideal is the violent aggressive man married to the violent aggressive woman. In the third, the Tchambuli, we found a genuine reversal of the attitudes of our own culture, with the woman the dominant, personal, managing partner, the man the less responsible and the emotionally dependent person. These three situations suggest, then, a very definite conclusion. If those mental attitudes which we have traditionally regarded as feminine—such as passivity, responsiveness, and a willingness to cherish children—can so easily be set up as the masculine pattern in one tribe, and in another be outlawed for the majority of women as well as for the majority of men, we no longer have any basis for regarding such aspects of behaviour as sex-linked. And this conclusion becomes even stronger when we consider the actual reversal in

Tchambuli of the position of dominance of the two sexes, in spite of the existence of formal patrilineal institutions.

The material suggests that we may say that many, if not all, of the personality traits which we have called masculine or feminine are as lightly linked to sex as are the clothing, the manners, and the form of head-dress that a society at a given period assigns to either sex. When we consider the behaviour of the typical Arapesh man or woman as contrasted with the behaviour of the typical Mundugumor man or woman, the evidence is overwhelmingly in favor of the strength of social conditioning. In no other way can we account for the almost complete uniformity with which Arapesh children develop into contented, passive, secure persons, while Mundugumor children develop characteristically into violent, aggressive, insecure persons. Only to the impact of the whole of the integrated culture upon the growing child can we lay the formation of the contrasting types. There is no other explanation of race, or diet, or selection that can be adduced to explain them. We are forced to conclude that human nature is almost unbelievably malleable, responding accurately and contrastingly to contrasting cultural conditions. The differences between individuals who are members of different cultures, like the difference between individuals within a culture, are almost entirely to be laid to differences in conditioning, especially during early childhood, and the form of this conditioning is culturally determined. Standardized personality differences between the sexes are of this order, cultural creations to which each generation, male and female, is trained to conform. . . .

If we then accept this evidence drawn from these simple societies which through centuries of isolation from the main stream of human history have been able to develop more extreme, more striking cultures than is possible under historical conditions of great intercommunication between peoples and the resulting heterogeneity, what are the implications of these results? What conclusions can we draw from a study of the way in which a culture can select a few traits from the wide gamut of human endowment and specialize these traits, either for one sex or for the entire community? . . . [M]ale and female personality are socially produced.

Name: _____   Class: _____

Date: _____   Section: _____

Reading Comprehension Activity Sheet

Sex and Temperament in Three Primitive Societies: The Malleability of Gender Roles, Margaret Mead

1. Compare and contrast the gender lifestyles of the Arapesh, Mundugumor, and Tchambuli peoples.

   _____
   _____
   _____
   _____
   _____
   _____
   _____
   _____
   _____
   _____
   _____

2. Based on Mead's analysis, describe how gender is "socially constructed." _____

   _____
   _____
   _____
   _____
   _____
   _____
   _____
   _____
   _____
   _____
   _____
   _____

Sexual Terrorism

Carole J. Sheffield

The right of men to control the female body is a cornerstone of patriarchy, it is expressed by their efforts to control pregnancy and childbirth and to define female health care in general. Male opposition to abortion is rooted in opposition to female autonomy. Violence and the threat of violence against females represent the need of patriarchy to deny that a woman's body is her own property and that no one should have access to it without her consent. Violence and its corollary, fear, serve to terrorize females and to maintain the patriarchal definition of woman's place.

The word *terrorism* invokes images of furtive organizations of the far right or left, whose members blow up buildings and cars, hijack airplanes, and murder innocent people in some country other than ours. But there is a different kind of terrorism, one that so pervades our culture that we have learned to live with it as though it were the natural order of things. Its target is females—of all ages, races, and classes. It is the common characteristic of rape, wife battery, incest, pornography, harassment, and all forms of sexual violence. I call it *sexual terrorism* because it is a system by which males frighten and, by frightening, control and dominate females.

The concept of terrorism captured my attention in an "ordinary" event. One afternoon I collected my laundry and went to a nearby laundromat. The place is located in a small shopping center on a very busy highway. After I had loaded and started the machines, I became acutely aware of my environment. It was just after 6:00 P.M. and dark, the other stores were closed, the laundromat was brightly lit, and my car was the only one in the lot. Anyone passing by could readily see that I was alone and isolated. Knowing that rape is often a crime of opportunity, I became terrified. I wanted to leaven and find a laundromat that was busier, but my clothes were well into the wash cycle, and, besides, I felt I was being "silly," "paranoid." The feeling of terror persisted, so I sat in my car, windows up and doors locked. When the wash was completed, I dashed in, threw the clothes into the dryer, and ran back out to

From *Women: A Feminist Perspective*, by Carole J. Sheffield. Copyright © 1995 by Carole J. Sheffield. Reprinted by permission.

my car. When the clothes were dry, I tossed them recklessly into the basket and hurriedly drove away to fold them in the security of my home.

Although I was not victimized in a direct, physical way or by objective or measurable standards, I felt victimized. It was, for me, a terrifying experience. I felt controlled by an invisible force. I was angry that something as commonplace as doing laundry after a day's work jeopardized my well-being. Mostly I was angry at being unfree: a hostage of a culture that, for the most part, encourages violence against females, instructs men in the methodology of sexual violence, and proves them with ready justification for their violence. I was angry that I could be victimized by being "in the wrong place at the wrong time." The essence of terrorism is that one never knows when is the wrong time and where is the wrong place.

Following my experience at the laundromat, I talked with my students about terrorization. Women students began to open up and reveal terrors that they had kept secret because of embarrassment: fears of jogging alone, shopping alone, going to the movies alone. One woman recalled feelings of terror in her adolescence when she did child care for extra money. Nothing had ever happened, and she had not been afraid of anyone in particular, but she had felt a vague terror when being driven home late at night by the man of the house.

The male students listened incredulously and then demanded equal time. The harder they tried, the more they realized how very different—qualitatively, quantitatively, and contextually—their fears were. All agreed that, while they experienced fear in a violent society, they did not experience terror, nor did they experience fear of rape or sexual mutilation. They felt more in control, either from a psychophysical sense of security that they could defend themselves or from a confidence in being able to determine wrong places and times. All the women admitted feeling fear and anxiety when walking to their cars on the campus, especially after an evening class or activity. None of the men experienced fear on campus at any time. The men could be rather specific in describing where they were afraid: in Harlem, for example, or in certain parts of downtown Newark, New Jersey—places that have a reputation for violence. But either they could avoid these places or they felt capable of self-protective action. Above all, male students said that they *never* feared being attacked simply because they were male. They *never* feared going to a movie or to a mall alone. Their daily activities were not characterized by a concern for their physical integrity.

The differences between men's and women's experiences of fear underscore the meaning of sexual terrorism: that women's lives are bounded by both the reality of pervasive sexual danger and the fear that reality engenders. In her study of rape, Susan Brownmiller argues that rape is "nothing more or less than a conscious process of intimidation by which all men keep all women in a state of fear."[1] In their study *The Female Fear,* Margaret T. Gordon and Stephanie Riger found that one-third of women said they worry at least once a month about being raped. Many said they worry daily about the possibility of being raped. When they think about rape, they feel terrified and somewhat paralyzed. A third of women indicated that the fear of rape is "part of the background" of their lives and "one of those things that's always there." Another third claimed they never worried about rape but reported taking precautions, "sometimes elaborate ones," to try to avoid being raped: Indeed, women's attempts to avoid sexual intrusion take many forms. To varying degrees, women change and restrict their behavior, life-styles, and physical appearances. They will pay higher costs for housing and transportation and even make educational and career choices to attempt to minimize sexual victimization.

Sexual terrorism includes nonviolent sexual intimidation and the threat of violence as well as overt sexual violence. For example, although an act of rape, an unnecessary hysterectomy, and the publishing of *Playboy* magazine appear to be quite different, they are in fact more similar than dissimilar. Each is based on fear, hostility, and a need to dominate women. Rape is an act of aggression and possession. Unnecessary hysterectomies are extraordinary abuses of power rooted in men's concept of women as primarily reproductive beings and in their need to asset power over that reproduction. *Playboy,* like all forms of pornography, attempts to control women through the power of definition. Male pornographers define women's sexuality for their male customers. The basis of pornography is men's fantasies about women's sexuality.

Components of Sexual Terrorism

The literature on terrorism does not provide a precise definition. Mine is taken from hacker, who says that "terrorism aims to frighten, and by frightening, to dominate and control."[2] Writers agree more readily on the characteristics and functions of terrorism than on a definition. This analysis will focus on five components to illuminate the similarities and distinctions between sexual terrorism and political terrorism. The five components are ideology, propaganda, indiscriminate and amoral violence, voluntary compliance, and society's perception of the terrorist and the terrorized.

And *ideology* is an integrated set of beliefs about the world that explains the way things are and provides a vision of how they ought to be. Patriarchy, meaning the "rule of the fathers," is the ideological foundation of sexism in our society. It asserts the superiority of males and the inferiority females. It also provides the rationale for sexual terrorism. The taproot of patriarchy is the masculine/warrior ideal. Masculinity must include not only a proclivity for violence but also all those characteristics claimed by warriors: aggression, control, emotional reserve, rationality, sexual potency, etc. Marc Feigen Fasteau, in *The Male Machine,* argues that "men are brought up with the idea that there ought to be some part of them, under control until released by necessity, that thrives on violence. This capacity, even affinity, for violence, lurking beneath the surface of every real man, is supposed to represent the primal untamed base of masculinity."[3]

Propaganda is the methodical dissemination of information for the purpose of promoting a particular ideology. Propaganda, by definition, is biased or even false information. Its purpose is to present one point of view on a subject and to discredit opposing points of view. Propaganda is essential to the conduct of terrorism. According to Francis Watson, in

Political Terrorism: The Threat and the Response, "Terrorism must not be defined only in terms of violence, but also in terms of propaganda. The two are in operation together. Violence of terrorism is a coercive means for attempting to influence the thinking and actions of people. Propaganda is a persuasive means for doing the same thing."[4] The propaganda of sexual terrorism is found in all expressions of the popular culture: films, television, music, literature, advertising, pornography. The propaganda of sexual terrorism is also found in the ideas of patriarchy expressed in science, medicine, and psychology.

The third component, which is common to all forms of political terrorism, consists of "indiscriminateness, unpredictability, arbitrariness, ruthless destructiveness and amorality."[5] Indiscriminate violence and amorality are also at the heart of sexual terrorism. Every female is a potential target of violence—at any age, at any time, in any place. Further, as we shall see, amorality pervades sexual violence. Child molesters, incestuous fathers, wife beaters, and rapists often do not understand that they have done anything wrong. Their views are routinely shared by police officers, lawyers, and judges, and crimes of sexual violence are rarely punished in American society.

The fourth component of the theory of terrorism is voluntary compliance. The institutionalization of a system of terror requires the development of mechanisms other than sustained violence to achieve its goals. Violence must be employed to maintain terrorism, but sustained violence can be costly and debilitating. Therefore, strategies for ensuring a significant degree of voluntary compliance must be developed. Sexual terrorism is maintained to a great extent by an elaborate system of sex-role socialization that in effect instructs men to be terrorists in the name of masculinity and women to be victims in the name of femininity.

Sexual and political terrorism differ in the final component, perceptions, of the terrorist and the victim. In political terrorism we know who is the terrorist and who is the victim. We may condemn or condone the terrorist, depending on our political views, but we sympathize with the victim. In sexual terrorism, however, we blame the victim and excuse the offender. We believe that the offender either is "sick" and therefore in need of our compassion or is acting out normal male impulses.

Types of Sexual Terrorism

While the discussion that follows focuses on four types of sexual terrorism—rape, wife abuse, sexual abuse of children, and sexual harassment—recent feminist research has documented other forms of sexual terrorism, including threats of violence, flashing, street hassling, obscene phone calls, stalking, coercive sex, pornography, prostitution, sexual slavery, and femicide. What women experience as sexually intrusive and violent is not necessarily reflected in our legal codes, and those acts that are recognized as criminal are often not understood specifically as crimes against women—as acts of sexual violence.

Acts of sexual terrorism include many forms of intrusion that society accepts as common and are therefore trivialized. For example, a recent study of women's experiences of obscene phone calls found that women respondents overwhelmingly found these calls to be a form of sexual intimidation and harassment. While obscene phone calls are illegal, only in rare cases do women report them and the police take them seriously. In contrast, some forms of sexual terrorism are so extraordinary that they are regarded not only as aberrant but also as incomprehensible. The execution of fourteen women students at the University of Montreal on December 6, 1`989, is one example of this. Separating the men from the women in a classroom and shouting. "You're all fucking feminists," twenty-five-year-old Marc Lepine systematically murdered fourteen women. In his suicide letter, claiming "the feminists have always enraged me," Lepine recognized his crime as a political act. For many women, this one act of sexual terrorism galvanized attention to the phenomenon of the murder of women because they are women. "Femicide," according to Jane Caputi and Diane E. H. Russell, described "the murders of women by men motivated by hatred, contempt, pleasure, or a sense of ownership of women."[6] Most femicide, unlike the Montreal massacre, is committed by a male acquaintance, friend, or relative. In *Surviving Sexual Violence,* Liz Kelly argues that sexual violence must be understood as a continuum—that is, "a continuous series of events that pass into one another" united by a "basic common character." Viewing sexual violence in this way furthers an understanding of both the "ordinary" and "extraordinary" forms of sexual terrorism and the range of abuse that women experience in their lifetimes.

Many types of sexual terrorism are crimes, yet when we look at the history of these acts, we see that they came to be considered criminal not so much to protect women as to adjust power relationships among men. Rape was originally a violation of a father's or husband's property rights; consequently, a husband by definition could not rape his wife. Wife beating was condoned by the law and still is condemned in name only. Although proscriptions against incest exist, society assumes a more serious posture toward men who sexually abuse other men's daughters. Sexual harassment is now a crime, and only recently has it been declared an actionable civil offense. Crimes of sexual violence are characterized by ambiguity and diversity in definition and interpretation. Because each state and territory has a separate system of law in addition to the federal system, crimes and punishments are assessed differently throughout the country.

RAPE

Rape statutes have been reformed in the past decade, largely to remove the exemption for wife rape and to use gender-neutral language. The essence of the definition of rape, however, remains the same: sexual penetration (typically defined as penile-vaginal, but may include oral and anal sodomy or penetration by fingers or other objects) of a female by force or threat of force, against her will and without her consent.

Traditional views of rape are shaped by male views of sexuality and by men's fear of being unjustly accused. Deborah Rhode argues, in *Justice and Gender,* that this reflects a "sexual schizophrenia." That is, forced sexual intercourse by a stranger against a chaste woman is unquestionably regarded as a heinous crime, whereas coercive sex that does not fit this model is largely denied. Since most women are raped by men they know, this construction excludes many forms of rape.

Because rape is considered a sexual act, evidence of force and resistance is often necessary to establish the nonconsent needed to convict rapists. Such proof is not demanded of a victim of any other crime. If females do not resist rape as much as possible, "consent" is assumed.

By 1990, forty-two states had adopted laws criminalizing rape in marriage: sixteen states recognize that wife rape is a crime and provide no exemptions; twenty-six states penalize wife rape but allow for some exemptions under which husbands cannot be prosecuted for raping their wives. Eight states do not recognize wife rape as a crime. In spite of statutory reform, wife rape remains a greatly misunderstood phenomenon, and the magnitude of sexual abuse by husbands is not known. In Diana E. H. Russell's pioneering study on rape in marriage [*Rape in Marriage*]; 14 percent of the female respondents reported having been raped by their husbands. The prevalence of wife rape, however, is believed to be much higher; approximately 40 percent of women in battered women's shelters also report having been raped by their husbands. Victims of wife rape, according to one study, are at a greater risk of being murdered by their husbands, or of murdering them, than women who are physically but not sexually assaulted.

WIFE ABUSE

For centuries it has been assumed that a husband had the right to punish or discipline his wife with physical force. The popular expression "rule of thumb" originated from English common law, which allowed a husband to beat his wife with a whip or stick no bigger in diameter than his thumb. The husband's prerogative was incorporated into American law. Several states once had statutes that essentially allowed a man to beat his wife without interference from the courts.

In 1871, in the landmark case of *Fulgham v. State,* an Alabama court ruled that "the privilege, ancient though it be, to beat her with a stick, to pull her hair, choke her, spit in her face or kick her about the floor or to inflict upon her other like indignities, is not now acknowledged by our law."[7] The law, however, has been ambiguous and often contradictory on the issue of wife abuse. While the courts established that a man had no right to beat his wife, it also held that a woman could not press charges against her abusive husband. In 1910, the U.S. Supreme Court ruled that a wife could not charge her husband with assault and battery because it "would open the doors of the court to accusations of all sorts of one spouse against the other and bring into public notice complaints for assaults, slander and libel."[8] The courts virtually condoned violence for the purpose of maintaining peace.

Laws and public attitudes about the illegality of wife abuse and the rights of the victim have been slowly evolving. During the 1980s, there was a proliferation of new laws designed to address the needs of victims of domestic violence and to reform police and judicial responses to wife abuse. These measures include temporary or permanent protection orders, state-funded or state-assisted shelters, state-mandated data collection, and proarrest or mandatory arrest policies. Most states, however, continue to define domestic violence as a misdemeanor crime, carrying jail sentences of less than one year. Felony crimes are punishable by more than one year in jail, and police officers tend to arrest more often for felony offenses. The distinction between misdemeanor and felony crimes is also based on the use of weapons and the infliction of serious injuries. While wife abuse is still considered a misdemeanor crime, a National Crime Survey revealed that at least 50 percent of the domestic "simple assaults" involved bodily injury as serious as or more serious than 90 percent of all rapes, robberies, and aggravated assaults.

Sexual Abuse of Children

Defining sexual abuse of children is very difficult. The laws are complex and often contradictory. Generally, sexual abuse of children includes statutory rape, molestation, carnal knowledge, indecent liberties, impairing the morals of a minor, child abuse, child neglect, and incest. Each of these is defined, interpreted, and punished differently in each state.

The philosophy underlying statutory-rape laws is that a child below a certain age—arbitrarily fixed by law—is not able to give meaningful consent. Therefore, sexual intercourse with a female below a certain age, even with consent, is rape. Punishment for statutory rape, although rarely imposed, can be as high as life imprisonment. Coexistent with laws on statutory rape are laws on criminal incest. Incest is generally interpreted as sexual activity, most often intercourse, with a blood relative. The difference, then, between statutory rape and incest is the relation of the offender to the child. Statutory rape is committed by someone outside the family; incest, by a member of the family. The penalty for incest, also rarely imposed, is usually no more than ten years in prison. This contrast suggests that sexual abuse of children is tolerated when it occurs within the family and that unqualified protection of children from sexual assault is not the intent of the law.

SEXUAL HARASSMENT

Sexual harassment is a new term for an old phenomenon. The research on sexual harassment, as well as the legal interpretation, centers on acts of sexual coercion or intimidation on the job and at school. Lin Farley, in *Sexual Shakedown: The Sexual Harassment of Women on the Job,* describes sexual harassment as "unsolicited nonreciprocal male behavior that asserts a woman's sex role over her function as a worker. It can be any or all of the following: staring at, commenting upon, or touching a woman's body; requests for acquiescence in sexual behavior; repeated nonreciprocated propositions for dates; demands for sexual intercourse; and rape."[9]

In 1980 the Equal employment Opportunity Commission issued federal guidelines that defined sexual harassment as any behavior that "has the purpose or effect of unreasonably interfering with an individual's work performance or creating an intimidating or hostile or offensive environment." Such behavior can include "unwelcome sexual advances, requests for sexual favors, and other verbal or physical conduct of a sexual nature."[10] It was not until six years later, however, that the Supreme Court, in *Meritor Savings Bank FSB v. Vinson,* ruled that sexual harassment was a form of sex discrimination under Title VII of the Civil Rights Act of 1964.

In October 1991 national attention was focused on the issue of sexual harassment as a result of allegations made against Supreme Court Justice nominee Clarence Thomas by Professor Anita Hill. (Thomas was subsequently confirmed as Supreme Court justice by a vote of fifty-two to forty-eight.) While there was a blizzard of media attention about sexual harassment, what emerged most clearly from the confirmation hearings was that the chasm between women's experiences of sexual harassment and an understanding of the phenomenon by society in general had not been bridged. Perhaps most misunderstood was the fact that Professor Hill's experience and her reaction to it were typical of sexually harassed women.

Characteristics of Sexual Terrorism

Those forms of sexual terrorism that are crimes share several common characteristics. Each will be addressed separately, but in the real world these characteristics are linked together and form a vicious circle, which functions to mask the reality of sexual terrorism and thus to perpetuate the system of oppression of females. Crimes of violence against females (1) cut across socioeconomic lines: (2) are the crimes least likely to be reported; (3) when reported, are the crimes least likely to be brought to trial or to result in conviction; (4) are often blamed on the victim; (5) are generally not taken seriously; and (6) fuse dominance and sexuality.

VIOLENCE AGAINST FEMALES CUTS ACROSS SOCIOECONOMIC LINES

The question "Who is the typical rapist, wife beater, incest offender, etc?" is raised constantly. The answer is simple: men. Female sexual offenders are exceedingly rare. The men who commit acts of sexual terrorism are of all ages, races, and religions; they come from all communities, income levels, and educational levels; they are married, single, separated, and divorced. The "typical" sexually abusive male does not exist.

One of the most common assumptions about sexual violence is that it occurs primarily among the poor, uneducated, and predominantly nonwhite populations. Actually, violence committed by the poor and non-white is simply more visible because of their lack of resources to secure the privacy that the middle and upper classes can purchase. Most rapes, indeed, most incidents of sexual assault, are not reported, and therefore the picture drawn from police records must be viewed as very sketchy.

The data on sexual harassment in work situations indicates that it occurs among all job categories and pay ranges. Sexual harassment is committed by academic men, who are among the most highly educated members of society. In a 1991 *New York Times* poll, five out of ten men said they had said or done something that "could have been construed by a female colleague as harassment."

All the studies on wife abuse testify to the fact that wife beating crosses socioeconomic lines. Wife beaters include high government officials, members of the armed forces, businessmen, policemen, physicians, lawyers, clergy, blue-collar workers, and the unemployed. According to Maria Roy, founder and director of New York's Abused Women's Aid in Crisis, "We see abuse of women on all levels of income, age, occupation, and social standing. I've had four women come in recently whose husbands are Ph.D.s—two them professors at top universities. Another abused woman is married to a very prominent attorney. We counseled battered wives whose husbands are doctors, psychiatrists, even clergymen."[11]

Similarly, in Vincent De Francis's classic study of 250 cases of sexual crimes committed against children, a major finding was that incidents of sexual assault against children cut across class lines. Since sexual violence is not "nice," we prefer to believe that nice men do not commit these acts and that nice girls and women are not victims. Our refusal to accept the fact that violence against females is widespread throughout society strongly inhibits our ability to develop meaningful strategies to eliminate it. Moreover, because of underreporting, it is difficult to ascertain exactly how widespread it is.

CRIMES OF SEXUAL VIOLENCE ARE THE LEAST LIKELY TO BE REPORTED

Underreporting is common for all crimes against females. There are two national sources for data on crime in the United States: the annual Uniform Crime Reports (UCR) of the Federal Bureau of Investigation, which collects information from police departments, and the National Crime Survey (NCS), conducted by the U.S. Department of Justice, which collects data on personal and household criminal victimizations from a nationally representative sample of households.

The FBI recognizes that rape is seriously underreported by as much as 80 to 90 percent. According to FBI data for 1990, 102,555 rapes were reported. The FBI Uniform Crime Report for 1990 estimates that a forcible rape occurs every five minutes. This estimate is based on reported rapes; accounting for the high rate of underreporting, the FBI estimates that a rape occurs every two minutes. The number of forcible rapes reported to the police has been increasing every year. Since 1986, the rape rate has risen 10 percent.

The National Crime Survey (renamed in 1991 as the National Crime Victimization Survey) data for 1990 reports 130,260 rapes. This data is only slightly higher than FBI data; researchers argue that NCS data has serious drawbacks as well. Just as victims are reluctant to report a rape to the police, many are also reluctant to reveal their victimization to an NCS interviewer, In fact, the NCS does not ask directly about rape (although it will in the future). A respondent may volunteer the information when asked questions about bodily harm. The NCS also excludes children under twelve, thus providing no data on childhood sexual assault.

In April 1992 the National Victim Center and the Crime Victims Research and Treatment Center released a report entitled "Rape in America," which summarized two nationwide studies: the National Women's Study, a three-year longitudinal survey of a national probability sample of 4,008 adult women, and the State of Services for Victims of Rape, which surveyed 370 agencies that provide rape crisis assistance. The National Women's Study sought information about the incidence of rape and information about a number of health issues related to rape, including depression, posttraumatic stress disorder, suicide attempts, and alcohol- and drug-related problems.

The results of the National Women's Study confirm a belief held by many experts that the UCR and NCS data seriously underrepresents the occurrence of rape. According to the National Women's Study, 683,000 adult women were raped during a twelve-month period from the fall of 1989 to the fall of 1990. This data is significantly higher than UCR and NCS data for approximately the same period. Moreover, since rapes of female children and adolescents under the age of eighteen and rapes of boys or men were not included in the study, the 683,000 rapes of adult women do not reflect an accurate picture of all rapes that occurred during that period. The data in this study also confirms the claim that acquaintance rape is far more pervasive than stranger rape. While 22 percent of victims were raped by someone unknown to them, 36 percent were raped by family members: 9 percent by husbands or ex-husbands, 11 percent by fathers or stepfathers, 16 percent by other relatives. Ten percent were raped by a boyfriend or ex-boyfriend and 29 percent by nonrelatives such as friends or neighbors, (3 percent were not sure or refused to answer).

Perhaps the most significant finding of the National Women's Study is that rape in the United States is "a tragedy of youth." The study found that 29 percent of rapes occurred to female victims under the age of eleven, 32 percent occurred to females between the ages of eleven and seventeen, and 22 percent occurred to females between the ages of eighteen and twenty-four. Other research suggests that one in four women will be the victim of rape or an attempted rape by the time they are in their midtwenties, and at least three-quarters of those assaults will be committed by men known to the victims. Lifetime probability for rape victimization is as high as 50 percent; that is, one out of two women will be sexually assaulted at least once in her lifetime.

The FBI's Uniform Crime Report indexes 10 million reported crimes a year but does not collect statistics on wife abuse. Since statutes in most states do not identify wife beating as a distinct crime, incidents of wife abuse are usually classified under "assault and battery" and "disputes." Estimates that 50 percent of American wives are battered every year are not uncommon in the literature. Recent evidence shows that violence against wives becomes greatest at and after separation. Divorced and separated women account for 75 percent of all battered women and report being battered fourteen times as often as women still living with their partners. These women are also at the highest risk of being murdered by their former husbands. Thirty-three percent of all women murdered in the United States between 1976 and 1987 were murdered by their husbands.

"The problem of sexual abuse of children is of unknown national dimensions," according to Vincent De Francis, "but findings strongly point to the probability of an enormous national incidence many times larger than the reported incidence of the physical abuse of children."[12] He discussed the existence of a wide gap between the reported incidence and the actual occurrence of sexual assaults against children and suggested that "the reported incidence represents the top edge of the moon as it rises over the mountain."[13] Research definitions as to what constitutes sexual abuse and research methodologies vary widely, resulting in reported rates ranging from 6 percent to 62 percent for female children and 3 percent to 31 percent for male children. David Finkelhor suggests that the lowest figures support the claim that child sexual abuse is far from a rare occurrence and that the higher reported rates suggest a "problem of epidemic proportions."

In a study of 126 African-American women and 122 white women in Los Angeles County, 62 percent reported at least one experience of sexual abuse before the age of eighteen. The same men who beat their wives often abuse their children. Researchers have found that "the worse the wife-beating, the worse the child abuse."[14] It is estimated that fathers may sexually abuse children in 25 percent to 33 percent of all domestic abuse cases. There is also a strong correlation between child abuse and the frequency of marital rape, particularly where weapons are involved.

Incest, according to author and researcher Florence rush, is the *Best Kept Secret*. The estimates, however speculative, are frightening. In a representative sample of 930 women in San Francisco, Diana E. H. Russell found that 16 percent of the women had been sexually abused by a relative before the age of eighteen and 4.5 percent had been sexually abused by their fathers (also before the age of eighteen). Extrapolating to the general population, this research suggests that 160,000 women per million may have been sexually abused before the age of eighteen, and 45,000 women per million may have been sexually abused by their fathers.

Accurate data on the incidence of sexual harassment is impossible to obtain. Women have traditionally accepted sexual innuendo as a fact of life and only recently have begun to report and analyze the dimensions of sexual coercion in the workplace. Research indicates that sexual harassment is pervasive. In 1978 Lin Farley found that accounts of sexual harassment within the federal government, the country's largest single employer, were extensive. In 1988 the U.S. Merit Systems Protection Board released an updated study that showed that 85 percent of working women experience harassing behavior at some point in their lives.

In 1976 over nine thousand women responded to a survey on sexual harassment conducted by *Redbook* magazine. More than 92 percent reported sexual harassment as a problem, a majority of the respondents described it as serious, and nine out of ten reported that they had personally experienced one or more forms of unwanted sexual attentions on the job. The Ad Hoc Group on Equal Rights for Women attempted to gather data on sexual harassment at the United Nations. Their questionnaire was confiscated by UN officials, but 875 staff members had already responded; 73 percent were women, and more than half of them said that they had personally experienced or were aware of incidents of sexual harassment at the UN. In May 1975, the Women's Section of the Human Affairs Program at Cornell University in Ithaca, New York, distributed the first questionnaire on sexual harassment. Of the 155 respondents, 92 percent identified sexual harassment as a serious problem, 70 percent had personally experienced some form of sexual harassment, and 56 percent reported incidents of physical harassment. A 1991 *New York Times*/CBS poll found that four out of ten women experienced sexual harassment at work, yet only 4 percent reported it.

In *The Lecherous Professor,* Billie Wright Dziech and Linda Weiner note that the low reportage of sexual harassment in higher education is due to the victims' deliberate avoidance of institutional processes and remedies. A pilot study conducted by the National Advisory Council on Women's Educational Programs on Sexual Harassment in Academia concluded:

> The sexual harassment of postsecondary students is an increasingly visible problem of great, but as yet unascertained, dimensions. Once regarded as an isolate, purely personal problem, it has gained civil rights credibility as its scale and consequences have become known, and is correctly viewed as a form of illegal sex-based discrimination.[15]

CRIMES OF VIOLENCE AGAINST FEMALES HAVE THE LOWEST CONVICTION RATES

The common denominator in the under reporting of all sexual assaults is fear. Females have been well trained in silence and passivity. Early and sustained sex-role socialization teaches that women are responsible for the sexual behavior of men and that women cannot be trusted. These beliefs operate together. They function to keep women silent about their victimization and to keep other people from believing women when they do come forward. The victim's fear that she will not be believed and, as a consequence, that the offender will not be punished is not unrealistic. Sex offenders are rarely punished in our society.

Rape has the lowest conviction rate of all violent crimes. The likelihood of a rape complaint ending in conviction is 2 to 5 percent. While the intent of rape reform legislation was to shift the emphasis from the victim's experiences to the perpetrator's acts, prosecutions are less likely to be pursued if the victim and perpetrator are acquainted, and juries are less likely to return a conviction in cases where the victim's behavior or *alleged behavior* (emphasis mine) departed from traditional sex-role expectations.

Data on prosecution and conviction of wife beaters is practically nonexistent. This is despite the fact that battery is, according to the U.S. Surgeon General, the "single largest cause of injury to women in the U.S." and accounts for one-fifth of all emergency room visits by women. Police departments have generally tried to conciliate rather than arrest. Guided by the "stitch rule," arrests were made only when the victim's injuries required stitches. Police routinely instructed the parties to "break it up" or "talk it out" or asked the abuser to "take a walk and cool off." Male police officers, often identifying with the male abuser, routinely failed to advise women of their rights to file a complaint.

As a result of sustained political activism on behalf of abused women, many states have revised their police training and have instituted pro- or even mandatory arrest policies. In 1984 the Attorney General's Task Force on Family Violence argued that the legal response to such violence be predicated on the abusive act and not on the relationship between the victim and the abuser. A key issue, however, is the implementation of such reform. The record shows that the criminal justice system has responded inconsistently.

Studies in the late 1970s and 1980s showed that batterers receive minimal fines and suspended sentences. In one study of 350 abused wives, none of the husbands served time in jail. And while the result of pro- and mandatory arrest policies is a larger number of domestic violence cases entering the judicial system, "there is considerable evidence that judges have yet to abandon the historical view of wife abuse."[16] In 1981 a Kansas judge suspended the fine of a convicted assailant on the condition that he buy his wife a box of candy. In 1984 a Colorado judge sentenced a man to two years on work release for fatally shooting his wife five times in the face. Although the sentence was less than the minimum required by law, the judge found that the wife had "provoked" her husband by leaving him. Recent task force reports on gender bias in the courts reveal a pattern of nonenforcement of protective orders, trivialization of complaints, and disbelief of females when there is no visible evidence of severe injuries. In 1987 a Massachusetts trial judge scolded a battered women for wasting his time with her request for a protective order. If she and her husband wanted to "gnaw" on each other, "fine," but they "shouldn't do it at taxpayers' expense." The husband later killed his wife, and taxpayers paid for a murder trial.

The lack of support and protection from the criminal justice system intensifies the double bind of battered women. Leaving the batterer significantly increases the risk of serious injury or death, while staying significantly increases the psychological terrorism and frequency of abuse. According to former Detroit Police Commander James Bannon, "You can readily understand why the women ultimately take the law into their own hands or despair of finding relief at all. Or *why the male feels protected by the system in his use of violence*" (emphasis mine).[17]

In his study of child sexual abuse, Vincent De Francis found that plea bargaining and dismissal of cases were the norm. The study sample consisted of 173 cases brought to prosecution. Of these, 44 percent (seventy-six cases) were dismissed, 22 percent (thirty-eight cases) voluntarily accepted a lesser plea, 11 percent (six cases) were found guilty of a lesser charge, and 2 percent (four cases) were found guilty as charged. Of the remaining thirty-five cases, either they were pending (fifteen) or terminated because the offender was committed to a mental institution (five) or because the offender absconded (seven), or no information was available (eight). Of the fifty-three offenders who were convicted or pleaded guilty, thirty offenders escaped a jail sentence. Twenty-one received suspended sentences and were placed on probation, seven received suspended sentences without probation, and two were fined a sum of money. The other 45 percent (twenty-three offenders) received prison terms from under six months to three years; five were given indeterminate sentences—that is, a minimum term of one year and a maximum term subject to the discretion of the state board of parole.

In Diana E. H. Russell's study of 930 women, 648 cases of child sexual abuse were disclosed. Thirty cases—5 percent—were reported to the police; four were cases of incestuous abuse, and twenty-six were extrafamilial child sexual abuse. Only seven cases resulted in conviction.

Most of the victims of sexual harassment in the Cornell University study were unwilling to use available procedures, such as grievances, to remedy their complaints, because they believed that nothing would be done. Their perception is based on reality; of the 12 percent who did complain, over half found that nothing was done in their cases. The low adjudication and punishment rates of sexual-harassment cases are particularly revealing in light of the fact that the offender is known and identifiable and that there is no fear of "mistaken identity," as there is in rape cases. While offenders accused of familial violence—incest and wife abuse—are also known, concern with keeping the family intact affects prosecution rates.

BLAMING THE VICTIM OF SEXUAL VIOLENCE IS PERVASIVE

The data on conviction rates of men who have committed acts of violence against females must be understood in the context of attitudes about women. Our male-dominated society evokes powerful myths to justify male violence against females and to ensure that these acts will rarely be punished. Victims of sexual violence are almost always suspect. We have developed an intricate network of beliefs and attitudes that perpetuate the idea that "victims of sex crimes have a hidden psychological need to be victimized."[18] We tend to believe either that the female willingly participated in her victimization or that she outright lied about it. Either way, we blame the victim and excuse or condone the offender.

Consider, for example, the operative myths about rape, wife battery, incest, and sexual harassment.

Rape
All women want to be raped.
No woman can be raped if she doesn't want it
   (you-can't-thread-a-moving-needle argument).
She asked for it.
She changed her mind afterward.
When she says no, she means yes.
If you are going to be raped, you might as well relax and enjoy it.

Wife Abuse
Some women need to be beaten.
A good kick in the ass will straighten her out.
She needs a punch in the mouth every so often to keep her in line.
She must have done something to provoke him.

Incest
The child was the seducer.
The child imagined it.

Sexual Harassment

> She was seductive.
> She misunderstood. I was just being friendly.

Underlying all the myths about victims of sexual violence is the belief that the victim causes and is responsible for her own victimization. In the National Women's Study, 69 percent of the rape victims were afraid that they would be blamed for their rape, 71 percent did not want their family to know they had been sexually abused, and 68 percent did not want people outside of their family knowing of their victimization. Diana Scully studied convicted rapists and found that these men both believed in the rape myths and used them to justify their own behavior. Underlying the attitudes about the male offender is the belief that he could not help himself: that is, he was ruled by his biology and/or he was seduced. The victim becomes the offender, and the offender becomes the victim. These two processes, blaming the victim and absolving the offender, protect the patriarchal view of the world by rationalizing sexual violence. Sexual violence by a normal male against an innocent female is unthinkable; therefore, she must have done something wrong or it would not have happened. This view was expressed by a Wisconsin judge who sentenced a twenty-four-year old man to ninety days' work release for sexually assaulting a five-year-old girl. The judge, claiming that the child was an "unusually promiscuous young lady," stated that "no way do I believe that [the defendant] initiated sexual contact." Making a victim believe she is at fault erases not only the individual offender's culpability but also the responsibility of the society as a whole. Sexual violence remains an individual problem, not a sociopolitical one.

One need only read the testimony of victims of sexual violence to see the powerful effects of blaming the victim. From the National Advisory Council on Women's Educational Programs Report on Sexual Harassment of Students:

> I was ashamed, thought it was my fault, and was worried that the school would take action against me (for "unearned" grades) if they found out about it.
>
> This happened seventeen years ago, and you are the first person I've been able to discuss it with in all that time. He's still at _____ , and probably still doing it.
>
> I'm afraid to tell anyone here about it, and I'm just hoping to get through the year so I can leave.[19]

From *Wife-Beating: The Silence Crisis,* Judge Stewart Oneglia comments,

> Many women find it shameful to admit they don't have a good marriage. The battered wife wraps her bloody head in a towel, goes to the hospital, and explains to the doctor she fell down the stairs. After a few years of the husband telling her he beats her because she is ugly, stupid, or incompetent, she is to psychologically destroyed that she believes it.

A battered woman from Boston related,

> I actually thought if I only learned to cook better or keep a cleaner house, everything would be okay. I put up with the beatings for five years before I got desperate enough to get help.[20]

Another battered woman said,

> When I came to, I wanted to die, the guilt and depression were so bad. Your whole sense of worth is tied up with being a successful wife and having a happy marriage. If your husband beats you, then your marriage is a failure, and you're a failure. It's so horribly the opposite of how it is supposed to be.[21]

Katherine Brady shared her experience as an incest survivor in *Father's Days: A True Story of Incest*. She concluded her story with the following:

> I've learned a great deal by telling my story. I hope other incest victims may experience a similar journey of discovery by reading it. If nothing else, I would wish them to hear in this tale the two things I needed most, but had to wait years to hear: "You are not alone and you are not to blame."[22]

SEXUAL VIOLENCE IS NOT TAKEN SERIOUSLY

Another characteristic of sexual violence is that these crimes are not taken seriously. Society manifests this attitude by simply denying the existence of sexual violence, denying the gravity of these acts, joking about them, and attempting to legitimate them.

Many offenders echo the societal norm by expressing genuine surprise when they are confronted by authorities. This seems to be particularly true in cases of sexual abuse of children, wife beating, and sexual harassment. In her study of incest, Florence rush found that child molesters very often do not understand that they have done anything wrong. Many men still believe that they have an inalienable right to rule "their women." Batterers, for example, often cite their right to discipline their wives; incestuous fathers cite their right to instruct their daughters in sexuality. These men are acting on the belief that women are the property of men.

The concept of females as the property of men extends beyond the family unit, as the evidence on sexual harassment indicates. "Are you telling me that this kind of horsing around may constitute an actionable offense?" queried a character on a television special on sexual harassment. This represents the typical response of a man accused of sexual harassment. Men have been taught that they are the hunters, and women—all women—are fair game. The mythology about the workaday world abounds with sexual innuendo. Concepts of "sleazy" (i.e., sexually accessible) nurses and dumb, big-breasted, blond secretaries are standard fare for comedy routines. When the existence of sexual violence can no longer be denied, a common response is to joke about it in order to belittle it. "If you are going to be raped, you might as well enjoy it" clearly belittles the violence of rape. The public still laughs when Ralph threatens Alice with "One of these days, POW—right in the kisser." Recently, a television talk-show host remarked that "incest is a game the whole family can play." The audience laughed uproariously.

SEXUAL VIOLENCE IS ABOUT VIOLENCE, POWER, AND SEX

The final characteristic common to all forms of violence against females is perhaps the most difficult to comprehend. During the past decade, many researchers argued (as I did in earlier versions of this article) that sexual violence is not about sex but about violence. I now believe, however, that the "either-or" dichotomy—either sexual violence is about sex or it's about violence—is false and misleading. Male supremacy identifies females as having a basic "flaw"—a trait that distinguishes males and females and legitimates women's inferior status. This "flaw" is female sexuality: it is tempting and seductive and therefore disruptive, capable of reproducing life itself and therefore powerful. Through sexual terrorism men seek to bring this force under control. The site of the struggle is the female body and female sexuality.

Timothy Beneke, in *Men on Rape,* argues that "not every man is a rapist but every man who grows up in America and learns American English learns all too much to think like a rapist" and that "for a man, rape has plenty to do with sex."[23] Twenty years of research and activism have documented that women largely experience rape, battery, incest, and sexual harassment as violence. That women and men often have vastly different experiences is not surprising. Under patriarchy men are entitled to sex; it is a primary vehicle by which they establish and signal their masculinity. From the male perspective, female sexuality is a commodity, something they must take, dominate, or own. Our popular culture routinely celebrates this particular notion of masculinity. Women are permitted to have sex, but only in marriage (the patriarchal ideal), or at least in love relationships. Women earn their femininity by managing their sexuality and keeping it in trust for a potential husband. The double standard of sexuality leads inevitably to coercion and sexual violence.

Many believe that re-visioning rape as violence not only accurately reflects many women's experiences but also is a more productive strategy for reforming legislation and transforming public attitudes. While arguing that "theoretically and strategically" the "rape as violence" position is the better one, attorney and author Susan Estrich points out that such an approach obscures the reality that the majority of rapes are coerced or forced but unaccompanied by conventional violence. In fact, one consequence of this approach is that it precludes protest from women who experience sexual intrusions in ways not typically seen as violent.

It is argued that in sexual harassment the motive is power, not sex. There is a wide consensus that sexual harassment is intended to "keep women in their place." Yet, the means by which this is attempted or accomplished are sexual: rude comments about sex or about a woman's body, pornographic gestures or posters, demands for sexual favors, rape, etc. Clearly, to the harassers, a woman's place is a largely sexual one; her very presence in the workplace sexualizes it. In the accounts of women's experiences with sexual harassment in *Sexual Harassment: Women Speak Out,* themes of sexual power and sexual humiliation resonate in each essay.

In wife battery the acts of violence are intended to inflict harm on the woman and ultimately to control her, but the message of the violence is explicitly sexual. For example, the most common parts of a woman's body attacked during battering are her face and her breasts—both symbols of her sexuality and her attractiveness to men. During pregnancy, the focus of the attack often shifts to the abdomen—a symbol of her reproductive power. In addressing the "either-or" debate in the sexual abuse of children, David Finkelhor points out "sex is always in the service of other needs. Just because it is infused with nonsexual motives does not make child sexual abuse different from other kinds of behavior that we readily call 'sexual'."[24]

Conclusion

The dynamic that underscores all manifestations of sexual terrorism is misogyny—the hatred of women. Violence against women is power expressed sexually. It is violence eroticized. Diana E. H. Russell argues that "we are socialized to sexualize power, intimacy, and affection, and sometimes hatred and contempt as well."[25] For women in the United States, sexual violence and its threat are central issues in their daily lives. Both violence and fear are functional. Without the power to intimidate and punish women sexually, the domination of women in all spheres of society—political, social, and economic—could not exist.

Notes

1. Susan Brownmiller, *Against Our Will: Men, Women and Rape* (New York: Simon and Schuster, 1975), 5.
2. Frederick F. Hacker, *Crusaders, Criminals and Crazies: Terrorism in Our Time* (New York: W. W. Norton and Co., 1976), xi.
3. Marc Feigen Fasteau, *The Male Machine* (New York: McGraw-Hill Book Co., 1974), 144.
4. Francis M. Watson, *Political Terrorism: The Threat and The Response* (Washington, DC: R. B. Luce, 1976), 15.
5. Paul Wilkinson, *Political Terrorism* (New York: John Wiley and Sons, 1974), 17.
6. Jane Caputi and Diana E. H. Russell. "Femicide: Speaking the Unspeakable," in "Everyday Violence Against Women. Special Report." *Ms,* 1, no. 2 (1990).
7. *Fulgham v. State,* 46 Ala. 143 (1871).
8. *Thompson v. Thompson,* 218 U.S. 611 (1910).
9. Lin Farley, *Sexual Shakedown: The Sexual Harassment of Women on the Job* (New York: McGraw-Hill Book Co., 1978), 14–15.
10. U.S. House of Representatives. Hearings on Sexual Harassment in the Federal Government, Committee on the Post Office and Civil Service, Subcommittee on Investigations. Washington, DC: U.S. Government Printing Office, 1980.
11. Roger Langley and Richard C. Levy, *Wife-Beating: The Silent Crisis* (New York: E. P. Dutton, 1977), 44.
12. Vincent De Francis, *Protecting the Child Victim of Sex Crimes Committed by Adults* (Denver: American Humane Society, 1969), vii.
13. Ibid.
14. Lee H. Bowker, Michelle Arbitell, and J. Richard McFerron. "On the Relationship Between Wife Beating and Child Abuse," in Kersti Yllo and Michele Bograd (eds.), *Feminist*

Perspectives on Wife Abuse. Newbury Park, CA: Sage Publications, Inc., 1988, 164.
15. Frank I. Till, *Sexual Harassment: A Report on the ?????*
16. Laura L. Crites. "Wife Abuse: The Judicial Record," in Laura L. Crites and Winifred L. Hepperle, *Women, the Courts and Equality.* Beverly Hills, CA: Sage Publications, Inc., 1987, 41.
17. James Bannon, as quoted in Del Martin, *Battered Wives* (New York: Pocket Books, 1977), 115.
18. Georgia Dullea, "Child Prostitution: Causes Are Sought" (*New York Times,* Sept. 4, 1979), p. C11.
19. Till, 28.
20. Ibid., 115.
21. Ibid., 116.
22. Katherine Brady, *Father's Days: A True Story of Incest* (New York: Dell Publishing Co., 1981), 253.
23. Timothy Beneke, *Men on Rape: What They Have to Say About Sexual Violence* (New York: St. Martin's Press, 1982), 16.
24. David Finkelhor (ed.). *Child Sexual Abuse: New Theory and Research.* New York: The Free Press, 1984, 34.

Name: _____   Class: _____

Date: _____   Section: _____

Reading Comprehension Activity Sheet

Sexual Terrorism, Carole J. Sheffield

1. What is sexual terrorism, and what is the outcome of sexual terrorism? _____

_____

_____

_____

_____

_____

_____

_____

_____

_____

_____

2. Briefly describe the components of sexual terrorism. _____

_____

_____

_____

_____

_____

_____

_____

_____

_____

_____

3. What purpose does "blaming the victim" serve?

chapter 9

Race and Ethnicity

The Problem of the Twentieth Century Is the Problem of the Color Line
W.E.B. Du Bois

Angry Women Are Building: Issues and Struggles Facing American Indian Women Today
Paula Gunn Allen

The Problem of the Twentieth Century Is the Problem of the Color Line

W.E.B. Du Bois

We are just finishing the first half of the twentieth century. I remember its birth in 1901. There was the usual discussion as to whether the century began in 1900 or 1901; but, of course, 1901 was correct. We expected great things . . . peace; the season of war among nations had passed; progress was the order . . . everything going forward to bigger and better things. And then, not so openly expressed, but even more firmly believed, the rule of white Europe and America over black, brown, and yellow peoples.

I was 32 years of age in 1901, married, and a father, and teaching at Atlanta University with a program covering a hundred years of study and investigation into the condition of American Negroes. Our subject of study at that time was education: the college-bred Negro in 1900, the Negro common school in 1901. My own attitude toward the twentieth century was expressed in an article which I wrote in the *Atlantic Monthly* in 1901. It said:

> The problem of the Twentieth Century is the problem of the color-line . . . I have seen a land right merry with the sun, where children sing, and rolling hills lie like passioned women wanton with harvest. And there in the King's Highway sat, and sits, a figure veiled and bowed, by which the Traveler's footsteps hasten as they go. On the tainted air broods fair. Three centuries' thought have been the raising and unveiling of that bowed human soul; and now behold, my fellows, a century now for the duty and the deed! The problem of the Twentieth Century is the problem of the color-line.

This is what we hoped, to this we Negroes looked forward; peace, progress and the breaking of the color line. What has been the result? We know it all too well . . . war, hate, the revolt of the colored peoples and the fear of more war.

From *Pittsburgh Courier* by W.E.B. Du Bois. Copyright © The estate of W.E.B. Du Bois. Reprinted by permission of David Graham Du Bois.

In the meantime, where are we; those 15,000,000 citizens of the United States who are descended from the slaves, brought here between 1600 and 1900? We formed in 1901, a separate group because of legal enslavement and emancipation into caste conditions, with the attendant poverty, ignorance, disease, and crime. We were in inner group and not an integral part of the American nation; but we were exerting ourselves to fight for integration.

The burden of our fight was in seven different lines. We wanted education; we wanted particularly the right to vote and civil rights; we wanted work with adequate wage; housing, without segregation or slums; a free press to fight our battles, and (although in those days we dare not say it) social equality.

In 1901 our education was in perilous condition, despite what we and our white friends had done for 30 years. The Atlanta University Conference said in its resolutions of 1901:

> We call the attention of the nation to the fact that less than one million of the three million Negro children of school age are at present regularly attending school, and these attend a session which lasts only a few months. We are today deliberately rearing millions of our citizens in ignorance and at the same time limiting the rights of citizenship by educational qualifications. This is unjust.

More particularly in civil rights, we were oppressed. We not only did not get justice in the courts, but we were subject to peculiar and galling sorts of injustice in daily life. In the latter half of the nineteenth century, where we first get something like statistics, no less than 3,000 Negroes were lynched without trial. An in addition to that we were subject continuously to mob violence and judicial lynching.

In political life we had, for 25 years, been disfranchised by violence, law, and public opinion. The 14th and 15th amendments were deliberately violated and the literature of the day in book, pamphlet, and daily press, was widely of opinion that the Negro was not ready for the ballot, could not use it intelligently, and that no action was called for to stop his political power from being exercised by Southern whites like Tillman and Vardaman.

We did not have the right or opportunity to work at an income which would sustain a decent and modern standard of life. Because of a past of chattel slavery, we were for the most part common laborers and servants, and a very considerable proportion were still unable to leave the plantations where they worked all their lives for next to nothing.

There were a few who were educated for the professions and we had many good artisans; that number was not increasing as it should have been, nor were new artisans being adequately trained. Industrial training was popular, but funds to implement it were too limited, and we were excluded from unions and the new mass industry.

We were housed in slums and segregated districts where crime and disease multiplied, and when we tried to move to better and healthier quarters we were met by segregation ordinance if not by mobs. We not only had no social equality, but we did not openly ask for it. It seemed a shameful thing to beg people to receive us as equals and as human beings; that was something we argued "that came and could not be fetched." And that meant not simply that we could not marry white women or legitimize mulatto bastards, but we could not stop in a decent hotel, nor eat in a public restaurant nor attend the theater, nor accept an invitation to a private white home, nor travel in a decent railway coach. When the "public" was invited, this did not include us and admission to colleges often involved special consideration if not blunt refusal.

Finally we had poor press . . . a few struggling papers with little news and inadequately expressed opinion, with small circulation or influence and almost no advertising.

This was our plight in 1901. It was discouraging, but not hopeless. There is no question but that we had made progress, and there also was no doubt but what that progress was not enough to satisfy us or to settle our problems.

We could look back on a quarter century of struggle which had its results. We had schools; we had teachers; a few had forced themselves into the leading colleges and were tolerated if not welcomed. We voted in Northern cities, owned many decent homes and were fighting for further progress. Leaders like Booker Washington had perceived wide popular approval and a Negro literature had begun to appear.

But what we needed was organized effort along the whole front, based on broad lines of complete emancipation. This came with the Niagara Movement in 1906 and the NAACP in 1909. In 1910 came the Crisis magazine and the real battle was on.

What have we gained and accomplished? The advance has not been equal on all fronts, nor complete on any. We have not progressed with closed ranks like a trained army, but rather with serried and broken ranks, with wide gaps and even temporary retreats. But we have advanced. Of that there can be no atom of doubt.

First of all in education; most Negro children today are in school and most adults can read and write. Unfortunately this literacy is not as great as the census says. The draft showed that at least a third of our youth are illiterate. But education is steadily rising. Six thousand bachelor degrees are awarded to Negroes each year and doctorates in philosophy and medicine are not uncommon. Nevertheless as a group, American Negroes are still in the lower ranks of learning and adaptability to modern conditions. They do not read widely, their travel is limited and their experience through contact with the modern world is curtailed by law and custom.

Secondly, in civil rights, the Negro has perhaps made his greatest advance. Mob violence and lynching have markedly decreased. Three thousand Negroes were lynched in the last half of the nineteenth century and five hundred in the first half of the twentieth. Today lynching is comparatively rare. Mob violence also has decreased, but is still in evidence, and summary and unjust court proceedings have taken the place of open and illegal acts. But the Negro has established, in the courts, his legal citizenship and his right to be included in the Bill of Rights. The question still remains of "equal but separate" public accommodations, and that is being attacked. Even the institution of "jim-crow" in travel is tottering. The infraction of the marriage situation by law and custom is yet to be brought before the courts and public opinion in a forcible way.

Third, the right to vote on the part of the Negro is being gradually established under the 14th and 15th amendments. It was not really until 1915 that the Supreme Court upheld this right of Negro citizens and even today the penalties of the 14th amendment have never been enforced. There are 7,000,000 possible voters among American Negroes and of these it is a question if more than 2,000,000 actually cast their votes. This is partly from the national inertia, which keeps half of all American voters away from the polls; but even more from the question as to what practical ends the Negro shall cast his vote.

He is thinking usually in terms of what he can do by voting to better his condition and he seldom gets a chance to vote on this matter. On the wider implications of political democracy he has not yet entered; particularly he does not see the economic foundations of present civilization and the necessity of his attacking the rule of corporate wealth in order to free the labor group to which he belongs.

Fourth, there is the question of occupation. There are our submerged classes of farm labor and tenants: our city laborers, washerwomen and scrubwomen and the mass of lower-paid servants. These classes still form a majority of American Negroes and they are on the edge of poverty, with the ignorance, disease, and crime that always accompany such poverty.

If we measure the median income of Americans, it is $3,000 for whites and $2,000 for Negroes. In Southern cities, seven percent of the white families and 30 percent of the colored families receive less that $1,000 a year. On the other hand, the class differentiation by income among Negroes is notable: the number of semiskilled and skilled artisans has increased or will as membership in labor unions. Professional men have increased, especially teachers and less notably, physicians, dentists, and lawyers.

The number of Negroes in business has increased; mostly in small retail businesses, but to a considerable extent in enterprises like insurance, real estate and small banking, where the color line gives Negroes certain advantages and where, too, there is a certain element of gambling. Also beyond the line of gambling, numbers of Negroes have made small fortunes in antisocial enterprises. All this means that there has arisen in the Negro group a distinct stratification from poor to rich. Recently I polled 450 Negro families belonging to a select organization 45 years old. Of these families, 127 received over $10,000 a year and a score of these over $25,000; 200 families received from $5,000 to $10,000 a year and 86 less than $5,000.

This is the start of a tendency which will grow; we are beginning to follow the American pattern of accumulating individual wealth and of considering that this will eventually settle the race problem. On the other hand, the whole trend of the thought of our age is toward social welfare; the prevention of poverty by more equitable distribution of wealth, and business for general welfare rather than private profit. There are few signs that these ideals are guiding Negro development today. We seem to be adopting increasingly the ideal of American culture.

Housing has, of course, been a point of bitter pressure among Negroes, because the attempt to segregate the race in its living conditions has not only kept the more fortunate ones from progress, but it has confined vast numbers of Negro people to the very parts of cities and country districts where they have fewest opportunities and least social contacts. They must live largely in slums, in contact with criminals and with fewest of the social advantages of government and human contact. The fight against segregation has been carried on in the courts and shows much progress against city ordinances, against covenants which make segregation hereditary.

Literature and art have made progress among Negroes; but with curious handicaps. An art expression is normally evoked by the conscious and unconscious demand of people for portrayal of their own emotion and experience. But in the case of the American Negroes, the audience, which embodies the demand and which pays sometimes enormous price for satisfaction, is not the Negro group, but the white group. And the pattern of what the white group wants does not necessarily agree with the natural desire of Negroes.

The whole of Negro literature is therefore curiously divided. We have writers who have written, not really about Negroes, but about the things which white people, and not the highest class of whites, like to hear about Negroes. And those who have expressed what the Negro himself thinks and feels, are those whose books sell to few, even of their own people; and whom most folk do not know. This has not made for the authentic literature which the early part of this century seemed to promise. To be sure, it can be said that American literature today has a considerable amount of Negro expressions and influence, although not as much as once we hoped.

Despite all this we have an increasing number of excellent Negro writers who make the promise for the future great by their real accomplishment. We have done something in sculpture and painting, but in drama and music we have markedly advanced. All the world listens to our singers, sings our music, and dances to our rhythms.

In science, our handicaps are still great. Turner, a great entomologist, was worked to death for lack of laboratory, just never had the recognition he richly deserved; and Carver was prisoner of his inferiority complex. Notwithstanding this, our real accomplishment in biology and medicine; in history and law; and in the social sciences has been notable and widely acclaimed. To this in no little degree is due our physical survival, our falling death rate, and our increased confidence in our selves and in our destiny.

The expression of Negro wish and desire through a free press has greatly improved as compared with 1900. We have a half dozen large weekly papers with circulations of a hundred thousand or more. Their news coverage is immense, even if not discriminating. But here again, the influence of the American press on us has been devastating. The predominance of advertising over opinion, the desire for income rather than literary excellence and the use of deliberate propaganda, had made our press less of a power than it could be, and leaves wide chance for improvement in the future.

In comparison with other institutions, the Negro church during the twentieth century has lost ground. It is no longer the dominating influence that it used to be, the center of social activity and of economic experiment. Nevertheless, it is still a powerful institution in the lives of a numerical majority of American Negroes if not upon the dominant intellectual classes. There has been a considerable increase in organized work for social progress through the church, but there has also been a large increase of expenditure for buildings, furnishings, and salaries; and it is not easy to find any increase in moral stamina or conscientious discrimination within church circles.

The scandal of deliberate bribery in election of bishops and in the holding of positions in the churches without a hierarchy has been widespread. It is a critical problem now as to just what part in the future the church among Negroes is going to hold.

Finally there comes the question of social equality, which, despite efforts on the part of thinkers, white and black, is after all the main and fundamental problem of race in the United States. Unless a human being is going to have all human rights, including not only work, but friendship, and if mutually desired, marriage and children, unless these avenues are open and free, there can be no real equality and no cultural integration.

It has hitherto seemed utterly impossible that any such solution of the Negro problem in America could take place. The situation was quite similar to the problem of the lower classes of laborers, serfs and servants in European nations during the sixteenth, seventeenth, and eighteenth centuries. All nations had to consist of two separate parts and the only relations between them was employment and philanthropy.

The problem has been partly solved by modern democracy, but modern democracy cannot succeed unless the peoples of different races and religions are also integrated into the democratic whole. Against this, large numbers of Americans have always fought and are still fighting, but the progress despite this has been notable. there are places in the United States, especially in large cities like New York and Chicago, where the social differences between the races has, to a large extent, been nullified and there is a meeting on terms of equality which would have been thought impossible a half century ago.

On the other hand, in the South, despite religion, education, and reason, the color line, although perhaps shaken, still stands, stark and unbending, and to the minds of most good people, eternal. Here lies the area of the last battle for the complete rights of American Negroes.

Within the race itself today there are disquieting signs. The effort of Negroes to become Americans of equal status with other Americans is leading them to a state of mind by which they not only accept what is good in America, but what is bad and threatening so long as the Negro can share equally. This is peculiarly dangerous at this epoch in the development of world culture.

After two world wars of unprecedented loss of life, cruelty, and destruction, we are faced by the fact that the industrial organization of our present civilization has in it something fundamentally wrong. It went to pieces in the first world war because of the determination of certain great powers excluded from world rule to share in that rule, by acquisition of the labor and materials of colonial peoples. The attempt to recover from the cataclysm resulted in the collapse of our industrial system, and a second world war.

In spite of the propaganda which has gone on, which represents America as the leading democratic state, we Negroes know perfectly well, and ought to know even better than most, that America is not a successful democracy and that until it is, it is going to drag down the world. This nation is ruled by corporate wealth to a degree which is frightening. One thousand persons own the United States and their power outweighs the voice of the mass of

American citizens. This must be cured, not by revolution, not by war and violence, but by reason and knowledge.

Most of the world is today turning toward the welfare state; turning against the idea of production for individual profit toward the idea of production for use and for the welfare of the mass of citizens. No matter how difficult such a course is, it is the only course that is going to save the world and this we American Negroes have got to realize.

We may find it easy now to get publicity, reward, and attention by going along with the reactionary propaganda and war hysteria which is convulsing this nation, but in the long run America will not thank its black children if they help it go the wrong way, or retard its progress.

Name: _____   Class: _____

Date: _____   Section: _____

Reading Comprehension Activity Sheet

The Problem of the Twentieth Century Is the Problem of the Color Line, W.E.B. Du Bois

1. Du Bois begins his essay with a discussion of the "different lines" that African Americans needed to fight. What are these different lines? _____

   _____

   _____

   _____

   _____

   _____

   _____

   _____

   _____

   _____

   _____

2. Discuss the "advances" made subsequent to the Niagara Movement and the creation of the NAACP? _____

   _____

   _____

   _____

   _____

   _____

   _____

   _____

   _____

   _____

   _____

3. Do you think the problems of the 20th century continue to be problems today in the 21st century?

Angry Women Are Building

Issues and Struggles Facing American Indian Women Today

Paula Gunn Allen

The central issue that confronts American Indian women throughout the hemisphere is survival, *literal survival,* both on a cultural and biological level. According to the 1980 census, population of American Indians is just over one million. This figure, which is disputed by some American Indians, is probably a fair estimate, and it carries certain implications. [Editors' note: The 1995 population is over two million.]

Some researchers put our pre-contact population at more than 45 million, while others put it at around 20 million. The U.S. government long put it at 450,000—a comforting if imaginary figure, though at one point it was put at around 270,000. If our current population is around one million; if, as some researchers estimate, around 25 percent of Indian women and 10 percent of Indian men in the United States have been sterilized without informed consent; if our average life expectancy is, as the best-informed research presently says, 55 years; if our infant mortality rate continues at well above national standards; if our average unemployment for all segments of our population—male, female, young, adult, and middle-ages—is between 60 and 90 percent; if the U.S. government continues its policy of termination, relocation, removal, and assimilation along with the destruction of wilderness, reservation land, and its resources, and severe curtailment of hunting, fishing, timber harvesting and water-use rights—then existing tribes are facing the threat of extinction which for several hundred tribal groups has already become fact in the past five hundred years.

From *The Sacred Hoop* by Paula Gunn Allen. Copyright © 1986, 1992 by Paula Gunn Allen. Reprinted with permission of Beacon Press, Boston.

In this nation of more than 200 million, the Indian people constitute less than one-half of one percent of the population. [Editors' note: In 1995, this figure was one percent.] In a nation that offers refuge, sympathy, and billions of dollars in aid from federal and private sources in the form of food to the hungry, medicine to the sick, and comfort to the dying, the indigenous subject population goes hungry, homeless, impoverished, cut out of the American deal, new, old, and in between. Americans are daily made aware of the world-wide slaughter of native peoples such as the Cambodians, the Palestinians, the Armenians, the Jews—who constitute only a few groups faced with genocide in this century.... The American Indian people are in a situation comparable to the imminent genocide in many parts of the world today. The plight of our people north and south of us is no better; to the south it is considerably worse. Consciously or unconsciously, deliberately, as a matter of national policy, or accidentally as a matter of "fate," *every single government, right,* left, or centrist in the western hemisphere is consciously or subconsciously dedicated to the extinction of those tribal people who live within its borders.

Within this geopolitical charnel house, American Indian women struggle on every front for the survival of our children, our people, our self-respect, our value systems, and our way of life. The past five hundred years testify to our skill at waging this struggle: for all the varied weapons of extinction pointed at our heads, we endure.

We survive war and conquest; we survive colonization, acculturation, assimilation; we survive beating, rape, starvation, mutilation, sterilization, abandonment, neglect, death of our children, our loved ones, destruction of our land, our homes, our past, and our future. We survive, and we do more than just survive. We bond, we care, we fight, we teach, we nurse, we bear, we feed, we earn, we laugh, we love, we hang in there, no matter what.

Of course, some, many of us, just give up. Many are alcoholics, many are addicts. Many abandon the children, the old ones. Many commit suicide. Many become violent, go insane. Many go "white" and are never seen or heard from again. But enough hold on to their traditions and their ways so that even after almost five hundred brutal years, we endure. And we even write songs and poems, make paintings and drawings that say "We walk in beauty. Let us continue."

Currently our struggles are on two fronts: physical survival and cultural survival. For women this means fighting alcoholism and drug abuse (our own and that of our husbands, lovers, parents, children);[1] poverty; affluence—a destroyer of people who are not traditionally socialized to deal with large sums of money; rape, incest, battering by Indian men; assaults on fertility and other health matters by the Indian Health Service and the Public Health Service; high infant mortality due to substandard medical care, nutrition, and health information; poor educational opportunities or education that takes us away from our traditions, language, and communities; suicide, homicide, or similar expressions of self-hatred; lack of economic opportunities; substandard housing; sometimes violent and always virulent racist attitudes and behaviors directed against us by an entertainment and educational system that wants only one thing from Indians: our silence, our invisibility, and our collective death.

A headline, in the *Navajo Times* . . . reported that rape was the number one crime on the Navajo reservation. In a professional mental health journal of the Indian Health Services, Phyllis Old Dog Cross reported that incest and rape are common among Indian women seeking services and that their incidence is increasing. "It is believed that at least 80 percent of the Native Women seen at the regional psychiatric service center (five state area) have experienced some sort of sexual assault."[2] Among the forms of abuse being suffered by Native American women, Old Dog Cross cites a recent phenomenon, something called "training." This form of gang rape is "a punitive act of a group of males who band together and get even or take revenge on a selected woman."[3]

These and other cases of violence against women are powerful evidence that the status of women within the tribes has suffered grievous decline since contact, and the decline has increased in intensity in recent years. The amount of violence against women, alcoholism, and violence, abuse, and neglect by women against their children and their aged relatives have all increased. These social ills were virtually unheard of among most tribes fifty years ago, popular American opinion to the contrary. As Old Dog Cross remarks:

> Rapid, unstable and irrational change was required of the Indian people if they were to survive. Incredible loss of all that had meaning was the norm. Inhuman treatment, murder, death, and punishment was a typical experience for all the tribal groups and some didn't survive.
>
> The dominant society devoted its efforts to the attempt to change the Indian into a white-Indian. No inhuman pressure to effect this change was overlooked. These pressures included starvation, incarceration and enforced education. Religious and healing customs were banished.
>
> In spite of the years of oppression, the Indian and the Indian spirit survived. Not, however, without adverse effect. One of the major effects was the loss of cultured values and the concomitant loss of personal identity . . . The Indian was taught to be ashamed of being Indian and to emulate the non-Indian. In short, "white was right." For the Indian male, the only route to be successful, to be good, to be right, and to have an identity was to be as much like the white man as he could.[4]

Often it is said that the increase of violence against women is a result of various sociological factors such as oppression, racism, poverty, hopelessness, emasculation of men, and loss of male self-esteem as their own place within traditional society has been systematically destroyed by increasing urbanization, industrialization, and institutionalization, but seldom do we notice that for the past forty to fifty years, American popular media have depicted American Indian men as bloodthirsty savages devoted to treating women cruelly. While traditional Indian men seldom did any such thing—and in fact among most tribes abuse of women was simply unthinkable, as was abuse of children of the aged—the lie about "usual" male Indian behavior seems to have taken root and now bears its brutal and bitter fruit.

Image casting and image control constitute the central process that American Indian women must come to terms with, for on that control rests our sense of self, our claim to a past and to a future that we define and that we build. Images of Indians in media and educational materials profoundly influence how we act, how we relate to the world and to each other, and how we value ourselves. They also determine to a large extent how our men act toward us, toward our children, and toward each other. The popular American media image of Indian people as savages with no conscience, no compassion, and no sense of the value of human life and human dignity was hardly true of the tribes—however true it was of the invaders. But as Adolf Hitler noted a little over fifty years ago, if you tell a lie big enough and often enough, it will be believed. Evidently, while Americans and people all over the world have been led into a deep and unquestioned belief that American Indians are cruel savages, a number of American Indian men have been equally deluded into internalizing that image and acting on it. Media images, literary images, and artistic images, particularly those embedded in popular culture, must be changed before Indian women will see much relief from the violence that destroys so many lives.

To survive culturally, American Indian women must often fight the United States government, the tribal governments, women and men of their tribe or their urban community who are virulently misogynist or who are threatened by attempts to change the images foisted on us over the centuries by whites. The colonizers' revisions of our lives, values, and histories have devastated us at the most critical level of all—that of our own minds, our own sense of who we are.

Many women express strong opposition to those who would alter our life supports, steal our tribal lands, colonize our cultures and cultural expressions, and revise our very identities. We must strive to maintain tribal status; we must make certain that the tribes continue to be legally recognized entities, sovereign nations within the large United States, and we must wage this struggle in many ways—political, educational, literary, artistic, individual, and communal. We are doing all we can: as mothers and grandmothers; as family members and tribal members; as professionals, workers, artists, shamans, leaders, chiefs, speakers, writers, and organizers; we daily demonstrate that we have no intention of disappearing, of being silent, or of quietly acquiescing in our extinction.

Notes

1. It is likely, say some researchers, that fetal alcohol syndrome, which is serious among many Indian groups, will be so serious among the White Mountain Apache and the Pine ridge Sioux that if present trends continue, by the year 2000 some people estimate that almost one-half of all children born on those reservations will in some way be affected by FAS. (Michael Dorris, Native American Studies, Dartmouth College, private conversation. Dorris has done extensive research into the syndrome as it affects native populations in the United States as well as in New Zealand.)
2. Phyllis Old Dog Cross, "Sexual Abuse, a New Threat to the Native American Woman: An Overview," *Listening Post: A Periodical of the Mental Health Programs of Indian Health Services,* vol. 6, no. 2 (April 1982), p. 18.
3. Old Dog Cross, p. 18.
4. Old Dog Cross, p. 20.

Name: _____ Class: _____

Date: _____ Section: _____

Reading Comprehension Activity Sheet

Angry Women Are Building: Issues and Struggles Facing American Indian Women Today, Paula Gunn Allen

1. Gunn Allen maintains that the American Indian woman is experiencing a struggle on two different "fronts." What are these fronts of struggle? _____

    _____

    _____

    _____

    _____

    _____

    _____

    _____

    _____

    _____

2. Select one "front" and discuss how you would assist the woman experiencing this particular crisis. What do you suggest can be done at the structural level to alleviate or eradicate this problem? _____

    _____

    _____

    _____

    _____

    _____

    _____

    _____

    _____

    _____

chapter 10

Sexual Orientation

He Defies You Still: The Memoirs of a Sissy
Tommi Avicolli

The New Gay Struggle
Richard Lacayo

He Defies You Still

The Memoirs of a Sissy

Tommi Avicolli

You're just a faggot
No history faces you this morning
A faggot's dreams are scarlet
Bad blood bled from words that scarred[1]

Scene One

A homeroom in a Catholic high school in South Philadelphia. They boy sits quietly in the first aisle, third desk, reading a book. He does not look up, not even for a moment. He is hoping no one will remember he is sitting there. He wishes he were invisible. The teacher is not yet in the classroom so the other boys are talking and laughing loudly.

Suddenly, a voice from beside him:

"Hey, you're a faggot, ain't you?"

The boy does not answer. He goes on reading his book, or rather pretending he is reading his book. It is impossible to actually read the book now.

"Hey, I'm talking to you!"

The boy still does not look up. He is so scared his heart is thumping madly; it feels like it is leaping out of his chest and into his throat. But he can't look up.

"Faggot, I'm talking to you!"

To look up is to meet the eyes of the tormentor.

Suddenly, a sharpened pencil point is thrust into the boy's arm. He jolts, shaking off the pencil, aware that there is blood seeping from the wound.

"What did you do that for?" he asks timidly.

From *Radical Teacher* by Tommi Avicolli. Reprinted with permission.

"Cause I hate faggots," the other boy says, laughing. Some other boys begin to laugh, too. A symphony of laughter. The boy feels as if he's going to cry. But he must not cry. Must not cry. So he holds back the tears and tries to read the book again. He must read the book. Read the book.

When the teacher arrives a few minutes later, the class quiets down. The boy does not tell the teacher what has happened. He spits on the wound to clean it, dabbing it with a tissue until the bleeding stops. For weeks he fears some dreadful infection from the lead in the pencil point.

Scene Two

The boy is walking home from school. A group of boys (two, maybe three, he is not certain) grab him from behind, drag him into an alley and beat him up. When he gets home, he races up to his room, refusing dinner ("I don't feel well," he tells his mother through the locked door) and spends the night alone in the dark wishing he would die. . . .

These are not fictitious accounts—I *was* that boy. Having been branded a sissy by neighborhood children because I preferred jump rope to baseball and dolls to playing soldiers, I was often taunted with "hey sissy" or "hey faggot" or "yoo hoo honey" (in a mocking voice) when I left the house.

To avoid harassment, I spent many summers alone in my room. I went out on rainy days when the street was empty.

I came to like being alone. I didn't need anyone, I told myself over and over again. I was an island. Contact with others meant pain. Alone, I was protected. I began writing poems then short stories. There was no reason to go outside anymore. I had a world of my own.

> In the schoolyard today
> they'll single you out
> Their laughter will leave your ears ringing
> like the church bells
> which once awed you. . . .[2]

School was one of the more painful experiences of my youth. The neighborhood bullies could be avoided. The taunts of the children living in those endless repetitive row houses could be evaded by staying in my room. But school was something I had to face day after day for some two hundred mornings a year.

I had few friends in school. I was a pariah. Some kids would talk to me, but few wanted to be known as my close friend. Afraid of labels. If I was a sissy, then he had to be a sissy, too. I was condemned to loneliness.

Fortunately, a new boy moved into our neighborhood and befriended me; he wasn't afraid of the labels. He protected me when the other guys threatened to beat me up. He walked me home from school; he broke through the terrible loneliness. We were in third or fourth grade at the time.

We spent a summer or two together. Then his parents sent him to camp and I was once again confined to my room.

Scene Three

High school lunchroom. The boy sits at a table near the back of the room. Without warning, his lunch bag is grabbed and tossed to another table. Someone opens it and confiscates a package of Tastykakes; another boy takes the sandwich. The empty bag is tossed back to the boy who stares at it, dumbfounded. He should be used to this; it has happened before.

Someone screams, "faggot," laughing. There is always laughter. It does not annoy him anymore.

There is no teacher nearby. There is never a teacher around. And what would he say if there were? Could he report the crime? He would be jumped after school if he did. Besides, it would be his word against theirs. Teachers never noticed anything. They never heard the taunts. Never heard the word, "faggot." They were the great deaf mutes, pillars of indifference; a sissy's pain was not relevant to history and geography and god made me to love honor and obey him, amen.

Scene Four

High school Religion class. Someone has a copy of *Playboy*. Father N. is not in the room yet; he's late, as usual. Someone taps the boy roughly on the shoulder. He turns. A finger points to the centerfold model, pink fleshy body, thin and sleek. Almost painted. Not real. The other asks, mocking voice, "Hey, does she turn you on? Look at those tits!"

The boy smiles, nodding meekly; turns away.

The other jabs him harder on the shoulder, "Hey, whatsamatter, don't you like girls?"

Laughter. Thousands of mouths; unbearable din of laughter. In the Arena: thumbs down. Don't spare the queer.

"Wanna suck my dick? Huh? That turn you on, faggot!"

The laughter seems to go on forever . . .

> Behind you, the sound of their laughter
> echoes a million times
> in a soundless place
> They watch you walk/sit/stand/breathe. . . .[3]

What did being sissy really mean? It was a way of walking (from the hips rather than the shoulders); it was a way of talking (often with a lisp or in a high-pitched voice); it was a way of relating to others (gently, not wanting to fight, or hurt anyone's feelings). It was being intelligent ("an egghead" they called it sometimes); getting good grades. It means not being interested in sports, not playing football in the street after school; not discussing teams and scores and playoffs. And it involved not showing fervent interest in girls, not talking about scoring with tits or *Playboy* centerfolds. Not concealing naked women in your history book; or porno books in your locker.

On the other hand, anyone could be a "faggot." It was a catch-all. If you did something that didn't conform to what was the acceptable behavior of the group, then you risked being called a faggot. If you didn't get along with the "in" crowd, you were a faggot. It was the most commonly used put-down. It kept guys in line. They became angry when somebody called them a faggot. More fights started over someone calling someone else a faggot than anything else. The word had power. It toppled the male ego, shattered his delicate facade, violated the image he projected. He was tough. Without feeling. Faggot cut through all this. It made him vulnerable. Feminine. And feminine was the worst thing he could possible be. Girls were fine for fucking, but no boy in his right mind wanted to be like them. A boy was the opposite of a girl. He was not feminine. He was not feeling. He was not weak.

Just look at the gym teacher who growled like a dog; or the priest with the black belt who threw kids against the wall in rage when they didn't know their Latin. They were men, they got respect.

But not the physics teacher who preached pacifism during lectures on the nature of atoms. Everybody knew what he was—and why he believed in the anti-war movement.

My parents only knew that the neighborhood kids called me names. They begged me to act more like the other boys. My brothers were ashamed of me. They never said it, but I knew. Just as I knew that my parents were embarrassed by my behavior.

At times, they tried to get me to act differently. Once my father lectured me on how to walk right. I'm still not clear on what that means. Not from the hips, I guess, don't "swish" like faggots do.

A nun in elementary school told my mother at Open House that there was "something wrong with me." I had draped my sweater over my shoulders like a girl, she said. I was a smart kid, but I should know better than to wear my sweater like a girl!

My mother stood there, mute. I wanted her to say something, to chastise the nun; to defend me. But how could she? This was a nun talking—representative of Jesus, protector of all that was good and decent.

An uncle once told me I should start "acting like a boy" instead of like a girl. Everybody seemed ashamed of me. And I guess I was ashamed of myself, too. It was hard not to be.

Scene Five

Priest: Do you like girls, Mark?
Mark: Uh-huh.
Priest: I mean *really* like them?
Mark: Yeah—they're okay.
Priest: There's a role they play in your salvation. Do you understand it, Mark?
Mark: Yeah.

Priest: You've got to like girls. Even if you should decide to enter the seminary, it's important to keep in mind God's plan for a man and a woman. . . .[4]

Catholicism of course condemned homosexuality. Effeminacy was tolerated as long as the effeminate person did not admit to being gay. Thus, priests could be effeminate because they weren't gay.

As a sissy, I could count on no support from the church. A male's sole purpose in life was to father children—souls for the church to save. The only hope a homosexual had of attaining salvation was by remaining totally celibate. Don't even think of touching another boy. To think of a sin was a sin. And to sin was to put a mark upon the soul. Sin—if it was a serious offense against god—led to hell. There was no way around it. If you sinned, you were doomed.

Realizing I was gay was not an easy task. Although I knew I was attracted to boys by the time I was about eleven, I didn't connect this attraction to homosexuality. I was not queer. Not I. I was merely appreciating a boy's good looks, his fine features, his proportions. It didn't seem to matter that I didn't appreciate a girl's looks in the same way. There was no twitching in my thighs when I gazed upon a beautiful girl. But I wasn't queer.

I resisted that label—queer—for the longest time. Even when everything pointed to it, I refused to see it. I was certainly not queer. Not I.

We sat through endless English classes, and History courses about the wars between men who were not allowed to love each other. No gay history was ever taught. No history faces you this morning. You're just a faggot. Homosexuals had never contributed to the human race. God destroyed the queers in Sodom and Gomorrah.

We learned about Michelangelo, Oscar Wilde, Gertrude Stein—but never that they were queer. They were not queer. Walt Whitman, the "father of American poetry," was not queer. No one was queer. I was alone, totally unique. One of a kind. Were there others like me somewhere? Another planet, perhaps?

In school, they never talked of the queers. They did not exist. The only hint we got of this other species was in religion class. And even then it was clouded in mystery—never spelled out. It was sin. Like masturbation. Like looking at *Playboy* and getting a hard-on. A sin.

Once a progressive priest in senior year religion class actually mentioned homosexuals—he said the word—but was into Erich Fromm, into homosexuals as pathetic and sick. Fixated at some early stage; penis, anal, whatever. Only heterosexuals passed on to the nirvana of sexual development.

No other images from the halls of the Catholic high school except those the other boys knew: swishy faggot sucking cock in an alley somewhere, grabbing asses in the bathroom. Never mentioning how much straight boys craved blow jobs, it was part of the secret.

It was all a secret. You were not supposed to talk about the queers. Whisper maybe. Laugh about them, yes. But don't be open, honest; don't try to understand. Don't cite their accomplishments. No history faces you this morning. You're just a faggot faggot no history just a faggot

Epilogue

The boy marching down the Parkway. Hundreds of queers. Signs proclaiming gay pride. Speakers. Tables with literature from gay groups. A miracle, he is thinking. Tears are coming loose now. Someone hugs him.

> You could not control
> the sissy in me
> nor could you exorcise him
> nor electrocute him
> You declared him illegal illegitimate
> insane and immature
> But he defies you still.[5]

Notes

1. From the poem "Faggot" by Tommi Avicolli, published in *GPU News,* Sept. 1979.
2. Ibid.
3. Ibid.
4. From the play *Judgment of the Roaches* by Tommi Avicolli, produced in Philadelphia at the Gay Community Center, the Painted Bride Arts Center and the University of Pennsylvania; aired over WXPN-FM, in four parts; and presented at the Lesbian/Gay Conference in Norfolk, VA, July, 1980.
5. From the poem "Sissy Poem," published in *Magic Doesn't Live Here Anymore* (Philadelphia: Spruce Street Press, 1976).

Name: _____ Class: _____

Date: _____ Section: _____

Reading Comprehension Activity Sheet

He Defies You Still: The Memoirs of a Sissy, Tommi Avicolli

1. Briefly discuss the role of religious ideology in the maintenance of demonizing homosexuality.

   _____
   _____
   _____
   _____
   _____
   _____
   _____
   _____
   _____
   _____
   _____
   _____

2. What is the "secret" that Avicolli mentions? What are the potential ramifications for keeping this secret? _____

   _____
   _____
   _____
   _____
   _____
   _____
   _____
   _____
   _____
   _____
   _____
   _____

The New Gay Struggle

Richard Lacayo

What people mean when they say Matthew Shepard's murder was a lynching is that he was killed to make a point. When he was 21 years old, the world's arguments reached him with deadly force and printed their worst conclusions across him. So he was stretched along a Wyoming fence not just as a dying young man but as a signpost. "When push comes to shove," it says, "this is what we have in mind for gays."

Three days after Shepard died, a crowd of around 5,000 gathered in the night on the steps of the Capitol in Washington, in a candlelight vigil that struggled to make another argument and extract another message from his death. Ellen DeGeneres, Ted Kennedy and Barney Frank, the openly gay Massachusetts Congressman—all the expected speakers took the microphone. What was less expected was the sheer turnout of lawmakers at a moment when Congress was embroiled in the crazy closing hours of the budget deal. So many members showed up to voice their grief and anger that House minority leader Dick Gephardt had time only to read their names. "It speaks volumes about how much progress we've made," says Winnie Stachelberg, lobbyist for the Human Rights Campaign, the nation's biggest gay-rights group. "Yet Matthew's death shows how much farther we have to go."

A lot farther, and through swamps. However much it revolted people all around the country, don't count on Shepard's murder to revolutionize the intractable politics of gay rights in Washington or elsewhere. In the aftermath of the killing, President Clinton urged Congress to pass the Hate Crimes Prevention Act, a bill long bottled up by conservatives and other groups in Congress because it would broaden the definition of hate crimes to include assaults on gays as well as women and the disabled. But with Congress adjourned until after Election Day, the momentum to pass the bill is no sure thing.

And while Shepard's death has forced even the most belligerently anti-gay conservatives to situate themselves carefully—condemning the murder while insisting they contributed nothing to the atmosphere that might legitimize it—the Republican Party, beholden to its Christian-activist base, doesn't dare compromise much on gay rights. One speaker at the

From *Time*, October 26, 1998. Used with permission of Time, Inc.

vigil was Wyoming's former Senator Alan Simpson, a Republican. But Wyoming's current G.O.P. Senators, Michael Enzi and Craig Thomas, didn't show.

Gay politics is more complicated than ever right now because what seems like an irresistible force of cultural change is meeting an immovable object of political resistance. For a long time, lesbians and gays have been defining themselves into the ordinary fabric of life. All the while, conservatives have been field-testing homosexuality as a defining issue for the Republican Party, especially for the next presidential election. This is all happening while Americans generally are drifting toward a bumpy accommodation, making judgments that are intricate, ad hoc and unpredictable. In a new TIME/CNN poll, 64% of those questioned thought homosexual relations are acceptable, but 48% thought they are morally wrong.

There may well be more *openly* gay men and women in America now than in any other country at any other time in history. The long-ago sexual revolution, gay visibility in the media, the reckonings forced by AIDS—there are any number of reasons for this emergence. It has changed straight America, of course. Just go rent *My Best Friend's Wedding,* or watch *Will & Grace* on NBC. What's less noticed is that it has also changed bay America, which is a very different place now than when Shepard was born, or even when he was a teenager. By a complex but not very surprising reciprocal relationship, the simple face that there are a greater number of visible and comfortable gays has created more of the same, more visible and comfortable gays. "I think we've done a great deal of persuading people that we are not a countercultural force," says Andrew Sullivan, author (*Love Undetectable*) and former *New Republic* editor, who epitomizes the argument that homosexuals should embrace the existing institutions of heterosexual society. "We are a mainstream force." Sullivan likes to point out that the richest gay group in the nation isn't a political group but a religious denomination, the Metropolitan Community Church, whose offerings totaled $17 million last year and whose membership across the nation has grown to 40,000. And the mainstreaming of gays isn't confined to New York City and Los Angeles; 21-year-olds are coming out everywhere, so that, for instance, a gay freshman landing this fall at Western Michigan University in Kalamazoo or at the University of Idaho in Moscow could find a group to join. In little Agency, Mo. (pop. 300), a woman named Liz Jalbert is president of Midland Empire Task Force, a gay group that has doubled in size, to nearly 100 paid members, in the past two years. Two Saturdays ago, more than 100 showed up at her house for the group's annual bonfire.

As a consequence, even the anti-gay right has had to shift the tone of its message as more straight Americans become acquainted with their own gay friends and family. Anita Bryant, the singer turned anti-gay campaigner of the 1970s said that what homosexuals really want is "the right to propose to our children." It says something about the difficulties of demonizing homosexuals these days when Senate majority leader Trent Lott merely compares them to kleptomaniacs, as he did this summer, or when Christian groups run ad campaigns insisting gays can be cured. While that language may try to throw the debate back more than 20 years, before psychologists concluded that homosexuality is not a mental illness, it represents a recognition that pure contempt is tricky when you are talking about people's children or friends.

At the same time, lesbian and gay organizations have gone from being outcasts of the left to being an expected presence in politics, or at least in Democratic coalitions, and a presence knocking at the door of the Republican Party. "The whole public attitude on gay issues has become much more mainstream," notes Al From, who runs the Democratic Leadership Council, which breeds centrist New Democrats like Clinton. "A lot of gay businessmen are New Democrats. A lot more people are dealing with gays in their families."

It has been a long road from there to here. Largely because of opposition from unions, blacks and church groups, it was not until 1983 that a gay organization, the National Gay and Lesbian Task Force, was admitted to the Leadership Conference on Civil Rights, one of Washington's most liberal legislative coalitions. It was 11 years more before the group took a consensus position on anything involving gay rights. In 1994 it backed a modest change in the Employment Non-Discrimination Act, or ENDA, that would prohibit discrimination on the basis of sexual orientation while permitting an exemption for churches. Two years later that amendment was defeated in the Senate by just a single vote.

For a long time, the most prominent nationwide gay-rights organization was the 35,000-member National Gay and Lesbian Task Force, which grew out of the scruffy radicalism of the old gay-liberation movement. But after 25 years, it still has virtually no lobbying presence on Capitol Hill. In the later 1980s the AIDS epidemic brought forth the street-theater militancy of ACT UP and in 1990 the in-your-face tribalism of Queer Nation. "We here, we're queer, get used to it" was an interesting statement of the facts. But the cutting edge of gay politics threatened to cut gays off altogether from the give and take of lawmaking.

The election of Bill Clinton was a psychological turning point, even though his support on gay-rights issues has been unsteady. His "Don't ask, don't tell" compromise on gays in the military satisfied no one. He signed the "Defense of Marriage" Act, which denies federal recognition to same-sex unions, then advertised the fact in '96 campaign spots on Christian radio stations. But he was canny about the symbolic gestures. He ended the federal policy of treating gays as security risks and invited gay activists to the White House for the first time. The message he sent was that gays were part of the American family and also part of the political game.

"The Clinton election took the wind out of the sails of street activists," says John Gallagher, national correspondent of the *Advocate,* the gay news monthly. "They used to be outside shouting. Now people have to be inside talking, which is a new experience." And during those years, a new kind of gay lobbying group has emerged. The Human Rights Campaign, founded in 1980, is the group that corresponds to mainstreaming impulses within the gay community. It's also the largest—membership 250,000, up from 85,000 just five years ago. Sedate and pragmatic, with a name so innocuous it could be transferred intact to a group devoted to fair labor practices, H.R.C. was established to speak to the middle class in middle-class terms. Its annual black-tie fund-raising dinner is the peak event of the gay political season. The guest speaker last year was Clinton; this year's was Al Gore. Executive director Elizabeth Birch is a corporate lawyer from Silicon Valley, former head of international litigation at Apple Computer; she has run H.R.C. like a software start-up—new image, new logo, fast growth. After she came to H.R.C. in 1995, she quickly changed its symbol to a yellow equal sign on a blue background. Cool as a computer-keyboard button, it has no visible connection to the pink triangle or rainbow flag, two more freighted symbols of the ragged glories of gay history.

"We're by far the largest gay organization," says Birch, "so something is working." Though the group channels most of its campaign gifts to Democrats, H.R.C. is determined to prove it is not an auxiliary of the Democratic Party. Its board includes former G.O.P. congressman Steve Gunderson. Of the 200 candidates the group endorsed this year, 14 were Republicans, including Pennsylvania Senator Arlen Specter, a chief sponsor of the hate-crimes bill. Now the group is locked in an internal struggle over whether to endorse New York Senator Alfonse D'Amato over his Democratic rival, Representative Charles Schumer. Though conservative on abortion rights and other liberal litmus tests, D'Amato has in recent years come around on most gay issues.

The White House has pressured some in H.R.C. to resist backing D'Amato. One way out is to endorse both candidates. But the logic of endorsing D'Amato runs this way: If a gay organization doesn't encourage Republicans who stick their neck out, why should they bother? And if H.R.C. backs a supportive Republican, wouldn't that foster a new generation of G.O.P. leaders who would respond to the more moderate politics of the G.O.P.'s growing younger and suburban base? "That party is at war with itself, and its best decision makers are not at the top," says Birch. "Trent Lott is making horrible mistakes."

In line with that thinking, there is small, careful movement within the G.O.P. to coincide with the August national convention of the Log Cabin Republicans, the 10,000-member gay G.O.P. group, Jim Nicholson, chairman of the Republican National Committee, made a point of welcoming gays into the party. "That's new," says Log Cabin executive director Rich Tafel. In the House this year, 30 Republicans joined Democrats to defeat a move to ban adoption by gays in the District of Columbia. Earlier, when Republican Joel Hefley of Colorado tried to revoke a Clinton Executive Order banning discrimination against gay federal employees, his measure was defeated, with the astonishing help of 63 Republican votes.

In the Senate, a handful of G.O.P. conservatives, including Utah's Orrin Hatch and Arizona's John McCain, have moved quietly, very quietly, in step with gay groups on issues like hate crimes, though not on more difficult ones like gay marriage. Eight years ago, Hatch was pivotal in helping overcome the resistance of Jesse Helms to win passage of the hate Crimes Statistics Act, which requires the Federal Government to keep data on bias crimes, including crimes against homosexuals. But he has not backed this year's hate-crimes bill publicly yet, lest he alienate conservative colleagues whose votes he will need for passage.

Indeed, so sensitive is the matter that neither Hatch nor H.R.C. would discuss the bill's exact status last week.

But at the same time that gay activists have become more sophisticated and accommodating, their opponents on the Christian right have become more militant and more powerful within the Republican Party. Gary Bauer, head of the Family Research Council, and his mentor James Dobson, the Christian broadcaster who heads Focus on the Family, with its 2.3 million-name mailing list, have made opposition to gay rights a defining issue. Republicans trying to bridge the gap complain that while the rhetoric of the Christian right makes compromise difficult, so does some of the language of gay activism. "They got to get off the stuff about Christians having this conspiracy to incite hate crimes," insists a Republican lawmaker. "When you have people so far apart, it makes it more difficult."

In the end and in the beginning, the struggle over gay rights is only partly political in the legislative sense. Much of the real action is in everyday life—from household arrangements to mass media to the simple yet crucial changes wrought by acquaintance and friendship. This debate has been carried on in the culture at large for years, around the ears of gays who, because they lived within it, came out and came out earlier, in a process that may not have been easy but that eventually seemed to them right and essential. If Washington reacts slowly and crudely, turning family dramas and internal dialogues into attack ads and legislative-floor fights, it only proves what conservatism has always argued—that government, even representative government, is a crude representative of ordinary lives. While the world tries to make sense out of Matthew Shepard's death, maybe his most important political act was his life. H was gay, and for a while he lived that way.

—Reported by Harriet Barovick and John Cloud/New York and Michael Duffy/Washington

Name: _____ Class: _____

Date: _____ Section: _____

Reading Comprehension Activity Sheet

The New Gay Struggle, Richard Lacayo

1. Can politics cause hate? _____

_____
_____
_____
_____
_____
_____
_____
_____
_____
_____
_____

2. Do you believe the political climate today is more, or less, accepting of homosexual rights? ____

_____
_____
_____
_____
_____
_____
_____
_____
_____
_____
_____
_____
_____

3. Should crimes against homosexuals be designated as "hate crimes"? How does an assault against a homosexual differ from an assault against a heterosexual? _____

PART III
Social Institutions

Social institutions, created and maintained by a society, represent manifestations of the "social fact" that Emile Durkheim described. These institutions are "larger" than the individuals who comprise them, a virtual 2+2=5 synergistic effect. Institutions embody patterns of interaction that have become routine and normative. The saying "You can't fight City Hall" reflects the difficult nature of negotiating change in social institutions. Individual attempts to impact an institution are met with resistance since it is difficult to overcome the 'inertia' that exists. Moreover, through the socialization process, members of a society are taught to accept the status quo and not challenge its existence. Those who challenge the existing social structure are defined as deviant, perhaps even as criminal, and are subsequently punished. They may be branded as "troublemakers," "instigators," or "non-conformists." This section will examine some of these social institutions, and how patterns within them become institutionalized and therefore made to be routine.

The first set of readings explores marriages and families. Although individuals make up the constellation of a family, the institution of family (variously defined) has been around as long as people have been. Yet, if you ask an American child, "What is a family?," their answer typically centers on the traditional definition of mother, father, siblings, and perhaps grandparents. Children, likewise, have very definitive ideas as to how "moms" and "dads" should act, and what a marriage represents, ideas which they then carry with them into adulthood. Little girls are socialized through storybooks, fairy tales, movies, and song to seek out their "Prince Charming" so that they may live "happily ever after." Families that do not look like the ones portrayed in popular television programming, or marriages that do not conform to the expectations instilled in us in terms of how husbands and wives should act, are seen as deviant. Alternative family forms or marital arrangements are viewed with suspicion. There are as many different families as there are individuals who make them up. The "institution of the family," however, has remained relatively stable.

The second set of readings explores the institution of education. Schools exist to teach our children the skills and knowledge necessary to succeed in a modern society. However, beyond the manifest functions of schools, the institution of education also teaches our children cultural values reflecting a middle-class orientation and lifestyle. This section will examine how children are taught, through a hidden curriculum, to be accepting of the status quo, to not challenge authority or question the existing social system, and to be socialized into future adult roles. The mechanisms of teaching these values are discussed, and inequities inherent in education are explored. As was demonstrated in the unit on social inequalities, children do not come to the school setting as equals. They arrive differentially prepared to acquire, assimilate, adopt, and embrace what is presented in the school arena. The degree to which children "go along with the program" will play no small role in their subsequent success.

The third social institution that will be explored is religion. Religion is so integral and fundamental to a large number of people, and involves such deeply held values and beliefs, that any discussion of religion is bound to result in heated debate. The purpose, however, is not to suggest that a particular religion is "right" or "wrong," but rather to explore the functions that religion has for a society. Religion is a social institution that was created and is maintained by a community of believers. As such, as examination of what a religion does for that community and the purposes that it serves should be conducted in an academic setting.

The fourth set of readings surrounding politics and government will probably be revisited in the near future as current research brings into the academic discussion the concerns surrounding domestic and international terrorism. The reading about the My Lai Massacre may not only shock and upset the reader, but it will also no doubt stimulate the discussion of potentially another My Lai. To think that such atrocities have been perpetrated in the past is no doubt distasteful, but to think that such an atrocity can be perpetrated again is down right unconscionable. In contrast, the article by C. Wright Mills calls back into the discussion the readings regarding social class. The assertion that was made earlier—that certain individuals in our society have differential access to social rewards—is made clear in the examination of power.

The last reading by George Ritzer looks at various trends in current American society. Based upon the fast-food industry, a model is presented in which social change is described using ideas associated with time, product, convenience, and self-service. This reading should lead to a discussion of anticipated future social trends. Moreover, dialogue can ensue concerning the upcoming trends and anticipated social changes of the social institutions explored in this section.

chapter 11

Marriages and Families

The Way We Really Are
Stephanie Coontz

The Two Marriages
Jessie Bernard

Ten Myths That Perpetuate Corporal Punishment
Murray A. Straus

The Way We Really Are

Stephanie Coontz

Introduction

Five years ago I wrote a book called *The Way We Never Were: American Families and the Nostalgia Trap.* As a family historian bothered by widespread misconceptions in the popular press about "traditional" families, I hoped to get people to look more realistically at the strengths, weaknesses, and surprising variability of family life in the past.

My book went to press just as Dan Quayle issued his famous condemnation of Murphy Brown, the fictional television character who decided to bear her child out of wedlock. The ensuing polemics over whether Murphy Brown was setting a bad example for our nation's youth were followed by an all-out war over family values as the 1992 election approached. Since much of the discussion focused on the contrast between today's families and "the way things used to be," I began to get calls from congressional committees, reporters, and television producers asking me for a historical perspective on these issues. Soon I found myself in the thick of a national debate over what was happening to the American family....

In my last book, I demonstrated the tremendous variety of family types that have worked—and not worked—in American history. When families succeeded, it was often for reasons quite different than stereotypes about the past suggest—because they were flexible in their living arrangements, for example, or could call on people and institutions beyond the family for assistance or support. And when families failed, the results were often devastating. There never was a golden age of family life, a time when all families were capable of meeting the needs of their members and protecting them from poverty, violence, or sexual exploitation.

The "traditional" sexual double standard, for example, may have led more middle-class girls to delay sex at the end of the nineteenth century than today, but it also created higher proportions of young female prostitutes. Respect for elders may have received more lip

From *The Way We Really Are* by Stephanie Coontz. Copyright © 1997 by Basic Books, a division of HarperCollins Publishers, Inc. Reprinted by permission of Basic Books, a member of Perseus Books, LLC.

service in the past, but elders were until very recently the segment of the population most likely to be destitute.

Yet knowing there was no golden age in history does not satisfy most people. Okay, they say, so the past wasn't great, and people have been lamenting the "breakdown of the family" or the "crisis of modern youth" since colonial days. It may be entertaining to know that John Watson, the most famous child psychiatrist of the early twentieth century, predicted in 1928 that marriage would be dead by 1977, and that in 1977, noted sociologist Amitai Etzioni announced that "by mid-1990 not one American family will be left." But even a stopped clock is right twice a day. What if these fears are finally coming true? Am I claiming that the more things change, the more they remain the same? Do I think people are crazy to feel anxious about recent trends in family life?

"Perhaps it's good to have our illusions about the past shattered," people often say, "but once we reject the lies and the myths, what do we put in their place?" Are the only lessons from history negative? Isn't there anything positive families can learn from history and sociology? . . .

BOOSTING OUR SOCIAL INTELLIGENCE: PUTTING FAMILY AND PERSONAL TRENDS IN CONTEXT

Understanding the history of families and the structural constraints under which they operate can prevent our emotional and social IQs from being stunted by what sometimes seems like a national campaign to "dumb us down." Politicians have become experts in squeezing the complexity out of issues to produce compressed, thirteen-second sound bites. Think-tank publicists bombard us with the out-of-context snippets of information sometimes called "factoids." . . .

Care must be taken in interpreting headlines about the explosion of unwed motherhood. Unwed motherhood has increased dramatically since 1970, but it's easy to overstate *how* dramatically, because much illegitimacy was covered up in the past and reporting methods have recently become much more sophisticated. In the past, notes Sam Roberts, many unwed mothers would tell census workers that they were separated, "resulting in the anomaly of many more 'separated' women than men." At least 80 percent of the increase in unwed motherhood reported between 1981 and 1983, explains Steve Rawlings of the Census Bureau, came from "refinements in survey procedures that were introduced early in the 1980s. This represents 10 to 15 percent of the total increase between 1970 and 1993 (or 20 to 25 percent of the increase since 1980)." And though newspapers routinely use unwed motherhood and single parenthood interchangeably, many unwed mothers are part of cohabiting couples. Five states, including California, further distort the statistics by assuming a woman is unmarried if she has a different last name than the father listed on the birth certificate!

It's also important to distinguish between the ratio of unmarried to married births and the rate of births to unmarried women. Between 1960 and 1990, the nonmarital birth ratio increased by more than 500 percent, from 5.3 percent of all births to 28 percent. But birth rates to unmarried women only increased by a factor of 1.73, not quite twofold. What explains the larger figure is that births to unmarried women rose while births to married women fell, increasing the *relative* proportion of unmarried births much more than their *absolute* numbers. In some cases, a fall in marital fertility may be so large that unwed births become a larger proportion of all births even when rates of unwed childbearing are flat or falling. The probability that an unmarried African-American woman would have a child actually fell from 9.8 to 9.0 percent between 1960 and 1990, for example; but because married-couple childbearing decreased among African Americans even more sharply, the proportion of black children born to unwed mothers rose.

I'm not saying that the media intend to mislead. But in many cases, lack of historical perspective makes intelligent, dedicated reporters vulnerable to manipulation by people who wish to magnify one particular set of the factoids that continuously streak across our information horizon. . . .

The result is that many pronouncements about the family, often by the same commentators, have a peculiarly manic-depressive quality. On the one hand, there are the doomsday predictions. New consensus spokesman David Popenoe warns that the decay of family life is "unique and unprecedented" and that the final collapse of "the last vestige of the traditional family unit" is imminent. "Marriage is dying," says Robert Rector of the Heritage Foundation; the next ten years will "decide whether or not marriage and family survive in this nation." Our failure to halt the decay of marriage, says the Council on Families in America, is "nothing less than an act of cultural suicide."

On the other hand, these catastrophic assertions are periodically interspersed with cheerful assurances that things may be turning around. Popenoe sees hopeful signs of a "new familism" in "the nation as a whole." Charles Murray of the American Enterprise Institute thinks we may be moving toward "the restoration of a culture in which family, parenthood, . . . morality, and the virtues are all perceived and valued in ways that our grandparents would find familiar."

Such wild fluctuations in assessments result from a lack of historical context. By contrast, once people understand the complicated *mix* of long-term changes in family trends, social institutions, and cultural mores, they are less likely to think that any one-size-fits-all quick fix can turn everything around, for better or for worse. They're more likely to be realistic about what can and can't be changed, what we need to adjust to and what we may be able to resist.

For example, take the question of whether marriage is a dying institution. In 1867 there were 9.6 marriages per 1,000 people. A hundred years later, in 1967, there were 9.7. The rate reached a low of 7.9 in 1932 and an all-time high of 16.4 in 1946, a peak quickly followed by a brief but huge surge in divorce. Marriage rates fell again from the early 1950s to 1958, rose slowly until the end of the 1960s, and then began to decline again. But the proportion of women who remain single all their lives is *lower* today than at the turn of the century, and fewer women now feel they have to forgo marriage entirely in order to do anything else in their lives. Periodic predictions to the contrary, it is unlikely that we will someday record the demise of the last married couple in America.

Nevertheless, marriage is certainly a *transformed* institution, and it plays a smaller role than ever before in organizing social and personal life. One reason is that marriage comes much later, for most people, than in the past. Men's average age at first marriage today is not unprecedented, though it has now regained the previous record high of 1890. But the average age of marriage for contemporary women is two years higher than its historical peak in 1890 and almost four years higher than in the 1950s. This figure approaches the highest age ever recorded for Western Europe, a region where marriage has always taken place later than almost anywhere else in the world. And although fewer women stay single all their lives than in 1900, a higher proportion of women than ever before experience a period of independent living and employment before marriage. Women's expectations of both marriage and work are unlikely to ever be the same as in the past.

The second reason for marriage's more limited role in people's lives is that it is no longer expected to last "until death do us part." Divorce rates in America rose steadily until World War II, fell briefly during the 1950s, and took off again during the late 1960s. The divorce rate crested near the end of the 1970s, leveled off in the 1980s, and very slightly receded from 1988 to 1993. This last trend was heralded by many commentators as a "real turnaround," a sign that Americans "are turning conservative, pro-family." but while demographers now say that only 40 percent, rather than 50 percent, of marriages will end in divorce, these remain among the highest divorce rates ever recorded. Furthermore, the cumulative effects of past divorces continue to mount. In 1960 there were 35 divorced men and women for every 1,000 married ones. By 1990 there were 140 divorced individuals for every 1,000 married ones.

People often misunderstand what statisticians mean when they estimate that one in every two or three marriages will end in divorce. The calculations refer to the chances of a marriage ending in divorce within 40 years. While rising divorce rates have increased the number of marriages at risk for dissolution, the gradual extension of life spans ensures that a marriage today has the potential to last three times longer than one of 200 years ago. Thus while the number of people who divorce is certainly unprecedented, so is the number of couples who celebrate their fortieth wedding anniversaries. In fact, the chances of doing so have never been better.

On the other hand, the average marriage that ends in divorce lasts only 6.3 years. We may be seeing more marriages that last longer and are more fulfilling than at any time in our history. But we are also seeing more marriages that are *less* committed and of shorter duration than in the past. Sociologist Valerie Oppenheimer suggests we are experiencing growing polarization between increasing numbers of very "high-quality," long-lasting marriages *and* increasing numbers of short-lived, medium- to "low-quality" ones where the partners are not committed enough to stay and work things through. Understanding this polarization helps explain some of the ambivalence Americans have about modern families. Very few people in a modern high-quality marriage would trade it for an older model where limited communication and a high degree of sexual dissatisfaction were taken for granted. And few adults in a very low-quality marriage, or their children, want to be trapped there for life. But the commitments and consequences of "medium-quality" marriages are more ambiguous, especially for kids, and this worries many Americans.

Often their worry takes the form of a debate over whether we should return to the family forms and values of the 1950s. That decade is still close enough that many people derive their political position on the issue from personal experience. At forums I've conducted across the country, some people raised in 1950s families tell of tormented childhoods in alcoholic, abusive, or conflict-ridden families. They cannot understand, they say vehemently, why anyone would regret the passing of the 1950s for a single moment. My research validates their experience. These individuals were not alone.

But other people remember 1950s families that shielded them from adult problems and disputes. Many had unmistakably happy parents. Others had secure childhoods but learned later that one or both of their parents were miserable. Some of these individuals are now sorry that their parents stayed together, but many more say they are glad not to have known about their parents' problems and grateful for whatever kept their families together. They are also thankful that the media did not expose them to many adult realities that today's children see or read about every day. My research validates their experience too.

The only way to get past the polarized personal testimonies for and against 1950s families is to put their strengths and weaknesses into historical perspective. This permits a more balanced assessment of what we have gained and lost since then. It also helps us distinguish historical precedents we may be able to draw on from new issues requiring new responses. . . .

Why Working Mothers Are Here to Stay

The 1950s was clearly out of balance in one direction, with almost half the adult population restricted in their access to economic and political roles beyond the family. But the last few decades have been out of balance in the opposite direction. Many of us now feel that our expanding roles beyond the family have restricted our access to family life.

At first glance, it appears that the new imbalance results from women, especially mothers, entering the workforce. Certainly, that trend has produced a dramatic change in relation to the decade that most people use as their measure of "traditional" family life. In 1950, only a quarter of all wives were in the paid labor force, and just 16 percent of all children had mothers who worked outside the home. By 1991, more than 58 percent of all married women, and nearly two-thirds of all married women with children, were in the labor force. Of the total number of children in the country, 59 percent, including a majority of preschoolers, had mothers who worked outside the home.

But to analyze today's family imbalance as a conflict between work and mothering is to misread family history and to misdirect future family policy. Historically, productive work by mothers as well as fathers (and by young people) has not only been compatible with family life but has also strengthened family relationships. What's really out of balance is the relationship between market activities and nonmarket ones (including community as well as family ties). Our jobs don't make room for family obligations. The purchase of goods and services often substitutes for family or neighborhood activities. Phone calls, beepers, faxes and e-mail constantly intrude into family time. To correct this imbalance, we need to reorganize work to make it more compatible with family life. We need to reorganize family life to make sure that all members share in the work needed to sustain it. We need to redirect technology so that it serves rather than dominates our social and interpersonal relationships.

Instead, however, the family consensus brokers encourage us to cobble together personal marital arrangements that combine what they consider to be the best family features from both the 1950s and the 1990s. They reason that if we could convince women to take time off from work while their children are young, bolster male wages enough that more families could afford to make this choice, increase the incentives for marriage, and combat the excesses of individualism that lead to divorce or unwed motherhood, then surely we could solve the conflicts that parents now experience in balancing work and family. While recommending that men should help out more at home and expressing abstract support for equal pay and promotion opportunities for women on the job, the family values think tanks nevertheless propose that parents revive "relatively traditional marital gender roles" for the period "when children are young," cutting back on mothers' paid work.

In the absence of wider social change in work policies and family support systems, this is the individual solution that many men and women try to work out. And it may be a reasonable stopgap measure for parents who can afford it. But when such personal accommodations are put forward as an overarching political program for family life, they cease to sound quite so reasonable. . . .

Women, the argument goes, are happy to care for children, but men's biological drives point them in a different direction. Men have to be coaxed and guided into responsible fatherhood, and societies have historically achieved this by granting husbands special status as moral educators, family authority figures, and breadwinners. When society stops viewing breadwinning "as a father's special task," we lose our most powerful way "to motivate fathers to provide for their children."

The family values crusaders believe that all men and women, at least during their parenting years, should organize their families with the man as primary provider and protector and the wife as primary nurturer. Before and after child rearing, a woman is welcome to work; but unless she has no other option, she should engage in "sequencing"—alternating work and child raising rather than trying to combine them. Popenoe proposes the wife take "at least a year" off work, then work part-time until her children are in their early to mid-teens. Even when both husband and wife are employed, the woman should remain primarily responsible for nurturing, with the man as "junior partner" at home. Husbands should help out more than in the past, but anything that smacks of "androgyny" is to be avoided like the plague. Society, he argues, must "disavow the popular notion of radical feminists that 'daddies can make good mommies.'"

Hostility to women's economic independence is a consistent subtext in "new consensus" writing. "Policies that encourage mothers to work instead of marry" are a large part of America's social problem, says Wade Horn of the National Fatherhood Initiative. Without providing any evidence, Dan Quayle claims studies show "that children whose parents work are *less likely* to have Mommy's undivided attention than children whose mothers stay home." Isn't it odd how quickly a discussion of working *parents* becomes an indictment of *Mommy?* According to this agenda, a male breadwinner–female homemaker division of labor is not an individual family choice but the correct model for every family. Women are told that there are compensations for giving up their aspirations to economic equality: "Even though the man is the head of the family, the woman is the neck, and she turns the head any way she wants." But if women are not willing to "give back" family leadership, groups such as the Promise Keepers advise men to "take it back. . . . Be sensitive. Treat the lady gently and lovingly. But lead!"

While we can debate the *merits* of these proposals for America's families, I am more interested in examining their *practicality*. How likely is it that a majority of mothers will once more withdraw from paid employment during the early years of child rearing? What can historical and sociological analysis teach us about how realistic it is to propose that we revive the breadwinner identity as the basis for men's commitment to marriage and child raising?

THE LATE BIRTH AND SHORT LIFE OF THE MALE BREADWINNER FAMILY

One of the most common misconceptions about modern marriage is the notion that coprovider families are a new invention in human history. In fact, today's dual-earner family represents a return to older norms, after a very short interlude that people mistakenly identify as "traditional."

Throughout most of humanity's history women as well as men were family breadwinners. Contrary to cartoons of cavemen dragging home food to a wife waiting at the campfire, in the distant past of early gathering and hunting societies women contributed as much or more to family subsistence as men. Mothers left the hearth to forage for food, hunt small animals, trade with other groups, or tend crops.

On this continent, neither Native American, African-American, nor white women were originally seen as economic dependents. Among European colonists, men dominated women, but their authority was based on legal, political, and religious coercion, not on men's greater economic importance. The most common words for wives in seventeenth- and eighteenth-century colonial America were "yoke-makes" or "meet-helps," labels that indicated women's economic partnership with men. Until the early nineteenth century, men and women worked together on farms or in small household businesses, alongside other family members. Responsibility for family life and responsibility for breadwinning were not two different, specialized jobs.

But in the early 1800s, as capitalist production for the market replaced home-based production for local exchange and a wage-labor system supplanted widespread self-employment and farming, more and more work was conducted in centralized work-places removed from the farm or home. A new division of labor then grew up within many families. Men (and older children) began to specialize in work outside the home, withdrawing from their traditional child-raising responsibilities. Household work and child care were delegated to wives, who gave up their older roles in production and barter. While slaves and free blacks continued to have high labor force participation by women, wives in most other ethnic and racial groups were increasingly likely to quit paid work outside the home after marriage.

But it's important to remember that this new division of work between husbands and wives came out of a *temporary* stage in the history of wage labor and industrialization. It corresponded to a transitional period when households could no longer get by primarily on things they made, grew, or bartered, but could not yet rely on purchased consumer goods. For example, families no longer produced their own homespun cotton, but ready-made clothing was not yet available at prices most families could afford. Women still had to sew clothes from cloth that men purchased with their pay. Most families still had to grow part of their food and bake their own bread. Food preparation and laundering required hours of work each day. Water often had to be hauled and heated.

Somebody had to go out to earn money in order to buy the things the family needed; but somebody else had to stay home and turn the things they bought into things they could actually use. Given the preexisting legal, political, and religious tradition of patriarchal dominance, husbands (and youths of both sexes) were assigned to work outside the home. Wives assumed exclusive responsibility for domestic matters that they had formerly shared with husbands or delegated to older children and apprentices. Many women supplemented their household labor with income-generating work that could be done at or around home—taking in boarders, doing extra sewing or laundering, keeping a few animals, or selling garden products. But this often arduous work was increasingly seen as secondary to wives' primary role of keeping house, raising the children, and getting dinner on the table.

The resulting identification of masculinity with economic activities and femininity with nurturing care, now often seen as the "natural" way of organizing the nuclear family, was in fact a historical product of this nineteenth-century transition from an agricultural household economy to an industrial wage economy. So even as an ideal, the male breadwinner family was a comparatively late arrival onto the historical scene. As a reality—a family form in which most people actually lived—it came about even later. . . .

THE REVIVAL OF WOMEN'S ROLE AS FAMILY COPROVIDER

. . . For approximately 50 years, from the 1920s through the 1960s, the growth in married women's work outside the home was smaller than the decline in child labor, so that the male breadwinner family became increasingly dominant. But even at its high point in the 1950s, less than 60 percent of American children spent their youth in an Ozzie and Harriet-type family where dad went to work and mom stayed home. And by the 1970s the fifty-year reign of this family form was definitely over. . . .

After 1973, real wages for young men began falling, creating a larger proportion of families where the mother worked just to keep the family afloat. Housing inflation meant that families with young children were especially likely to need the wife to work, in order to afford the new home that their growing family motivated them to buy. By 1989, almost 80 percent of all home buyers came from two-income households. Another incentive was the rising cost of higher education, which increased nearly three times faster than household income between 1980 and 1994.

Today most families can no longer think of the earnings that wives and mothers bring home as a bonus that can be put aside when family needs call. Nor, increasingly, do the jobs women hold allow them the luxury of choosing to cut back or quit when family priorities change, any more than their husbands' jobs would. By 1993, married women working full-time contributed 41 percent of their families' incomes. Indeed, in 23 percent of two-earner couples, the wives earned *more* than their husbands.

The sequencing of mothering and paid employment that characterized many women's activities over the past 100 years is becoming a thing of the past. Through most of this century, even though labor participation rates for women rose steadily, they dropped significantly when women were in their twenties and thirties. By 1990, however, labor-force participation rates no longer dipped for women in their child-raising years. Today, fewer and fewer women leave their jobs while their children are very young.

Proponents of the modified male breadwinner family believe that if we could drastically reduce the number of single-mother households, raise wages for men, and convince families to get by on a little less, we might be able to get wives to quit work during their child-raising years. Polls consistently show that many women would like to cut back on work hours, though not quit entirely (and it's interesting that an almost equal number of men would also like to cut back their hours). But a return to the norm of male breadwinner families is simply not feasible for most Americans.

WHY WIVES AND MOTHERS WILL CONTINUE TO WORK OUTSIDE THE HOME

It's not just a dollars-and-cents issue. Most women would not give up the satisfactions of their jobs even if they could afford to quit. They consistently tell interviewers they like the social respect, self-esteem, and friendship networks they gain from the job, despite the stress they may face finding acceptable child care and negotiating household chores with their husbands. In a 1995 survey by Louis Harris & Associates, for example, less than a third of working women said they would prefer to stay home even if money were no object.

Another reason women do not want to quit work is that they are not willing to surrender the increased leverage it gives them in the family. The simple truth is that women who do not earn income have much less decision-making power in marital relations than women who do. And no amount of goodwill on the part of husbands seems to lessen this imbalance. In one in-depth study of American families, researchers found that the primary determinant of power in all couples was who brings in the money. The only exception was among lesbians. Lesbian couples might be persuaded to have one partner stay home with the kids and the other earn the money, but I doubt that the Institute for American Values would consider this a positive step in the direction of "marital role complementarity."

Aside from women's own motivations to remain at work, the issue of whether a family can afford to have the wife stay home is quite debatable. One of the most longstanding American traditions, much older than the ideal of the male breadwinner, is the search for socioeconomic mobility. That's why many families came to America in the first place. It's what people were seeking when they crossed the plains in covered wagons, why farmers switched from diversified family crops to specialized market production, what parents have expected education to provide for their children.

From the mid-nineteenth to the mid-twentieth century, there were three main routes to family economic advancement. One was child labor, allowing parents to accumulate enough to buy a house and possibly send a later generation to school. Another was the move from farm to city, to take advantage of higher wage rates in urban areas. The third was investment in increased training and education for male members of the family.

But child labor was abolished in the early twentieth century, and even before 1950 most men had already obtained nonfarm jobs. By the mid-1960s there were diminishing returns to the gains families could expect from further education or training for men. As these older strategies ceased to guarantee continued mobility, women's employment became so central to family economic advancement that it could less and less often be postponed or interrupted for full-time child raising.

In other words, even for families where the uninterrupted work of wives isn't essential for minimum family subsistence, it is now the main route to even a modest amount of upward mobility. Those who tell women who "don't need to work" that they should go back to full-time child rearing are contradicting many of the other ideals most Americans hold dear. We're talking about abandoning the American dream here. The only way to get a significant number of families to make this choice would be to foster a thoroughly untraditional—some might even say un-American—acceptance of a stationary standard of living, a no-growth family economy. Some families may harbor such subversive ideals; yet the chances are slim that this will become a mass movement any time soon.

Name: _____ Class: _____

Date: _____ Section: _____

Reading Comprehension Activity Sheet

The Way We Really Are, Stephanie Coontz

1. What are the consequences for both females and males when females are socialized to believe their value can only be realized through the full-time homemaker role? _____

_____

_____

_____

_____

_____

_____

_____

_____

_____

2. In what ways do the conflicts between work and family in the 21st century mirror work and family conflicts of an earlier era? _____

_____

_____

_____

_____

_____

_____

_____

_____

_____

_____

3. How do you think that conflict between work and family can be negotiated? _____

The Two Marriages
Jessie Bernard

The Future of Whose Marriage?

Both Uncle Honoré and Gigi's grandmother remembered it well, according to Alan Jay Lerner's lyric. And this is what it had been like according to Uncle Honoré: "It was a lovely moonlit evening in May. You arrived at nine o'clock in your gold dress only a little late for our dinner engagement with friends. Afterward there was that delightful carriage ride when we were so engrossed in one another that we didn't notice you had lost your glove." Ah, yes, Uncle Honoré remembered it well indeed, down to the last detail.

Or, come to think of it, did he? For Gigi's grandmother remembered it too, but not at all the same way. "There was no moon that rainy June evening. For once I was on time when we met at eight o'clock at the restaurant where we dined alone. You complimented me on my pretty blue dress. Afterwards we took a long walk and we were so engrossed in one another that we didn't notice I had lost my comb until my hair came tumbling down."

The Japanese motion picture *Rashomon* was built on the same idea—four different versions of the same events. So, also, was Robert Gover's story of the college boy and the black prostitute in his *One Hundred Dollar Misunderstanding*. Also in this category is the old talmudic story of the learned rabbi called upon to render a decision in a marital situation. After listening carefully to the first spouse's story, he shook his head, saying, "You are absolutely right"; and, after listening equally carefully to the other spouse's story, he again shook his head, saying, "You are absolutely right."

There is no question in any of these examples of deliberate deceit or prevarication or insincerity or dishonesty. Both Uncle Honoré and Grandmamma are equally sincere, equally honest, equally "right." The discrepancies in their stories make a charming duet in *Gigi*. And even the happiest of mates can match such differences in their own memories.

From *The Future of Marriage* by Jessie Bernard, 1972 Yale University Press. Reprinted by permission of Yale University Press.

In the Case of Uncle Honoré and Grandmamma, we can explain the differences in the pictures they had in their heads of that evening half a century earlier: memories play strange tricks on all of us. But the same differences in the accounts of what happened show up also among modern couples even immediately after the event. In one study, for example, half of all the partners gave differing replies to questions about what had happened in a laboratory decision-making session they had just left. Other couples give different responses to questions about ordinary day-by-day events like lawn mowing as well as about romantic events. Once our attention has been called to the fact that both mates are equally sincere, equally honest, equally "right," the presence of two marriages in every marital union becomes clear—even obvious, as artists and wise persons have been telling us for so long.

Anyone, therefore, discussing the future of marriage has to specify whose marriage he is talking about: the husband's or the wife's. For there is by now a very considerable body of well-authenticated research to show that there really are two marriages in every marital union, and that they do not always coincide.

"His" and "Her" Marriages

Under the jargon "discrepant responses," the differences in the marriages of husbands and wives have come under the careful scrutiny of a score of researchers. They have found that when they ask husbands and wives identical questions about the union, they often get quite different replies. There is usually agreement on the number of children they have and a few other such verifiable items, although not, for example, on length of premarital acquaintance and of engagement, on age at marriage and interval between marriage and birth of first child. Indeed, with respect to even such basic components of the marriage as frequency of sexual relations, social interaction, household tasks, and decision making, they seem to be reporting on different marriages. As, I think, they are.

In the area of sexual relations, for example, Kinsey and his associates found different responses in from one- to two-thirds of the couples they studied. Kinsey interpreted these differences in terms of selective perception. In the generation he was studying, husbands wanted sexual relations more often than the wives did, thus "the females may be overestimating the actual frequencies" and "the husbands . . . are probably underestimating the frequencies." The differences might also have been vestiges of the probable situation earlier in the marriage when the desired frequency of sexual relations was about six to seven times greater among husbands than among wives. This difference may have become so impressed on the spouses that it remained in their minds even after the difference itself had disappeared or even been reversed. In a sample of happily married, middle-class couples a generation later, Harold Feldman found that both spouses attributed to their mates more influence in the area of sex than they did to themselves.

Companionship, as reflected in talking together, Feldman found, was another area where differences showed up. Replies differed on three-fourths of all the items studied, including the topics talked about, the amount of time spent talking with each other, and which partner initiated conversation. Both partners claimed that whereas they talked more about topics of interest to their mates, their mates initiated conversations about topics primarily of interest to themselves. Feldman concluded that projection in terms of needs was distorting even simple, everyday events, and lack of communication was permitting the distortions to continue. It seemed to him that "if these sex differences can occur so often among these generally well satisfied couples, it would not be surprising to find even less consensus and more distortion in other less satisfied couples."

Although, by and large, husbands and wives tend to become more alike with age, in this study of middle-class couples, differences increased with length of marriage rather than decreased, as one might logically have expected. More couples in the later than in the earlier years, for example, had differing pictures in their heads about how often they laughed together, discussed together, exchanged ideas, or worked together on projects, and about how well things were going between them.

The special nature of sex and the amorphousness of social interaction help to explain why differences in response might occur. But household tasks? They are fairly objective and clear-cut and not all that emotion-laden. Yet even here there are his-and-her versions. Since the division of labor in the household is becoming increasingly as issue in marriage, the uncovering of differing replies in this area is especially relevant. Hard as it is to believe, Granbois and Willett tell us that more than half of the partners in one sample disagreed on who kept track of money and bills. On the question, who mows the lawn? more than a fourth disagreed. Even family income was not universally agreed on.

These differences about sexual relations, companionship, and domestic duties tell us a great deal about the two marriages. But power or decision making can cover all aspects of a relationship. The question of who makes decisions or who exercises power has therefore attracted a great deal of research attention. If we were interested in who really had the power or who really made the decisions, the research would be hopeless. Would it be possible to draw any conclusion from a situation in which both partners agree that the husband ordered the wife to make all the decisions? Still, an enormous literature documents the quest of researchers for answers to the question of marital power. The major contribution it has made has been to reveal the existence of differences in replies between husbands and wives.

The presence of such inconsistent replies did not at first cause much concern. The researchers apologized for them but interpreted them as due to methodological inadequacies; if only they could find a better way to approach the problem, the differences would disappear. Alternatively, the use of only the wife's responses, which were more easily available, was justified on the grounds that differences in one direction between the partners in one marriage compensated for differences in another direction between the partners in another marriage and thus canceled them out. As, indeed, they did. For when Granbois and Willett, two market researchers, analyzed the replies of husbands and wives separately, the overall picture was in fact the same for both wives and husbands. Such canceling out of differences in the total sample, however, concealed almost as much as it revealed about the individual couples who composed it. Granbois and Willet concluded, as Kinsey had earlier, that the "discrepancies . . . reflect differing perceptions on the part of responding partners." And this was the heart of the matter.

Differing reactions to common situations, it should be noted, are not at all uncommon. They are recognized in the folk wisdom embedded in the story of the blind men all giving different replies to questions on the nature of the elephant. One of the oldest experiments in juridical psychology demonstrates how different the statements of witnesses of the same act can be. Even in laboratory studies, it takes intensive training of raters to make it possible for them to arrive at agreement on the behavior they observe.

It has long been known that people with different backgrounds see things differently. We know, for example, that poor children perceive coins as larger than do children from more affluent homes. Boys and girls perceive differently. A good deal of the foundation for projective tests rests on the different ways in which individuals see identical stimuli. And this perception—or, as the sociologists put it, definition of the situation—is reality for them. In this sense, the realities of the husband's marriage are different from those of the wife's.

Finally, one of the most perceptive of the researchers, Constantina Safilios-Rothschild, asked the crucial question: Was what they were getting, even with the best research techniques, family sociology or wives' family sociology? She answered her own question: What the researchers who relied on wives' replies exclusively were reporting on was the wife's marriage. The husband's was not necessarily the same. There were, in fact, two marriages present:

> One explanation of discrepancies between the responses of husbands and wives may be the possibility of two "realities," the husband's subjective reality and the wife's subjective reality—two perspectives which do not always coincide. Each spouse perceives "facts" and situations differently according to his own needs, values, attitudes, and beliefs. An "objective" reality could possibly exist only in the trained observer's evaluation, if it does exist at all.

Interpreting the different replies of husbands and wives in terms of selective perception, projection of needs, values, attitudes, and beliefs, or different definitions of the situation by no means renders them trivial or incidental or justifies dismissing or ignoring them. They are, rather, fundamental for an understanding of the two marriages, his and hers, and we ignore them at the peril of serious misunderstanding of marriage, present as well as future.

Is There an Objective Reality in Marriage?

Whether or not husbands and wives perceive differently or define situations differently, still, sexual relations are taking place, companionship is or is not occurring, tasks about the house are being performed, and decisions are being made every day by someone. In this sense, some sort of "reality" does exist. David Olson went to the laboratory to see if he could uncover it.

He first asked young couples expecting babies such questions as these: Which one of them would decide whether to buy insurance for the newborn child? Which one would decide the husband's part in diaper changing? Which one would decide whether the new mother would return to work or to school? When there were differences in the answers each gave individually on the questionnaire, he set up a situation in which together they had to arrive at a decision in his laboratory. He could them compare the results of the questionnaire with the results in the simulated situation. He found neither spouse's questionnaire response any more accurate than the other's; that is, neither conformed better to the behavioral "reality" of the laboratory than the other did.

The most interesting thing, however, was that husbands, as shown on their questionnaire response, perceived themselves as having more power than they actually did have in the laboratory "reality," and wives perceived that they had less. Thus, whereas three-fourths (73 percent) of the husbands overestimated their power in decision making, 70 percent of the wives underestimated theirs. Turk and Bell found similar results in Canada. Both spouses tend to attribute decision-making power to the one who has the "right" to make the decision. Their replies, that is, conform to the model of marriage that has characterized civilized mankind for millennia. It is this model rather than their own actual behavior that husbands and wives tend to perceive.

We are now zeroing in on the basic reality. We can remove the quotation marks. For there is, in fact, an objective reality in marriage. It is a reality that resides in the cultural—legal, moral, and conventional—prescriptions and proscriptions and, hence, expectations that constitute marriage. It is the reality that is reflected in the minds of the spouses themselves. The differences between the marriages of husbands and of wives are structural realities, and it is these structural differences that constitute the basis for the different psychological realities.

The Authority Structure of Marriage

Authority is an institutional phenomenon; it is strongly bound up with faith. It must be believed in; it cannot be enforced unless it also has power. Authority resides not in the person on whom it is conferred by the group or society, but in the recognition and acceptance it elicits in others. Power, on the other hand, may dispense with the prop of authority. It may take the form of the ability to coerce or to veto; it is often personal, charismatic, not institutional. This kind of personal power is self-enforcing. It does not require shoring up by access to force. In fact, it my even operate subversively. A woman with this kind of power may or may not know that she possesses it. If she does know she has it, she will probably disguise her exercise of it.

In the West, the institutional structure of marriage has invested the husband with authority and backed it by the power of church and state. The marriages of wives have thus been officially dominated by the husband. Hebrew, Christian, and Islamic versions of deity were in complete accord on this matter. The laws, written or unwritten, religious or civil, which have defined the marital union have been based on male conceptions, and they have undergirded male authority.

Adam came first. Eve was created to supply him with companionship, not vice versa. And God himself had told her that Adam would rule over her; her wishes had to conform to his. The New Testament authors agreed. Women were created for men, not men for women; women were therefore commanded to be obedient. If they wanted to learn anything, let them ask their husbands in private, for it was shameful for them to talk in the church. They should submit themselves to their husbands, because husbands were superior to wives; and wives should be as subject to their husbands as the church was to Christ. Timothy wrapped it all up: "Let the woman learn in silence with all subjection. But I suffer not a woman to teach, nor to usurp authority over the man, but to be in silence." Male Jews continued for millennia to thank God three times a day that they were not women. And the Koran teaches women that men are naturally their superiors because God made them that way; naturally, their own status is one of subordination.

The state as well as the church had the same conception of marriage, assigning to the husband and father control over his dependents, including his wife. Sometimes this power was well-nigh absolute, as in the case of the Roman patria potestas—or the English common law, which flatly said, "The husband and wife are as one and that one is the husband." There are rules still lingering today with the same, though less extreme, slant. Diane B. Schulder has summarized the legal framework of the wife's marriage as laid down in the common law.

> The legal responsibilities of a wife are to live in the home established by her husband; to perform the domestic chores (cleaning, cooking, washing, etc.) necessary to help maintain that home; to care for her husband and children.... A husband may force his wife to have sexual relations as long as his demands are reasonable and her health is not endangered....
> The law allows a wife to take a job if she wishes. However, she must see that her domestic chores are completed, and, if there are children, that they receive proper care during her absence.

A wife is not entitled to payment for household work; and some jurisdictions in the United States expressly deny payment for it. In some states, the wife's earnings are under the control of her husband, and in four, special court approval and in some cases husband's consent are required if a wife wishes to start a business of her own.

The male counterpart to these obligations includes that of supporting his wife. He may not disinherit her. She has a third interest in property owned by him, even if it is held in his name only. Her name is required when he sells property.

Not only divine and civil law but also rules of etiquette have defined authority as a husband's prerogative. One of the first books published in England was a *Boke of Good Manners,* translated from the French of Jacques Le Grand in 1487, which included a chapter on "How Wymmen Ought to Be Gouerned." The thirty-third rule of Plutarch's *Rules for Husbands and Wives* was that women should obey their husbands; if they "try to rule over their husbands they make a worse mistake than the husbands do who let themselves be ruled." The husband's rule should not, of course, be brutal; he should not rule his wife "as a master does his chattel, but as the soul governs the body, by feeling with her and being linked to her by affection." Wives, according to Richard Baxter, a seventeenth-century English divine, had to obey even a wicked husband, the only exception being that wife need not obey a husband if he ordered her to change her religion. But, again, like Plutarch, Baxter warned that the husband should love his wife; his authority should not be so coercive or so harsh as to destroy love. Among his twelve rules for carrying out the duties of conjugal love, however, was one to the effect that love must not be so imprudent as to destroy authority.

As late as the nineteenth century, Tocqueville noted that in the United States the ideals of democracy did not apply between husbands and wives.

> Nor have the Americans ever supposed that one consequence of democratic principles is the subversions of marital power, or the confusion of the natural authorities in families. They hold that every association must have a head in order to accomplish its objective, and that the natural head of the conjugal association is man. They do not therefore deny him the right of directing his partner; and they maintain, that in the smaller association of husband and wife, as well as in the great social community, the object of democracy is to regulate and legalize the powers which are necessary, not to subvert all power.
>
> This opinion is not peculiar to men and contested by women; I never observed that the women of America consider conjugal authority as a fortunate usurpation [by men] of their rights, not that they thought themselves degraded by submitting to it. It appears to me, on the contrary, that they attach a sort of pride to the voluntary surrender of their own will, and make it their boast to bend themselves to the yoke, not to shake it off.

The point here is not to document once more the specific ways (religious, legal, moral, traditional) in which male authority has been built into the marital union—that has been done a great many times—but merely to illustrate how different (structurally or "objectively" as well as perceptually or "subjectively") the wife's marriage has actually been from the husband's throughout history.

The Subversiveness of Nature

The rationale for male authority rested not only on biblical grounds but also on nature or natural law, on the generally accepted natural superiority of men. For nothing could be more self-evident than that the patriarchal conception of marriage, in which the husband was unequivocally the boss, was natural, resting as it did on the unchallenged superiority of males.

Actually, nature, if not deity, is subversive. Power, or the ability to coerce or to veto, is widely distributed in both sexes, among women as well as among men. And whatever the theoretical or conceptual picture may have been, the actual, day-by-day relationships between husbands and wives have been determined by the men and women themselves. All that the institutional machinery could do was to confer authority; it could not create personal power, for such power cannot be conferred, and women can generate it as well as men. Thus, keeping women in their place has been a universal problem in spite of the fact that almost without exception institutional patterns give men positions of superiority over them.

If the sexes were, in fact, categorically distinct, with no overlapping, so that no man was inferior to any woman or any woman superior to any man, or vice versa, marriage would have been a great deal simpler. But there is not such sharp cleavage between the sexes except with respect to the presence or absence of certain organs. With all the other characteristics of each sex, there is greater or less overlapping, some men being more "feminine" than the average woman and some women more "masculine" than the average man. The structure of families and societies reflects the positions assigned to men and women. The bottom stratum includes children, slaves, servants, and outcasts of all kinds, males as well as females. As one ascends the structural hierarchy, the proportion of males increases, so that at the apex there are only males.

When societies fall back on the lazy expedient—as all societies everywhere have done—of allocating the rewards and punishments of life on the basis of sex, they are bound to create a host of anomalies, square pegs in round holes, societal misfits. Roles have been allocated on the basis of sex which did not fit a sizable number of both sexes—women, for example, who chafed a subordinate status and men who could not master superordinate status. The history of the relations of the sexes is replete with examples of such misfits. Unless a modus vivendi is arrived at, unhappy marriages are the result.

There is, though, a difference between the exercise of power by husbands and by wives. When women exert power, they are not rewarded; they may even be punished. They are "deviant." Turk and Bell note that "wives who . . . have the greater influence in decision making may experience guilt over this fact." They must therefore dissemble to maintain the illusion, even to themselves, that they are subservient. They tend to feel less powerful than they are because they *ought* to be.

When men exert power, on the other hand, they are rewarded; it is the natural expression of authority. They feel no guilt about it. The prestige of authority goes to the husband whether or not he is actually the one who exercises it. It is not often even noticed when the wife does so. She sees to it that it is not.

There are two marriages, then, in every marital union, his and hers. And his is better than hers. The questions, therefore, are these: In what direction will they change in the future? Will one change more than the other? Will they tend to converge or to diverge? Will the future continue to favor the husband's marriage? And if the wife's marriage is improved, will it cost the husband's anything, or will his benefit along with hers?

References

Bell, Norman. *See* Turk, James L.

Bernard, Jessie. *American Family Behavior.* New York: Harper, 1942.

———. *Remarriage: A Study of Marriage.* New York: Dryden Press, 1956; New York: Russell and Russell, 1971.

———. *The Sex Game.* Englewood Cliffs, N.J.: Prentice Hall, 1968: New York: Atheneum, 1972.

———. *Women and the Public Interest: An Essay on Policy and Protest.* Chicago, Ill.: Aldine-Atherton, 1971.

Brown, George W., and Ritter, Michael. "The Measurement of Family Activities and Relationships." *Human Relations* 19 (August 1966): 241–63.

Cheraskin, E., and Ringsdorf, W. M. "Familial Factors in Psychic Adjustment," *Journal of the American Geriatric Society* 17 (June 1969): 609–11.

1 Cor. 14:35; 1 Cor. 11:3.

De Tocqueville, Alexis. *Democracy in America.* New York: J. and H. G. Langley, 1840.

Elinson, Jack. *See* Haberman, Paul W.

Eph. 5:22–24.

Feld, Sheila, *See* Veroff, Joseph.

Feldman, Harold. *Development of the Husband-Wife Relationship.* Ithaca, N.Y.: Cornell University Press, 1967.

Feldman, Harold. *See* Rollins, Boyd C.

Ferber, Robert. "On the Reliability of Purchase Influence Studies." *Journal of Marketing* 19 (January 1955): 225–32.

Gen. 1, 2, and 3.

Gover, R. *One Hundred Dollar Misunderstanding*. New York: Grove Press, 1962.

Granbois, Donald H., and Willett, Ronald P. "Equivalence of Family Role Measures Based on Husband and Wife Data." *Journal of Marriage and the Family* 32 (February 1970).

Haberman, Paul W., and Elinson, Jack. "Family Income Reported in Surveys: Husbands Versus Wives." *Journal of Marketing Research* 4 (May 1967): 191–94.

Heer, David M. "Husband and Wife Perceptions of Family Power Structure." *Marriage and Family Living* 24 (February 1962): 67.

Hoffman, Dean K. See Kenkel, W. F.

Kenkel, W. F., and Hoffman, Dean K. "Real and Conceived Roles in Family Decision Making." *Marriage and Family Living* 18 (November 1956): 314.

Kinsey, A. C., Pomeroy, Wardell B., and Martin, Clyde E. *Sexual Behavior in the Human Male.* Philadelphia, Pa.: W. B. Saunders, 1948.

Lerner, Alan Jay. "I Remember It Well." From Gigi.

Maccoby, Eleanor E. "Women's Intellect." In *The Potential of Woman,* edited by Seymour M. Farber and Roger H. L. Wilson, 29. New York: McGraw-Hill, 1963.

Michels, Roberto. "Authority." *Encyclopedia of the Social Sciences,* 2:319. New York: Macmillan, 1933.

Morrison, Denton E. *See* Wilkening, E. A.

Olson, David H. "The Measurement of Family Power by Self-Report and Behavioral Methods." *Journal of Marriage and the Family* 31 (August 1969): 549.

Ringsdorf, W. M. *See* Cheraskin, E.

Ritter, Michael. *See* Brown, George W.

Rollins, Boyd C., and Feldman, Harold. "Marital Satisfaction over the Family Life Cycle." *Journal of Marriage and the Family* 32 (February 1970): 24.

Safilios-Rochschild, Constantina. "Family Sociology or Wives' Family Sociology? A Cross-Cultural Examination of Decision-Making." *Journal of Marriage and the Family* 31 (May 1969).

———. "The Study of Family Power Structure: A Review 1960–1969." *Journal of Marriage and the Family* 32 (November 1970): 539–52.

Scanzoni, John. "Note on the Sufficiency of Wife Responses in Family Research." *Pacific Sociological Review,* fall 1965, 12.

Schulder, Diane B. "Does the Law Oppress Women?" In *Sisterhood Is Powerful,* edited by Robin Morgan, 147. New York: Vintage Books, 1970.

1 Tim. 2:11.

Turk, James L., and Bell, Norman. "The Measurement of Family Behavior: What They Perceive, What They Report, What We Observe." Paper read at meeting of American Sociological Association, September 1970.

Veroff, Joseph, and Feld, Sheila. *Marriage and Work in America,* 120–21. New York: Van Nostrand-Reinhold, 1970.

Wilkening, E. A., and Morrison, Denton E. "A Comparison of Husband-Wife Responses Concerning Who Makes Farm and Home Decisions." *Journal of Marriage and the Family* 25 (August 1963): 351.

Willett, Ronald P. *See* Granbois, Donald H.

Wolgast, Elizabeth. "Do Husbands or Wives Make the Purchasing Decisions?" *Journal of Marketing* 23 (October 1958): 151–58.

Zelditch, Morris. "Family, Marriage, and Kinship." In *Handbook of Modern Sociology,* edited by Robert E. L. Faris, Chicago, Ill.: Rand McNally, 1964.

Name: _____   Class: _____

Date: _____   Section: _____

Reading Comprehension Activity Sheet

The Two Marriages, Jessie Bernard

1. Briefly compare and contrast "her" and "his" marriages. _____

_____

_____

_____

_____

_____

_____

_____

_____

_____

_____

_____

2. At then end of the article, Bernard states that "there are two marriages . . . his and hers. And his is better than hers." What other reasons beyond "marital power" would lead the author to this conclusion? _____

_____

_____

_____

_____

_____

_____

_____

_____

_____

_____

_____

Ten Myths That Perpetuate Corporal Punishment

Murray A. Straus

Hitting children is legal in every state of the United States and 84 percent of a survey of Americans agreed that it is sometimes necessary to give a child a good hard spanking. Study after study shows that almost 100 percent of parents with toddlers hit their children. There are many reasons for the strong support of spanking. Most of them are myths.

Myth 1: Spanking Works Better

There has been a huge amount of research on the effectiveness of corporal punishment of animals, but remarkably little on the effectiveness of spanking children. That may be because almost no one, including psychologists, feels a need to study it because it is assumed that spanking is effective. In fact, what little research there is on the effectiveness of corporal punishment of children agrees with the research on animals. Studies of both animals and children show that punishment is *not* more effective than other methods of teaching and controlling behavior. Some studies show it is less effective.

Ellen Cohn and I asked 270 students at two New England colleges to tell us about the year they experienced the most corporal punishment. Their average age that year was eight, and they recalled having been hit an average of six times that year. We also asked them what percentage of time they thought the corporal punishment was effective. It averaged a little more than half (53 percent). Of course, 53 percent also means that corporal punishment was *not* perceived as effective about half the time it was used.

From *Beating the Devil Out of Them: Corporal Punishment in American Families and Effects on Children* by Murray A. Straus. Copyright © 2001 by Murray A. Straus. Reprinted by permission of Transaction Publishers.

LaVoie (1974) compared the use of a loud noise (in place of corporal punishment) with withdrawal of affection and verbal explanation in a study of first- and second-grade children. He wanted to find out which was more effective in getting the children to stop touching certain prohibited toys. Although the loud noise was more effective initially, there was not difference over a longer period of time. Just explaining was as effective as the other methods.

A problem with LaVoie's study is that it used a loud noise rather than actual corporal punishment. That problem does not apply to an experiment by Day and Roberts (1983). They studied three-year-old children who had been given "time out" (sitting in a corner). Half of the mothers were assigned to use spanking as the mode of correction if their child did not comply and left the corner. The other half put their non-complying child behind a low plywood barrier and physically enforced the child staying there. Keeping the child behind the barrier was just as effective as the spanking in correcting the misbehavior that led to the time out.

A study by Larzelere also found that a combination of *non*-corporal punishment and reasoning was as effective as corporal punishment and reasoning in correcting disobedience.

Crozier and Katz (1979), Patterson (1982), Webster-Stratton (1990), and Webster-Stratton et al. (1988) all studied children with serious conduct problems. Part of the treatment used in all three experiments was to get parents to stop spanking. In all three, the behavior of the children improved after spanking ended. Of course, many other things in addition to no spanking were part of the intervention. But, as you will see, parents who on their own accord to do not spank also do many other things to manage their children's behavior. It is these other things, such a setting clear standards for what is expected, providing lots of love and affection, explaining things to the child, and recognizing and rewarding good behavior, that account for why children of non-spanking parents tend to be easy to manage and well-behaved. What about parents who do these things and also spank? Their children also tend to be well-behaved, but it is illogical to attribute that to spanking since the same or better results are achieved without spanking, and also without adverse side effects.

Such experiments are extremely important, but more experiments are needed to really understand what is going on when parents spank. Still, what Day and Roberts found can be observed in almost any household. Let's look at two examples.

In a typical American family there are many instances when a parent might say, "Mary! You did that again! I'm going to have to send you to your room again." This is just one example of a non-spanking method that did *not* work.

The second example is similar: A parent might say, "Mary! You did that again! I'm going to have to spank you again." This is an example of spanking that did *not* work.

The difference between these two examples is that when spanking does not work, parents tend to forget the incident because it contradicts the almost-universal American belief that spanking is something that works when all else fails. On the other hand, they tend to remember when a *non*-spanking method did not work. The reality is that nothing works all the time with a toddler. Parents think that spanking is a magic charm that will cure the child's misbehavior. It is not. There is no magic charm. It takes many interactions and many repetitions to bring up children. Some things work better with some children than with others.

Parents who favor spanking can turn this around and ask, If spanking doesn't work any better, isn't that the same as saying that it works just as well? So what's wrong with a quick slap on the wrist or bottom? There are at least three things that are wrong:

- Spanking becomes less and less effective over time, and when children get bigger, it becomes difficult or impossible.
- For some children, the lessons learned through spanking include the idea that they only need to be good if Mommy or Daddy is watching or will know about it.
- There are a number of very harmful side effects, such as a greater chance that the child will grow up to be depressed or violent. Parents don't perceive these side effects because they usually show up only in the long run.

Myth 2: Spanking Is Needed as a Last Resort

Even parents and social scientists who are opposed to spanking tend to think that it may be needed when all else fails. There is no scientific evidence supporting this belief, however. It is a myth that grows out of our cultural and psychological commitment to corporal punishment. You can prove this to yourself by a simple exercise with two other people. Each of the three should, in turn, think of the most extreme situation where spanking is necessary. The other two should try to think of alternatives. Experience has shown that it is very difficult to come up with a situation for which the alternatives are not as good as spanking. In fact, they are usually better.

Take the example of a child running out into the street. Almost everyone thinks that spanking is appropriate then because of the extreme danger. Although spanking in that situation may help *parents* relieve their own tension and anxiety, it is not necessary or appropriate for teaching the child. It is not necessary because spanking does not work better than other methods, and it is not appropriate because of the harmful side effects of spanking. The only physical force needed is to pick up the child and get him or her out of danger, and, while hugging the child, explain the danger.

Ironically, if spanking is to be done at all, the "last resort" may be the worst. The problem is that parents are usually very angry by that time and act impulsively. Because of their anger, if the child rebels and calls the parent a name or kicks the parent, the episode can escalate into physical abuse. Indeed, most episodes of physical abuse started as physical punishment and got out of hand (Straus 1994; Kadushin and Martin 1981). Of course, the reverse is not true, that is, most instances of spanking do not escalate into abuse. Still, the danger of abuse is there, and so is the risk of psychological harm.

The second problem with spanking as a last resort is that, in addition to teaching that hitting is the way to correct wrongs, hitting a child impulsively teaches another incorrect lesson—that being extremely angry justifies hitting.

Myth 3: Spanking Is Harmless

When someone says, I was spanked and I'm OK, he or she is arguing that spanking does no harm. This is contrary to almost all the available research. One reason the harmful effects are ignored is because many of us (including those of us who are social scientists) are reluctant to admit that their own parents did something wrong and even more reluctant to admit that we have been doing something wrong with our own children. But the most important reason may be that it is difficult to see the harm. Most of the harmful effects do not become visible right away, often not for years. In addition, only a relatively small percentage of spanked children experience obviously harmful effects.

The delayed reaction and the small proportion seriously hurt are the same reasons the harmful effects of smoking were not perceived for so long. In the case of smoking, the research shows that one-third of very heavy smokers die of lung cancer or some other smoking-induced disease. That, of course, means that two-thirds of heavy smokers do *not* die of these diseases (Mattson et al. 1987). So, most heavy smokers can say, "I've smoked more than a pack a day for 30 years and I'm OK." Similarly, most people who were spanked can say, "My parents spanked me, and I'm not a wife beater or depressed."

Another argument in defense of spanking is that it is not harmful if the parents are loving and explain why they are spanking. The research does show that the harmful effects of spanking are reduced if it is done by loving parents who explain their actions. However, a study by Larzelere (1986) shows that although the harmful effects are reduced, they are not eliminated. The harmful side effects include an increased risk of delinquency as a child and crime as an adult, wife beating, depression, masochistic sex, and lowered earnings (Straus 1994).

In addition to having harmful psychological effects on children, hitting children also makes life more difficult for parents. Hitting a child to stop misbehavior may be the easy way in the short run, but in the slightly longer run, it makes the job of being a parent more difficult. This is because spanking reduces the ability of parents to influence their children, especially in adolescence when they are too big to control by physical force. Children are more likely to do what the parents want if there is a strong bond of affection with the parent. In short, being able to influence a child depends in considerable part on the bond between parent and child (Hirschi 1969). An experiment by Redd, Morris, and Martin (1975) shows that children tend to avoid caretaking adults who use punishment. In the natural setting, of course, there are many things that tie children to their parents. I suggest that each spanking chips away at the bond between parent and child.

Part of the process by which corporal punishment eats away at the parent-child bond is shown in the study of 270 students mentioned earlier. We asked the students for their reactions to "the first time you can remember being hit by one of your parents" and the most recent instance. We used a check list of 33 items, one of which was "hated him or her." That item was checked by 42 percent for both the first and the most recent instance of corporal punishment they could remember. The large percentage who hated their parents for hitting them is important because it is evidence that corporal punishment does chip away at the bond between child and parent.

Contrary to the "spoiled child" myth, children of non-spanking parents are likely to be easier to manage and better behaved than the children of parents who spank. This is partly because they tend to control their own behavior on the basis of what their own conscience tells them is right and wrong rather than to avoid being hit. This is ironic because almost everyone thinks that spanking "when necessary" makes for better behavior.

Myth 4: One or Two Times Won't Cause Any Damage

The evidence indicates that the greatest risk of harmful effects occurs when spanking is very frequent. However, that does not necessarily mean that spanking just once or twice is harmless. Unfortunately, the connection between spanking once or twice and psychological damage has not been addressed by most of the available research. This is because the studies seem to be based on this myth. They generally cluster children into "low" and "high" groups in terms of the frequency they were hit. This prevents the "once or twice is harmless" myth from being tested scientifically because the low group may include parents who spank once a year or as often as once a month. Studies show that even one or two instances of corporal punishment are associated with a slightly higher probability of later physically abusing your own child, slightly more depressive symptoms, and a greater probability of violence and other crime later in life (Straus 1994). The increase in these harmful side effects when parents use only moderate corporal punishment (hit only occasionally) may be small, but why run even that small risk when the evidence shows that corporal punishment is no more effective than other forms of discipline in the short run, and less effective in the long run?

Myth 5: Parents Can't Stop Without Training

Although everyone can use additional skills in child management, there is no evidence that it takes some extraordinary training to be able to stop spanking. The most basic step in eliminating corporal punishment is for parent educators, psychologists, and pediatricians to make a simple and unambiguous statement that hitting a child is wrong and that a child *never,* ever, under any circumstances except literal physical self-defense should be hit.

That idea has been rejected almost without exception everytime I suggest it to parent educators or social scientists. They believe it would turn off parents and it could even be harmful because parents don't know what else to do. I think that belief is an unconscious defense of corporal punishment. I say that because I have never heard a parent educator say that before we can tell parents to never *verbally* attack a child, parents need training in alternatives. Some do need training, but everyone agrees that parents who use *psychological* pain as a method of discipline, such as insulting or demeaning the child, should stop immediately. But when it comes to causing *physical* pain by spanking, all but a small minority of parent educators say that before parents are told to stop spanking, they need to learn alternative modes of discipline. I believe they should come right out, as they do for verbal attacks, and say without qualification that a child should *never* be hit.

This is not to say that parent education programs are unnecessary, just that they should not be a precondition for ending corporal punishment. Most parents can benefit from parent education programs such as The Nurturing Program (Bavolek et al. 1983 to 1992), STEP (Dinkmeyer and McKay 1989), Parent Effectiveness Training (Gordon 1975), Effective Black Parenting (Alvy and Marigna 1987), and Los Niños Bien Educado Program (Tannatt and Alvy 1989). However, even without such programs, most parents already use a wide range of non-spanking methods, such as explaining, reasoning, and rewarding. The problem is that they also spank. Given the fact that parents already know and use many methods of teaching and controlling, the solution is amazingly simple. In most cases, parents only need the patience to keep on doing what they were doing to correct misbehavior. Just leave out the spanking! Rather than arguing that parents need to learn certain skills *before* they can stop using corporal punishment, I believe that parents are more likely to use and cultivate those skills if they decide or are required to stop spanking.

This can be illustrated by looking at one situation that almost everyone thinks calls for spanking: when a toddler runs out into the street. A typical parent will scream in terror, rush out and grab the child, and run to safety, telling the child, No! No! and explaining the danger—all of this accompanied by one or more slaps to the legs or behind.

The same sequence is as effective or more effective *without the spanking.* The spanking is not needed because even tiny children can sense the terror in the parent and understand, No! No! Newborn infants can tell the difference between when a mother is relaxes and when she is tense (Stern 1977). Nevertheless, the fact that a child understands that something is wrong does not guarantee never again running into the street; just as spanking does not guarantee the child will not run into the street again.

If the child runs out again, non-spanking parents should use one of the same strategies as spanking parents—repetition. Just as spanking parents will spank as many times as necessary until the child learns, parents who don't spank should continue to monitor the child, hold the child's hand, and take whatever other means are needed to protect the child until the lesson is learned. Unfortunately, when non-spanking methods do not work, some parents quickly turn to spanking because they lose patience and believe it is more effective. But spanking parents seldom question its effectiveness, they just keep on spanking.

Of course, when the child misbehaves again, most spanking parents do more than just repeat the spanking or spank harder. They usually also do things such as explain the danger to the child before letting the child go out again or warn the child that if it happens again, he or she will have to stay in the house for the afternoon, and so on. The irony is that when the child finally does learn, the parent attributes the success to the spanking, not the explanation.

Myth 6: If You Don't Spank, Your Children Will Be Spoiled or Run Wild

It is true that some non-spanked children run wild. But when that happens it is not because the parent didn't spank. It is because some parents think the alternative to spanking is to ignore a child's misbehavior or to replace spanking with verbal attacks such as, "Only a dummy like you can't learn to keep your toys where I won't trip over them." The best alternative is to take firm action to correct the misbehavior without hitting. Firmly condemning what the child has done and explaining why it is wrong are usually enough. When they are not, there are a host of other things to do, such as requiring a time out or depriving the child of a privilege, neither of which involves hitting the child.

Suppose the child hits another child. Parents need to express outrage at this or the child may think it is acceptable behavior. The expression of outrage and a clear statement explaining why the child should never hit another person, except in self-defense, will do the trick in most cases. That does not mean one such warning will do the trick, any more than a single spanking will do the trick. It takes most children a while to learn such things, whatever methods the parents use.

The important of how parents go about teaching children is clear from a classic study of American parenting—*Patterns of Child Rearing* by Sears, Maccoby, and Levin (1957). This study found two actions by parents that are linked to a high level of aggression by the child: permissiveness of the child's aggression, namely ignoring it when the child hits them or another child, and spanking to correct misbehavior. The most aggressive children are children of parents who permitted aggression by the child and who also hit them for a variety of misbehavior. The least aggressive children are children of parents who clearly condemned acts of aggression and who, by not spanking, acted in a way that demonstrated the principle that hitting is wrong.

There are other reasons why, on the average, the children of parents who do not spank are better behaved than children of parents who spank:

- Non-spanking parents pay more attention to their children's behavior, both good and bad, than parents who spank. Consequently, they are more likely to reward good behavior and less likely to ignore misbehavior.
- Their children have fewer opportunities to get into trouble because they are more likely to child-proof the home. For older children, they have clear rules about where they can go and who they can be with.
- Non-spanking parents tend to do more explaining and reasoning. This teaches the child how to use these essential tools to monitor his or her own behavior, whereas

children who are spanked get less training in thinking things through.
- Non-spanking parents treat the child in ways that tend to bond the child to them and avoid acts that weaken the bond. They tend to use more rewards for good behavior, greater warmth and affection, and fewer verbal assaults on the child (see Myth 9). By not spanking, they avoid anger and resentment over spanking. When there is a strong bond, children identify with the parent and want to avoid doing things the parent says are wrong. The child develops a conscience and lets that direct his or her behavior.

Myth 7: Parents Spank Rarely or Only for Serious Problems

Contrary to this myth, parents who spank tend to use this method of discipline for almost any misbehavior. Many do not even give the child a warning. They spank before trying other things. Some advocates of spanking even recommend this. At any supermarket or other public place, you can see examples of a child doing something wrong, such as taking a can of food off the shelf. The parent then slaps the child's hand and puts back the can, sometimes without saying a word to the child. John Rosemond, the author of *Parent Power* (1981), says, "For me, spanking is a first resort. I seldom spank, but when I decide . . . I do it, and that's the end of it."

The high frequency of spanking also shows up among the parents. The typical parent of a toddler told us of about 15 instances is which he or she had hit the child during the previous 12 months. That is surely a minimum estimate because spanking a child is generally such a routine and unremarkable event that most instances are forgotten. Other studies, such as that of Newson and Newson (1963), report much more chronic hitting of children. My tabulations for mothers of three- to five-year-old children in the National Longitudinal Study of Youth found that almost two-thirds hit their children during the week of the interview, and they did it more than three times in just that one week. As high as that figure may seem, I think that daily spanking is not at all uncommon. It has been documented because the parents who do it usually don't realize how often they are hitting their children.

Myth 8: By the Time a Child Is a Teenager, Parents Have Stopped Spanking

Parents of children in their early teens are also heavy users of corporal punishment, although at that age it is more likely to be a slap on the face than on the behind. More than half of the parents of 13- to 14-year-old children in our two national surveys hit their children in the previous 12 months. The percentage drops each year as children get older, but even at age 17, one out of five parents is still hitting. To make matters worse, these are minimum estimates.

Of the parents of teenagers who told us about using corporal punishment, 84 percent did it more than once in the previous 12 months. For boys, the average was seven times and for girls, five times. These are minimum figures because we interviewed the mother in half the families and the father in the other half. The number of times would be greater if we had information on what the parent who was not interviewed did.

Myth 9: If Parents Don't Spank, They will Verbally Abuse Their Child

The scientific evidence is exactly the opposite. Among nationally representative samples of parents, those who did the least spanking also engaged in the least verbal aggression.

It must be pointed out that non-spanking parents are an exceptional minority. They are defying the cultural prescription that says a good parent should spank if necessary. The depth of their involvement with their children probably results from the same underlying characteristics that lead them to reject spanking. There is a danger that if more ordinary parents are told to never spank, they might replace spanking by ignoring misbehavior or by verbal attacks. Consequently, a campaign to end spanking must also stress the importance of avoiding verbal attacks as well as physical attacks, and also the importance of paying attention to misbehavior.

Myth 10: It Is Unrealistic to Expect Parents to Never Spank

It is no more unrealistic to expect parents to never hit a child than to expect that husbands should never hit their wives, or that no one should go through a stop sign, or that a supervisor should never hit an employee. Despite the legal prohibition, some husbands hit their wives, just as some drivers go through stop signs, and a supervisor occasionally may hit an employee.

If we were to prohibit spanking, as is the law in Sweden (Deley 1988; Haeuser 1990), there still would be parents who would continue to spank. But that is not a reason to avoid passing such a law here. Some people kill, even though murder has been a crime since the dawn of history. Some husbands continue to hit their wives even though it has been more than a century since the courts stopped recognizing the common law right of a husband to "physically chastise an errant wife" (Calvert 1974).

A law prohibiting spanking is unrealistic only because spanking is such an accepted part of American culture. That also was true of smoking. Yet in less than a generation we have made tremendous progress toward eliminating smoking. We can make similar progress toward eliminating spanking by showing parents that spanking is dangerous, that their children will be easier to bring up if they do not spank, and by clearly saying that a child should *never*, under any circumstances, be spanked.

References

Alvy, Kirby T., and Marilyn Marigna. 1987. *Effective Black Parenting.* Studio City, CA: Center for the Improvement of Child Caring.

Bavolek, Stephen J., et al. 1983 to 1992. *The Nurturing Programs.* Park City, Utah: Family Development Resources.

Calvert, Robert. 1974. "Criminal and Civil Liability in Husband-Wife Assaults." Chapter 9 in *Violence in the Family,* ed. Suzanne K. Steinmetz and Murray A. Straus. NY: Harper & Row.

Crozier, Jill, and Roger C. Katz. 1979. "Social Learning Treatment of Child Abuse." *Journal of Behavioral Therapy and Psychiatry* 10: 213–220.

Day, Dan E., and Mark W. Roberts. 1983. "An Analysis of the Physical Punishment Component of a Parent Training Program." *Journal of Abnormal Child Psychology* 11(1):141–152.

Deley, W. (1988). Physical Punishment of Children: Sweden and the USA. *Journal of Comparative Family Studies* 19(3):419–431.

Dinkmeyer, Don, Sr., and Gary D. McKay. 1989. *Systematic Training for Effective Parenting.* Circle Pines, MN: American Guidance Service.

Gelles, Richard J., and Murray A. Straus. 1988. *Intimate Violence.* New York: Simon & Schuster.

Gordon, T. 1975. *Parent Effectiveness Training.* New York: New American Library.

Haeuser, Adrienne Ahlgren. 1990. "Banning Parental Use of Physical Punishment: Success in Sweden." Presented at 8th International Congress on Child Abuse and Neglect, Hamburg, Federal Republic of Germany, September 2–6, 1990.

Hirsch, Travis. 1969. *The Causes of Delinquency.* Berkeley and Los Angeles: University of California Press.

Kadushin, Alfred, and Judith A. Martin. 1981. *Child Abuse: An Interactional Event.* New York: Columbia University press.

Larzelere, Robert E. 1986. "Moderate Spanking: Model or Deterrent of Children's Aggression in the Family?" *Journal of Family Violence* 1(1):27–36.

———. 1993. "Response to Oosterhuis: Empirically Justified Uses of Spanking: Toward a Discriminating View of Corporal Punishment." *Journal of Psychology and Theory* 21:142–147.

———. 1993. "Should Corporal Punishment by Parents Be Considered Abusive—No" In Eileen Gambrill and Mary Ann Mason, eds. *Children and Adolescents: Controversial Issues.* Newbury Park, CA: Sage.

LaVoie, Joseph C. 1974. "Type of Punishment as a Determination of Resistance to Deviation." *Developmental Psychology* 10:181–189.

Mattson, Margaret E., Earl S. Pollack, and Joseph W. Cullen. 1987. "What Are the Odds That Smoking Will Kill You?" *American Journal of Public Health* 77(4):425–431.

Newson, John, and Elizabeth Newson. 1963. *Patterns of Infant Care in an Urban Community.* Baltimore: Penguin Books.

Patterson, Gerald R. 1982. *A Social Learning Approach to Family Intervention: III. Coercive Family Process.* Eugene, OR: Castalia.

Redd, William H., Edward K. Morris, and Jerry A. Martin. 1975. "Effects of positive and negative adult-child interactions on children's social preferences." *Journal of Experimental Child Psychology* 19:153–164.

Rosemond, John K. 1981. *Parent Power: A Common Sense Approach to Raising Your Children in the 80s.* Charlotte, NC: East Woods Press.

Sears, Robert R., Eleanor C. Maccoby, and Harry Levin. 1957. *Patterns of Child Rearing.* Evanston, IL: Row, Peterson, and Company.

Stern, Daniel. 1977. *The First Relationship: Mother and Infant.* Cambridge, MA: Harvard University Press.

Straus, Murray A. 1991. "Discipline and Deviance: Physical Punishment of Children and Violence and Other Crime in Adulthood." *Social Problems* 38(2):101–123.

———. 1993. "Corporal Punishment of Children and Depression and Suicide in Adulthood." In Joan McCord, ed., *Coercion and Punishment in Long-Term Perspective.* New York: Cambridge University Press.

Straus, Murray A., with Denise A. Donnelly. 1994. *Beating the Devil Out of Them: Corporal Punishment in American Families.* New York: Macmillan.

Straus, Murray A., and Richard J. Gelles. 1990. *Physical Violence in American Families: Risk Factors and Adaptations to Violence in 8,145 Families.* New Brunswick, MJ: Transaction.

Straus, Murray A., and Holley S. Gimpel. 1992. "Corporal Punishment by Parents and Economic Achievement: A Theoretical Model and Some Preliminary Empirical Data." Paper presented at the 1992 meeting of the American Sociological Association. Durham, NH: Family Research Laboratory, University of New Hampshire.

Straus, Murray A., Richard J. Gelles, and Suzanne K. Steinmetz. 1980. *Behind Closed Doors: Violence in the American Family.* New York: Doubleday/Anchor.

Tannatt, Lupita Montoya, and Kirby T. Alvy. 1989. *Los Niños Bien Educados Program.* Studio City, CA: Center for the Improvement of Child Caring.

Webster-Stratton, Carolyn. 1990. "Enhancing the Effectiveness of Self-Administered Videotape Parent Training for Families with Conduct-Problem Children." *Journal of Abnormal Child Psychology* 18(5):479–492.

Webster-Stratton, Carolyn, Mary Kolpacoff, and Terri Hollinsworth. 1988. "Self-Administered Videotape Therapy for Families with Conduct-Problem Children: Comparison with Two Cost-Effective Treatments and a Control Group." *Journal of Consulting and Clinical Psychology* 56(4):558–566.

Name: _____   Class: _____

Date: _____   Section: _____

Reading Comprehension Activity Sheet

Ten Myths that Perpetuate Corporal Punishment, Murray A. Straus

1. Straus states that there are many reasons for the strong support of spanking, and that most of them are myths. Briefly describe each of these myths. _____

   _____

   _____

   _____

   _____

   _____

   _____

   _____

   _____

   _____

   _____

   _____

2. What role, if any, do you think awareness about child abuse has altered social perception relative to child discipline? _____

   _____

   _____

   _____

   _____

   _____

   _____

   _____

   _____

   _____

   _____

   _____

chapter 12

Education

Learning the Student Role: Kindergarten
as Academic Boot Camp
Harry L. Gracey

Civilize Them with a Stick
Mary Crow Dog
Richard Erdoes

Learning the Student Role: Kindergarten as Academic Boot Camp

Harry L. Gracey

. . . Kindergarten is generally conceived by educators as a year of preparation for school. It is thought of as a year in which small children, five or six years old, are prepared socially and emotionally for the academic learning which will take place over the next twelve years. It is expected that a foundation of behavior and attitudes will be laid in kindergarten on which the children can acquire the skills and knowledge they will be taught in the grades. A booklet prepared for parents by the staff of a suburban New York school system says that the kindergarten experience will stimulate the child's desire to learn and cultivate the skills he will need for learning in the rest of his school career. It claims that the child will find opportunities for physical growth, for satisfying his "need for self-expression," acquire some knowledge, and provide opportunities for creative activity. It concludes, "The most important benefit that your five-year-old will receive from kindergarten is the opportunity to live and grow happily and purposefully with others in a small society." The kindergarten teachers in one of the elementary schools in this community, one we shall call the Wilbur Wright School, said their goals were to see that the children "grew" in all ways: physically, of course, emotionally, socially, and academically. They said they wanted children to like school as a result of their kindergarten experiences and that they wanted them to learn to get along with others. . . .

The unique job of the kindergarten in the educational division of labor seems rather to be teaching children the student role. The student role is the repertoire of behavior and attitudes regarded by educators as appropriate to children in school. Observation in the kindergartens of the Wilbur Wright School revealed a great variety of activities through which children are shown and then drilled in the behavior and attitudes defined as appropriate for

From *Readings in Introductory Sociology,* 3rd ed. by Harry L. Gracey. Copyright © 1977 by Harry Gracey. Reprinted by permission.

school and thereby induced to learn the role of student. Observations of the kindergartens and interviews with the teachers both pointed to the teaching and learning of classroom routines as the main element of the student role. The teachers expended most of their efforts, for the first half of the year at least, in training the children to follow the routines which teachers created. The children were, in a very real sense, *drilled* in tasks and activities created by the teachers for their own purposes and beginning and ending quite arbitrarily (from the child's point of view) at the command of the teacher. One teacher remarked that she hated September, because during the first month "everything has to be done rigidly, and repeatedly, until they know exactly what they're supposed to do." However, "by January," she said, "they know exactly what to do [during the day] and I don't have to be after them all the time." Classroom routines were introduced gradually from the beginning of the year in all the kindergartens, and children were drilled in them as long as was necessary to achieve regular compliance. By the end of the school year, the successful kindergarten teacher has a well-organized group of children. They follow classroom routines automatically, having learned all the command signals and the expected responses to them. They have, in our terms, learned the student role. The following observations shows one such classroom operating at optimum organization on an afternoon late in May. It is the class of an experienced and respected kindergarten teacher.

An Afternoon in Kindergarten

At about 12:20 in the afternoon on a day in the last week of May, Edith Kerr leaves the teachers' room where she has been having lunch and walks to her classroom at the far end of the primary wing of Wright School. A group of five- and six-year-olds peer at her through the glass doors leading from the hall cloakroom to the play area outside. Entering her room, she straightens some material in the "book corner" of the room, arranges music on the piano, takes colored paper from her closet, and places it on one of the shelves under the window. Her room is divided into a number of activity areas through the arrangement of furniture and play equipment. Two easels and a paint table near the door create a kind of passageway inside the room. A wedge-shaped area just inside the front door is made into a teacher's area by the placing of "her" things there: her desk, file, and piano. To the left is the book corner, marked off from the rest of the room by a puppet stage and a movable chalkboard. In it are a display rack of picture books, a record player, and a stack of children's records. To the right of the entrance are the sink and cleanup area. . . .

At 12:25 Edith opens the outside door and admits the waiting children. They hang their sweaters on hooks outside the door and then go to the center of the room and arrange themselves in a semicircle on the floor, facing the teacher's chair which she has placed in the center of the floor. Edith follows them in and sits in her chair checking attendance while waiting for the bell to ring. When she has finished attendance, which she takes by sight, she asks the children what the date is, what day and month it is, how many children are enrolled in the class, how many are present, and how many are absent.

The bell rings at 12:30 and the teacher puts away her attendance book. She introduces a visitor, who is sitting against the right wall taking notes, as someone who wants to learn about schools and children. She then goes to the back of the room and takes down a large chart labeled "Helping Hands." Bringing it to the center of the room, she tells the children it is time to change jobs. Each child is assigned some task on the chart by placing his name, lettered on a paper "hand," next to a picture signifying the task—e.g., a broom, a blackboard, a milk bottle, a flag, and a Bible. She asks the children who wants each of the jobs and rearranges their "hands" accordingly. Returning to her chair, Edith announces, "One person should tell us what happened to Mark." A girl raises her hand and when called on says, "Mark fell and hit his head and had to go to the hospital." The teacher adds that Mark's mother had written saying he was in the hospital. . . .

At 12:35 two children arrive. Edith asks them why they are late and then sends them to join the circle on the floor. The other children vie with each other to tell the newcomers what happened to Mark. When this leads to a general disorder Edith asks, "Who has serious time?" The children become quiet, and a girl raises her hand. Edith nods and the child gets a Bible and hands it to Edith. She reads the Twenty-third Psalm while the children sit quietly. Edith helps the child in charge being reciting the Lord's Prayer, while the other children follow along for the first unit of sounds and then trail off as Edith finishes for them. Everyone stands and faces the American flag hung to the right of the door. Edith leads the pledge to the flag, with the children again following the familiar sounds as far as they remember them. Edith then asks the girl in charge what song she wants and the child replies, "My Country." Edith goes to the piano and plays "America," singing as the children follow her words.

Edith returns to her chair in the center of the room, and the children sit again in the semicircle on the floor. It is 12:40 when she tells the children, "Let's have boys' sharing time first." She calls the name of the first boy sitting on the end of the circle, and he comes up to her with a toy helicopter. He turns and holds it up for the other children to see. He says, "It is a helicopter." Edith asks, "What is it used for?" and he replies, "For the army. Carry men. For the war." Other children join in, "For shooting submarines." "To bring back men from space when they are in the ocean." Edith sends the boy back to the circle and asks the next boy if he has something. He replies "No" and she passes on to the next. He says "Yes" and brings a bird's nest to her. He holds it for the class to see, and the teacher asks, "What kind of bird made the nest?" The boy replies, "My friend says a rain bird made it." Edith asks what the nest is made of and different children reply, "mud," "leaves," and "sticks." There is also a bit of moss woven into the nest and Edith tries to describe it to the children. They, however, are more interested in seeing if anything is inside it, and Edith lets the boy carry it around the semicircle showing the children its insides. Edith tells the children of some baby robins in a nest in her yard, and some of the children tell about baby birds they have seen. Some children are asking about a small object in the next which they say looks like an egg, but all have seen the nest now, and Edith calls on the next boy. . . .

At 1:30 Edith has the children line up in the center of the room; she says, "Table one, line up in front of me," and children ask, "What are we going to do?" Then she moves a few steps to the side and says, "Table two over her, line up next to table one," and more children ask, "What for?" She does this for table three and table four and each time the children ask, "Why, what are we going to do?" When the children are lined up in four lines of five each, spaced so that they are not touching one another, Edith puts on a new record and leads the class in calisthenics, to the accompaniment of the record. The children just jump around every which way in their places instead of doing the exercises, and by the time the record is finished, Edith, the only one following it, seems exhausted. She is apparently adopting the president's new "Physical Fitness" program in her classroom.

At 1:35 Edith pulls her chair to the easels and calls the children to sit on the floor in front of her, table by table. When they are all seated she asks, "What are you going to do for worktime today?" Different children raise their hands and tell Edith what they are going to draw. Most are going to make pictures of animals they saw in the zoo. Edith asks if they want to make pictures to send to Mark in the hospital, and the children agree to this. Edith gives drawing paper to the children, calling them to her one by one. After getting a piece of paper, the children go to the crayon box on the right-hand shelves, select a number of colors, and go to the tables, where they begin drawing. Edith is again trying to quiet the perpetually talking girls. She keeps two of them standing by her so they won't disrupt the others. She asks them, "Why do you feel you have to talk all the time?" and then scolds them for not listening to her. Then she sends them to their tables to draw. . . .

At 2:15 Edith walks to the entrance of the room, switches off the lights, and sits at the piano and plays. The children begin spontaneously singing the song, which is "Clean up, clean up. Everybody clean up." Edith walks around the room supervising the cleanup. Some children put their toys, the blocks, puzzles, games and so on back on their shelves under the windows. The children making a collage keep right on working. A child from another class comes in to borrow the 45-rpm adapter for the record player. At more urging from Edith the rest of the children shelve their toys and work. The children are sitting around their tables now, and Edith asks, "What record would you like to hear while you have your milk?" There is some confusion and no general consensus, so Edith drops the subject and begins to call the children, table by table, to come get their milk. "Table one," she says, and the five children come to the sink, wash their hands and dry them, pick up a carton of milk and a straw, and take it back to their table. Two talking girls wander about the room interfering with the children getting their milk and Edith calls out to them to "settle down." As the children sit, many of them call out to Edith the name of the record they want to hear. When all the children are seated at tables with milk, Edith plays one of these records called "Bozo and the Birds" and shows the children pictures in a book which go with the record. The record recites, and the book shows the adventures of the clown, Bozo, as he walks through a woods meeting many different kinds of birds who, of course, display the characteristics of many kinds of people or, more accurately, different stereotypes. As children finish their milk they take blankets or pads from the shelves under the windows and lie on them in the center of the room where Edith sits on her chair showing the pictures. By 2:30 half the class is lying on the floor on their blankets, the record is still playing, and the teacher is turning the pages of the book. The child who came in previously returns the 45-rpm adapter, and one of the kindergartners tells Edith what the boy's name is and where he lives.

The record ends at 2:40. Edith says, "Children, down on your blankets." All the class is lying on blankets now. Edith refuses to answer the various questions individual children put to her because, she tells them, "it's rest time now." Instead she talks very softly about what they will do tomorrow. They are going to work with clay, she says. The children lie quietly and listen. One of the boys raises his hand and when called on tells Edith, "The animals in the zoo looked so hungry yesterday." Edith asks the children what they think about this and a number try to volunteer opinions, but Edith accepts only those offered in a "rest-time tone," that is, softly and quietly. . . .

At 2:50 Edith sits at the piano and plays. The children sit on the floor in the center of the room and sing. They have a repertoire of songs about animals, including one in which each child sings a refrain alone. They know these by heart and sing along through the ringing of the 2:55 bell. When the song is finished Edith gets up and coming to the group says, "Okay, rhyming words to get your coats today." The children raise their hands and as Edith calls on them, they tell her two rhyming words, after which they are allowed to go into the hall to get their coats and sweaters. They return to the room with these and sit at their tables. At 2:59 Edith says, "When you have your coats on, you may line up at the door." Half of the children go to the door and stand in a long line. When the three o'clock bell rings, Edith returns to the piano and plays. The children sing a song called "Goodbye," after which Edith sends them out.

Training for Learning and Life

The day in kindergarten at Wright School illustrates both the content of the student role as it has been learned by these children and the processes by which the teacher has brought about this learning or "taught" them the student role. The children have learned to go through routines and to follow orders with unquestioning obedience, even when these make no sense to them. They have been disciplined to do as they are told by an authoritative person without significant protest. Edith has developed this discipline in the children by creating and enforcing a rigid social structure in the classroom through which she effectively controls the behavior of most of the children for most of the school day. The "living with others in a small society" which the school pamphlet tells parents is the most important thing the children will learn in kindergarten can be seen now in its operational meaning, which is learning to live by the routines imposed by the school. This learning appears to be the principal content of the student role.

Children who submit to school-imposed discipline and come to identify with it, so that being a "good student" comes to be an important part of their developing identities, *become* the good students by the school's definitions. Those who submit to the routines of the school but do not come to identify with them will be adequate students who find the more important part of their identities elsewhere, such as in the play group outside school. Children who refuse to submit to the school routines are rebels, who become known as "bad students" and often "problem children" in the school, for they do not learn the academic curriculum and their behavior is often disruptive in the classroom. Today, schools engage clinical psychologists in part to help teachers deal with such children.

In looking at Edith's kindergarten at Wright School, it is interesting to ask how the children learn this role of student—come to accept school-imposed routines—and what, exactly, it involves in terms of behavior and attitudes. The most prominent features of the classroom are its physical and social structures. The room is carefully furnished and arranged in ways adults feel will interest children. The play store and play kitchen in the back of the room, for example, imply that children are interested in mimicking these activities of the adult world. The only space left for the children to create something of their own is the empty center of the room, and the materials at their disposal are the blocks, whose use causes anxiety on the part of the teacher. The room, being carefully organized physically by the adults, leaves little room for the creation of physical organization on the part of the children.

The social structure created by Edith is a far more powerful and subtle force for fitting the children to the student role. This structure is established by the very rigid and tightly controlled set of rituals and routines through which the children are put during the day. There is first the rigid "locating procedure" in which the children are asked to find themselves in terms of the month, date, day of the week, and the number of the class who are present and absent. This puts them solidly in the real world as defined by adults. The day is then divided into six periods whose activities are for the most part determined by the teacher. In Edith's kindergarten the children went through serious time, which opens the school day, sharing time, play time (which in clear weather would be spent outside), work time, cleanup time, after which they have their milk, and rest time, after which they go home. The teacher has programmed activities for each of these times.

Occasionally the class is allowed limited discretion to choose between proffered activities such as stories or records, but original ideas for activities are never solicited from them. Opportunity for free individual action is open only once in the day, during the part of the work time left after the general class assignment has been completed (on the day reported, the class assignment was drawing animal pictures for the absent Mark). Spontaneous interests or observations from the children are never developed by the teacher. It seems that her schedule just does not allow room for developing such unplanned events. During sharing time, for example, the child who brought a bird's nest told Edith, in reply to her question of what kind of bird made it, "My friend says it's a rain bird." Edith does not think to ask about this bird, probably because the answer is "childish," that is, not given in accepted adult categories of birds. . . .

While children's perceptions of the world and opportunities for genuine spontaneity and creativity are being systematically eliminated from the kindergarten, unquestioned obedience to authority and rote learning of meaningless material are being encouraged. When the children are called to line up in the center of the room they ask "Why?" and "What for?" as they are in the very process of complying. They have learned to go smoothly through a programmed day, regardless of whether parts of the program make any sense to them or not. Here the student role involves what might be called "doing what you're told and never mind why." Activities which might "make sense" to the children are effectively ruled out, and they are forced or induced to participate in activities which may be "senseless," such as the calisthenics.

At the same time the children are being taught by rote meaningless sounds in the ritual oaths and songs, such as the Lord's Prayer, the Pledge to the Flag, and "America." As they go through the grades children learn more and more of the sounds of these ritual oaths, but the fact that they have often learned meaningless sounds rather than meaningful statements is shown when they are asked to write these out in the sixth grade; they write them as groups of sounds rather than as a series of words, according to the sixth-grade teachers at Wright School. Probably much learning in the elementary grades is of this character, that is, having no intrinsic meaning to the children but rather being tasks inexplicably required of them by authoritative adults. . . .

The kindergarten has been conceived of here as the year in which children are prepared for their schooling by learning the role of student. In the classrooms of the rest of the school grades the children will be asked to submit to systems and routines imposed by the teachers and the curriculum. The days will be much like those of kindergarten, except that academic subjects will be substituted for the activities of the kindergarten. Once out of the school system, young adults will more than likely find themselves working in large-scale bureaucratic organizations, perhaps on the assembly line in the factory, perhaps in the paper routines of the white collar occupations, where they will be required to submit to rigid routines imposed by "the company" which may make little sense to them. Those who can operate well in this situation will be successful bureaucratic functionaries. Kindergarten, therefore, can be seen as preparing children not only for participation in the bureaucratic organization of large modern school systems, but also for the large-scale occupational bureaucracies of modern society.

Name: _____   Class: _____

Date: _____   Section: _____

Reading Comprehension Activity Sheet

Learning the Student Role: Kindergarten as Academic Boot Camp, Harry L. Gracey

1. Gracey states that the educational system socializes and teaches children their "student role." What is this student role? _____

   _____
   _____
   _____
   _____
   _____
   _____
   _____
   _____
   _____
   _____
   _____

2. Based on the reading, how are the values of discipline, conformity, and behaviors supporting capitalism instilled in grades K–12? _____

   _____
   _____
   _____
   _____
   _____
   _____
   _____
   _____
   _____
   _____
   _____

Civilize Them with a Stick

Mary Crow Dog
Richard Erdoes

Few students are aware of our nation's policies toward Native Americans, which included the separation of Indian children from their families and cultures so that these children could be "civilized" into the dominant society. Consequently, thousands of Native American children were forced to leave the reservation to attend boarding schools, day schools, or schools in converted Army posts. These total institutions used tactics similar to those used by the military to resocialize the young Native Americans. In the following selection, Mary Crow Dog and Richard Erdoes reveal how the institution of education can be an agent of social control whose purpose is to assimilate racial-ethnic populations, such as Native Americans into the dominate culture.

> *... Gathered from the cabin, the wickiup, and the tepee,*
> *partly by cajolery and partly by threats;*
> *partly by bribery and partly by force,*
> *they are induced to leave their kindred*
> *to enter these schools and take upon themselves*
> *the outward appearance of civilized life.*
> —ANNUAL REPORT OF THE DEPARTMENT OF INTERIOR, 1901

It is almost impossible to explain to a sympathetic white person what a typical old Indian boarding school was like; how it affected the Indian child suddenly dumped into it like a small creature from another world, helpless, defenseless, bewildered, trying desperately and instinctively to survive and sometimes not surviving at all. I think such children were like the victims of Nazi concentration camps trying to tell average, middle-class Americans what their experience had been like. Even now, when these schools are much improved, when the buildings are new, all gleaming steel and glass, the food tolerable, the teachers well trained and well intentioned, even trained in child psychology—unfortunately the psychology of

From *Lakota Woman* by Mary Crow Dog with Richard Erdoes. Copyright (1990) by Mary Crow Dog and Richard Erdoes. used by permission of Grove/Atlantic, Inc.

white children, which is different from ours—the shock to the child upon arrival is still tremendous. Some just seem to shrivel up, don't speak for days on end, and have an empty look in their eyes. I know of an 11-year-old on another reservation who hanged herself, and in our school, while I was there, a girl jumped out of the window, trying to kill herself to escape an unbearable situation. That first shock is always there.

Although the old tiyospaye has been destroyed, in the traditional Sioux families, especially in those where there is no drinking, the child is never left alone, It is always surrounded by relatives, carried around, enveloped in warmth. It is treated with the respect due to any human being, even a small one. It is seldom forced to do anything against its will, seldom screamed at, and never beaten. That much, at least, is left of the old family group among full-bloods. And then suddenly a bus or car arrives, full of strangers, usually white strangers, who yank the child out of the arms of those who love it, taking it screaming to the boarding school. The only word I can think of for what is done to these children is kidnapping.

Even now, in a good school, there is impersonality instead of close human contact; a sterile, cold atmosphere, an unfamiliar routine, language problems, and above all the maza-skan-skan, that damn clock—white man's time as opposed to Indian time, which is natural time. Like eating when you are hungry and sleeping when you are tired, not when that damn clock says you must. But I was not taken to one of the better, modern schools. I was taken to the old-fashioned mission school at St. Francis, run by the nuns and Catholic fathers, built sometime around the turn of the century and not improved a bit when I arrived, not improved as far as the buildings, the food, the teachers, or their methods were concerned.

In the old days, nature was our people's only school and they needed no other. Girls had their toy tipis and dolls, boys their toy bows and arrows. Both rode and swam and played the rough Indian games together. Kids watched their peers and elders and naturally grew from children into adults. Life in the tipi circle was harmonious—until the whiskey peddlers arrived with their wagons and barrels of "Injun whiskey." I often wished I could have grown up in the old, before-whiskey days.

Oddly enough, we owed our unspeakable boarding schools to the do-gooders, the white Indian-lovers. The schools were intended as an alternative to the outright extermination seriously advocated by generals Sherman and Sheridan, as well as by most settlers and prospectors overrunning our land. "You don't have to kill those poor benighted heathen," the do-gooders said, "in order to solve the Indian Problem. Just give us a chance to turn them into useful farmhands, laborers, and chambermaids who will break their backs for you at low wages." In that way the boarding schools were born. The kinds were taken away from their villages and pueblos, in their blankets and moccasins, kept completely isolated from their families—sometimes for as long as ten years—suddenly coming back, their short hair slick with pomade, their necks raw from stiff, high collars, their thick jackets always short in the sleeves and pinching under the arms, their tight patent leather shoes giving them corns, the girls in starched white blouses and clumsy, high-buttoned boots—caricatures of white people. When they found out—and they found out quickly—that they were neither wanted by whites nor by Indians, they got good and drunk, many of them staying drunk for the rest of their lives. I still have a poster I found among my grandfather's stuff, given to him by the missionaries to tack up on his wall. It reads:

1. Let Jesus save you.
2. Come out of your blanket, cut your hair, and dress like a white man.
3. Have a Christian family with one wife for life only.
4. Live in a house like your white brother. Work hard and wash often.
5. Learn the value of a hard-earned dollar. Do not waste your money on giveaways. Be punctual.
6. Believe that property and wealth are signs of divine approval.
7. Keep away from saloons and strong spirits.
8. Speak the language of your white brother. Send your children to school to do likewise.
9. Go to church often and regularly.
10. Do not go to Indian dances or to the medicine men.

The people who were stuck upon "solving the Indian Problem" by making us into whites retreated from this position only step by step in the wake of Indian protests.

The mission school at St. Francis was a curse for our family for generations. My grandmother went there, then my mother, then my sisters and I. At one time or other every one of us tried to run away. Grandma told me once about the bad times she had experienced at St. Francis. In those days they let students go home only for one week every year. Two days were used up for transportation, which meant spending just five days out of 365 with her family. And that was an improvement. Before grandma's time, on many reservations they did not let the students go home at all until they had finished school. Anybody who disobeyed the nuns was severely punished. The building in which my grandmother stayed had three floors, for girls only. Way up in the attic were little cells, about five by five by ten feet. One time she was in church and instead of praying she was playing jacks. As punishment they took her to one of those little cubicles where she stayed in darkness because the windows had been boarded up. They left her there for a whole week with only bread and water for nourishment. After she came out she promptly ran away, together with three other girls. They were found and brought back. The nuns stripped them naked and whipped them. They used a horse buggy whip on my grandmother. Then she was put back into the attic—for two weeks.

My mother had much the same experiences but never wanted to talk about them, and then there I was, in the same place. The school is now run by the BIA—the Bureau of Indian Affairs—but only since about 15 years ago. When I was there, during the 1960s, it was still run by the Church. The Jesuit fathers ran the boys' wing and the Sisters of the Sacred Heart ran us—with the help of the strap. Nothing had changed since my grandmother's days. I have been told recently that even in the '70s they were still beating children at that school.

All I got out of school was being taught how to pray. I learned quickly that I would be beaten if I failed in my devotions or, God forbid, prayed the wrong way, especially prayed in Indian to Wakan Tanka, the Indian Creator.

The girls' wing was built like an F and was run like a penal institution. Every morning at five o'clock the sisters would come into our large dormitory to wake us up, and immediately we had to kneel down at the sides of our beds and recite the prayers. At six o'clock we were herded into the church for more of the same. I did not take kindly to the discipline and to marching by the clock, left-right, left-right. I was never one to like being forced to do something. I do something because I feel like doing it. I felt this way always, as far as I can remember, and my sister Barbara felt the same way. An old medicine man once told me: "Us Lakotas are not like dogs who can be trained, who can be beaten and keep on wagging their tails, licking the hand that whipped them. We are like cats, little cats, big cats, wildcats, bobcats, mountain lions. It doesn't matter what kind, but cats who can't be tamed, who scratch if you step on their tails." But I was only a kitten and my claws were still small.

Barbara was still in the school when I arrived and during my first year or two she could still protect me a little bit. When Barb was a seventh grader she ran away together with five other girls, early in the morning before sunrise. They brought them back in the evening. The girls had to wait for two hours in front of the mother superior's office. They were hungry and cold, frozen through. It was wintertime and they had been running the whole day without food, trying to make good their escape. The mother superior asked each girl, "Would you do this again?" She told them that as punishment they would not be allowed to visit home for a month and that she'd keep them busy on work details until the skin on their knees and elbows had worn off. At the end of her speech she told each girl, "Get up from this chair and lean over it." She then lifted the girls' skirts and pulled down their underpants. Not little girls either, but teenagers. She had a leather strap about a foot long and four inches wide fastened to a stick, and beat the girls, one after another, until they cried. Barb did not give her that satisfaction but just clenched her teeth. There was one girl, Barb told me, the nun kept on beating and beating until her arm got tired.

I did not escape my share of the strap. Once, when I was 13 years old, I refused to go to Mass. I did not want to go to church because I did not feel well. A nun grabbed me by the hair, dragged me upstairs, made me stoop over, pulled my dress up (we were not allowed at the time to wear jeans), pulled my panties down, and gave me what they called "swats"—25 swats with a board around which Scotch tape had been wound. She hurt me badly.

My classroom was right next to the principal's office and almost every day I could hear him swatting the boys. Beating was the common punishment for not doing one's homework, or for being late to school. It had such a bad effect upon me that I hated and mistrusted every white person on sight, because I met only one kind. It was not until much later that I met sincere white people I could relate to and be friends with. Racism breeds racism in reverse.

The routine at St. Francis was dreary. Six A.M., kneeling in church for an hour or so; seven o'clock, breakfast; eight o'clock, scrub the floor, peel spuds, make classes. We had to mop the dining room twice every day and scrub the tables. If you were caught taking a rest, doodling on the bench with a fingernail or knife, or just rapping, the nun would come up with a dish towel and just slap it across your face, saying, "You're not supposed to be talking, you're supposed to be working!" Monday mornings we had cornmeal mush, Tuesday oatmeal, Wednesday rice and raisins, Thursday cornflakes, and Friday all the leftovers mixed together or sometimes fish. Frequently the food had bugs or rocks in it. We were eating hot dogs that were weeks old, while the nuns were dining on ham, whipped potatoes, sweet peas, and cranberry sauce. In winter our dorm was icy cold while the nuns' rooms were always warm.

I have seen little girls arrive at the school, first graders, just fresh from home and totally unprepared for what awaited them, little girls with pretty braids, and the first thing the nuns did was chop their hair off and tie up what was left behind their ears. Next they would dump the children into tubs of alcohol, a sort of rubbing alcohol, "to get the germs off." Many of the nuns were German immigrants, some from Bavaria, so that we sometimes speculated whether Bavaria was some sort of Dracula country inhabited by monsters. For the sake of objectivity I ought to mention that two of the German fathers were great linguists and that the only Lakota-English dictionaries and grammars which are worth anything were put together by them.

At night some of the girls would huddle in bed together for comfort and reassurance. Then the nun in charge of the dorm would come in and say, "What are the two of you doing in bed together? I smell evil in this room. You girls are evil incarnate. You are sinning. You are going to hell and burn forever. You can act that way in the devil's frying pan." She would get them out of bed in the middle of the night, making them kneel and pray until morning. We had not the slightest idea what it was all about. At home we slept two and three in a bed for animal warmth and a feeling of security.

The nuns and the girls in the two top grades were constantly battling it out physically with fists, nails, and hair-pulling. I myself was growing from a kitten into an undersized cat. My claws were getting bigger and were itching for action. About 1969 or 1970 a strange young white girl appeared on the reservation. She looked about 18 to 20 years old. She was pretty and had long, blond hair down to her waist, patched jeans, boots, and a backpack. She was different from any other white person we had met before. I think her name was Wise. I do not know how she managed to overcome our reluctance and distrust, getting us into a corner, making us listen to her, asking us how we were treated. She told us that she was from New York. She was the first real hippie or Yippie we had come across. She told us of people called the Black Panthers, Young Lords, and Weathermen. She said, "Black people are getting it on. Indians are getting it on in St. Paul and California. How about you?" She also said, "Why don't you put out an underground paper, mimeograph it. It's easy. Tell it like it is. Let it all hang out." She spoke a strange lingo but we caught on fast.

Charlene Left Hand Bull and Gina One Star were two full-blood girls I used to hang out with. We did everything together. They were willing to join me in a Sioux uprising. We put together a newspaper which we called the *Red Panther*. In it we wrote how bad the school was, what kind of slop we had to eat—slimy, rotten blackened potatoes for two weeks—the way we were beaten. I think I was the one who wrote the worst article about our principal of the moment, Father Keeler. I put all my anger and venom into it. I called him a goddam wasičun son of a bitch. I wrote that he knew nothing about Indians and should go back to where he came from, teaching white children whom he could relate to. I wrote that we knew which priests slept with which nuns and that all they ever could think about was filling their bellies and buying a new car. It was the kind of writing which foamed at the mouth, but which also lifted a great deal of weight from one's soul.

On Saint Patrick's Day, when everybody was at the big powwow, we distributed our newspapers. We put them on windshields and bulletin boards, in desks and pews, in dorms and toilets. But someone saw us and snitched on us. The shit hit the fan. The three of us were taken before a board meeting. Our parents, in my case my mother, had to come. They were told that ours was a most serious matter, the worst thing that had ever happened in the school's long history. One of the nuns told my mother, "Your daughter really needs to be talked to." "What's wrong with my daughter?" my mother asked. She was given one of our *Red Panther* newspapers. The nun pointed out its name to her and then my piece, waiting for mom's reaction. After a while she asked, "Well, what have you got to say to this? What do you think?"

My mother said, "Well, when I went to school here, some years back, I was treated a lot worse than these kids are. I really can't see how they can have any complaints, because we was treated a lot stricter. We could not even wear skirts halfway up our knees. These girls have it made. But you should forgive them because they are young. And it's supposed to be a free country, free speech and all that. I don't believe what they done is wrong." So all I got out of it was scrubbing six flights of stairs on my hands and knees, every day. And no boy-side privileges.

The boys and girls were still pretty much separated. The only time one could meet a member of the opposite sex was during free time, between 4 and 5:30, in the study hall or on benches or the volleyball court outside, and that was strictly supervised. On day Charlene and I went over to the boys' side. We were on the ball team and they had to let us practice. We played three extra minutes, only three minutes more than we were supposed to. Here was the nuns' opportunity for revenge. We got 25 swats. I told Charlene, "We are getting too old to have our bare asses whipped that way. We are old enough to have babies. Enough of this shit. Next time we fight back." Charlene only said, "Hoka-hay!"

. . .

In a school like this there is always a lot of favoritism. At St. Francis it was strongly tinged with racism. Girls who were near-white, who came from what the nuns called "nice families," got preferential treatment. They waited on the faculty and got to eat ham or eggs and bacon in the morning. they got the easy jobs while the skins, who did not have the right kind of back-ground—myself among them—always wound up in the laundry room sorting out 10-bushel baskets of dirty boys' socks every day. Or we wound up scrubbing the floors and doing all the dishes. The school therefore fostered fights and antagonism between whites and breeds, and between breeds and skins. At one time Charlene and I had to iron all the robes and vestments the priests wore when saying Mass. We had to fold them up and put them into a chest in the back of the church. In a corner, looking over our shoulders, was a statue of the crucified Savior, all bloody and beaten up. Charlene looked up and said, "Look at the poor Indian. The pigs sure worked him over." That was the closest I ever came to seeing Jesus.

I was held up as a bad example and didn't mind. I was old enough to have a boyfriend and promptly got one. At the school we had an hour and a half for ourselves. Between the boys' and the girls' wings were some benches where one could sit. My boyfriend and I used to go there just to hold hands and talk. The nuns were very uptight about any boy-girl stuff. They had an exaggerated fear of anything having even the faintest connection with sex. One day in religion class, an all-girl class, Sister Bernard singled me out for some remarks, pointing me out as a bad example, an example that should be shown. She said that I was too free with my body. That I was holding hands which meant that I was not a good example to follow. She also said that I wore unchaste dresses, skirts which were too short, too suggestive, shorter than regulations permitted, and for that I would be punished. She dressed me down before the whole class, carrying on and on about my unchastity.

. . .

We got a new priest in English. Curing one of his first classes he asked one of the boys a certain question. The boy was shy. He spoke poor English, but he had the right answer. The priest told him, "You did not say it right. Correct yourself. Say it over again." The boy got flustered and stammered. He could hardly get out a word. But the priest kept after him: "Didn't you hear? I told you to do the whole thing over. Get it right this time." He kept on and on.

I stood up and said, "Father, don't be doing that. If you go into an Indian's home and try to talk Indian, they might laugh at you and say, 'Do it over correctly. Get it right this time!'"

He shouted at me, "Mary, you stay after class. Sit down right now!'

I stayed after class, until after the bell. He told me, "Get over here!" He grabbed me by the arm, pushing me against the blackboard, shouting, "Why are you always mocking us? You have no reason to do this."

I said, "Sure I do. You were making fun of him. You embarrassed him. He needs strengthening, not weakening. You hurt him. I did not hurt you."

He twisted my arm and pushed real hard. I turned around and hit him in the face, giving him a bloody nose. After that I ran out of the room, slamming the door behind me. He and I went to Sister Bernard's office. I told her, "Today I quit school. I'm not taking any more of this, none of this shit anymore. None of this treatment. Better give me my diploma. I can't waste any more time on you people."

Sister Bernard looked at me for a long, long time. She said, "All right, Mary Ellen, go home today. Come back in a few days and get your diploma." And that was that. Oddly enough, that priest turned out okay. He taught a class in grammar, orthography, composition, things like that. I think he wanted more respect in class. He was still young and unsure of himself. But I was in there too long. I didn't feel like hearing it. Later he became a good friend of the Indians, a personal friend of myself and my husband. He stood up for us during Wounded Knee and after. He stood up to his superiors, stuck his neck way out, became a real people's priest. He even learned our language. He died prematurely of cancer. It is not only the good Indians who die young, but the good whites, too. It is the timid ones who know how to take care of themselves who grow old. I am still grateful to that priest for what he did for us later and for the quarrel he picked with me—or did I pick it with him?—because it ended a situation which had become unendurable for me. The day of my fight with him was my last day in school.

Name: _____ Class: _____

Date: _____ Section: _____

Reading Comprehension Activity Sheet

Civilize Them with a Stick, Mary Crow Dog and Richard Erdoes

1. Compare and contrast the Indian way of life to the white boarding school way of life for Native American children. _____

   _____

   _____

   _____

   _____

   _____

   _____

   _____

   _____

   _____

   _____

2. What rationale was cited for taking the children from their Indian families and isolating them in the schools? _____

   _____

   _____

   _____

   _____

   _____

   _____

   _____

   _____

   _____

   _____

   _____

3. The authors state "Racism breeds racism in reverse." Explain the meaning behind this statement.

chapter 13

Religion

The Elementary Forms of the Religious Life
Emile Durkheim

Miami's Little Havana: Yard Shrines, Cult Religion, and Landscape
James R. Curtis

The Elementary Forms of the Religious Life

Emile Durkheim

The institution of religion is the topic of the following four selections. Sociologists have long studied now religion affects the social structure and the personal experience of individuals in society. Emile Durkheim (1858–1917), for example, often placed religion at the center of his social analyses. Durkheim was especially concerned with the meaning of religion and how it contributed to social cohesion. This selection is an excerpt from his definitive study of religion among the Australian aborigines, "The Elementary Forms of Religious Life." In his analysis of the functions of religion in society, Durkheim states that religious beliefs and rituals are real and reflect the societies in which they exist. Moreover, Durkheim argues for a separation between the knowledge of religion and the knowledge of science.

The theorists who have undertaken to explain religion in rational terms have generally seen in it before all else a system of ideas, corresponding to some determined object. This object has been conceived in a multitude of ways: nature, the infinite, the unknowable, the ideal, etc.; but these differences matter but little. In any case, it was the conceptions and beliefs which were considered as the essential elements of religion. As for the rites, from this point of view they appear to be only an external translation, contingent and material, of these internal states which alone pass as having any intrinsic value. This conception is so commonly held that generally the disputes of which religion is the theme turn about the question whether it can conciliate itself with science or not, that is to say, whether or not there is a place beside our scientific knowledge for another form of thought which would be specifically religious.

But the believers, the men who lead the religious life and have a direct sensation of what it really is, object to this way of regarding it, saying that it does not correspond to their daily experience. In fact, they feel that the real function of religion is not to make us think, to

From *The Elementary Forms of Religious Life,* translated from the French by Joseph Ward Swain, Allen & Urwin, 1915.

enrich our knowledge, nor to add to the conceptions which we owe to science others of another origin and another character, but rather, it is to make us act, to aid us to live. The believer who has communicated with his god is not merely a man who sees new truths of which the unbeliever is ignorant; he is a man who is *stronger*. He feels within him more force, either to endure the trials of existence, or to conquer them. It is as though he were raised above the miseries of the world, because he is raised above his condition as a mere man; he believes that he is saved from evil, under whatever form he may conceive this evil. The first article in every creed is the belief in salvation by faith. But it is hard to see how a mere idea could have this efficacy. An idea is in reality only a part of ourselves; then how could it confer upon us powers superior to those which we have of our own nature? Howsoever rich it might be in affective virtues, it could add nothing to our natural vitality; for it could only release the motive powers which are within us, neither creating them nor increasing them. From the mere fact that we consider an object worthy of being loved and sought after, it does not follow that we feel ourselves stronger afterwards; it is also necessary that this object set free energies superior to these which we ordinarily have at our command and also that we have some means of making these enter into us and unite themselves to our interior lives. Now for that, it is not enough that we think of them; it is also indispensable that we place ourselves within their sphere of action, and that we set ourselves where we may best feel their influence; in a word, it is necessary that we act, and that we repeat the acts thus necessary evey time we feel the need of renewing their effects. From this point of view, it is readily seen how that group of regularly repeated acts which form the cult get their importance. In fact, whoever has really practised a religion knows very well that it is the cult which gives rise to these impressions of joy, of interior peace, of serenity, of enthusiasm which are, for the believer, an experimental proof of his beliefs. The cult is not simply a system of signs by which the faith is outwardly translated; it is a collection of the means by which this is created and recreated periodically. Whether it consists in material acts or mental operations, it is always this which is efficacious.

Our entire study rests upon this postulate that the unanimous sentiment of the believers of all times cannot be purely illusory. Together with a recent apologist of the faith[1] we admit that these religious beliefs rest upon a specific experience whose demonstrative value is, in one sense, not one bit inferior to that of scientific experiments, though different from them. We, too, think that "a tree is known by its fruits," and that fertility is the best proof of what the roots are worth. But from the fact that a "religious experience," if we choose to call it this, does exist and that it has a certain foundation—and, by the way, is there any experience which has none?—it does not follow that the reality which is its foundation conforms objectively to the idea which believers have of it. The very fact that the fashion in which it has been conceived has varied infinitely in different times is enough to prove that none of these conceptions express it adequately. If a scientist states it as an axiom that the sensations of heat and light which we feel correspond to some objective cause, he does not conclude that this is what it appears to the senses to be. Likewise, even if the impressions which the faithful feel are not imaginary, still they are in no way privileged intuitions; there is no reason for believing that they inform us better upon the nature of their object than do ordinary sensations upon the nature of bodies and their properties. In order to discover what this object consists of, we must submit them to an examination and elaboration analogous to that which has substituted for the sensuous idea of the world another which is scientific and conceptual.

This is precisely what we have tried to do, and we have seen that this reality, which mythologies have represented under so many different forms, but which is the universal and eternal objective cause of these sensations *sui generis* out of which religious experience is made, is society. We have shown what moral forces it develops and how it awakens this sentiment of a refuge, of a shield and of a guardian support which attaches the believer to his cult. It is that which raises him outside himself; it is even that which made him. For that which makes a man is the totality of the intellectual property which constitutes civilization, and civilization is the work of society. Thus is explained the preponderating role of the cult in all religions, whichever they may be. This is because society cannot make its influence felt unless it is in action, and it is not in action unless the individuals who compose it are assembled together and act in common. It is by common action that it takes consciousness of itself and realizes its position; it is before all else an active cooperation. The collective ideas and sentiments are even possible only owing to these exterior movements which symbolize them, as we have established. Then it is action which dominates the religious life, because of the mere fact that it is society which is its source. . . .

Religious forces are therefore human forces, moral forces. It is true that since collective sentiments can become conscious of themselves only by fixing themselves upon external objects, they have not been able to take form without adopting some of their characteristics from other things: They have thus acquired a sort of physical nature; in this way they have come to mix themselves with the life of the material world, and then have considered themselves capable of explaining what passes there. But when they are considered only from this point of view and in this role, only their most superficial aspect is seen. In reality, the essential elements of which these collective sentiments are made have been borrowed by the understanding. It ordinarily seems that they should have a human character only when they are conceived under human forms;[2] but even the most impersonal and the most anonymous are nothing else than objectified sentiments. . . .

Some reply that men have a natural faculty for idealizing, that is to say, of substituting for the real world another different one, to which they transport themselves by thought. But that is merely changing the terms of the problem; it is not resolving it or even advancing it. This systematic idealization is an essential characteristic of religions. Explaining them by an innate power of idealization is simply replacing one word by another which is the equivalent of the first; it is as if they said that men have made religions because they have a religious nature. Animals know only one world, the one which they perceive by experience, internal as well as external. Men alone have the faculty of conceiving the ideal, of adding something to the real. Now where does this singular privilege come from? Before making it an initial fact or a mysterious virtue which escapes science, we must be sure that it does not depend upon empirically determinable conditions.

The explanation of religion which we have proposed has precisely this advantage, that it gives an answer to this question. For our definition of the sacred is that it is something added to and above the real: Now the ideal answers to this same definition; we cannot explain one without explaining the other. In fact, we have seen that if collective life awakens religious thought on reaching a certain degree of intensity, it is because it brings about a state of effervescence which changes the conditions of psychic activity. Vital energies are overexcited, passions more active, sensations stronger; there are even some which are produced only at this moment. A man does not recognize himself; he feels himself transformed and consequently he transforms the environment which surrounds him. In order to account for the very particular impressions which he receives, he attributes to the things with which he is in most direct contact properties which they have not, exceptional powers and virtues which the objects of everyday experience do not posses. In a word, above the real world where his profane life passes he has placed another which, in one sense, does not exist except in thought, but to which he attributes a higher sort of dignity than to the first. Thus, from a double point of view it is an ideal world.

The formation of the ideal world is therefore not an irreducible fact which escapes science; it depends upon conditions which observation can touch; it is a natural product of social life. For a society to become conscious of itself and maintain at the necessary degree of intensity the sentiments which it thus attains, it must assemble and concentrate itself. Now this concentration brings about an exaltation of the mental life which takes form in a group of ideal conceptions where is portrayed the new life thus awakened; they correspond to this new set of psychical forces which is added to those which we have at our disposition for the daily tasks of existence. A society can neither create itself nor recreate itself without at the same time creating an ideal. This creation is not a sort of work of supererogation for it, by which it would complete itself, being already formed; it is the act by which it is periodically made and remade. Therefore when some oppose the ideal society to the real society, like two antagonists which would lead us in opposite directions, they materialize and oppose abstractions. The ideal society is not outside of the real society; it is a part of it. Far from being divided between them as between two poles which mutually repel each other, we cannot hold to one without holding to the other. For a society is not made up merely of the mass of individuals who compose it, the ground which they occupy, the things which they use and the movements which they perform, but above all is the idea which it forms of itself. It is undoubtedly true that it hesitates over the manner in which it ought to conceive itself; it feels itself drawn in divergent directions. But these conflicts which break forth are not between the ideal and reality, but between two different ideals, that of yesterday and that of today, that which has the authority of tradition and that which has the hope of the future. There is surely a place for investigating whence these ideals evolve; but whatever solution may be given to thi problem, it still remains that all passes in the world of the ideal.

Thus the collective ideal which religion expresses is far from being due to a vague innate power of the individual, but it is rather at the school of collective life that the individual has learned to idealize. It is in assimilating the ideals elaborated by society that he has become capable of conceiving the ideal. It is society which, by leading him within its sphere of action, had made him acquire the need of raising himself above the world of experience and has at the same time furnished him with the means of conceiving another. For society has constructed this new world in constructing itself, since it is society which this expresses. This both with the individual and in the group, the faculty of idealizing has nothing mysterious about it. It is not a sort of luxury which a man could get along without, but a condition of his very existence. He could not be a social being, that is to say, he could not be a man, if he had not acquired it. It is true that in incarnating themselves in individuals, collective ideals tend to individualize themselves. Each understands them after his own fashion and marks them with his own stamp; he suppresses certain elements and adds others. Thus the personal ideal disengages itself from the social ideal in proportion as the individual personality develops itself and becomes an autonomous source of action. But if we wish to understand this aptitude, so singular in appearance, of living outside of reality, it is enough to connect it with the social conditions upon which it depends.

Therefore it is necessary to avoid seeing in this theory of religion a simple restatement of historical materialism: That would be misunderstanding our thought to an extreme degree. In showing that religion is something essentially social, we do not mean to say that it confines itself to translating into another language the material forms of society and its immediate vital necessities. It is true that we take it as evident that social life depends upon its material foundation and bears its mark, just as the mental life of an individual depends upon his nervous system and in fact his whole organism. But collective consciousness is something more than a mere epiphenomenon of its morphological basis, just as individual consciousness is something more than a simple efflorescence of the nervous system. In order that the former may appear, a synthesis *sui generis* of particular consciousnesses is required. Now this synthesis has the effect of disengaging a whole world of sentiments, ideas, and images which, once born, obey laws all their own. They attract each other, repel each other, unite, divide themselves, and multiply, though these combinations are not commanded and necessitated by the condition of the underlying reality. The life thus brought into being even enjoys so great an independence that it sometimes indulges in manifestations with no purpose or utility of any sort, for the mere pleasure of affirming itself. We have shown that this is often precisely the case with ritual activity and mythological thought.[3] . . .

That is what the conflict between science and religion really amounts to. It is said that science denies religion in principle. But religion exists; it is a system of given facts; in a word, it is a reality. How could science deny this reality? Also, insofar as religion is action, and insofar as it is a means of making men live, science could not take its place, for even if this expresses life, it does not create it; it may well seek to explain the faith, but by the very act it presupposes it. Thus there is no conflict except upon one limited point. Of the two functions which religion originally fulfilled, there is one, and only one, which tends to escape it more and more: That is its speculative function. That which science refuses to grant to religion is not its right to exist, but its right to dogmatize upon the nature of things and the special competence which it claims for itself for knowing man and the world. As a matter of fact, it does not know itself. It does not even know what it is made of, nor to what need it answers. It is itself a subject for science, so far is it from being able to make the law for science! And from another point of view, since there is no proper subject for religious speculation outside that reality to which scientific reflection is applied, it is evident that this former cannot play the same role in the future that it has played in the past.

However, it seems destined to transform itself rather than to disappear. . . .

Notes

1. James, William. 1902. *The Varieties of Religious Experience.* New York: Longmans, Green.
2. It is for this reason that Frazer and even Preuss set impersonal religious forces outside of, or at least on the threshold of religion, to attach them to magic.
3. On this same question, see out article, "Representations individuelles et representations collectives." In *Revue du Metaphysique,* May, 1898.

Name: _____ Class: _____

Date: _____ Section: _____

Reading Comprehension Activity Sheet

The Elementary Forms of the Religious Life, Emile Durkheim

1. Durkheim indirectly suggests that religious life is social constructed. Explain this relationship.

   _____
   _____
   _____
   _____
   _____
   _____
   _____
   _____
   _____
   _____
   _____
   _____
   _____

2. In what way does Durkheim encourage the separation of the knowledge of religion from the knowledge of science? _____

   _____
   _____
   _____
   _____
   _____
   _____
   _____
   _____
   _____
   _____
   _____
   _____
   _____

Miami's Little Havana

Yard Shrines, Cult Religion, and Landscape

James R. Curtis

In the summer of 1978 a brief article entitled "Neighbors Irate over Family's Shrine" appeared in *The Miami Herald*.[1] The story told of a group of residents in the predominantly non-Latin City of South Miami who feared that a newly-erected, seven-foot shrine in the front yard of a Cuban neighbor would lower property values. City officials called in to investigate found that the shrine was located too close to the front property line, and thus was in violation of municipal building and zoning laws. Confused and saddened by the turmoil created the Cuban family stated that the shrine had been built (at a cost of $1,500) in gratitude to Santa Barbara "for answering all of our prayers."

More than an isolated human interest story, the above incident is perhaps symbolic of the bicultural social adjustments, and urban landscape transformations, which have taken place and are continuing to occur in the greater Miami area as a result of Cuban in-migration. In the short span of only 20 years, beginning in 1959, the Cuban population of Dade County has ballooned from about 20,000 to a current estimate of 430,000.[2] Counting the 94,000 non-Cuban Latins residing in the county—mostly Puerto Ricans, Mexicans and Central and South Americans—Latins constitute approximately 35 per cent of the county's population, as compared to only 5 percent in 1960.[3] Moreover, Latins have settled in distinct residential concentrations, thereby greatly accentuating the "Latinization" of selected locales.[4] The city of Miami, for example, is almost 56 percent Latin (207,000 out of 370,000); Hialeah, with a population of 133,000, is over 65 percent Latin, most of whom are Cuban. The impact of such sudden and fundamental change in the pattern of ethnicity has profoundly altered both material and nonmaterial elements of culture in the region. Nowhere are these transformations

Browne, Ray B., ed. Rituals and Ceremonies in Popular Culture, © 1980. Reprinted by permission of The University of Wisconsin Press.

better manifested than in Little Havana, a four-square-mile enclave of Cuban culture located a scant mile southwest of downtown Miami.

Often referred to as "a city (or "nation") within a city," Little Havana is the nucleus, the core, of Cuban life in Miami. Once a healthy middle-class Anglo neighborhood, dating from the immediate post–World War I era, by the mid-1950s it had deteriorated and was declining in population as urban growth and increased mobility opened up newer housing areas for the middle-class in the outlying suburbs.[5] For the newly arriving Cuban refugees this area was preferred in respect to having available and affordable housing units and vacant shops for potential business endeavors.[6] It was also served by public transportation and near the central business district where social services and employment opportunities were most abundant. The neighborhood was reborn as "Little Havana" almost literally overnight. Although its function as the principal receptor area has declined in recent years as the Cuban population has grown in numbers and affluence,[7] and has since spread out to other settlement areas, Little Havana remains in spirit, if not in landscape, the traditional Cuban quarter.

In most important respect, Little Havana is a self-contained community which has evolved, by design, to suit the needs and tastes of its residents, and in so doing has embellished the landscape with a pronounced Cuban flavor. Along West Flagler and Southwest Eighth Streets (the latter know locally as *"Calle Ocho"*), the two principal commercial strips which cut through the district, a full complement of goods and services is offered which cater to the Cuban population. If so desired, a Cuban who lives in Little Havana and speaks only Spanish, could shop, dine out, be medically cared for, attend churches, schools, shows and theaters, die, and be buried without a word of English being uttered.

The commercial landscape of Little Havana reflects in both vivid and subtle ways this impress of Cuban culture. From the older stucco buildings of Spanish and art deco styles, and from the small shopping plazas which have been built of late, neon store signs flash *"Joyeria," "Ferreteria," "Muebleria," "Farmacia," "Mercado," "Zapateria,"* and so on. One frequently encounters small groups of three and four gathered at the countless vest-pocket, open-air coffee counters to sip the syrupy-dark, bittersweet *cafe cubano* and consume fresh *pasteles* (pastry).

The newsstands and bookstores in the district display a plethora of Spanish-language books, magazines, and newspapers, including *El Miami Herald* with a circulation in excess of 50,000. The acrid smell of cured tobacco wafts from the 30 or so small cigar factories located in the area where old men (*tabaqueros*) patiently roll cigars *a mano* (by hand).[8] At Antonio Maceo Mini Park, on *Calle Ocho,* men play continuous games of dominoes on permanently fixed tables and benches designed specifically for that purpose. Fresh fruits and vegetables are sold in open-air markets and stands which dot the district. The sweet smell of simmering garlic hangs heavy over the hundred-plus restaurants featuring Cuban and Spanish cuisine, ranging from elegant supper clubs with valet parking to four-stool cafes.

The life and vitality of these places, however, stand in stark contrast to the somberness surrounding the Cuban Memorial Plaza, where flowers and wreaths are faithfully placed at the base of the Bay of Pigs monument in memory of loved ones who feel during that ill-fated invasion. To be sure, the landscape of Little Havana conveys a strong feeling of pre-revolutionary Cuba, but the sense of a people in exile remains pervasive. The existence of nearly one hundred officially recognized "municipalities in exile," which function as social and quasi-political organizations composed of former residents of particular municipalities in Cuba, attests to their vitality.[9] Many of these groups, in fact, have converted houses and other buildings in Little Havana into meeting halls where lectures, concerts and dances are periodically held, and where informational and historical newsletters are published.

Thus, as befitting a people caught inextricably between two cultures, Little Havana is not an isolated community devoid of contact and consequence with the surrounding society and environment. Rather, in culture and landscape, it is a mixture of both Cuban and American influences. Cuban and American flags, for example, proudly bedeck the streets of Little Havana during national holidays of both countries. Cuban (grocery) shoppers may patronize the neighborhood Winn Dixie or Pantry Pride supermarkets, and then walk to the back parking lot of these stores and barter with itinerant Cuban peddlers selling fresh fish, poultry, fruit, and vegetables. Teenagers sip on *batidos* (exotic fruit milkshakes) from Cuban ice cream shops and eat *grandes macs* from the local McDonald's. In language as well, especially among the younger Cubans, one now hears a curious mixture of Spanish and English ("Spanglish," as it is known).[10] Signs on some store windows, for example, announce "*Gran Sale*." Young people may be heard shouting to one another, "*Tenga un* nice day."

Although the housing area of Little Havana has been significantly upgraded and changed as a consequence of the Cuban tenure, the residential landscape is not nearly as "Latinized" as the commercial strips in the district. In fact, a quick drive through the area would probably leave the impression that it is largely indistinguishable from neighboring Anglo residential areas. Yet, upon closer inspection, differences unfold. Fences, for example, now enclose many front yards, and wrought iron and tile have been added to some houses for decorative purposes. Even these characteristically Hispanic features, however, remain relatively minor in comparison to what one might expect to find in most Latin communities. If anything, one is impressed more by how little these embellishments reflect the fundamental replacement of culture groups which has occurred in the area. This observation, however, is somewhat misleading, for it fails to include the single most conspicuous landscape element which clearly distinguished Little Havana from non-Cuban residential areas.

Yard Shrines

If the Cuban family in the story recounted at the beginning of this article had lived in Little Havana, it would not have aroused the resentment, or even stirred the curiosity, of neighbors over the construction of its yard shrine. City officials would not have been brought in to search for some minor infraction of local building or zoning laws to force its removal. More common-place than exceptional, there are literally hundreds of yard shrines gracing the cultural landscape of Little Havana.[11]

The shrines may be found anywhere in the yard area—front, back, or along the sides—although the front yard, especially near the sidewalk, appears to be a favored location. Regardless of placement, however, the front of the shrine always faces the street. Since these are personal shrines, built to suit the religious needs and preferences of individuals, no two are exactly alike; diversity is the standard. In size, the shrines range from about two to ten feet in height, and two to six feet in width. Most are rectangular in shape, although octagonal and circular structures are not uncommon. The most frequently used building materials include brick, cement, stone, and glass; wood is rarely, if ever, used except for trimming. Exterior walls, though, are often stuccoed or tiled. A single cross may adorn the top of a shrine, and use of latticework and other forms of ornamentation are occasionally found, but in general the degree of exterior embellishment is more austere than ornate.

Regardless of size, materials used, or shape, the interiors of the shrines remain visible through either sealed glass side panels or a single glass door enclosing the front of the sanctuary. Pedestaled inside, usually on an elevated platform or altar, stands a single statue. At the base of the statue, and occasionally on a small stair well leading to the base, one finds an utterly baffling array of items, including, for example, fresh-cut or artificial flowers, candles, crucifixes, jars of leaves, bowls of water, beads, stones, miniature figures of men or animals, and other assorted paraphernalia.

The statues themselves are of Catholic saints, the Madonna and Jesus, each identifiable (at least to the knowing eye) by sex, colors, adornment, and particular symbols, such as a cup, a cane, or a cross. By far, the three saints which are enshrined most commonly in Little Havana are, in order, Santa Barbara, Our Lady of Charity (Patron saint of Cuba), and Saint Lazarus. Other saints, particularly Saint Francis of Assisi, Saint Christopher, and Saint Peter are also found, but with much less frequency. Likewise, shrines built in honor of the Madonna and Jesus are not nearly as numerous as those erected to the main three saints.

Santa Barbara is most often portrayed as a young woman dressed in a white tunic with a red mantle bordered with gold trimming. She wears a golden crown and holds a golden goblet in her right hand and a golden sword in her left. Our Lady of Charity is similarly represented as a young woman dressed in a white tunic. Her cloak, however, is either blue or white. She holds a child in her left arm. At her feet, seated or kneeling in a boat, are two or three small male figures looking reverently upward. Saint Lazarus is usually depicted as a bent and crippled man of middle age, with open wounds and sores, supported with the aid of crutches. Two or three small dog figures often stand at his feet. This particular portrayal of Lazarus is not the image officially recognized or sanctioned by the Church; it has evolved from Cuban tradition.

Sacred elements in the landscape often convey much less religious context from which they spring than observation alone would suggest. The religious beliefs which inspire the construction of yard shrines in Little Havana are illustrative of this contention. Considering, for example, that a vast majority of Cubans are Roman Catholics, and that most of the shrines are built in apparent homage to saints, one might logically suspect that these shrines are erected by followers of the Catholic faith. This assumption, however, is neither entirely correct nor incorrect. In truth, many of the shrines are built by Catholics, but perhaps an equal number, if not more, are erected by followers of a fascinating, syncretic Afro-Cuban cult religion called *Santeria*.

Santeria: An Afro-Cuban Religion

This history of the West Indies is rich in examples of the spontaneous melding of European and African culture traits and complexes. This process of transculturation—in which different cultural elements are jumbled, mixed, and fused—played an important role in the shaping of present cultural patterns in the region, particularly in the nonmaterial aspects of culture such as language, music, and religion. More notable examples of religious syncretism in the New World in which elements of Catholicism were combined with ancient African tribal beliefs and practices include *Vodun* (i.e., voodoo) in Haiti, *Xango* in Trinidad, and *Santeria* in Cuba.[12]

Santeria, like other syncretic Afro-Christian folk religions, combines an elaborate ensemble of ritual, magical, medical, and theological beliefs to form a total magico-religious world view. The *Santeria* religion evolved among descendants of the Yoruba slaves who had been brought to Cuba from Nigeria beginning in the sixteenth century, but particularly in the first half of the nineteenth century.[13] These descendants—known in Cuba as the *Lucumi*—learned from oral history the tribal religion of their ancestral home. It was a complex polytheistic religion involving a pantheon of gods and goddesses called *orishas*.[14] It was also colorful in its mythology. In many respects it was extraordinarily reminiscent of ancient Greek mythology.[15] The African religion was rather quickly altered, however, as the Cuban *Lucumis* fell increasingly under the sway of the Spanish culture.[16] Exposure to the Catholic religion, particularly its veneration of numerous saints, greatly influenced the nature of the emergent folk religion.[17] In time, the Yoruba deities came to be identified with the images of Catholic saints.[18] The *orishas* then became *santos* (saints), and their worship became known as *Santeria*—literally the worship of saints. Thus, to the *santero* (i.e., the practitioner of *Santeria*), a shrine may be built to house a statue in the image of a Catholic saint, but the saint is actually representative of a Yoruba god. It is exceedingly difficult to determine accurately, based solely on appearance, whether a yard shrine in Little Havana actually belongs to a Catholic or a follower of *Santeria*. In general, however, yard shrines built by practitioners of *Santeria* are more likely to contain nontraditional religious items such as bowls of water, stones, and jars of leaves.

The followers of *Santeria* believe in a supreme god called *Olodumare, Olofi,* or *Olorún*. He is thought to be a distant, lofty figure. Contact with this supreme deity is attainable only through the *orishals* who serve as intermediaries.[19] Thus, worship of god-saints serves as the focus for formal and informal devotional practices; there are no subcults or special rites exclusively in honor of *Olodumare*.

The saints "who are known both by their Catholic names and their Yoruba appellations" are associated with specific colors, particular symbols or "weapons," such as thunder, fire, or swords, and are considered to have the same supernatural powers ascribed to the African deities.[20] Each is believed to possess specific attributes, which in total govern all aspects of human life and natural phenomena. A *santero* might seek to invoke the power, for example, of *Babalu-Aye* (associated with Saint Lazarus), god of illness and disease, to cure a particular ailment, or *Orúnmila* (associated with Saint Francis of Assisi), god of wisdom and divination, to bestow knowledge. Others, purportedly, can assure success in a job, ward off an evil spirit, bring back a former lover, and so on.

The numerous deities, however, are not all venerated equally; some are more favored than others, often leading to the formation of a special subcult devoted to a particular god-saint. In Cuba, as in Miami now *Changó* (Associated with Saint Barbara), god of fire, thunder, and lightning, is the most popular of all the *orishas*.[21] *Changó* represents a curious form of syncretism involving a change of sex from the male Yoruba god to the female Catholic saint. *Oshún* (associated with Our Lady of Charity, patron saint of Cuba), god of love, marriage, and gold, and *Babalu-Aye* are also extremely popular in Miami. Seven of the most revered and powerful *orishas* are often worshipped collectively. This group is known among *santeros* as the "Seven African Powers." The *orishas* which make up this septet, their associated Catholic images, colors, human aspects controlled, and weapons are shown in Table 13.1.

The ritual and devotional activities of *santeros* are confined, in most cases, to private residences. The more important functions, such as an initiation into the cult, a funeral, or a consultation in which some form of divination is sought is presided over by a high "priest"

TABLE 13.1
The Seven African Powers

Orisha	Catholic Image	Colors	Human Aspect Controlled	Weapons or Symbols
Changó	Santa Barbara	red/white	passion, enemies	thunder, sword, cup
Elegguá	Holy Guardian Angel	red/black	messages	iron nails, small iron rooster
Obatalá	Our Lady of Mercy	white	peace, purity	all white substances
Oggún	Saint Peter	green/black	war, employment	iron, knives, steel
Orúnmila	Saint Francis of Assisi	green/yellow	divination	Table (a divination board) of Ifa
Oshún	Our Lady of Charity	yellow/red/green	love, marriage, gold	mirror, seashells, pumpkins
Yemayá	Our Lady of Regla	blue/white	maternity, womenhood	canoe, seashells, fans

Source: Migene Gonzalez-Wippler, *Santeria: African Magic in Latin American* (New York: Julian Press), 1973.

of the religion, called a *babaloa*.[22] Lesser orders of priesthood attend to the more mundane rites and rituals. The rituals themselves are primitive, bizzare affairs, often involving the consumption of beverages concocted from exotic herbs and roots, the use of incense, oils, and foreign perfumes, drumming, dancing, trance inducement, and animal sacrifices.[23] Many of the liturgical practices including phraseology used in prayers and incantations, as well as various paraphernalia needed for ritualistic purposes, are also borrowed from Catholicism. A *Santeria* priest might even suggest to a follower that he or she attend a Catholic mass; in many cases simply to obtain holy water or even a piece of the consecrated host for use in a subsequent ritual.[24]

The Expansion of Santeria

As surprising as it may seem, *Santeria* today is neither a predominantly rural nor a lower socioeconomic class phenomenon. Indeed, authorities on the religion confirm that *Santeria* has permeated all racial groups and socioeconomic classes in Cuba, and now in the Cuba community in exile.[25] With the Cuban immigration to the United States. Santeria is known to be thriving in the larger cities where Cuba refugees have settled, including New York, Los Angeles, Detroit, Chicago, and particularly Miami. A precise determination of the numbers of adherents to *Santeria* in Miami is virtually impossible to ascertain, since they do not build public churches or publish membership records. It is believed, however, that their numbers run into the thousands. One rough indication is provide by anthropologist William Bascom who estimated in 1969 that there were at least 83 *babaloas,* or high priests, practicing in Miami.[26] This may be compared to Havana, which is the stronghold of *Santeria* with tens of thousands of followers, where Bascom estimated the number of *babaloas* at about 200 just prior to the Cuban Revolution.[27] Perhaps a better indicator is the existence in Miami of over 12 *botanicas,* which are retail supply outlets catering to the *Santeria* trade.

By all scholarly accounts, *Santeria* is becoming increasingly popular among certain segments of the Cuban exile community. The reason most commonly cited for this kindling of interest is the fear of some Cuban refugees of losing their cultural identity through acculturation to the American way of life.[28] Such a conversion would perhaps represent an attempt to maintain linkage to a more stable past in the face of rapidly changing values and lifestyles. Disenchantment with the Catholic faith is another factor also frequently mentioned as contributing to the apparent expansion of *Santeria* in the United States. In this respect, the Catholic church's questioning of the historical validity of certain saints who were popular in Cuba (such as Saint Lazarus and Saint Christopher), the elimination of many rituals practiced in Cuba, and just the size and institutionalized nature of the Catholic religion have reportedly prompted some Cuban-Americans to seek out alternative religious affiliation, including *Santeria.*[29] Furthermore, the adaptive nature of the Santeria religion itself has apparently contributed to its expansion. Mercedes Sandoval, for example, concludes: "Its intrinsic flexibility, eclecticism and heterogeneity have been advantages in helping ensure functional, dogmatic and ritual changes which enable it to meet the different needs of its many followers."[30] Evidently one of the more important and attractive aspects of *Santeria* for the Cuban community in Miami is its function as a mental health care system.[31]

In the process of change and modification as practiced in the United States, however, many African chants and dances, the use of certain herbs and roots and other medicinal and ritualistic elements have been abandoned. One of the more interesting adaptations, for example, involves a change in the Oil of the Seven African Powers, used in the worship of those deities. The "oil" is now available in *botanicas* in Miami as an aerosol spray. Directions on the side of the container read as follows: "Repeat as necessary. Make your petition. Make the sign of the cross. Air freshener, deodorizer."

Perhaps the apparent expansion of interest in *Santeria* among certain members of the Cuban exile community is only a transitional phenomenon which will subside, or die out completely, as the process of acculturation speeds ahead: [this] occurred, for example, in Italian American cult religions.[32] At the present time, however, as one follower of *Santeria* said, "When we hear thunder in Miami, we know that Changó is in exile."[33] Regardless of the future of this particular religious cult, the yard shrines and other contributions to the cultural landscape associated with the Cuban sector reflect the growing social diversity of this rapidly changing cosmopolitan city.

Notes

1. Sam Jacobs, "Neighbors Irate over Family's Shrine," *The Miami Herald* (July 2, 1978), section A, p. 23.
2. Strategy Research Corporation, "Latin Market Survey," Miami, Florida, 1977, p. 78; Metropolitan Dade County Office of the County Manager, "Profile of the Latin Population in the Metropolitan Dade County Area," Miami, Florida, 1976.
3. Strategy Research Corporation, p. 78.
4. Metropolitan Dade County Planning Department, "Ethnic Breakdown by Census Tract," Miami, Florida, 1975.
5. Metropolitan Dade County Office of the City Manager, "Impact of the Community Development Program on Private Involvement in the Commercial Rehabilitation of the 'Little Havana' Neighborhood," Miami, Florida, 1978, p. 2.
6. Kimball D. Woodbury, "The Spatial Diffusion of the Cuban Community in Dade County, Florida" (unpublished M.A. thesis, University of Florida, Department of Geography, 1978) p. 33.
7. F. Pierce Eichelberger, "The Cubans in Miami: Residential Movements and Ethnic Group Differentiation" (unpublished M.A. thesis, University of Cincinnati, Department of Geography, 1974), p. 83.
8. William D. Montalbano, "Vanishing Hands," *The Miami Herald* (Feb. 4, 1979), Tropic section, pp. 19–21.
9. Ileana Oroza, "The Traditionalist," *The Miami Herald* (July 4, 1978), section A, p. 16.
10. John Dorschner, "Growing up Spanglish in Miami," *The Miami Herald* (Sept. 11, 1977), Tropic section, pp. 6–13.

11. Matthew Creelman, "Count Your Built-In Blessings," *The Miami Herald* (July 21, 1979), Section D, p. 3.
12. George E. Simpson, *Religious Cults of the Caribbean: Trinidad, Jamaica, and Haiti* (Rio Piedras, Puerto Rico: Institute of Caribbean Studies, 1970), p. 11.
13. Migene Gonzalez-Wippler, *Santeria: African Magic in Latin America* (New York: Julian Press, 1973), p. 1.
14. D. E. Baldwin, *The Yoruba of Southwest Nigeria* (Boston: G. K. Hall, 1976).
15. J. O. Lucas, *The Religions of the Yorubas* (Lagos: C.M.S. Bookshop, 1942).
16. William Bascom, "The Yoruba in Cuba," *Nigeria,* 37 (1951).
17. William Bascom, "The Focus of Cuban Santeria," *Southwestern Journal of Anthropology,* 6 (Spring, 1950): 64–68.
18. Gonzalez-Wippler, p. 3; Melville J. Herskovits, "African Gods and Catholic Saints in New World Negro Belief," *American Anthropologist,* 39 (Oct–Dec., 1937): 635–43.
19. Isabel Mercedes Castellanos, "The Use of Language in Afro-Cuban Religion" (unpublished Ph.D. dissertation, Georgetown University, Dept. of Languages and Linguistics, 1976), pp. 31–33.
20. Gonzalez-Wippler, p. 16.
21. Mercedes C. Sandoval, "Santeria as a Mental Health Care System: An Historical Overview," *Social Science and Medicine,* 13B (April, 1979): 139; William R. Bascom, *Shango in the New World* (Austin, Texas: Univ. of Texas Press, 1972), pp. 13–15.
22. Castellanos, "The Use of Language in Afro-Cuban Religion," p. 35.
23. Mercedes C. Sandoval, *La Religion Afro-Cubana* (Madrid, Spain: Playor, S.A., 1975); Lydia Cabrera, *El Monte* (Miami: Ediciones, C.R., 1971); Ellen Hampton, "Drums Beating and Animals Shrieking Frightening Southwest Dade Residents," *The Miami Herald* (Nov. 25, 1979), section B, p. 19.
24. Gonzalez-Wippler, p. 4.
25. Sandoval, *La Religion Afro-Cubana,* pp. 270–72; Castellanos, pp. 163–64.
26. Bascom, *Shango in the New World,* p. 20.
27. *Ibid.*
28. Castellanos, p. 164.
29. Sandoval, *La Religion Afro-Cubana,* p. 272.
30. Sandoval, "Santeria as a Mental Health Care System," p. 137.
31. *Ibid.,* pp. 137–51; Clarrisa S. Scott, "Health and Healing Practices among Five Ethnic Groups in Miami, Florida," *Public Health Reports,* 89 (Nov.–Dec., 1974): 526–27.
32. Rudolph J. Vecoli, "Cult and Occult in Italian-American Culture: The Persistence of a Religious Heritage," in *Immigrants and Religion in Urban Culture,* ed. Randall M. Miller and Thomas D. Marzik (Philadelphia: Temple University Press, 1977), pp. 25–47.
33. Sandoval, *La Religion Afro-Cubana,* p. 274.

Name: _____ Class: _____

Date: _____ Section: _____

Reading Comprehension Activity Sheet

Miami's Little Havana: Yard Shrines, Cult Religion, and Landscape, James R. Curtis.

1. In what ways have the residents of Miami's Little Havana combined elements of Catholicism and Santeria? _____

_____

_____

_____

_____

_____

_____

_____

_____

_____

_____

2. Is such a combination antithetical to the notion of what is a religion (or that of being religious)?

_____

_____

_____

_____

_____

_____

_____

_____

_____

_____

_____

chapter 14

Politics and the Government

The Power Elite
C. Wright Mills

The My Lai Massacre: A Military Crime of Obedience
Herbert Kelman
V. Lee Hamilton

The Power Elite

C. Wright Mills

The powers of ordinary men are circumscribed by the everyday worlds in which they live, yet even in these rounds of job, family, and neighborhood they often seem driven by forces they can neither understand nor govern. "Great changes" are beyond their control, but affect their conduct and outlook nonetheless. The very framework of modern society confines them to projects not their own, but from every side, such changes now press upon the men and women of the mass society, who accordingly feel that they are without purpose in an epoch in which they are without power.

But not all men are in this sense ordinary. As the means of information and of power are centralized, some men come to occupy positions in American society from which they can look down upon, so to speak, and by their decisions mightily affect, the everyday worlds of ordinary men and women. They are not made by their jobs; they set up and break down jobs for thousands of others; they are not confined by simple family responsibilities; they can escape. They may live in many hotels and houses, but they are bound by no one community. They need not merely "meet the demands of the day and hour"; in some part, they create these demands, and cause others to meet them. Whether or not they profess their power, their technical and political experience of it far transcends that of the underlying population. What Jacob Burckhardt said of "great men," most Americans might well say of their elite: "They are all that we are not."

The power elite is composed of men whose positions enable them to transcend the ordinary environments of ordinary men and women; they are in positions to make decisions having major consequences. Whether they do or do not make such decisions is less important than the fact that they do occupy such pivotal positions: Their failure to act, their failure to make decisions, is itself an act that is often of greater consequence than the decisions they do make. For they are in command of the major hierarchies and organizations of modern society. They rule the big corporations. They run the machinery of the state and claim its prerogatives. They direct the military establishment. They occupy the strategic command

From *The Power Elite*. New Edition by C. Wright Mills, copyright © 1956, 2000 by Oxford University Press, Inc. Used by permission of Oxford University Press, Inc.

posts of the social structure, in which are now centered the effective means of the power and the wealth and the celebrity which they enjoy.

The power elite are not solitary rulers. Advisers and consultants, spokesmen and opinion makers are often the captains of their higher thought and decision. Immediately below the elite are the professional politicians of the middle levels of power, in the Congress and in the pressure groups, as well as among the new and old upper classes of town and city and region. Mingling with them, in curious ways which we shall explore, are those professional celebrities who live by being continually displayed but are never, so long as they remain celebrities, displayed enough. If such celebrities are not at the head of any dominating hierarchy, they do often have the power to distract the attention of the public or afford sensations to the masses, or, more directly, to gain the ear of those who do occupy positions of direct power. More or less unattached, as critics of morality and technicians of power, ad spokesmen of God and creators of mass sensibility, such celebrities and consultants are part of the immediate scene in which the drama of the elite is enacted. But the drama itself is centered in the command posts of the major institutional hierarchies.

The truth about the nature and the power of the elite is not some secret which men of affairs know but will not tell. Such men hold quite various theories about their own roles in the sequence of event and decision. Often they are uncertain about their roles, and even more often they allow their fears and their hopes to affect their assessment of their own power. No matter how great their actual power, they tend to be less acutely aware of it than of the resistances of others to its use. Moreover, most American men of affairs have learned well the rhetoric of public relations, in some cases even to the point of using it when they are alone, and thus coming to believe it. The personal awareness of the actors is only one of the several sources one must examine in order to understand the higher circles. Yet many who believe that there is no elite, or at any rate none of any consequence, rest their argument upon what men of affairs believe about themselves, or at least assert in public.

There is, however, another view: Those who feel, even if vaguely, that a compact and powerful elite of great importance does now prevail in America often base that feeling upon the historical trend of our time. They have felt, for example, the domination of the military event, and from this they infer that generals and admirals, as well as other men of decision influenced by them, must be enormously powerful. They hear that the Congress has again abdicated to a handful of men decisions clearly related to the issue of war or peace. They know that the bomb was dropped over Japan in the name of the United States of America, although they were at no time consulted about the matter. They feel that they live in a time of big decisions; they know that they are not making any. Accordingly, as they consider the present as history, they infer that at its center, making decisions or failing to make them, there must be an elite of power.

On the one hand, those who share this feeling about big historical events assume that there is an elite and that its power is great. On the other hand, those who listen carefully to the reports of men apparently involved in the great decisions often do not believe that there is an elite whose powers are of decisive consequence.

Both views must be taken into account, but neither is adequate. The way to understand the power of the American elite lies neither solely in recognizing the historic scale of events nor in accepting the personal awareness reported by men of apparent decision. Behind such men and behind the events of history, linking the two, are the major institutions of modern society. These hierarchies of state and corporation and army constitute the means of power; as such they are now of a consequence not before equaled in human history—and at their summits, there are now those command posts of modern society which offer us the sociological key to an understanding of the role of the higher circles in America.

Within American society, major national power now resides in the economic, the political, and the military domains. Other institutions seem off to the side of modern history, and, on occasion, duly subordinated to these. No family is as directly powerful in national affairs as any major corporation; no church is as directly powerful in the external biographies of young men in America today as the military establishment; no college is as powerful in the shaping of momentous events as the National Security Council. Religious, educational, and family institutions are not autonomous centers of national power; on the contrary, these decentralized areas are increasingly shaped by the big three, in which developments of decisive and immediate consequence now occur.

Families and churches and schools adapt to modern life; governments and armies and corporations shape it; and, as they do so, they turn these lesser institutions into means for their ends. Religious institutions provide chaplains to the armed forces where they are used as a means of increasing the effectiveness of its morale to kill. Schools select and train men for their jobs in corporations and their specialized tasks in the armed forces. The extended family has, of course, long been broken up by the industrial revolution, and now the son and the father are removed from the family, by compulsion if need be, whenever the army of the state sends out the call. And the symbols of all these lesser institutions are used to legitimate the power and the decisions of the big three.

The life-fate of the modern individual depends not only upon the family into which he was born or which he enters by marriage, but increasingly upon the corporation in which he spends the most alert hours of his best years; not only upon the school where he is educated as a child and adolescent, but also upon the state which touches him throughout his life; not only upon the church in which on occasion he hears the word of God, but also upon the army in which he is disciplined.

If the centralized state could not rely upon the inculcation of nationalist loyalties in public and private schools, its leaders would promptly seek to modify the decentralized educational system. If the bankruptcy rate among the top 500 corporations were as high as the general divorce rate among the 37 million married couples, there would be economic catastrophe on an international scale. If members of armies gave to them no more of their lives than do believers to the churches to which they belong, there would be a military crisis.

Within each of the big three, the typical institutional unit has become enlarged, has become administrative, and, in the power of its decisions, has become centralized. Behind these developments there is a fabulous technology, for as institutions, they have incorporated this technology and guide it, even as it shapes and paces their developments.

The economy—once a great scatter of small productive units in autonomous balance—has become dominated by two or three hundred giant corporations, administratively and politically interrelated, which together hold the keys to economic decisions.

The political order, once a decentralized set of several dozen states with a weak spinal cord, has become a centralized, executive establishment which has taken up into itself many powers previously scattered, and now enters into each and every cranny of the social structure.

The military order, once a slim establishment in a context of distrust fed by state militia, has become the largest and most expensive feature of government, and, although well-versed in smiling public relations, now has all the grim and clumsy efficiency of a sprawling bureaucratic domain.

In each of these institutional areas, the means of power at the disposal of decision makers have increased enormously; their central executive powers have been enhanced; within each of them modern administrative routines have been elaborated and tightened up.

At each of these domains becomes enlarged and centralized, the consequences of its activities become greater, and its traffic with the others increases. The decisions of a handful of corporations bear upon military and political as well as upon economic developments around the world. The decisions of the military establishment rest upon and grievously affect political life as well as the very level of economic activity. The decisions made within the political domain determine economic activities and military programs. There is no longer, on the one hand, an economy, and, on the other hand, a political order containing a military establishment unimportant to politics and to money making. There is a political economy linked, in a thousand ways, with military institutions and decisions. On each side of the world-split running through central Europe and around the Asiatic rimlands, there is an ever-increasing interlocking of economic, military, and political structures. If there is government intervention in the corporate economy, so is there corporate intervention in the governmental process. In the structural sense, this triangle of power is the source of the interlocking directorate that is most important for the historical structure of the present.

The fact of the interlocking is clearly revealed at each of the points of crisis of modern capitalist society—slump, war, and boom. In each, men of decision are led to an awareness of the interdependence of the major institutional orders. In the nineteenth century, when the scale of all institutions was smaller, their liberal integration was achieved in the automatic economy, by an autonomous play of market forces, and in the automatic political domain, by the bargain and the vote. It was then assumed that out of the imbalance and friction that followed the limited decisions then possible a new equilibrium would in due course emerge. That can no longer be assumed, and it is not assumed by the men at the top of each of the three dominant hierarchies.

For given the scope of their consequences, decisions—and indecisions—in any one of these ramify into the others, and hence top decisions tend either to become coordinate or to lead to a commanding indecision. It has not always been like this. When numerous small entrepreneurs made up the economy, for example, many of them could fail and the consequences still remain local; political and military authorities did not intervene. But now, given political expectations and military commitments, can they afford to allow key units of the private corporate economy to break down in slump? Increasingly, they do intervene in economic affairs, and as they do so, the controlling decisions in each order are inspected by agents of the other two, and economic, military, and political structures are interlocked.

At the pinnacle of each of the three enlarged and centralized domains, there have arisen those higher circles which make up the economic, the political, and the military elites. At the top of the economy, among the corporate rich, there are the chief executives; at the top of the political order, the members of the political directorate; at the top of the military establishment, the elite of soldier-statesmen clustered in and around the Join Chiefs of Staff and the upper echelon. As each of these domains has coincided with the other, as decisions tend to become total in their consequence, the leading men in each of the three domains of power—the warlords, the corporation chieftains, the political directorate—tend to come together, to form the power elite of America.

The higher circles in and around these command posts are often thought of in terms of what their members possess: They have a greater share than other people of the things and experiences that are most highly valued. From this point of view, the elite are simply those who have the most of what there is to have, which is generally held to include money, power, and prestige—as well as all the ways of life to which these lead. But the elite are not simply those who have the most, for they could not "have the most" were it not for their positions in the great institutions. For such institutions are the necessary bases of power, of wealth, and of prestige, and at the same time, the chief means of exercising power, of acquiring and retaining wealth, and of cashing in the higher claims for prestige.

By the powerful we mean, of course, those who are able to realize their will, even if others resist it. No one, accordingly, can be truly powerful unless he has access to the command of major institutions, for it is over these institutional means of power that the truly powerful are, in the first instance, powerful. Higher politicians and key officials of government command such institutional power; so do admirals and generals, and so do the major owners and executives of the larger corporations. Not all power, it is true, is anchored in and exercised by means of such institutions, but only within and through them can power be more or less continuous and important.

Wealth also is acquired and held in and through institutions. The pyramid of wealth cannot be understood merely in terms of the very rich; for the great inheriting families, as we shall see, are now supplemented by the corporate institutions of modern society: Every one of the very rich families has been and is closely connected—always legally and frequently managerially as well—with one of the multimillion-dollar corporations.

The modern corporation is the prime source of wealth, but, in latter-day capitalism, the political apparatus also opens and closes many avenues to wealth. The amount as well as the source of income, the power over consumer's goods as well as over productive capital, are determined by position within the political economy. If our interest in the very rich goes beyond their lavish or their miserly consumption, we must examine their relations to modern forms of corporate property as well as to the state; for such relations now determine the chances of men to secure big property and to receive high income.

Great prestige increasingly follows the major institutional units of the social structure. It is obvious that prestige depends, often quite decisively, upon access to the publicity machines that are now a central and normal feature of all the big institutions of modern America. Moreover, one feature of these hierarchies of corporation, state, and military establishment is that their top positions are increasingly interchangeable. One result of this is the accumulative nature of prestige. Claims for prestige, for example, may be initially based on military roles, then expressed in and augmented by an educational institution run by corporate executives, and cashed in, finally, in the political order, where, for General Eisenhower and those he represents, power and prestige finally meet at the very peak. Like wealth and power, prestige tends to be cumulative: The more of it you have, the more you can get. These values also tend to be translatable into one another: The wealthy find it easier than the poor to gain power; those with status find it easier than those without it to control opportunities for wealth.

If we took the one hundred most powerful men in America, the one hundred wealthiest, and the one hundred most celebrated away from the institutional positions they now occupy, away from their resources of men and women and money, away from the media of mass communication that are now focused upon them—then they would be powerless and poor and uncelebrated. For power is not of a man. Wealth does not center in the person of the wealthy. Celebrity is not inherent in any personality. To be celebrated, to be wealthy, to have power requires access to major institutions, for the institutional positions men occupy determine in large part their chances to have and to hold these valued experiences.

The people of the higher circles may also be conceived as members of a top social stratum, as a set of groups whose members know one another, see one another socially and at business, and so, in making decisions, take one another into account. The elite, according to this conception, feel themselves to be, and are felt by others to be, the inner circle of "the upper social classes." They form a more or less compact social and psychological entity; they have become self-conscious members of a social class. People are either accepted into this class or they are not, and there is a qualitative split, rather than merely a numerical scale, separating them from those who are not elite. They are more or less aware of themselves as a social class and they behave toward one another differently from the way they do toward members of other classes. They accept one another, understand one another, marry one another, tend to work and to think if not together at least alike.

Now, we do not want by our definition to prejudge whether the elite of the command posts are conscious members of such a socially recognized class, or whether considerable proportions of the elite derive from such a clear and distinct class. These are matters to be investigated. Yet in order to be able to recognize what we intend to investigate, we must note something that all biographies and memoirs of the wealthy and the powerful and the eminent make clear: No matter what else they may be, the people of these higher circles are involved in a set of overlapping "crowds" and intricately connected "cliques." There is a kind of mutual attraction among those who "sit on the same terrace"—although this often becomes clear to them, as well as to others, only at the point at which they feel the need to draw the line; only when, in their common defense, they come to understand what they have in common, and so close their ranks against outsiders.

The idea of such ruling stratum implies that most of its members have similar social origins, that throughout their lives they maintain a network of informal connections, and that to some degree there is an interchangeability of position between the various hierarchies of money and power and celebrity. We must, of course, note at once that if such an elite stratum does exist, its social visibility and its form, for very solid historical reasons, are quite different from those of the noble cousinhoods that once ruled various European nations.

That American society has never passed through a feudal epoch is of decisive importance to the nature of the American elite, as well as to American society as a historic whole. For it means that no nobility or aristocracy, established before the capitalist era, has stood in tense opposition to the higher bourgeoisie. It means that this bourgeoisie has monopolized not only wealth but prestige and power as well. It means that no set of noble families has commanded the top positions and monopolized the values that are generally held in high esteem; and certainly that no set has done so explicitly by inherited right. It means that no high church dignitaries or court nobilities, no entrenched landlords with honorific accouterments, no monopolists of high army posts have opposed the enriched bourgeoisie and in the name of birth and prerogative successfully resisted its self-making.

But this does *not* mean that there are no upper strata in the United States. That they emerged from a "middle class" that had no recognized aristocratic superiors does not mean they remained middle class when enormous increases in wealth made their own superiority possible. Their origins and their newness may have made the upper strata less visible in America than elsewhere. But in America today there are in fact tiers and ranges of wealth and power of which people in the middle and lower ranks know very little and may not even dream. There are families who, in their well-being, are quite insulated from the economic jolts and lurches felt by the merely prosperous and those farther down the scale. There are also men of power who in quite small groups make decisions of enormous consequence for the underlying population.

The My Lai Massacre

A Military Crime of Obedience

Herbert Kelman
V. Lee Hamilton

March 16, 1968, was a busy day in U.S. history. Stateside, Robert F. Kennedy announced his presidential candidacy, challenging a sitting president from his own party—in part out of opposition to an undeclared and disastrous war. In Vietnam, the war continued. In many ways, March 16 may have been a typical day in that war. We will probably never know. But we do know that on that day a typical company went on a mission—which may or may not have been typical—to a village called Son (or Song) My. Most of what is remembered from that mission occurred in the subhamlet known to Americans as My Lai 4.

The My Lai massacre was investigated and charges were brought in 1969 and 1970. Trails and disciplinary actions lasted into 1971. Entire books have been written about the army's year-long cover-up of the massacre (for example, Hersh, 1972), and the cover-up was a major focus of the army's own investigation of the incident. Our central concern here is the massacre itself—a crime of obedience—and public reactions to such crimes, rather than the lengths to which many went to deny the event. Therefore this account concentrates on one day: March 16, 1968.

Many verbal testimonials to the horrors that occurred at My Lai were available. More unusual was the fact that an army photographer, Ronald Haeberle, was assigned the task of documenting the anticipated military engagement at My Lai—and documented a massacre instead. Later, as the story of the massacre emerged, his photographs were widely distributed and seared the public conscience. What might have been dismissed as unreal or exaggerated was depicted in photographs of demonstrable authenticity. The dominant image appeared on the cover of *Life:* piles of bodies jumbled together in a ditch along a trail—the

From *Crimes of Obedience* by Herbert Kelman and V. Lee Hamilton. 1989 Yale University Press. Reprinted by permission of Yale University Press.

dead all apparently unarmed. All were Oriental, and all appeared to be children, women, or old men. Clearly there had been a mass execution, one whose image would not quickly fade.

So many bodies (over twenty in the cover photo alone) are hard to imagine as the handiwork of one killer. These were not. They were the product of what we call a crime of obedience. Crimes of obedience begin with orders. But orders are often vague and rarely survive with any clarity the transition from one authority down a chain of subordinates to the ultimate actors. The operation at Son My was no exception.

"Charlie" Company, Company C, under Lt. Col. Frank Barker's command, arrived in Vietnam in December 1967. As the army's investigative unit, directed by Lt. Gen. William R. Peers, characterized the personnel, they "contained no significant deviation from the average" for the time. Seymour S. Hersh (1970) described the "average" more explicitly: "Most of the men in Charlie Company had volunteered for the draft; only a few had gone to college for even one year. Nearly half were black, with a few Mexican-Americans. Most were eighteen to twenty-two years old. The favorite reading matter of Charlie Company, like that of other line infantry units in Vietnam, was comic books" (p. 18). The action at My Lai, like that throughout Vietnam, was fought by a cross-section of those Americans who either believed in the war or lacked the social resources to avoid participating in it. Charlie Company was indeed average for that time, that place, and that war.

Two key figures in Charlie Company were more unusual. The company's commander, Capt. Ernest Medina, was an upwardly mobile Mexican-American who wanted to make the army his career, although he feared that he might never advance beyond captain because of his lack of formal education. His eagerness had earned him a nickname among his men: "Mad Dog Medina." One of his admirers was the platoon leader Second Lt. William L. Calley, Jr., an undistinguished, five-foot-three-inch junior-college dropout who had failed four of the seven courses in which he had enrolled his first year. Many viewed him as one of those "instant officers" made possible only by the army's then-desperate need for manpower. Whatever the cause, he was an insecure leader whose frequent claim was "I'm the boss." His nickname among some of the troops was "Surfside 5½," reference to the swashbuckling heroes of a popular television show, "Surfside 6."

The Son My operation was planned by Lieutenant Colonel Barker and his staff as a search-and-destroy mission with the objective of rooting out the Forty-eight Viet Con Battalion from their base area of Son My village. Apparently no written orders were ever issued. Barker's superior, Col. Oran Henderson, arrived at the staging point the day before. Among the issues he reviewed with the assembled officers were some of the weaknesses of prior operations by their units, including their failure to be appropriately aggressive in pursuit of the enemy. Later briefings by Lieutenant Colonel Barker and his staff asserted that no one except Viet Cong was expected to be in the village after 7 A.M. on the following day. The "innocent" would all be at the market. Those present at the briefings gave conflicting accounts of Barker's exact orders, but he conveyed at least a strong suggestion that the Son My area was to be obliterated. As the army's inquiry reported: "While there is some conflict in the testimony as to whether LTC Barker ordered the destruction of houses, dwellings, livestock, and other foodstuffs in the Son My area, the preponderance of the evidence indicates that such destruction was implied, if not specifically directed, by his orders of 15 March" (Peers Report, in Goldstein et al., 1976, p. 94).

Evidence that Barker ordered the killing of civilians is even more murky. What does seem clear, however, is that—having asserted that civilians would be away at the market—he did not specify what was to be done with any who might nevertheless be found on the scene. The Peers Report therefore considered it "reasonable to conclude that LTC Barker's minimal or nonexistent instructions concerning the handling of noncombatants created the potential for grave misunderstandings as to his intentions and for interpretation of his orders as authority to fire, without restriction, on all persons found in target area" (Goldstein et al., 1976, p. 95). Since Barker was killed in action in June 1968, his own formal version of the truth was never available.

Charlie Company's Captain Medina was briefed for the operation by Barker and his staff. He then transmitted the already vague orders to his own men. Charlie Company was spoiling for a fight, having been totally frustrated during its months in Vietnam—first by waiting for battles that never came, then by incompetent forays led by inexperienced commanders, and finally by mines and booby traps. In fact, the emotion-laden funeral of a sergeant killed by a booby trap was held on March 15, the day before May Lai. Captain Medina gave the orders for the next day's action at the close of that funeral. Many were in a mood for revenge.

It is again unclear what was ordered. Although all participants were alive by the time of the trials for the massacre, they were either on trial or probably felt under threat of trial. Memories are often flawed and self-serving at such times. It is apparent that Medina relayed to the men at least some of Barker's general message—to expect Viet Cong resistance, to burn, and to kill livestock. It is not clear that he ordered the slaughter of the inhabitants, but some of the men who heard him thought he had. One of those who claimed to have heard such orders was Lt. William Calley.

As March 16 dawned, mush was expected of the operation by those who had set it into motion. Therefore a full complement of "brass" was present in helicopters overhead, including Barker, Colonel Henderson, and their superior, Major General Koster (who went on to become commandant of West Point before the story of May Lai broke). On the ground, the troops were to carry with them one reporter and one photographer to immortalize the anticipated battle.

The action for Company C began at 7:30 as their first wave of helicopters touched down near the subhamlet of My Lai 4. By 7:47 all of Company C was present and set to fight. But instead of the Viet Cong Forty-eighth Battalion, My Lai was filled with the old men, women, and children who were supposed to have gone to market. By this time, in their version of the war, and with whatever orders they thought they had heard, the men from Company C were nevertheless ready to find Viet Cong everywhere. By nightfall, the official tally was 128 VC killed and three weapons captured, although later, unofficial body counts ran as high as 500. The operation at Son My was over. And by nightfall, as Hersh reported: "the Viet Cong were back in My Lai 4, helping the survivors bury the dead. It took five days. Most of the funeral speeches were made by the Communist guerrillas. Nguyen Bat was not a Communist at the time of the massacre, but the incident changed his mind. 'After the shooting,' he said, 'all the villagers became Communists'" (1970, p. 74). To this day, the memory of the massacre is kept alive by markers and plaques designating the spots where groups of villagers were killed, by a large statue, and by the My Lai Museum, established in 1975 (Williams, 1985).

But what could have happened to leave American troops reporting a victory over Viet Cong when in fact they had killed hundreds of noncombatants? It is not hard to explain the report of victory; that is the essence of a cover-up. It is harder to understand how the killings came to be committed in the first place, making a cover-up necessary.

Mass Executions and the Defense of Superior Orders

Some of the atrocities on March 16, 1968, were evidently unofficial, spontaneous acts: rapes, tortures, killings. For example, Hersh (1970) describes Charlie Company's Second Platoon as entering "My Lai 4 with guns blazing" (p. 50); more graphically, Lieutenant "Brooks and his men in the second platoon to the north had begun to systematically ransack the hamlet and slaughter the people, kill the livestock, and destroy the crops. Men poured rifle and machinegun fire into huts without knowing—or seemingly caring—who was inside" (pp. 49–50).

Some atrocities toward the end of the action were part of an almost casual "mopping-up," much of which was the responsibility of Lieutenant LaCross's Third Platoon of Charlie Company. The Peers Report states: "The entire 3rd Platoon then began moving into the western edge of My Lai (4), for the mop-up operation. . . . The squad . . . began to burn the houses in the southwestern portion of the hamlet" (Goldstein et al., 1976, p. 133). They became mingled with other platoons during a series of rapes and killings of survivors for which it was impossible to fix responsibility. Certainly to a Vietnamese all GIs would by this point look alike: "Nineteen-year-old Nguyen Thi Ngoc Tuyet watched a baby trying to open her slain mother's blouse to nurse. A soldier shot the infant while it was struggling with the blouse, and then slashed it with his bayonet." Tuyet also said she saw another baby hacked to death by GIs wielding their bayonets. "Le Tong, a twenty-eight-year-old rice farmer, reported seeing one woman raped after GIs killed her children. Nguyen Khoa, a thirty-seven-year-old peasant, told of a thirteen-year-old girl who was raped before being killed. GIs then attacked Khoa's wife, tearing off her clothes. Before they could rape her, however, Khoa said, their six-year-old son, riddled with bullets, fell and saturated her with blood. The GIs left her alone" (Hersh, 1970, p. 72). All the Company C was implicated in a pattern of death and destruction throughout the hamlet, much of which seemingly lacked rhyme or reason.

But a substantial amount of the killing was *organized* and traceable to one authority: the First Platoon's Lt. William Calley. Calley was originally charged with 109 killings, almost all of them mass executions at the trial and other locations. He stood trail for 102 of these killings, was convicted of 22 in 1971, and at first received a life sentence. Through others—both superior and subordinate to Calley—were brought to trial, he was the only one convicted for the My Lai crimes. Thus, the only actions of My Lai for which *anyone* was ever convicted were mass executions, ordered and committed. We suspect that there are common-sense reasons why this one type of killing was singled out. In the midst of rapidly moving events with people running about, an execution of stationary targets is literally a still life that stands out and whose participants are clearly visible. It can be proven that specific people committed specific deeds. An execution, in contrast to the shooting of someone on the run, is also more likely to meet the legal definition of an act resulting from intent—with malice aforethought. Moreover, American military law specifically forbids the killing of unarmed civilians or military prisoners, as does the Geneva Convention between nations. Thus common sense, legal standards, and explicit doctrine all made such actions the likeliest target for prosecution.

When Lieutenant Calley was charged under military law it was for violation of the Uniform Code of Military Justice (UCMJ) Article 118 (murder). This article is similar to civilian codes in that it provides for conviction if an accused:

without justification or excuse, unlawfully kills a human being, when he—

1. has a premeditated design to kill;
2. intends to kill or inflict great bodily harm;
3. is engaged in an act which is inherently dangerous to others and evinces a wanton disregard of human life; or
4. is engaged in the perpetration or attempted perpetration of burglary, sodomy, rape, robbery, or aggravated arson. (Goldstein et al., 1976, p. 507)

For a soldier, one legal justification for killing is warfare; but warfare is subject to many legal limits and restrictions, including, of course, the inadmissibility of killing unarmed noncombatants or prisoners whom one has disarmed. The pictures of the trial victims at My Lai certainly portrayed one or the other of these. Such an action would be illegal under military law; ordering another to commit such an action would be illegal; and following such an order would be illegal.

But following an order may provide a second and pivotal justification for an act that would be murder when committed by a civilian. American military law assumes that the subordinate is inclined to follow orders, as that is the normal obligation of the role. Hence, legally, obedient subordinates are protected from unreasonable expectations regarding their capacity to evaluate those orders:

An order requiring the performance of a military duty may be inferred to be legal. An act performed manifestly beyond the scope of authority, or pursuant to an order that a man of ordinary sense and understanding would know to be illegal, or in a wanton manner in the discharge of a lawful duty, is not excusable. (Par. 216, Subpar. *d,* Manual for Courts Martial, United States, 1969 Rev.)

Thus what *may* be excusable is the good-faith carrying out of an order, as long as that order appears to the ordinary soldier to be a legal one. In military law, invoking superior orders moves the question from one of the action's consequences—the body count—to one of evaluating the actor's motives and good sense.

In sum, if anyone is to be brought to justice for a massacre, common sense and legal codes decree that the most appropriate targets are those who make themselves executioners. This is the kind of target the government selected in prosecuting Lieutenant Calley with the greatest fervor. And in a military context, the most promising way in which one can redefine one's undeniable deeds into acceptability is to invoke superior orders. This is what Calley did in attempting to avoid conviction. Since the core legal issues involved points of mass execution—the ditches and trail where America's image of My Lai was formed—we review these events in greater detail.

The day's quiet beginning has already been noted. Troops landed and swept unopposed into the village. The three weapons eventually reported as the haul from the operation were picked up from three apparent Viet Cong who fled the village when the troops arrived and were pursued and killed by helicopter gunships. Obviously the Viet Cong did frequent the area. But it appears that by about 8:00 A.M. no one who met the troops was aggressive, and no one was armed. By the laws of war Charlie Company had no argument with such people.

As they moved into the village, the soldiers began to gather its inhabitants together. Shortly after 8:00 A.M. Lieutenant Calley told Pfc. Paul Meadlo that "you know what to do with" a group of villagers Meadlo was guarding. Estimates of the numbers in the group ranged as high as eighty women, children, and old men, and Meadlo's own estimate under oath was thirty to fifty people. As Meadlo later testified, Calley returned after ten or fifteen minutes: "He [Calley] said, 'How come they're not dead?' I said, 'I didn't know we were supposed to kill them.' He said, 'I want them dead.' He backed off twenty or thirty feet and started shooting into the people—the Viet Cong—shooting automatic. He was beside me. He burned four or five magazines. I burned off a few, about three. I helped shoot 'em" (Hammer, 1971, p. 155). Meadlo himself and others testified that Meadlo cried as he fired; others reported him later to be sobbing and "all broke up." It would appear that to Lieutenant Calley's subordinates something was unusual, and stressful, in these orders.

At the trial, the first specification in the murder charge against Calley was for this incident; he was accused of premeditated murder of "an unknown number, not less than 30, Oriental human beings, males and females of various ages, whose names are unknown, occupants of the village of My Lai 4, by means of shooting them with a rifle" (Goldstein et al., 1976, p. 497).

Among the helicopters flying reconnaissance above Son My was that of CWO Hugh Thompson. By 9:00 or soon after, Thompson had noticed some horrifying events from his perch. As he spotted wounded civilians, he sent down smoke markers so that soldiers on the ground could treat them. They killed them instead. He reported to headquarters, trying to persuade someone to stop what was going on. Barker, hearing the message, called down to Captain Medina. Medina, in turn, later claimed to have told Calley that it was "enough for today." But it was not yet enough.

At Calley's orders, his men began gathering the remaining villagers—roughly seventy-five individuals, mostly women and children—and herding them toward a drainage ditch. Accompanied by three or four enlisted men, Lieutenant Calley executed several batches of civilians who had been gathered into ditches. Some of the details of the process were entered into testimony in such accounts as Pfc. Dennis Conti's: "A lot of them, the people, were trying to get up and mostly they was just screaming and pretty bad shot up. . . . I seen a woman tried to get up. I seen Lieutenant Calley firs. He hit the side of her head and blew it off" (Hammer, 1971, p. 125).

Testimony by other soldiers presented the shooting's aftermath. Specialist Four Charles Hall, asked by Prosecutor Aubrey Daniel how he knew the people in the ditch were dead, said: "There was blood coming from them. They were just scattered all over the ground in the ditch, some in piles and some scattered out 20, 25 meters perhaps up the ditch. . . . They were very old people, very young children, and mothers. . . . There was blood all over them" (Goldstein et al., 1976, pp. 501–502). And Pfc. Gregory Olsen corroborated the general picture of the victims: "They were—the majority were women and children, some babies. I distinctly remember one middle-aged Vietnamese male dressed in white right at my feet as I crossed. None of the bodies were mangled in any way. There was blood. Some appeared to be dead, others followed me with their eyes as I walked across the ditch" (Goldstein et al., 1976, p. 502).

The second specification in the murder charge stated that Calley did "with premeditation, murder an unknown number of Oriental human beings, not less than seventy, males and females of various ages, whose names are unknown, occupants of the village of My Lai 4, by means of shooting them with a rifle" (Goldstein et al., 1976, p. 497). Calley was also charged with and tried for shootings of individuals (an old man and a child); these charges were clearly supplemental to the main issue at trial—the mass killings and how they came about.

It is noteworthy that during these executions more than one enlisted man avoided carrying out Calley's orders, and more than one, by sworn oath, directly refused to obey them. For example, Pfc. James Joseph Dursi testified, when asked if he fired when Lieutenant Calley ordered him to: "No I just stood there. Meadlo turned to me after a couple of minutes and said 'Shoot! Why don't you shoot! Why don't you fire!' He was crying and yelling. I said, 'I can't! I won't!' And the people were screaming and crying and yelling. They kept firing for a couple of minutes, mostly automatic and semi-automatic" (Hanner, 1971, p. 143). . . .

Disobedience of Lieutenant Calley's own orders to kill represented a serious legal and moral threat to a defense *based* on superior orders, such as Calley was attempting. This defense had to assert that the orders seemed reasonable enough to carry out; that they appeared to be legal orders. Even if the orders in question were not legal, the defense had to assert that an ordinary individual could not and should not be expected to see the distinction. In short, if what happened was "business as usual," even though it might be bad business, then the defendant stood a chance of acquittal. But under direct command from "Surfside 5½," some ordinary enlisted men managed to refuse, to avoid, or at least to stop doing what they were ordered to do. As "reasonable men" of "ordinary sense and understanding," they had apparently found something awry that morning; and it would have been hard for an officer to plead successfully that he was more ordinary than his men in his capacity to evaluate the reasonableness of orders.

Even those who obeyed Calley's orders showed great stress. For example, Meadlo eventually began to argue and cry directly in front of Calley. Pfc. Herbert Carter shot himself in the foot, possibly because he could no longer take what he was doing. We were not destined to hear a sworn version of the incident, since neither side at the Calley trail called him to testify.

The most unusual instance of resistance to authority came from the skies. CWO Hugh Thompson, who had protested the apparent carnage of civilians, was Calley's inferior in rank but was not in his line of command. He was also watching the ditch from his helicopter and noticed some people moving after the first round of slaughter—chiefly children who had been shielded by their mothers' bodies. Landing to rescue the wounded, he also found some villagers hiding in a nearby bunker. Protecting the Vietnamese with his own body, Thompson ordered his men to train their guns on the Americans and to open fire if the Americans fired on the Vietnamese. He then radioed for additional rescue helicopters and stood between the Vietnamese and the Americans under Calley's command until the Vietnamese could be evacuated. He later returned to the ditch to unearth a child buried, unharmed, beneath layers of bodies. In October 1969, Thompson was awarded the Distinguished Flying Cross for heroism at My Lai, specifically (albeit inaccurately) for the rescue of children hiding in a bunker "between Viet Cong forces and advancing friendly forces" and for the rescue of a wounded child "caught in the intense crossfire" (Hersh, 1970, p. 119). Four months earlier, at the Pentagon, Thompson had identified Calley as having been at the ditch.

By about 10:00 A.M., the massacre was winding down. The remaining actions consisted largely of isolated rapes and killings, "clean-up" shootings of the wounded, and the destruction of the village by fire. We have already seen some examples of these more indiscriminate and possibly less premeditated acts. By the 11:00 A.M. lunch break, when the exhausted men of Company C were relaxing, two young girls wandered back from a hiding place only to be invited to share lunch. This surrealist touch illustrates the extent to which the soldiers' action had become dissociated from its meaning. As hour earlier, some of these men were making sure that not even a child would escape the executioner's bullet. But now the job was done and it was time for lunch—and in this new context it seemed only natural to ask the children who had managed to escape execution to join them. The massacre had ended. It remained only for the Viet Cong to reap the political rewards among the survivors in hiding.

The army command in the area knew that something had gone wrong. Direct commanders, including Lieutenant Colonel Barker, had firsthand reports, such as Thompson's complaints. Others had such odd bits of evidence as the claim of 128 Viet Cong dead with a booty of only three weapons. But the cover-up of My Lai began at once. The operation was reported as a victory over a stronghold of the Viet Cong Forty-eighth. . . .

William Calley was not the only man tried for the event at My Lai. The actions of over thirty soldiers and civilians were scrutinized by investigators; over half of these had to face charges or disciplinary action of some sort. Targets of investigation included Captain Medina, who was tried, and various higher-ups, including General Koster. But Lieutenant Calley was the only person convicted, the only person to serve time.

The core of Lieutenant Calley's defense was superior orders. What this meant to him—in contrast to what it meant to the judge and jury—can be gleaned from his responses to a series of questions from his defense attorney, George Latimer, in which Calley sketched out his understanding of the laws of war and the actions that constitute doing one's duty within those laws:

> *Latimer:* Did you receive any training which had to do with the obedience to orders?
> *Calley:* Yes, sir.
> *Latimer:* . . . what were you informed [were] the principles involved in that field?
> *Calley:* That all orders were to be assumed legal, that the soldier's job was to carry out any order given him to the best of his ability.
> *Latimer:* . . . what might occur if you disobeyed an order by a senior officer?
> *Calley:* You could be court-martialed for refusing an order and refusing an order in the face of the enemy, you could be sent to death, sir.
> *Latimer:* [I am asking] whether you were required in any way, shape or form to make a determination of the legality or illegality of an order?
> *Calley:* No, sir. I was never told that I had the choice, sir.
> *Latimer:* If you had a doubt about the order, what were you supposed to do?
> *Calley:* . . . I was supposed to carry the order out and then come back and make my complaint. (Hammer, 1971, pp. 240–241)

Lieutenant Calley steadfastly maintained that his actions within My Lai had constituted, in his mind, carrying out orders from Captain Medina. Both his own actions and the orders he gave to others (such as the instruction to Meadlo to "waste 'em") were entirely in response to superior orders. He denied any intent to kill individuals and any but the most passing awareness of distinctions among the individuals: "I was ordered to go in there and destroy the enemy. That was my job on that day. That was the mission I was given. I did not sit down and think in terms of men, women, and children. They were all classified the same, and that was the classification that we dealt with, just as enemy soldiers." When Latimer asked if in his own opinion Calley had acted "rightly and according to your understanding of your directions and orders," Calley replied, "I felt then and I still do that I acted as I was directed, and I carried out the orders that I was given, and I do not feel wrong in doing so, sir" (Hammer, 1971, p. 257).

His court-martial did not accept Calley's defense of superior orders and clearly did not share his interpretation of his duty. The jury evidently reasoned that, even if there had been orders to destroy everything in sight and to "waste the Vietnamese," any reasonable person would have realized that such orders were illegal and should have refused to carry them out. The defense of superior orders under such conditions is inadmissible under international and military law. The U.S. Army's *Law of Land Warfare* (Dept. of the Army, 1956), for example, states that "the fact that the law of war has been violated pursuant to an order of a superior authority, whether military or civil, does not deprive the act in question of its character of a war crime, nor does it constitute a defense in the trial of an accused individual, unless he did not know and could not reasonably have been expected to know that the act was unlawful" and that "members of the armed forces are bound to obey only lawful orders" (in Falk et al., 1971, pp. 71–72).

The disagreement between Calley and the court-martial seems to have revolved around the definition of the responsibilities of a subordinate to obey, on the one hand, and to evaluate, on the other. This tension . . . can best be captured via the charge to the jury in the Calley court-martial, made by the trail judge, Col. Reid Kennedy. The forty-one pages of the charge included the following:

> Both combatants captured by and noncombatants detained by the opposing force . . . have the right to be treated as prisoners. . . . Summary execution of detainees or prisoners is forbidden by law. . . . I therefore instruct you . . . that if unresisting human beings were killed at My Lai (4) while within the effective custody and control of our military forces, their deaths cannot be considered justified. . . . Thus if you find that Lieutenant Calley received an order directing him to kill unresisting Vietnamese within his control or within the control of his troops, *that order would be an illegal order.*
>
> A determination that an order is illegal does not, of itself, assign criminal responsibility to the person following the order for acts done in compliance with it. Soldiers are taught to follow orders, and special attention is given to obedience of orders on the battlefield. Military effectiveness depends on obedience to orders. On the other hand, the obedience of a soldier is not the obedience of an automation. A soldier is a reasoning agent, obliged to respond, not as a machine, but as a person. The law takes these factors into account in assessing criminal responsibility for acts done in compliance with illegal orders.
>
> The acts of a subordinate done in compliance with an unlawful order given him by this superior are excused and impose no criminal liability upon him unless the superior's order is one which a man of *ordinary sense and understanding* would, under the circumstances, know to be unlawful, or if the order in question is actually known to the accused to be unlawful. (Goldstein et al., 1976, pp. 525–526; emphasis added)

By this definition, subordinates take part in a balancing act, one tipped toward obedience but tempered by "ordinary sense and understanding."

A jury of combat veterans proceeded to convict William Calley of the premeditated murder of no less than twenty-two human beings. (The army, realizing some unfortunate connotations in referring to the victims as "Oriental human beings," eventually referred to them as "human beings.") Regarding the first specification in the murder charge, the bodies on the trial, [Calley] was convicted of premeditated murder of not less than one person. (Medical testimony had been able to pinpoint only one person whose wounds as revealed in Haeberle's photos were sure to be immediately fatal.) Regarding the second specification, the bodies in the ditch, Calley was convicted of the premeditated murder of not less than twenty human beings. Regarding additional specifications that he had killed an old man and a child, Calley was convicted of premeditated murder in the first case and of assault with intent to commit murder in the second.

Lieutenant Calley was initially sentenced to life imprisonment. That sentence was reduced: first to twenty years, eventually to ten (the latter by Secretary of Defense Callaway in 1974). Calley served three years before being released on bond. The time was spent under house arrest in his apartment, where he was able to receive visits from his girlfriend. He was granted parole on September 10, 1975.

Sanctioned Massacres

The slaughter at My Lai is an instance of a class of violent acts that can be described as sanctioned massacres (Kelman, 1973): acts of indiscriminate, ruthless, and often systematic mass violence, carried out by military or paramilitary personnel while engaged in officially sanctioned campaigns, the victims of which are defenseless and unresisting civilians, including old men, women, and children. Sanctioned massacres have occurred throughout history. Within American history, My Lai had its precursors in the Philippine war around the turn of the century (Schirmer, 1971) and in the massacres of American Indians. Elsewhere in the world, one recalls the Nazis' "final solution" for European Jews, the massacres and deportations of Armenians by Turks, the liquidation of the kulaks and the great purges in the Soviet Union, and more recently the massacres in Indonesia and Bangladesh, in Biafra and Burundi, in South Africa and Mozambique, in Cambodia and Afghanistan, in Syria and Lebanon. . . .

The occurrence of sanctioned massacres cannot be adequately explained by the existence of psychological forces—whether these be characterological dispositions to engage in murderous violence or profound hostility against the target—so powerful that they must find expression in violent acts unhampered by moral restraints. Instead, the major instigators for this class of violence derive from the policy process. The question that really calls for psychological analysis is why so many people are willing to formulate, participate in, and condone policies that call for the mass killings of defenseless civilians. Thus it is more instructive to look not at the motives for violence but at the conditions under which the usual moral inhibitions against violence become weakened. Three social processes that tend to create such conditions can be identified: authorization, routinization, and dehumanization. Through authorization, the situation becomes so defined that the individual is absolved of the responsibility to make personal moral choices. Through routinization, the action becomes so organized that there is no opportunity for raising moral questions. Through dehumanization, the actors' attitudes toward the target and toward themselves become so structured that it is neither necessary nor possible for them to view the relationship in moral terms.

AUTHORIZATION

Sanctioned massacres by definition occur in the context of an authority situation, a situation in which, at least for many of the participants, the moral principles that generally govern human relationships do not apply. Thus, when acts of violence are explicitly ordered, implicitly encouraged, tacitly approved, or at least permitted by legitimate authorities, people's readiness to commit or condone them is enhanced. That such acts are authorized seems to carry automatic justification for them. Behaviorally, authorization obviates the necessity of making judgments or choices. Not only do normal moral principles become inoperative, but—particularly when the actions are explicitly ordered—a different kind of morality, linked to the duty to obey superior orders, tends to take over.

In an authority situation, individuals characteristically feel obligated to obey the orders of the authorities, whether or not these correspond with their personal preferences. They see themselves as having no choice as long as they accept the legitimacy of the orders and of the authorities who give them. Individuals differ considerably in the degree to which—and the conditions under which—they are prepared to challenge the legitimacy of an order on the grounds that the order itself is illegal, or that those giving it have overstepped their authority, or that it stems from a policy that violates fundamental societal values. Regardless of such individual differences, however, the basic structure of a situation of legitimate authority requires subordinates to respond in terms of their role obligations rather than their personal preferences; they can openly disobey only by challenging the legitimacy of the authority. Often people obey without question even though the behavior they engage in may entail great personal sacrifice or great harm to others.

An important corollary of the basic structure of the authority situation is that actors often do not see themselves as personally responsible for the consequences of their actions. Again, there are individual differences, depending on actors' capacity and readiness to evaluate the legitimacy of orders received. Insofar as they see themselves as having had no choice in their actions, however, they do not feel personally responsible for them. They were not personal agents, but merely extensions of the authority. Thus, when their actions cause harm to others, they can feel relatively free of guilt. A similar mechanism operates when a person engages in antisocial behavior that was not ordered by the authorities but was tacitly encouraged and approved by them—even if only by making it clear that such behavior will not be punished. In this situation, behavior that was formerly illegitimate is legitimized by the authorities' acquiescence.

In the My Lai massacre, it is likely that the structure of the authority situation contributed to the massive violence in both ways—that is, by conveying the message that acts of violence against Vietnamese villagers were *required,* as well as the message that such acts, even if not ordered, were *permitted* by the authorities in charge. The actions at My Lai represented, at least in some respects, responses to explicit or implicit orders. Lieutenant Calley indicated, by orders and by example, that he wanted large numbers of villagers killed. Whether Calley himself had been ordered by his superiors to "waste" the whole area, as he claimed, remains a matter of controversy. Even if we assume, however, that he was not explicitly ordered to wipe out the village, he had reason to believe that such actions were expected by his superior officers. Indeed, the very nature of the war conveyed this expectation. The principal measure of military success was the "body count"—the number of enemy soldiers killed—and any Vietnamese killed by the U.S. military was commonly defined as a "Viet Cong." Thus, it was not totally bizarre for Calley to believe that what he was doing at My Lai was to increase his body count, as any good officer was expected to do.

Even to the extent that the actions at My Lai occurred spontaneously, without reference to superior orders, those committing them had reason to assume that such actions might be tacitly approved of by the military authorities. Not only had they failed to punish such acts in most cases, but the very strategies and tactics that the authorities consistently devised were based on the proposition that the civilian population of South Vietnam—whether "hostile" or "friendly"—was expendable. Such policies as search-and-destroy missions, the establishment of free-shooting zones, the use of antipersonnel weapons, the bombing of entire villages if they were suspected of harboring guerrillas, the forced migration of masses of the rural population, and the defoliation of vast forest areas helped legitimize acts of massive violence of the kind occurring at My Lai.

Some of the actions at My Lai suggest an orientation to authority based on unquestioning obedience to superior orders, no matter how destructive the actions these orders call for. Such obedience is specifically fostered in the course of military training and reinforced by the structure of the military authority situation. It also reflects, however, an ideological orientation that may be more widespread in the general population. . . .

ROUTINIZATION

Authorization processes create a situation in which people become involved in an action without considering its implications and without really making a decision. Once they have taken the initial step, they are in a new psychological and social situation in which the pressures to continue are powerful. As Lewin (1947) has pointed out, many forces that might originally have kept people out of a situation reverse direction once they have made a commitment (once they have gone through the "gate region") and now serve to keep them in the situation. For example, concern about the criminal nature of an action, which might originally have inhibited a person from becoming involved, may now lead to deeper involvement in efforts to justify the action and to avoid negative consequences.

Despite these forces, however, given the nature of the actions involved in sanctioned massacres, one might still expect moral scruples to intervene; but the likelihood of moral resistance is greatly reduced by transforming the action into routine, mechanical, highly programmed operations. Routinization fulfills two functions. First, it reduces the necessity of making decisions, thus minimizing the occasions in which moral questions may arise. Second, it makes it easier to avoid the implications of the action, since the actor focuses on the details of the job rather than on its meaning. The later effect is more readily achieved among those who participate in sanctioned massacres from a distance—from their desks or even from the cockpits of their bombers.

Routinization operates both at the level of the individual actor and at the organizational level. Individual job performance is broken down into a series of discrete steps, most of them carried out in automatic, regularized fashion. It becomes easy to forget the nature of the product that emerges from this process. When Lieutenant Calley said of My Lai that is was "no great deal," he probably implied that it was all in a day's work. Organizationally, the task is divided among different offices, each of which has responsibility for a small portion of it. This arrangement diffuses responsibility and limits the amount and scope of decision making that is necessary. There is no expectation that the moral implications will be considered at any of these points, nor is there any opportunity to do so. The organizational processes also help further legitimize the actions of each participant. By proceeding in routine fashion—processing papers, exchanging memos, diligently carrying out their assigned tasks—the different units mutually reinforce each other in the view that what is going on must be perfectly normal, correct, and legitimate. The shared illusion that they are engaged in a legitimate enterprise helps the participants assimilate their activities to other purposes, such as the efficiency of their performance, the productivity of their unit, or the cohesiveness of their group (see Janis, 1972).

Normalization of atrocities is more difficult to the extent that there are constant reminders of the true meaning of the enterprise. Bureaucratic inventiveness in the use of language helps to cover up such meaning. For example, the SS had a set of *Sprachregelungen,* or "language rules," to govern descriptions of their extermination program. As Arendt (1964) points out, the term *language rule* in itself was "a code name; it meant what in ordinary language would be called a lie" (p. 85). The code names for killing and liquidation were "final solution," "evacuation," and "special treatment." The war in Indochina produced its own set of euphemisms, such as "protective reaction," "pacification," and "forced-draft urbanization and modernization." The use of euphemisms allows participants in sanctioned massacres to differentiate their actions from ordinary killing and destruction and thus to avoid confronting their true meaning.

DEHUMANIZATION

Authorization processes override standard moral considerations; routinization processes reduce the likelihood that such considerations will arise. Still, the inhibitions against murdering one's fellow human beings are generally so strong that the victims must also be stripped of their human status if they are to be subjected to systematic killing. Insofar as they are dehumanized, the usual principles of morality no longer apply to them.

Sanctioned massacres become possible to the extent that the victims are deprived in the perpetrators' eyes of the two qualities essential to being perceived as fully human and included in the moral compact that governs human relationships: *identity*—standing as independent, distinctive individuals, capable of making choices and entitled to live their own lives—and *community*—fellow membership in an interconnected network of individuals who care for each other and respect each other's individuality and rights (Kelman, 1973; see also Bakan, 1966, for a related distinction between "agency" and "communion"). Thus, when a group of people is defined entirely in terms of a category to which they belong, and when this category is excluded from the human family, moral restraints against killing them are more readily overcome.

Dehumanization of the enemy is a common phenomenon in any war situation. Sanctioned massacres, however, presuppose a more extreme degree of dehumanization, insofar as the killing is not in direct response to the target's threats or provocations. It is not what they have done that marks such victims for death but who they are—the category to which they happen to belong. They are the victims of policies that regard their systematic destruction as a desirable end or an acceptable means. Such extreme dehumanization becomes possible when the target group can readily be identified as a separate category of people who have historically been stigmatized and excluded by the victimizers; often the victims belong to a distinct racial, religious, ethnic, or political group regarded as inferior or sinister. The traditions, the habits, the images, and the vocabularies for dehumanizing such groups are already well established and can be drawn upon when the groups are selected for massacre. Labels help deprive the victims of identity and community, as in the epithet "gooks" that was commonly used to refer to Vietnamese and other Indochinese peoples.

The dynamics of the massacre process itself further increase the participants' tendency to dehumanize their victims. Those who participate as part of the bureaucratic apparatus increasingly come to see their victims as bodies to be counted and entered into their reports, as faceless figures that will determine their productivity rates and promotions. Those who participate in the massacre directly—in the field, as it were—are reinforced in their perception of the victims as less than human by observing their very victimization. The only way they can justify what is being done to these people—both by others and by themselves—and they only way they can extract some degree of meaning out of the absurd events in which they find themselves participating (see Lifton, 1971, 1973) is by coming to believe that the victims are subhuman and deserve to be rooted out. And thus the process of dehumanization feeds on itself.

References

Arendt, H. (1964). *Eichmann in Jerusalem: A report on the banality of evil.* New York: Viking Press.

Bakan, D. (1966). *The duality of human existence.* Chicago: Rand McNally.

Department of the Army. (1956). *The law of land warfare* (Field Manual, No. 27-10). Washington, DC: U.S. Government Printing Office.

Falk, R. A.; Kolko, G.: & Lifton, R. J. (Eds.). (1971). *Crimes of war.* New York: Vintage Books.

French, P. (Ed.). (1972). *Individual and collective responsibility: The massacre at My Lai.* Cambridge, MA: Schenkman.

Goldstein, J.; Marshall, B.; & Schwartz, J. (Eds.). (1976). *The My Lai massacre and its cover-up: Beyond the reach of law?* (The Peers report with a supplement and introductory essay on the limits of law). New York: Free Press.

Hammer, R. (1971). *The court-martial of Lt. Calley.* New York: Coward, McCann, & Geoghegan.

Hersh, S. (1970). *My Lai 4: A report on the massacre and its aftermath.* New York: Vintage Books.

———. (1972). *Cover-up.* New York: Random House.

Janis, I. L. (1972). *Victims of groupthink: A psychological study of foreign-policy decisions and fiascoes.* Boston: Houghton Mifflin.

Kelman, H. C. (1973). Violence without moral restraint: Reflections on the dehumanization of victims and victimizers. *Journal of Social Issues, 29*(4), 25–61.

Lewin, K. (1947). Group decision and social change. In T. M. Newcomb & E. L. Hartley (Eds.), *Readings in social psychology.* New York: Holt.

Lifton, R. J. 91971). Existential evil. In N. Sanford, C. Comstock, & Associates, *Sanctions for evil: Sources of social destructiveness.* San Francisco: Jossey-Bass.

———. (1973). *Home from the war—Vietnam veterans: Neither victims nor executioners.* New York: Simon & Schuster.

Manual for courts martial, United States (rev. ed.). (1969). Washington, DC: U.S. Government Printing Office.

Schirmer, D. B. (1971, April 24). My Lai was not the first time. *New Republic,* pp. 18–21.

Williams, B. (1985, April 14–15). "I will never forgive," say My Lai survivor. *Jordan Times* (Amman), p. 4.

Name: _____   Class: _____

Date: _____   Section: _____

Reading Comprehension Activity Sheet

The May Lai Massacre: A Military Crime of Obedience, Herbert Kelman and V. Lee Hamilton

1. Briefly discuss what happed on March 16, 1968. _____

_____

_____

_____

_____

_____

_____

_____

_____

_____

_____

_____

2. What was Lieutenant Calley's defense, and what was the outcome of the court martial? _____

_____

_____

_____

_____

_____

_____

_____

_____

_____

_____

_____

_____

3. Define "sanctioned massacres" and what three specific characteristics make such a massacre possible.

The McDonaldization of Society

George Ritzer

A wide-ranging process of *rationalization* is occurring across American society and is having an increasingly powerful impact in many other parts of the world. It encompasses such disparate phenomena as fast-food restaurants, TV dinners, packaged tours, industrial robots, plea bargaining, and open-heart surgery on an assembly-line basis. As widespread and as important as these developments are, it is clear that we have barely begun a process that promises even more extraordinary changes (e.g., genetic engineering) in the years to come. We can think of rationalization as a historical process and rationality as the end result of that development. As a historical process, rationalization has distinctive roots in the western world. Writing in the late nineteenth and early twentieth centuries, the great German sociologist Max Weber saw his society as the center of the ongoing process of rationalization and the bureaucracy as its paradigm case. The model of rationalization, at least in contemporary America, is no longer the bureaucracy, but might be better though of as the fast-food restaurant. As a result, our concern here is with what might be termed the "McDonaldization of Society." While the fast-food restaurant is not the ultimate expression of rationality, it is the current exemplar for future developments in rationalization.

A society characterized by rationality is one which emphasizes *efficiency, predictability, calculability, substitution of nonhuman of human technology, and control over uncertainty.* In discussing the various dimensions of rationalization, we will be little concerned with the gains already made, and yet to be realized, by greater rationalization. These advantages are widely discussed in schools and in the mass media. In fact, we are in danger of being seduced by the innumerable advantages already offered, and promised in the future, by rationalization. The glitter of these accomplishments and promises has served to distract most people from the grave dangers posed by progressive rationalization. In other words, we

From *Journal of American Comparative Cultures,* 1983, Volume 6(1), pages 100–107. Reprinted by permission of Blackwell Publishing.

are ultimately concerned here with the irrational consequences that often flow from rational systems. Thus, the second major theme of this essay might be termed "the irrationality of rationality." . . .

Efficiency

The process of rationalization leads to a society in which a great deal of emphasis is placed on finding the best or optimum means to any given end. Whatever a group of people define as an end, and everything they so define, is to be pursued by attempting to find the best means to achieve the end. Thus, in the Germany of Weber's day, the bureaucracy was seen as the most efficient means of handling a wide array of administrative tasks. Somewhat later, the Nazis came to develop the concentration camp, its ovens, and other devices as the optimum method of collecting and murdering millions of Jews and other people. The efficiency that Weber described in turn-of-the-century Germany, and which later came to characterize many Nazi activities, has become a basic principle of life in virtually every sector of a rational society.

The modern American family, often with two wage earners, has little time to prepare elaborate meals. For the relatively few who still cook such meals, there is likely to be great reliance on cookbooks that make cooking from scratch much more efficient. However, such cooking is relatively rare today. Most families take as their objective quickly and easily prepared meals. To this end, much use is made of prepackaged meals and frozen TV dinners.

For many modern families, the TV dinner is no longer efficient enough. To many people, eating out, particularly in a fast-food restaurant, is a far more efficient way of obtaining their meals. Fast-food restaurants capitalize on this by being organized so that diners are fed as efficiently as possible. They offer a limited, simple menu that can be cooked and served in an assembly-line fashion. The latest development in fast-food restaurants, the addition of drive-through windows, constitutes an effort to increase still further the efficiency of the dining experience. The family now can simply drive through, pick up its order, and eat it while driving to the next, undoubtedly efficiently organized, activity. The success of the fast-food restaurant has come full circle with frozen food manufacturers now touting products for the home modeled after those served in fast-food restaurants.

Increasingly, efficiently organized food production and distribution systems lie at the base of the ability of people to eat their food efficiently at home, in the fast-food restaurant, or in their cars. Farms, groves, ranches, slaughterhouses, warehouses, transportation systems, and retailers are all oriented toward increasing efficiency. A notable example is chicken production where they are mass-bred, force-fed (often with many chemicals), slaughtered on an assembly line, iced or fast frozen, and shipped to all parts of the country. Some may argue that such chickens do not taste as good as the fresh-killed, local variety, but their complaints are likely to be drowned in a flood of mass-produced chickens. Then there is bacon which is more efficiently shipped, stored, and sold when it is preserved by sodium nitrate, a chemical which is unfortunately though by many to be carcinogenic. Whatever one may say about the quality or the danger of the products, the fact remains that they are all shaped by the drive for efficiency. . . .

One of the most interesting and important aspects of efficiency is that it often comes to be not a means but an end in itself. This "displacement of goals" is a major problem in a rationalizing society. We have, for example, the bureaucrats who slavishly follow the rules even though their inflexibility negatively affects the organization's ability to achieve its goals. Then there are the bureaucrats who are so concerned with efficiency that they lose sight of the ultimate goals the means are designed to achieve. A good example was the Nazi concentration camp officers who, in devoting so much attention to maximizing the efficiency of the camps' operation, lost sight of the fact that the ultimate purpose of the camps was the murder of millions of people.

Predictability

A second component of rationalization involves the effort to ensure predictability from one place to another. In a rational society, people want to know what to expect when they enter a given setting or acquire some sort of commodity. They neither want nor expect surprises. They want to know that if they journey to another locale, the setting they enter or the commodity they buy will be essentially the same as the setting they entered or product they purchased earlier. Furthermore, people want to be sure that what they encounter is much like what they encountered at earlier times. In order to ensure predictability over time and place a rational society must emphasize such things as discipline, order, systemization, formalization, routine, consistency, and methodical operation.

One of the attractions of TV dinners for modern families is that they are highly predictable. The TV dinner composed of fried chicken, mashed potatoes, green peas, and peach cobbler is exactly the same from one time to another and one city to another. Home cooking from scratch is, conversely, a notoriously unpredictable enterprise with little assurance that dishes will taste the same time after time. However, the cookbook cannot eliminate all unpredictability. There are often simply too many ingredients and other variables involved. Thus the cookbook dish is far less predictable than the TV dinner or a wide array of other prepared dishes.

Fast-food restaurants rank very high on the dimension of predictability. In order to help ensure consistency, the fast-food restaurant offers only a limited menu. Predictable end products are made possible by the use of similar raw materials, technologies, and preparation and serving techniques. Not only the food is predictable; the physical structures, the logo, the "ambience," and even the personnel are as well.

The food that is shipped to our homes and our fast-food restaurants is itself affected by the process of increasing predictability. Thus our favorite white bread is indistinguishable from one place to another. In fact, food producers have made great efforts to ensure such predictability.

On packaged tours travelers can be fairly sure that the people they travel with will be much like themselves. The planes, buses, hotel accommodations, restaurants, and at least the way in which the sites are visited are very similar from one location to another. Many people go on packaged tours *because* they are far more predictable than travel undertaken on an individual basis.

Amusement parks used to be highly unpredictable affairs. People could never be sure, from one park to another, precisely what sorts of rides, events, foods, visitors, and employees they would encounter. All of that has changed in the era of the theme parks inspired by Disneyland. Such parks seek to ensure predictability in various ways. For example, a specific type of young person is hired in these parks, and they are all trained in much the same way, so that they have a robot-like predictability.

Other leisure-time activities have grown similarly predictable. Camping in the wild is loaded with uncertainties—bugs, bears, rain, cold, and the like. To make camping more predictable, organized grounds have sprung up around the country. Gone are many of the elements of unpredictability replaced by RVs, paved-over parking lots, sanitized campsites, fences and enclosed camp centers that provide laundry and food services, recreational activities, television, and video games. Sporting events, too, have in a variety of ways been made more predictable. The use of artificial turf in baseball makes for a more predictable bounce of a ball. . . .

Calculability or Quantity Rather than Quality

It could easily be argued that the emphasis on quantifiable measures, on things that can be counted, is *the* most defining characteristic of a rational society. Quality is notoriously difficult to evaluate. How do we assess the quality of a hamburger, or a physician, or a student? Instead of even trying, in an increasing number of cases, a rational society seeks to develop a series of quantifiable measures that it takes as surrogates for quality. This urge to quantify has given great impetus to the development of the computer and has, in turn, been spurred by the widespread use and increasing sophistication of the computer.

The fact is that many aspects of modern rational society, especially as far as calculable issues are concerned, are made possible and more widespread by the computer. We need not belabor the ability of the computer to handle large numbers of virtually anything, but somewhat less obvious is the use of the computer to give the illusion of personal attention in a world made increasingly impersonal in large part because of the computer's capacity to turn virtually everything into quantifiable dimensions. We have all now had many experiences where we open a letter personally addressed to us only to find a computer letter. We are aware that the names and addresses of millions of people have been stored on tape and that with the aid of a number of word processors a form letter has been sent to every name on the list. Although the computer is able to give a sense of personal attention, most people are nothing more than an item on a huge mailing list.

Our main concern here, though, is not with the computer, but with the emphasis on quantity rather than quality that it has helped foster. One of the most obvious examples in the university is the emphasis given to grades and cumulative grade point averages. With less and less contact between professor and student, there is little real effort to assess the quality of what students know, let alone the quality of their overall abilities. Instead, the sole measure of the quality of most college students is their grade in a given course and their grade point averages. Another blatant example is the emphasis on a variety of uniform exams such as SATs and GREs in which the essence of an applicant is reduced to a few simple scores and percentiles.

Within the educational institution, the importance of grades is well known, but somewhat less known is the way quantifiable factors have become an essential part of the process of evaluating college professors. For example, teaching ability is very hard to evaluate. Administrators have difficulty assessing teaching quality and thus substitute quantitative scores. Of course each score involves qualitative judgments, but this is conveniently ignored. Student opinion polls are taken and the scores are summed, averaged, and compared. Those who score well are deemed good teachers while those who don't are seen as poor teachers. There are many problems involved in relying on these scores such as the fact that easy teachers in "gut" courses may well obtain high ratings while rigorous teachers of difficult courses are likely to score poorly. . . .

In the workworld we find many examples of the effort to substitute quantity for quality. Scientific management was heavily oriented to turning everything work-related into quantifiable dimensions. Instead of relying on the "rule of thumb" of the operator, scientific management sought to develop precise measures of how much work was to be done by each and every motion of the worker. Everything that could be was reduced to numbers and all these numbers were then analyzable using a variety of mathematical formulae. The assembly line is similarly oriented to a variety of quantifiable dimensions such as optimizing the speed of the line, minimizing time for each task, lowering the price of the finished product, increasing sales and ultimately increasing profits. The divisional system pioneered by General Motors and thought to be one of the major reasons for its past success was oriented to the reduction of the performance of each division to a few, bottom-line numbers. By monitoring and comparing these numbers, General Motors was able to exercise control over the results without getting involved in the day-to-day activities of each division. . . .

Thus, the third dimension of rationalization, calculability or the emphasis on quantity rather than quality, has wide applicability to the social world. It is truly central, if not the central, component of rationalizing society. To return to our favorite example, it is the case that McDonald's expends far more effort telling us how many billions of hamburgers it has sold than it does in telling us about the quality of those burgers. Relatedly, it touts the size of its product (the "Big Mac") more than the quality of the product (it is not the "Good Mac"). The bottom line in many settings is the number of customers processed, the speed with which they are processed, and the profits produced. Quality is secondary, if indeed there is any concern at all for it.

Substitution of Nonhuman Technology

In spite of Herculean efforts, there are important limits to the ability to rationalize what human beings think and do. Seemingly no matter what one does, people still retain at least the ultimate capacity to think and act in a variety of unanticipated ways. Thus, in spite of great efforts to make human behavior more efficient, more predictable, more calculable, people continue to act in unforeseen ways. People continue to make home-cooked meals from scratch, to camp in tents in the wild, to eat in old-fashioned diners, and to sabotage the assembly lines. Because of these realities, there is great interest among those who foster increasing rationality in using rational technologies to limit individual independence and ultimately to replace human beings with machines and other technologies that lack the ability to think and act in unpredictable ways.

McDonald's does not yet have robots to serve us food, but it does have teenagers whose ability to act autonomously is almost completely eliminated by techniques, procedures, routines, and machines. There are numerous examples of this including rules which prescribe all the things a counterperson should do in dealing with a customer as well as a large variety of technologies which determine the actions of workers such as drink dispensers which shut themselves off when the cup is full; buzzers, lights, and bells which indicate when food (e.g., french fries) is done; and cash registers which have the prices of each item programmed in. One of the latest attempts to constrain individual action is Denny's use of pre-measured packages of dehydrated food that are "cooked" simply by putting them under the hot water tap. Because of such tools and machines, as well as the elaborate rules dictating worker behavior, people often feel like they are dealing with human robots when they relate to the personnel of a fast-food restaurant. When human robots are found, mechanical robots cannot be far behind. Once people are reduced to a few robot-like actions, it is a relatively easy step to replace them with mechanical robots. Thus Burgerworld is reportedly opening a prototypical restaurant in which mechanical robots serve the food.

Much of the recent history of work, especially manual work, is a history of efforts to replace human technology with nonhuman technology. Scientific management was oriented to the development of an elaborate and rigid set of rules about how jobs were to be done. The workers were to blindly and obediently follow those rules and not to do the work the way they saw fit. The various skills needed to perform a task were carefully delineated and broken down into a series of routine steps that could be taught to all workers. The skills, in other words, were built into the routines rather than belonging to skilled craftspersons. Similar points can be made about the assembly line which is basically as set of nonhuman technologies that have the needed steps and skills built into them. The human worker is reduced to performing a limited number of simple, repetitive operations. However, the control of this technology over the individual worker is so great and omnipresent that individual workers have reacted negatively manifesting such things as tardiness, absenteeism, turnover, and even sabotage. We are now witnessing a new stage in this technological development with automated processes now totally replacing many workers with robots. With the coming of robots we have reached the ultimate stage in the replacement of humans with nonhuman technology.

Even religion and religious crusades have not been unaffected by the spread of nonhuman technologies. The growth of large religious organizations, the use of Madison Avenue techniques, and even drive-in churches all reflect the incursion of modern technology. But it is in the electronic church, religion through the TV screens, that replacement of human by nonhuman technology in religion is most visible and has its most important manifestation. . . .

Control

This leads us to the fifth major dimension of rationalization—control. Rational systems are oriented toward, and structured to expedite, control in a variety of senses. At the most general level, we can say that rational systems are set up to allow for greater control over the uncertainties of life—birth, death, food production and distribution, housing, religious salvation, and many, many others. More specifically, rational systems are oriented to gaining greater control over the major source of uncertainty in social life—other people. Among other things, this means control over subordinates by superiors and control of clients and customers by workers.

There are many examples of rationalization oriented toward gaining greater control over the uncertainties of life. The burgeoning of the genetic engineering movement can be seen as being aimed at gaining better control over the production of life itself. Similarly, amniocentesis can be seen as a technique which will allow the parents to determine the kind of child they will have. The efforts to rationalize food production and distribution can be seen as being aimed at gaining greater control over the problems of hunger and starvation. A steady and regular supply of food can make life itself more certain for large numbers of people who today live under the threat of death from starvation.

At a more specific level, the rationalization of food preparation and serving at McDonald's gives it great control over its employees. The automobile assembly line has a similar impact. In fact, the vast majority of the structures of a rational society exert extraordinary control over the people who labor in them. But because of the limits that still exist on the degree of control that rational structures can exercise over individuals, many rationalizing employers are driven to seek to more fully rationalize their operations and totally eliminate the worker. The result is an automated, robot-like technology over which, barring some *2001* rebellion, there is almost total control.

In addition to control over employees, rational systems are also interested in controlling the customer/clients they serve. For example, the fast-food restaurant with its counter, the absence of waiters and waitresses, the limited seating, and the drive-through windows all tend to lead customers to do certain things and not to do others.

IRRATIONALITY OF RATIONALITY

Although not an inherent part of rationalization, the *irrationality of rationality* is a seemingly inevitable byproduct of the process. We can think of the irrationality of rationality in several ways. At the most general level it can simply be seen as an overarching label for all the negative effects of rationalization. More specifically, it can be seen as the opposite of rationality, at least in some of its senses. For example, there are the inefficiencies and unpredictabilities that are often produced by seemingly rational systems. Thus, although bureaucracies are constructed to bring about greater efficiency in organizational work, the fact is that there are notorious inefficiencies such as the "red tape" associated with the operation of most bureaucracies. Or, take the example of the arms race in which a focus on quantifiable aspects of nuclear weapons may well have made the occurrence of nuclear war more, rather than less, unpredictable.

Of greatest importance, however, is the variety of negative effects that rational systems have on the individuals who live, work, and are served by them. We might say that *rational systems are not reasonable systems.* As we've already discussed, rationality brings with it great dehumanization as people are reduced to acting like robots. Among the dehumanizing aspects of a rational society are large lecture classes, computer letters, pray TV, work on the automobile assembly line, and dining at a fast-food restaurant. Rationalization also tends to bring with it disenchantment leaving much of our lives without any mystery or excitement. Production by a hand craftsman is far more mysterious than an assembly-line technology where each worker does a single, very limited operation. Camping in an RV tends to suffer in comparison to the joys to be derived from camping in the wild. Overall a fully rational society would be a very bleak and uninteresting place.

CONCLUSIONS

Rationalization, with McDonald's as the paradigm case, is occurring throughout America, and, increasingly, other societies. In virtually every sector of society more and more emphasis is placed on efficiency, predictability, calculability, replacement of human by nonhuman technology, and control over uncertainty. Although progressive rationalization has brought with it innumerable advantages, it has also created a number of problems, the various irrationalities of rationality, which threaten to accelerate in the years to come. These problems, and their acceleration should not be taken as a case for the return to a less rational form of society. Such a return is not only impossible but also undesirable. What is needed is not a less rational society, but greater control over the process of rationalization involving, among other things, efforts to ameliorate its irrational consequences.

Name: _____ Class: _____

Date: _____ Section: _____

Reading Comprehension Activity Sheet

The McDonaldization of Society, George Ritzer

1. What is "McDonaldization" and what impact does it have on society? _____
_____
_____
_____
_____
_____
_____
_____
_____
_____
_____
_____

2. Briefly describe the five major dimensions of the process of rationalization. _____
_____
_____
_____
_____
_____
_____
_____
_____
_____
_____
_____
_____

3. Ritzer states "Rational systems are not reasonable systems." What does this statement mean?

Name: _____ Class: _____

Date: _____ Section: _____

Student Information Sheet

Please supply your e-mail address or another way to contact you. _____
_____

What year are you in school (freshman, sophomore, junior, senior)? _____
_____

What is your intended major or program? _____
_____

Where is your hometown? _____
_____

What is the population of your hometown? _____
_____

Have you ever taken a sociology class before? If so, which class and when? _____
_____
_____

Why did you decide to take this course? _____
_____
_____

Which topics or issues would you find most interesting to study from a sociological viewpoint?
_____
_____
_____
_____
_____
_____
_____

Name: _____ Class: _____

Date: _____ Section: _____

Course Assessment Sheet

Which topics or issues did you find most interesting to study from a sociological viewpoint? Why?

_____

_____

_____

Which topics or issues did you find least interesting to study from a sociological viewpoint? Why?

_____

_____

_____

Which articles in *A Sociological Tapestry* did you find most interesting and why?

_____

_____

_____

_____

Which articles in *A Sociological Tapestry* did you find least interesting and why?

_____

_____

_____

_____

What is your overall impression of this course? Do you feel that you have acquired a sharper "sociological imagination"? Please explain your answer.

_____

_____

_____

_____

_____

_____